YAMATONADESHIKO SHICHIHENGE

18

Tomoko Hayakawa

**Translated and adapted by
David Ury**

**Lettered by
North Market Street Graphics**

DEL
REY

Ballantine Books • New York

The Wallflower volume 18 is a work of fiction. Names, characters, places, and incidents are the products of the author's imagination or are used fictitiously. Any resemblance to actual events, locales, or persons, living or dead, is entirely coincidental.

A Del Rey Manga/Kodansha Trade Paperback Original

Published in the United States by Del Rey Books, an imprint of The Random House Publishing Group, a division of Random House, Inc., New York.

Publication rights arranged through Kodansha Ltd.

First published in Japan in 2007 by Kodansha Ltd., Tokyo, as *Yamatonadeshiko Shichihenge*

ISBN 978-0-345-50660-3

Printed in the United States of America

www.delreymanga.com

9 8 7 6 5 4 3 2 1

Translator/Adapter—David Ury
Lettering—North Market Street Graphics

Contents

A Note from the Author

♥ OH MY GOD! IT FINALLY HAPPENED. SUNAKO AND KYOHEI
KISSED! COULD THIS BE THE BEGINNING OF A STEAMY LOVE
AFFAIR? WILL THEY BECOME A REAL COUPLE? EVEN I DON'T
KNOW THE ANSWER TO THAT ONE! WHATEVER HAPPENS, I
HOPE YOU GUYS WILL STAND BY THEM.

—Tomoko Hayakawa

Honorifics Explained

Throughout the Del Rey Manga books, you will find Japanese honorifics left intact in the translations. For those not familiar with how the Japanese use honorifics and, more important, how they differ from American honorifics, we present this brief overview.

Politeness has always been a critical facet of Japanese culture. Ever since the feudal era, when Japan was a highly stratified society, use of honorifics—which can be defined as polite speech that indicates relationship or status—has played an essential role in the Japanese language. When addressing someone in Japanese, an honorific usually takes the form of a suffix attached to one's name (example: "Asuna-san"), is used as a title at the end of one's name, or appears in place of the name itself (example: "Negi-sensei," or simply "Sensei!").

Honorifics can be expressions of respect or endearment. In the context of manga and anime, honorifics give insight into the nature of the relationship between characters. Many English translations leave out these important honorifics and therefore distort the feel of the original Japanese. Because Japanese honorifics contain nuances that English honorifics lack, it is our policy at Del Rey not to translate them. Here, instead, is a guide to some of the honorifics you may encounter in Del Rey Manga.

-san: This is the most common honorific and is equivalent to Mr., Miss, Ms., or Mrs. It is the all-purpose honorific and can be used in any situation where politeness is required.

-sama: This is one level higher than "-san" and is used to confer great respect.

-dono: This comes from the word "tono," which means "lord." It is an even higher level than "-sama" and confers utmost respect.

-kun: This suffix is used at the end of boys' names to express famil-iarity or endearment. It is also sometimes used by men among friends, or when addressing someone younger or of a lower station.

-chan: This is used to express endearment, mostly toward girls. It is also used for little boys, pets, and even among lovers. It gives a sense of childish cuteness.

Bozu: This is an informal way to refer to a boy, similar to the English terms "kid" and "squirt."

Sempai/
Senpai: This title suggests that the addressee is one's senior in a group or organization. It is most often used in a school setting, where underclassmen refer to their upperclassmen as "sempai." It can also be used in the workplace, such as when a newer em-ployee addresses an employee who has seniority in the com-pany.

Kohai: This is the opposite of "sempai" and is used toward underclass-men in school or newcomers in the workplace. It connotes that the addressee is of a lower station.

Sensei: Literally meaning "one who has come before," this title is used for teachers, doctors, or masters of any profession or art.

-[blank]: This is usually forgotten in these lists, but it is perhaps the most significant difference between Japanese and English. The lack of honorific means that the speaker has permission to ad-dress the person in a very intimate way. Usually, only family, spouses, or very close friends have this kind of permission. Known as *yobisute*, it can be gratifying when someone who has earned the intimacy starts to call one by one's name with-out an honorific. But when that intimacy hasn't been earned, it can be very insulting.

THE wallFLOWER

YAMATONADESHIKO SHICHIHENGE

ヤマトナデシコ七変化♡

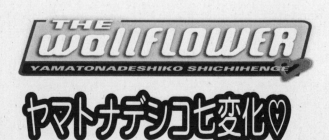

CONTENTS

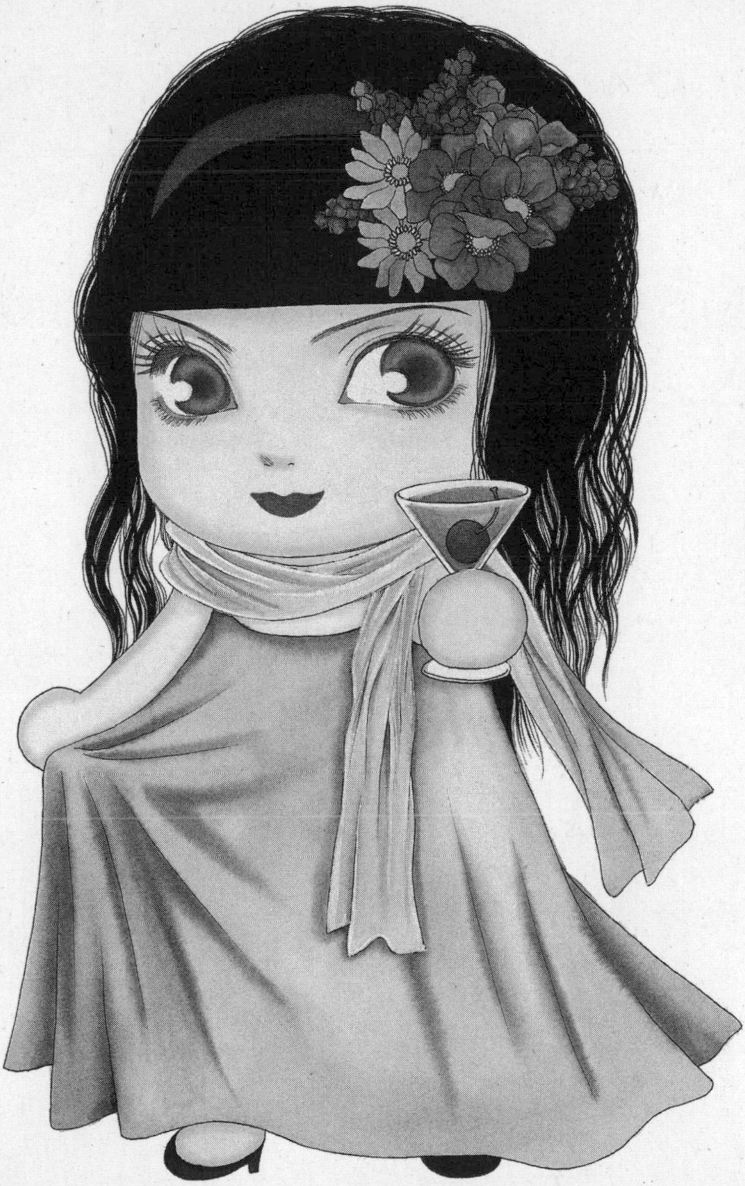

Chapter 71

VICTORY OVER SOCIETY! VICTORY OVER POVERTY!

WALLFLOWER'S BEAUTIFUL CAST OF CHARACTERS (?)

SUNAKO IS A DARK LONER WHO LOVES HORROR MOVIES. WHEN HER AUNT, THE LANDLADY OF A BOARDING-HOUSE, LEAVES TOWN WITH HER BOYFRIEND, SUNAKO IS FORCED TO LIVE WITH FOUR HANDSOME GUYS. SUNAKO'S AUNT MAKES A DEAL WITH THE BOYS, WHICH CAUSES NOTHING BUT HEADACHES FOR SUNAKO: "MAKE SUNAKO INTO A LADY, AND YOU CAN LIVE RENT FREE FOR THREE YEARS." WITH THE NAKAHARA HOUSEHOLD UNDERGOING REMODELING, THE GANG HAS BEEN RELOCATED TO A FANCY, FIVE-STAR HOTEL. UNABLE TO DEAL WITH THE LUXURY OF IT ALL, SUNAKO RUNS AWAY AND FINDS A CHEAP APARTMENT ALONG WITH, OF ALL PEOPLE, KYOHEI. NOW THEY'RE LIVING IT UP IN THE LAP OF POVERTY.

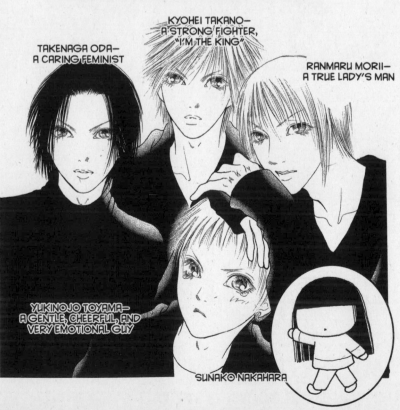

KYOHEI TAKANO—
A STRONG FIGHTER,
"I'M THE KING"
RANMARU MORII—
A TRUE LADY'S MAN
TAKENAGA ODA—
A CARING FEMINIST
YUKINOJO TOYAMA—
A GENTLE, CHEERFUL, AND
VERY EMOTIONAL GUY
SUNAKO NAKAHARA

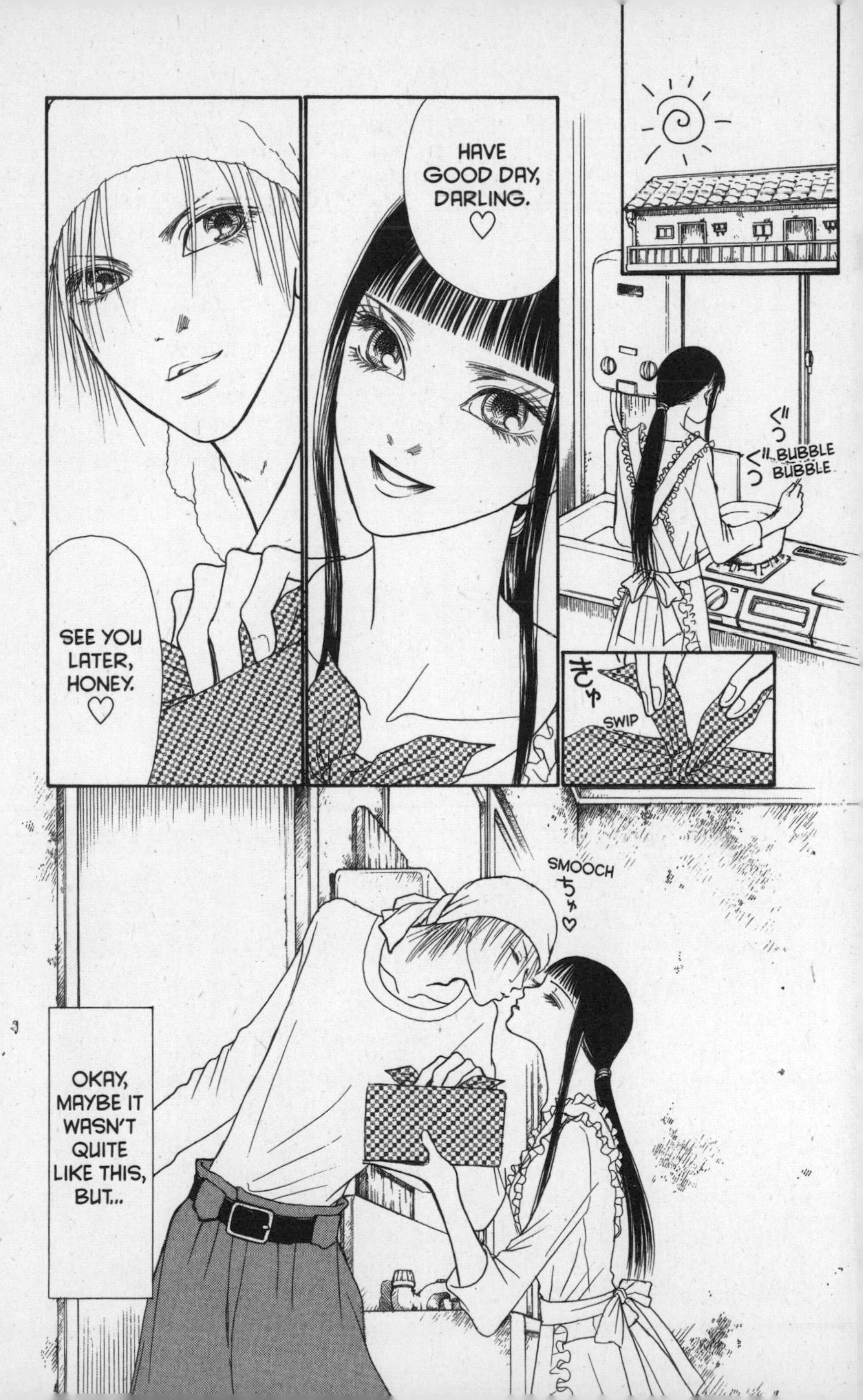
ぐつぐつ
BUBBLE BUBBLE
きゅ
SWIP
HAVE GOOD DAY, DARLING. ♡
SEE YOU LATER, HONEY. ♡
SMOOCH
ちゅ♡
OKAY, MAYBE IT WASN'T QUITE LIKE THIS, BUT...

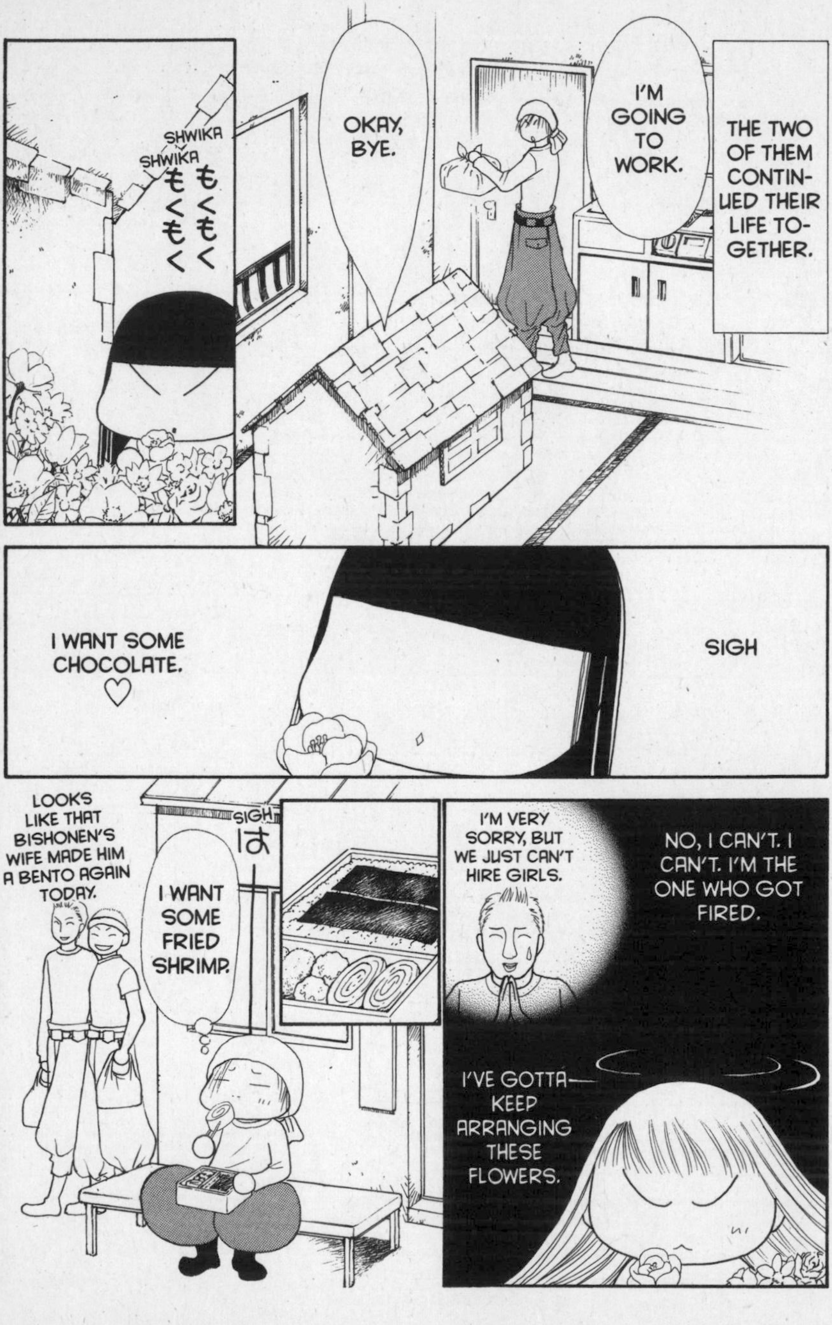
THE TWO OF THEM CONTINUED THEIR LIFE TOGETHER.
I'M GOING TO WORK.
OKAY, BYE.
SHWIKA SHWIKA
もくもく もくもく
SIGH
I WANT SOME CHOCOLATE. ♡
I'M VERY SORRY, BUT WE JUST CAN'T HIRE GIRLS.
NO, I CAN'T. I CAN'T. I'M THE ONE WHO GOT FIRED.
I'VE GOTTA— KEEP ARRANGING THESE FLOWERS.
SIGH
は
I WANT SOME FRIED SHRIMP.
LOOKS LIKE THAT BISHONEN'S WIFE MADE HIM A BENTO AGAIN TODAY.

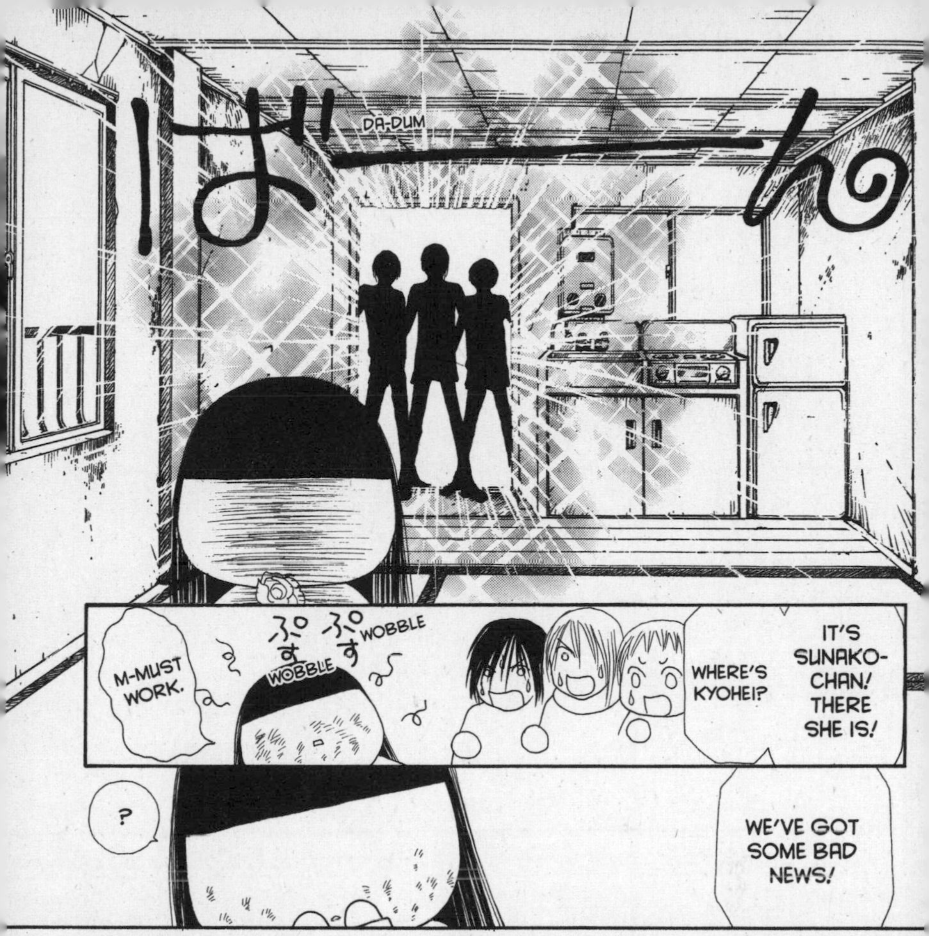
ばーん
DA-DUM
IT'S SUNAKO-CHAN! THERE SHE IS!
WHERE'S KYOHEI?
ぷす WOBBLE
ぷす WOBBLE
M-MUST WORK.
WE'VE GOT SOME BAD NEWS!
?

BEHIND THE SCENES

I'M SURE ALL OF YOU *BESSATSU FRIEND* READERS (AND *BEST C* READERS TOO) ♥ ALREADY KNOW ABOUT THIS, BUT WHILE I WAS WORKING ON THE STORYBOARDS FOR THIS CHAPTER, I GOT TO DO AN INTERVIEW WITH KIYOHARU-SAMA FOR *BESSATSU FRIEND*. ♥ ♥ ♥

AS YOU CAN IMAGINE, I COULD BARELY EVEN TALK . . . SIGH . . . HE WAS SO HOT! HE HAS SUCH A POWERFUL AURA. ♥ ♥ ♥

AROUND THE SAME TIME, I ALSO HAD TO DO AN INTERVIEW FOR *FOOL'S MATE* MAGAZINE. ALL I TALKED ABOUT WAS KIYOHARU. IT WAS SO FUN. ♥ WHEN I READ THE INTERVIEW WITH KIYOHARU IN *FOOL'S*, I TOTALLY CRIED. I'D FOLLOW YOU ANYWHERE, KIYOHARU-SAMA! ♥ ♥ ♥ YOU ARE THE HOTTEST GUY ON EARTH. ♥ ♥ ♥

I WAS SO EXCITED TO BE ABLE TO WORK WITH TOJO-SAN. ♥ THANK YOU SO MUCH. I'LL KEEP ON BUYING *FOOL'S*!

SIGH...I WAS SO HAPPY TO WORK WITH ONE OF MY FAVORITE WRITERS. ♥

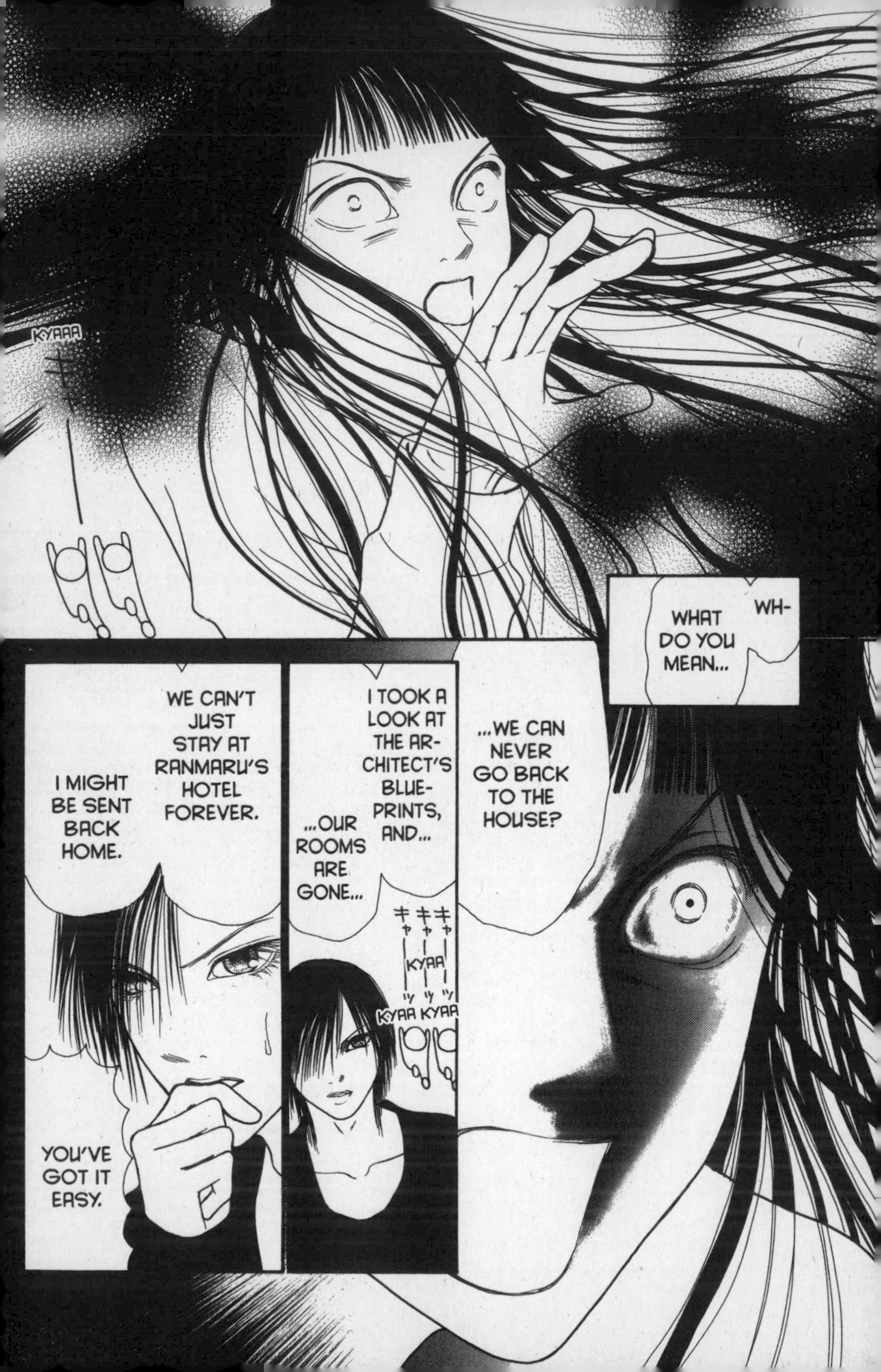
KYAAA
WH-
WHAT DO YOU MEAN...
...WE CAN NEVER GO BACK TO THE HOUSE?
I TOOK A LOOK AT THE ARCHITECT'S BLUEPRINTS, AND...
...OUR ROOMS ARE GONE...
KYAA
KYAA KYAA
WE CAN'T JUST STAY AT RANMARU'S HOTEL FOREVER.
I MIGHT BE SENT BACK HOME.
YOU'VE GOT IT EASY.

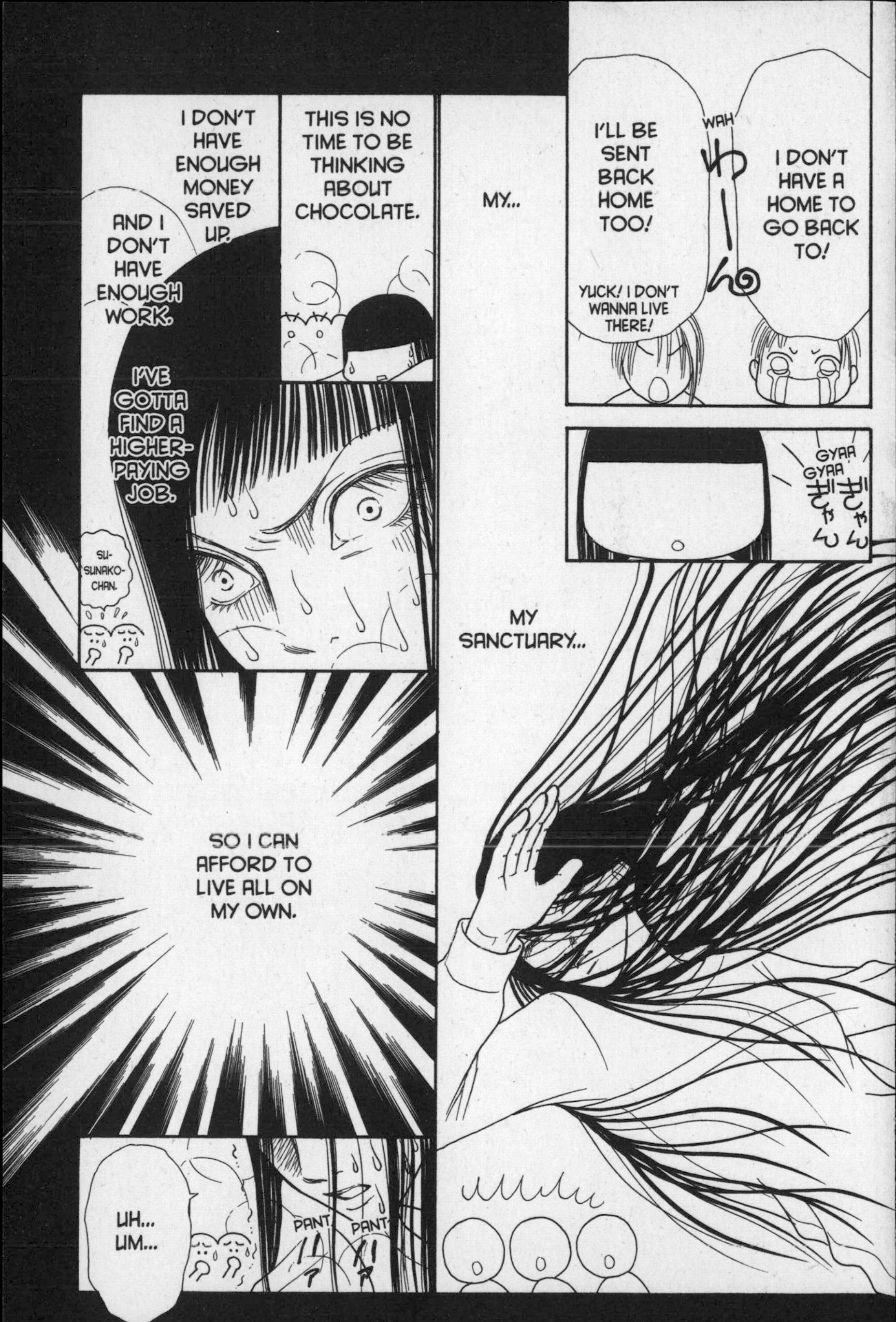
I DON'T HAVE A HOME TO GO BACK TO!
WAH
I'LL BE SENT BACK HOME TOO!
YUCK! I DON'T WANNA LIVE THERE!
GYAA GYAA
MY...
MY SANCTUARY...
THIS IS NO TIME TO BE THINKING ABOUT CHOCOLATE.
I DON'T HAVE ENOUGH MONEY SAVED UP.
AND I DON'T HAVE ENOUGH WORK.
I'VE GOTTA FIND A HIGHER-PAYING JOB.
SU-SUNAKO-CHAN.
SO I CAN AFFORD TO LIVE ALL ON MY OWN.
PANT
PANT
UH... UM...

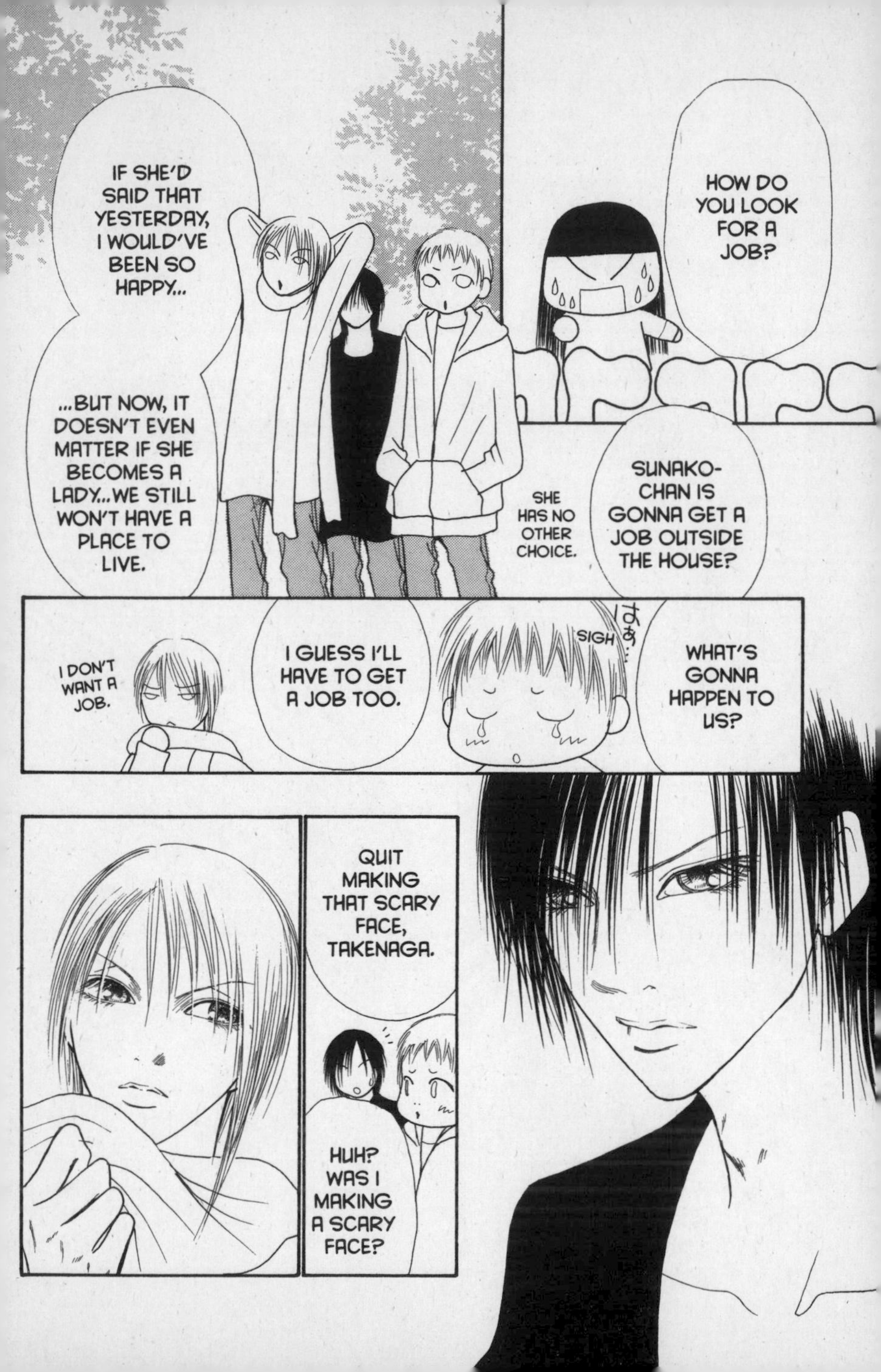
HOW DO YOU LOOK FOR A JOB?
SUNAKO-CHAN IS GONNA GET A JOB OUTSIDE THE HOUSE?
SHE HAS NO OTHER CHOICE.
IF SHE'D SAID THAT YESTERDAY, I WOULD'VE BEEN SO HAPPY...
...BUT NOW, IT DOESN'T EVEN MATTER IF SHE BECOMES A LADY...WE STILL WON'T HAVE A PLACE TO LIVE.
WHAT'S GONNA HAPPEN TO US?
はぁ…
SIGH
I GUESS I'LL HAVE TO GET A JOB TOO.
I DON'T WANT A JOB.
QUIT MAKING THAT SCARY FACE, TAKENAGA.
HUH? WAS I MAKING A SCARY FACE?

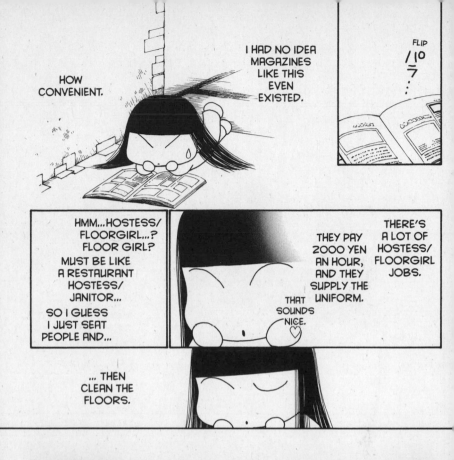

FLIP
I HAD NO IDEA MAGAZINES LIKE THIS EVEN EXISTED.
HOW CONVENIENT.
THERE'S A LOT OF HOSTESS/ FLOORGIRL JOBS.
THEY PAY 2000 YEN AN HOUR, AND THEY SUPPLY THE UNIFORM.
THAT SOUNDS NICE. ♡
HMM...HOSTESS/ FLOORGIRL...? FLOOR GIRL?
MUST BE LIKE A RESTAURANT HOSTESS/ JANITOR...
SO I GUESS I JUST SEAT PEOPLE AND...
... THEN CLEAN THE FLOORS.

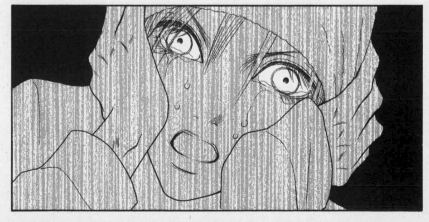

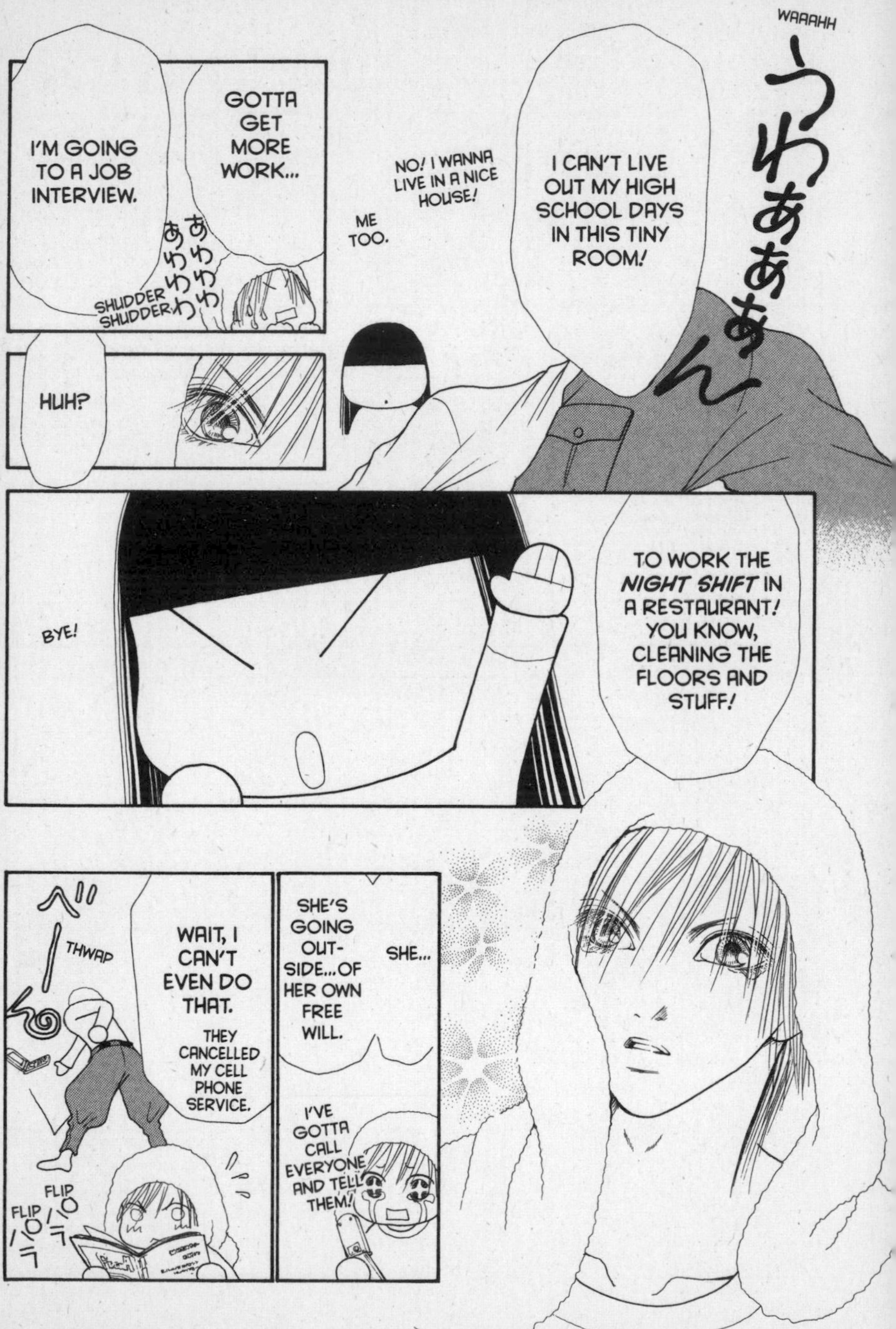
WAAAHH
うわあああん
I CAN'T LIVE OUT MY HIGH SCHOOL DAYS IN THIS TINY ROOM!
NO! I WANNA LIVE IN A NICE HOUSE!
ME TOO.
GOTTA GET MORE WORK...
あわわわ あわわわ
SHUDDER SHUDDER
I'M GOING TO A JOB INTERVIEW.
HUH?
TO WORK THE *NIGHT SHIFT* IN A RESTAURANT! YOU KNOW, CLEANING THE FLOORS AND STUFF!
BYE!
SHE...
SHE'S GOING OUT-SIDE...OF HER OWN FREE WILL.
I'VE GOTTA CALL EVERYONE AND TELL THEM!
WAIT, I CAN'T EVEN DO THAT.
THEY CANCELLED MY CELL PHONE SERVICE.
THWAP
FLIP FLIP

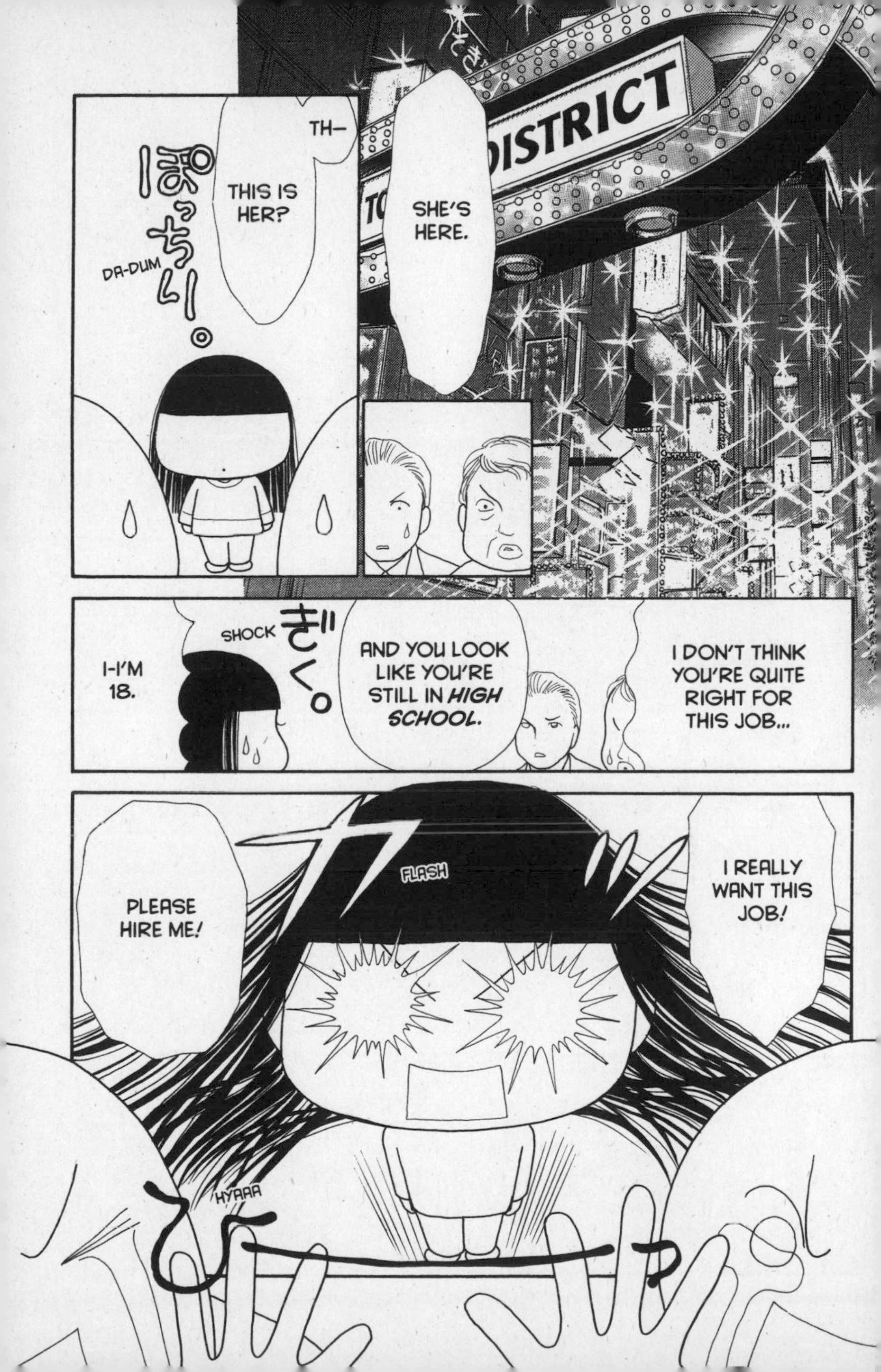

TO DISTRICT
SHE'S HERE.
TH—
THIS IS HER?
DA-DUM
I DON'T THINK YOU'RE QUITE RIGHT FOR THIS JOB...
AND YOU LOOK LIKE YOU'RE STILL IN *HIGH SCHOOL*.
ぎく。
SHOCK
I-I'M 18.
I REALLY WANT THIS JOB!
カッ
FLASH
PLEASE HIRE ME!
HYAAA

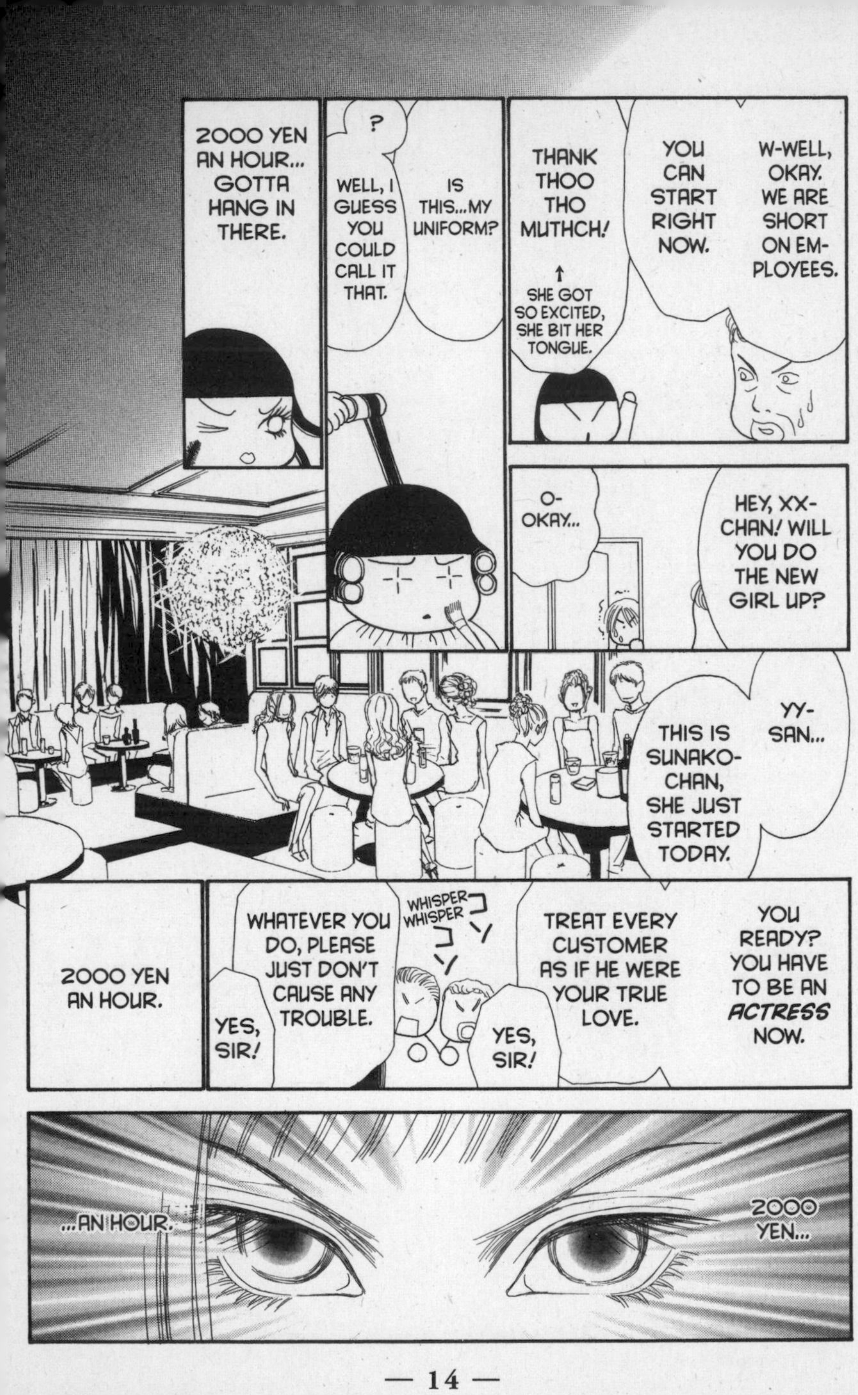
W-WELL, OKAY. WE ARE SHORT ON EMPLOYEES.
YOU CAN START RIGHT NOW.
THANK THOO THO MUTHCH!
↑ SHE GOT SO EXCITED, SHE BIT HER TONGUE.
HEY, XX-CHAN! WILL YOU DO THE NEW GIRL UP?
O-OKAY...
?
IS THIS...MY UNIFORM?
WELL, I GUESS YOU COULD CALL IT THAT.
2000 YEN AN HOUR... GOTTA HANG IN THERE.
YY-SAN...
THIS IS SUNAKO-CHAN, SHE JUST STARTED TODAY.
YOU READY? YOU HAVE TO BE AN *ACTRESS* NOW.
TREAT EVERY CUSTOMER AS IF HE WERE YOUR TRUE LOVE.
YES, SIR!
WHISPER WHISPER
WHATEVER YOU DO, PLEASE JUST DON'T CAUSE ANY TROUBLE.
YES, SIR!
2000 YEN AN HOUR.
2000 YEN...
...AN HOUR.

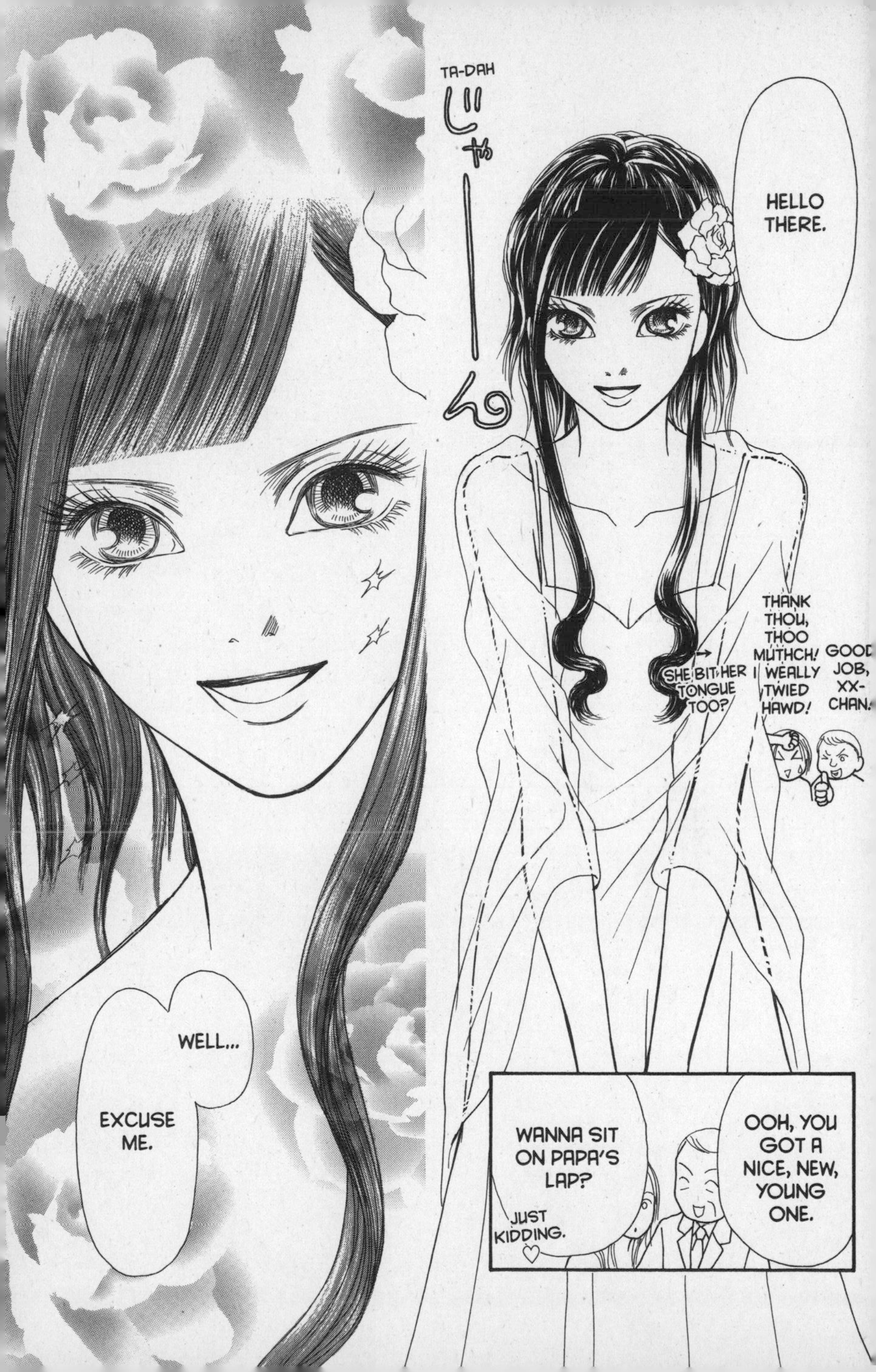

TA-DAH
じゃーん
HELLO THERE.
GOOD JOB, XX-CHAN.
THANK THOU, THOO MUTHCH! I WEALLY TWIED HAWD!
SHE BIT HER TONGUE TOO?
OOH, YOU GOT A NICE, NEW, YOUNG ONE.
WANNA SIT ON PAPA'S LAP?
JUST KIDDING. ♡
WELL...
EXCUSE ME.

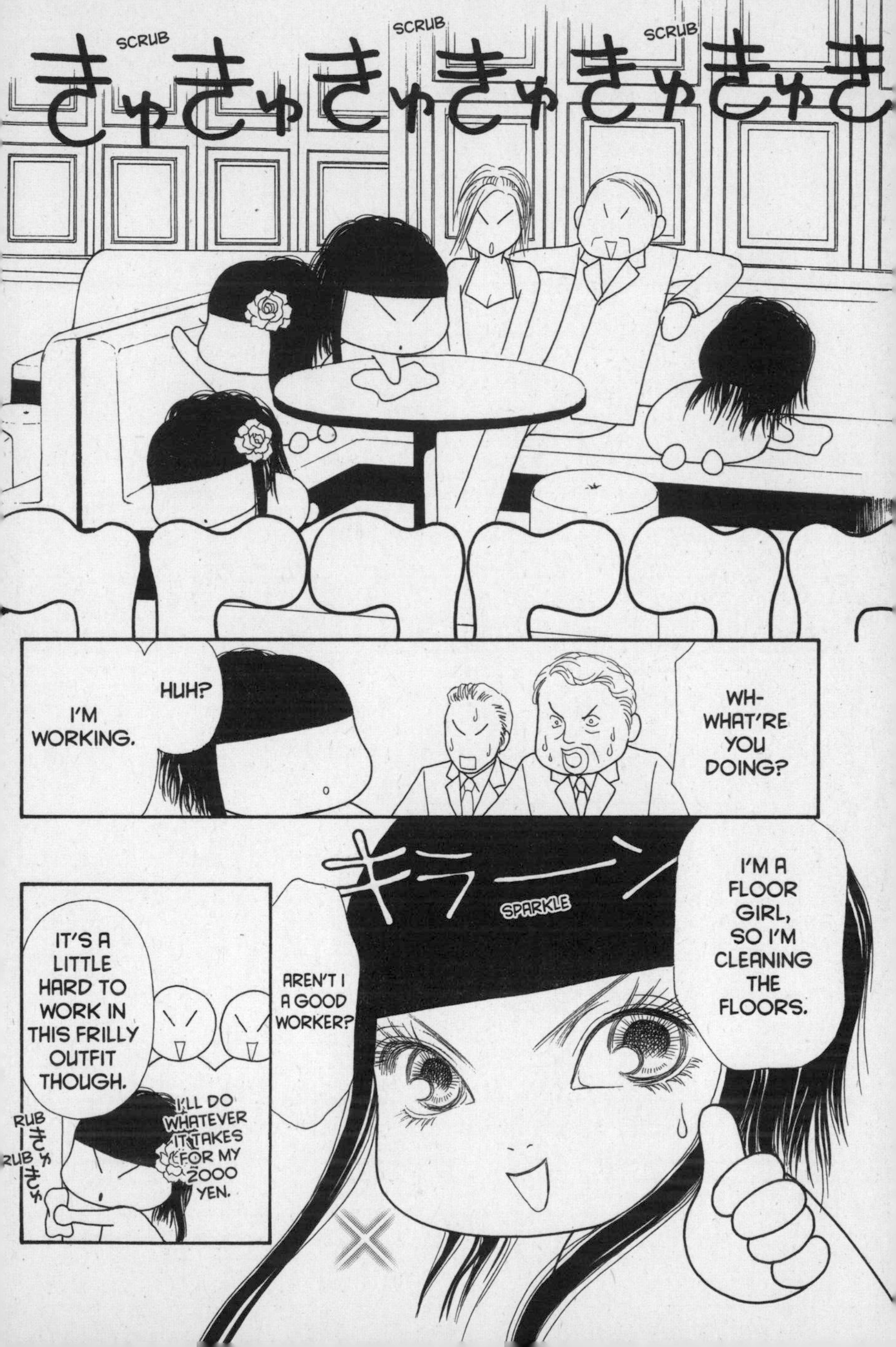
SCRUB SCRUB SCRUB
きゅきゅきゅきゅきゅきゅき
WH- WHAT'RE YOU DOING?
HUH?
I'M WORKING.
I'M A FLOOR GIRL, SO I'M CLEANING THE FLOORS.
キラーン
SPARKLE
AREN'T I A GOOD WORKER?
IT'S A LITTLE HARD TO WORK IN THIS FRILLY OUTFIT THOUGH.
I'LL DO WHATEVER IT TAKES FOR MY 2000 YEN.
RUB きゅ
RUB きゅ

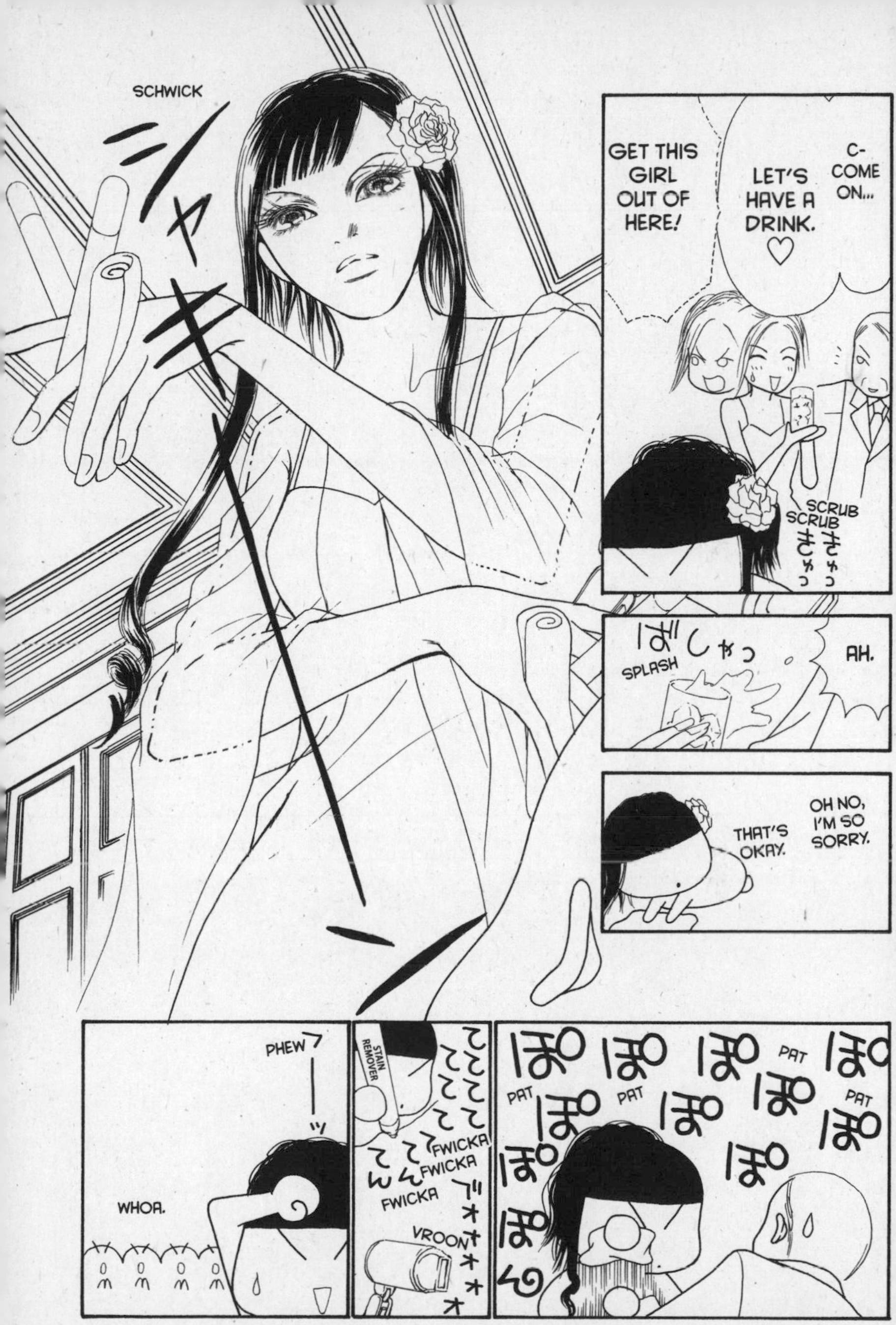
C- COME ON...
LET'S HAVE A DRINK. ♡
GET THIS GIRL OUT OF HERE!
SCRUB SCRUB
きゅっ きゅっ
AH.
ぱしゃっ
SPLASH
OH NO, I'M SO SORRY.
THAT'S OKAY.
SCHWICK
PAT PAT PAT PAT
STAIN REMOVER
FWICKA FWICKA FWICKA
VROON
PHEW
WHOA.

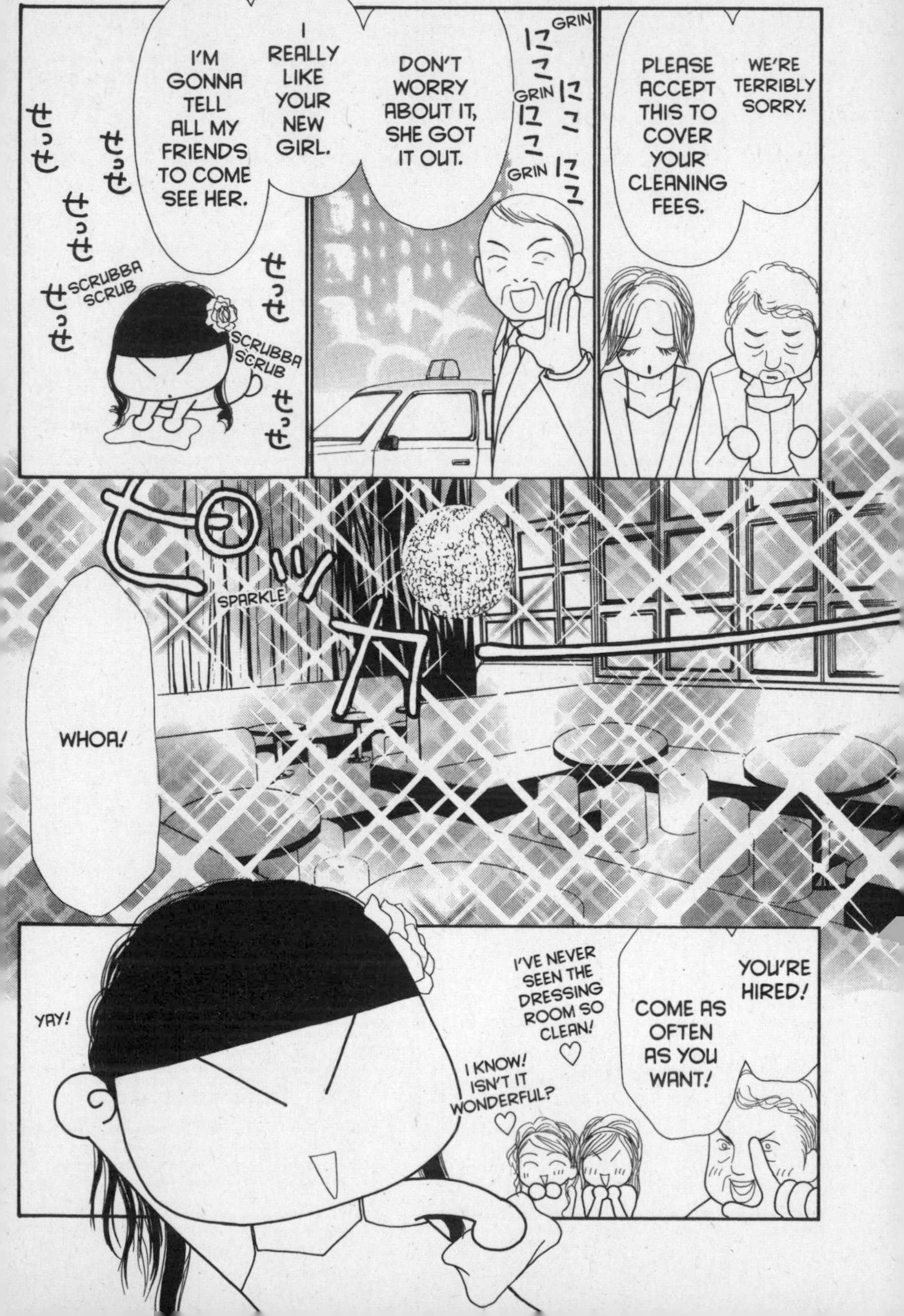
WE'RE TERRIBLY SORRY.
PLEASE ACCEPT THIS TO COVER YOUR CLEANING FEES.
にこ GRIN
にこ GRIN
にこ GRIN
DON'T WORRY ABOUT IT, SHE GOT IT OUT.
I REALLY LIKE YOUR NEW GIRL.
I'M GONNA TELL ALL MY FRIENDS TO COME SEE HER.
せっせ せっせ SCRUBBA SCRUB
せっせ せっせ SCRUBBA SCRUB
SPARKLE
WHOA!
YOU'RE HIRED!
COME AS OFTEN AS YOU WANT!
I'VE NEVER SEEN THE DRESSING ROOM SO CLEAN! ♡
I KNOW! ISN'T IT WONDERFUL? ♡
YAY!

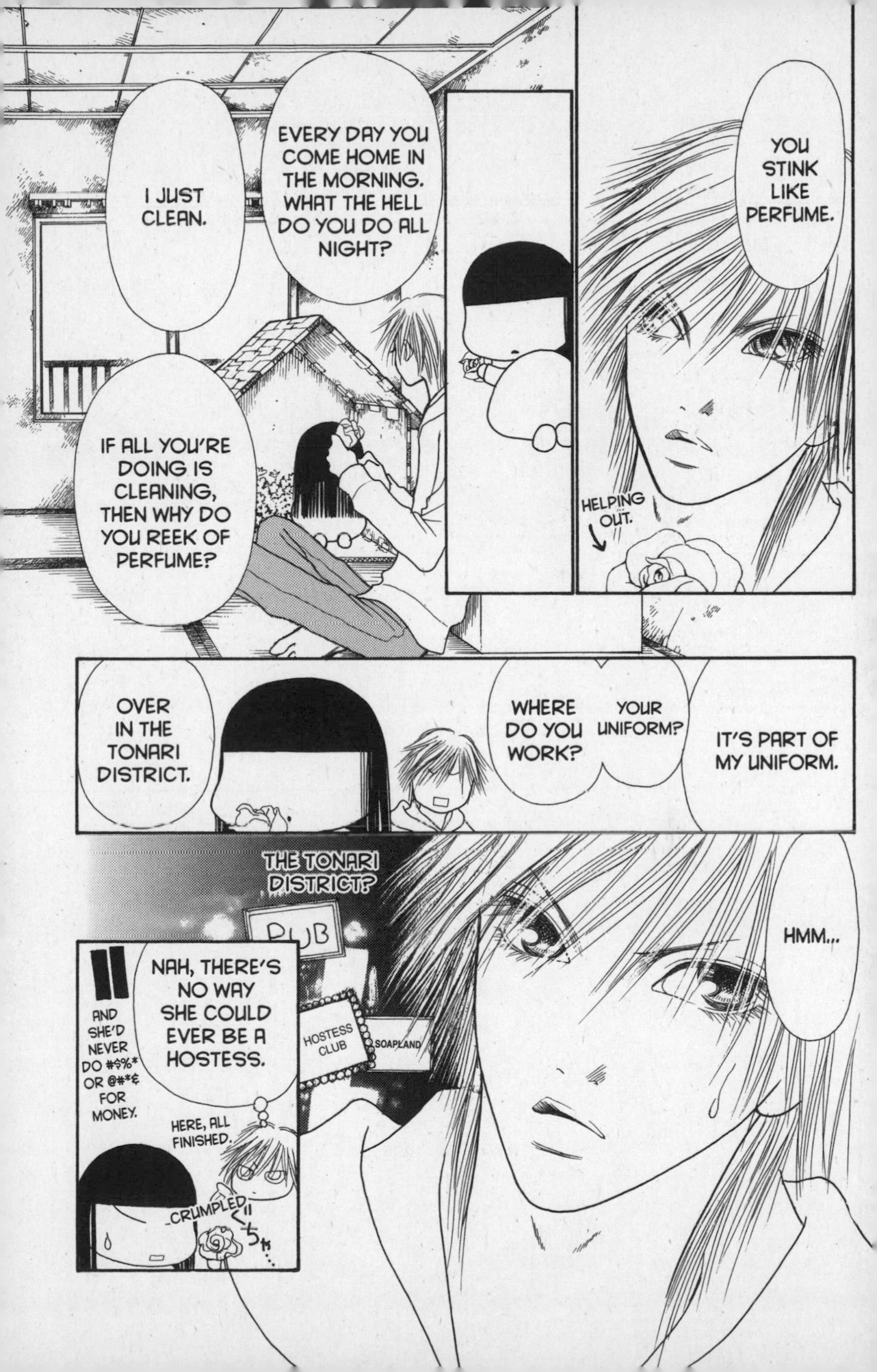
YOU STINK LIKE PERFUME.
HELPING OUT.
EVERY DAY YOU COME HOME IN THE MORNING. WHAT THE HELL DO YOU DO ALL NIGHT?
I JUST CLEAN.
IF ALL YOU'RE DOING IS CLEANING, THEN WHY DO YOU REEK OF PERFUME?
IT'S PART OF MY UNIFORM.
YOUR UNIFORM?
WHERE DO YOU WORK?
OVER IN THE TONARI DISTRICT.
HMM...
THE TONARI DISTRICT?
PUB
HOSTESS CLUB
SOAPLAND
NAH, THERE'S NO WAY SHE COULD EVER BE A HOSTESS.
AND SHE'D NEVER DO #$%* OR @#*& FOR MONEY.
HERE, ALL FINISHED.
CRUMPLED

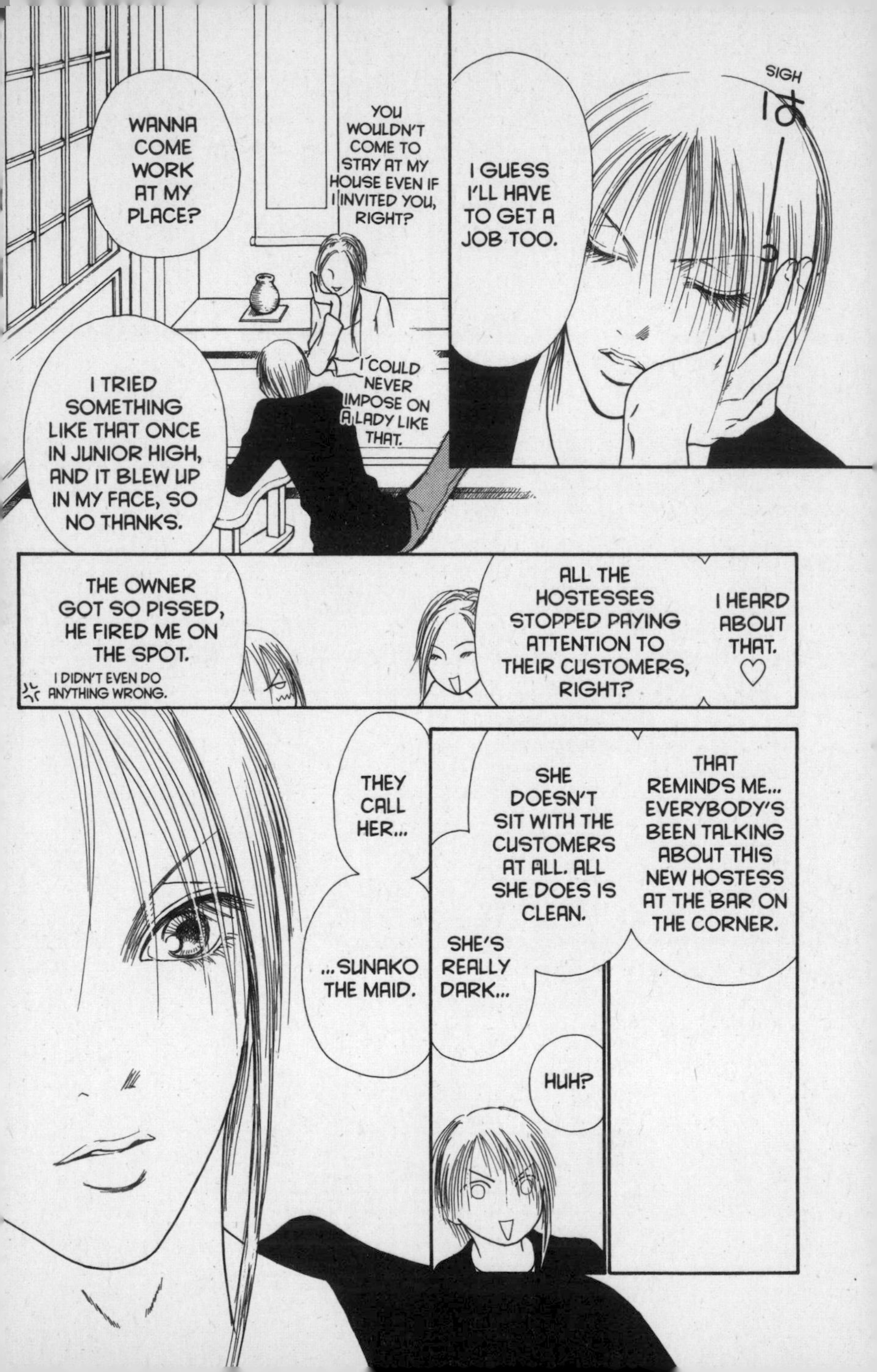
SIGH
は
I GUESS I'LL HAVE TO GET A JOB TOO.
YOU WOULDN'T COME TO STAY AT MY HOUSE EVEN IF I INVITED YOU, RIGHT?
I COULD NEVER IMPOSE ON A LADY LIKE THAT.
WANNA COME WORK AT MY PLACE?
I TRIED SOMETHING LIKE THAT ONCE IN JUNIOR HIGH, AND IT BLEW UP IN MY FACE, SO NO THANKS.
THE OWNER GOT SO PISSED, HE FIRED ME ON THE SPOT.
I DIDN'T EVEN DO ANYTHING WRONG.
I HEARD ABOUT THAT. ♡
ALL THE HOSTESSES STOPPED PAYING ATTENTION TO THEIR CUSTOMERS, RIGHT?
THAT REMINDS ME... EVERYBODY'S BEEN TALKING ABOUT THIS NEW HOSTESS AT THE BAR ON THE CORNER.
SHE DOESN'T SIT WITH THE CUSTOMERS AT ALL. ALL SHE DOES IS CLEAN.
SHE'S REALLY DARK...
THEY CALL HER...
...SUNAKO THE MAID.
HUH?

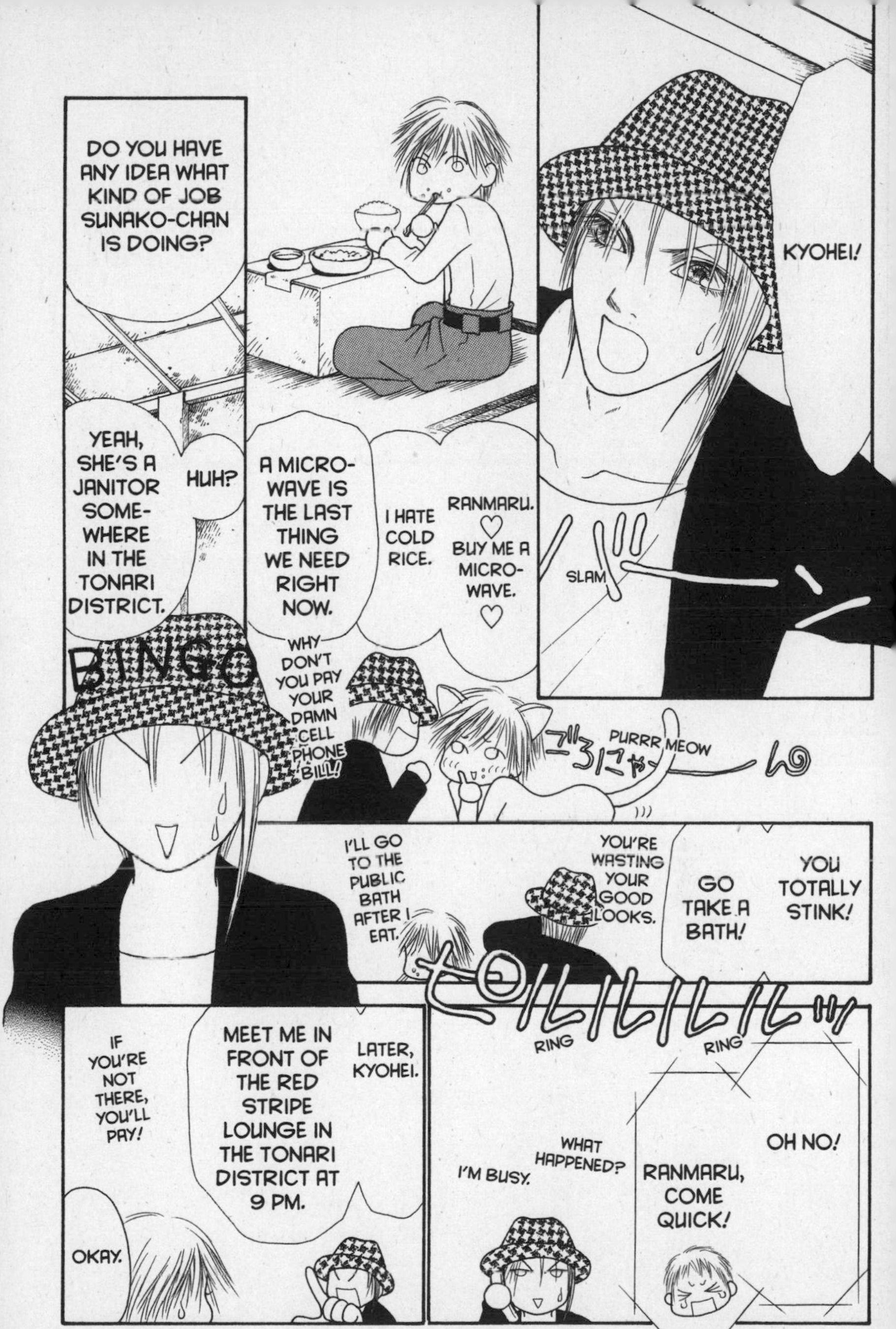
KYOHEI!
SLAM
RANMARU. ♡ BUY ME A MICRO-WAVE. ♡
I HATE COLD RICE.
A MICRO-WAVE IS THE LAST THING WE NEED RIGHT NOW.
WHY DON'T YOU PAY YOUR DAMN CELL PHONE BILL!
ごろにゃーん
PURRR MEOW
DO YOU HAVE ANY IDEA WHAT KIND OF JOB SUNAKO-CHAN IS DOING?
HUH?
YEAH, SHE'S A JANITOR SOME-WHERE IN THE TONARI DISTRICT.
BINGO
YOU TOTALLY STINK!
GO TAKE A BATH!
YOU'RE WASTING YOUR GOOD LOOKS.
I'LL GO TO THE PUBLIC BATH AFTER I EAT.
RING
RING
OH NO!
RANMARU, COME QUICK!
WHAT HAPPENED?
I'M BUSY.
LATER, KYOHEI.
MEET ME IN FRONT OF THE RED STRIPE LOUNGE IN THE TONARI DISTRICT AT 9 PM.
IF YOU'RE NOT THERE, YOU'LL PAY!
OKAY.

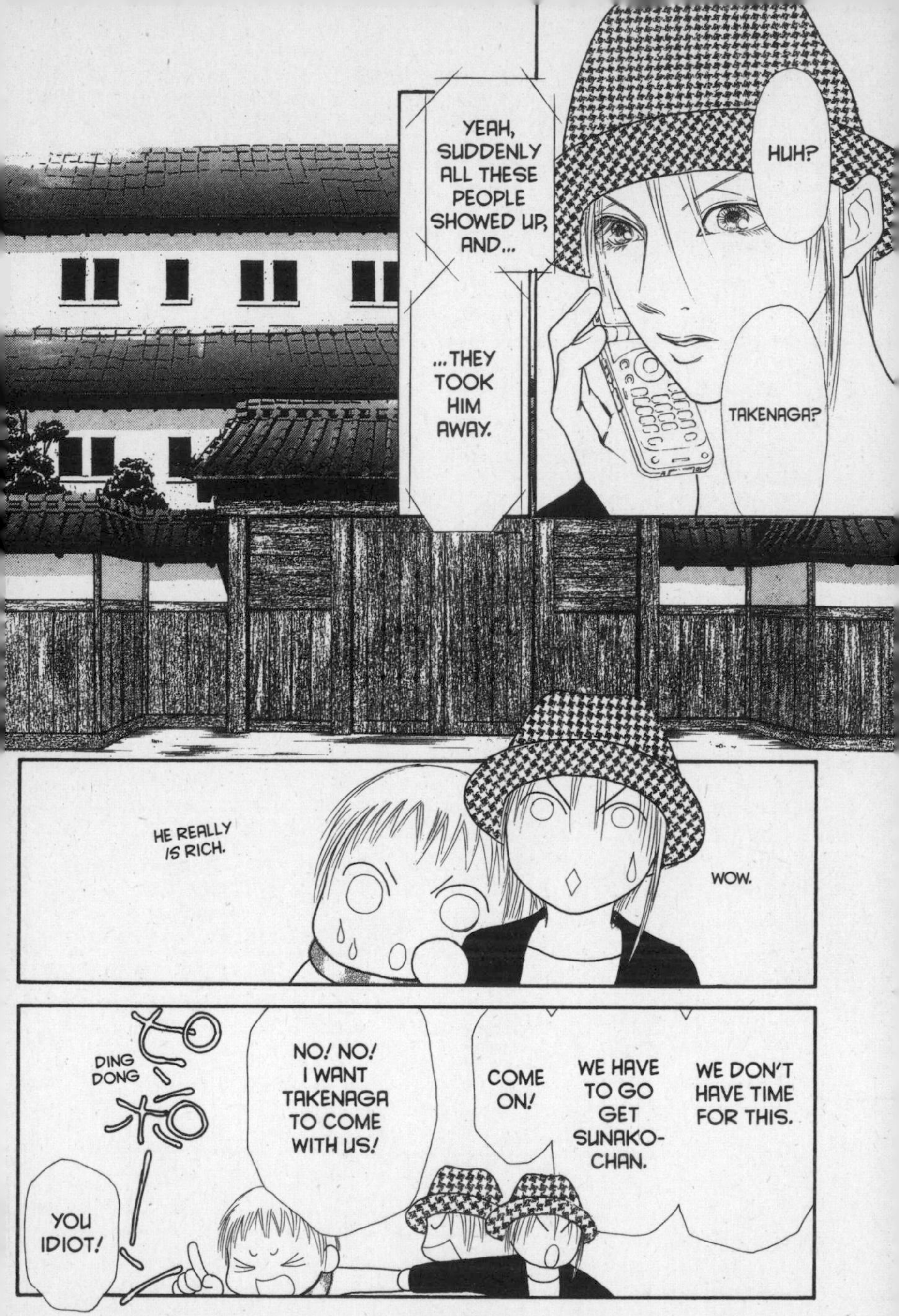
HUH?
TAKENAGA?
YEAH, SUDDENLY ALL THESE PEOPLE SHOWED UP, AND...
...THEY TOOK HIM AWAY.
WOW.
HE REALLY IS RICH.
WE DON'T HAVE TIME FOR THIS.
WE HAVE TO GO GET SUNAKO-CHAN.
COME ON!
NO! NO! I WANT TAKENAGA TO COME WITH US!
DING DONG
YOU IDIOT!

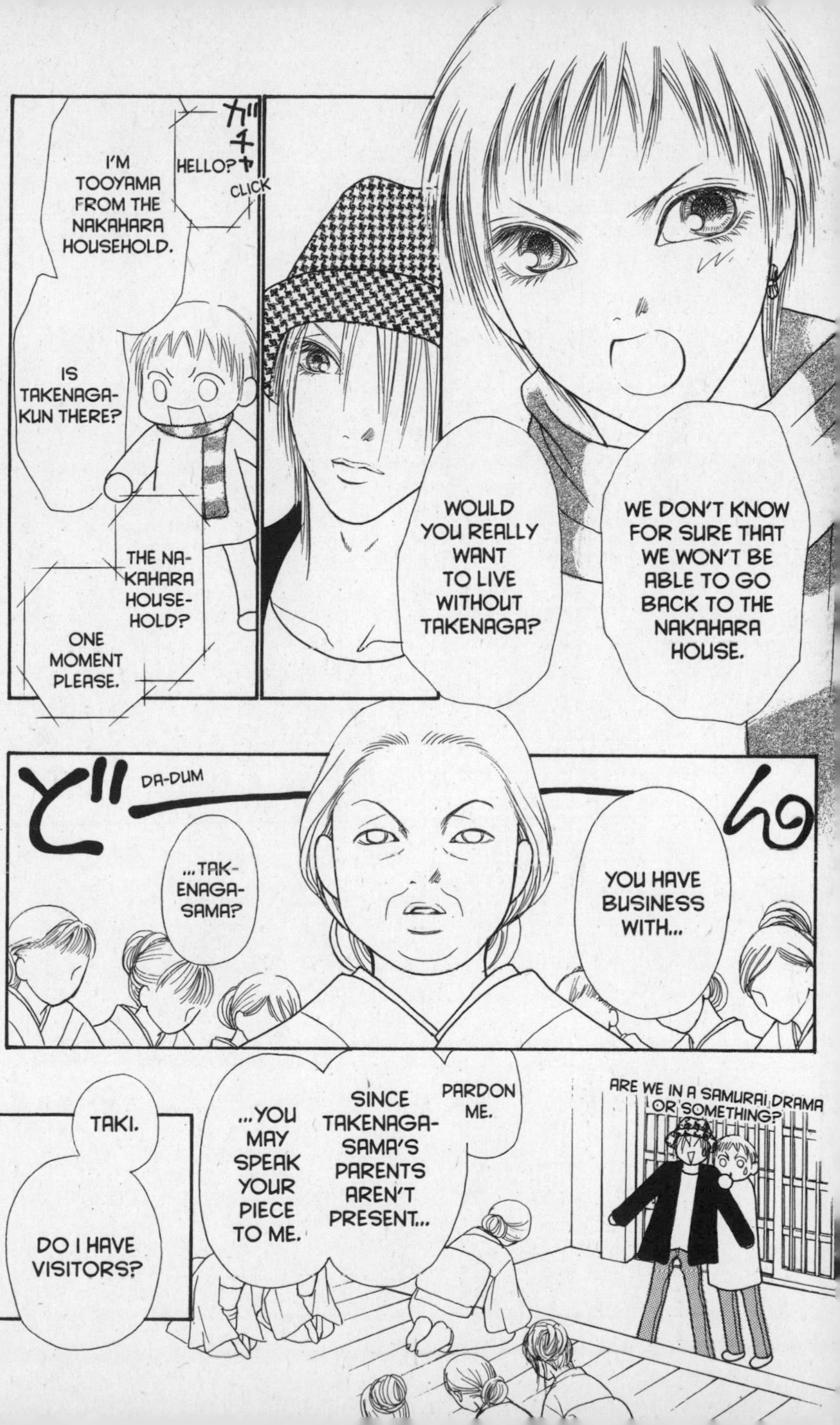
WE DON'T KNOW FOR SURE THAT WE WON'T BE ABLE TO GO BACK TO THE NAKAHARA HOUSE.
WOULD YOU REALLY WANT TO LIVE WITHOUT TAKENAGA?
ガチャ
CLICK
HELLO?
I'M TOOYAMA FROM THE NAKAHARA HOUSEHOLD.
IS TAKENAGA-KUN THERE?
THE NAKAHARA HOUSEHOLD?
ONE MOMENT PLEASE.
どーん
DA-DUM
YOU HAVE BUSINESS WITH...
...TAKENAGA-SAMA?
ARE WE IN A SAMURAI DRAMA OR SOMETHING?
PARDON ME.
SINCE TAKENAGA-SAMA'S PARENTS AREN'T PRESENT...
...YOU MAY SPEAK YOUR PIECE TO ME.
TAKI.
DO I HAVE VISITORS?

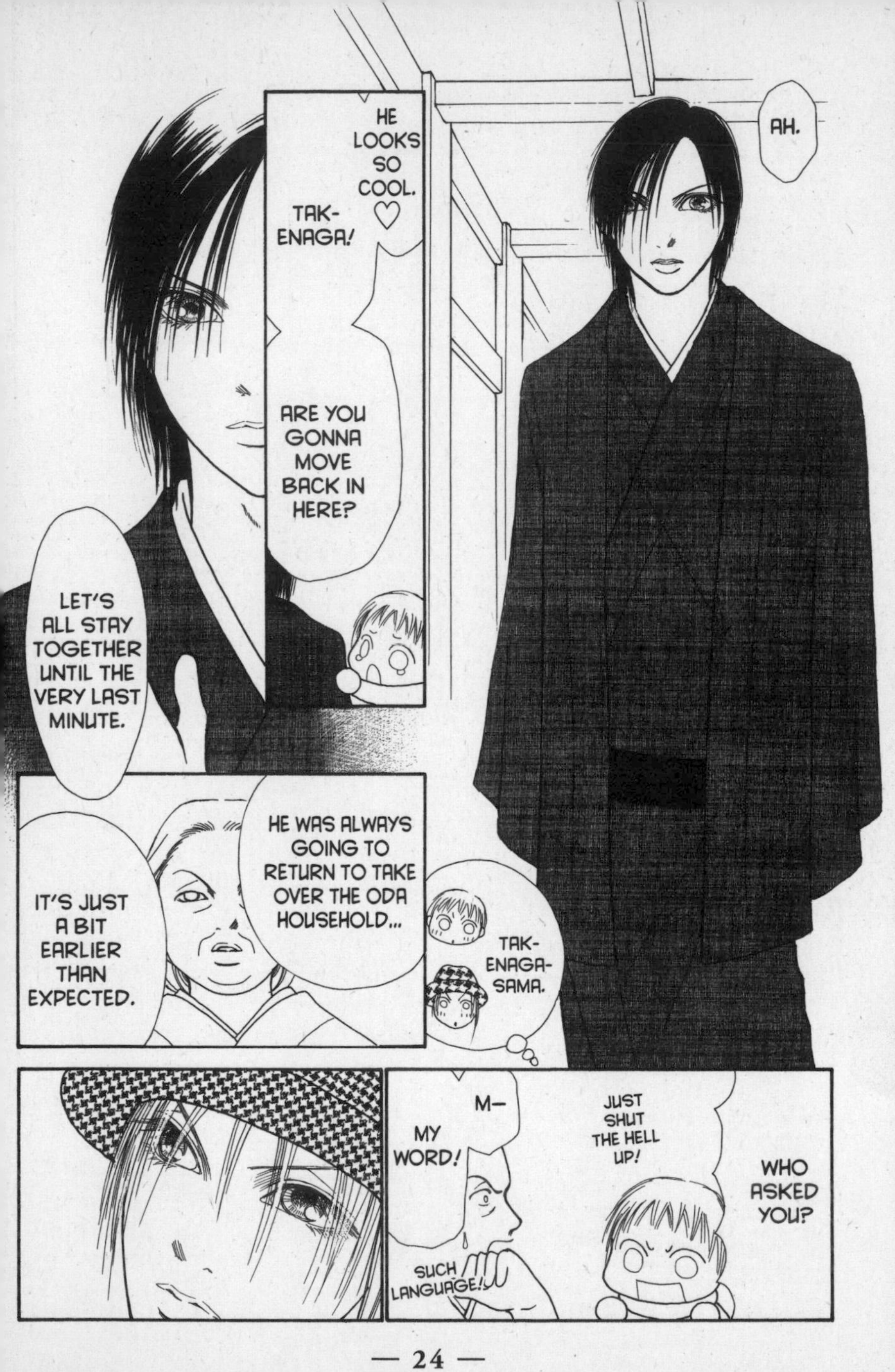
AH.
HE LOOKS SO COOL. ♡
TAK-ENAGA!
ARE YOU GONNA MOVE BACK IN HERE?
LET'S ALL STAY TOGETHER UNTIL THE VERY LAST MINUTE.
TAK-ENAGA-SAMA.
HE WAS ALWAYS GOING TO RETURN TO TAKE OVER THE ODA HOUSEHOLD...
IT'S JUST A BIT EARLIER THAN EXPECTED.
WHO ASKED YOU?
JUST SHUT THE HELL UP!
M—
MY WORD!
SUCH LANGUAGE!

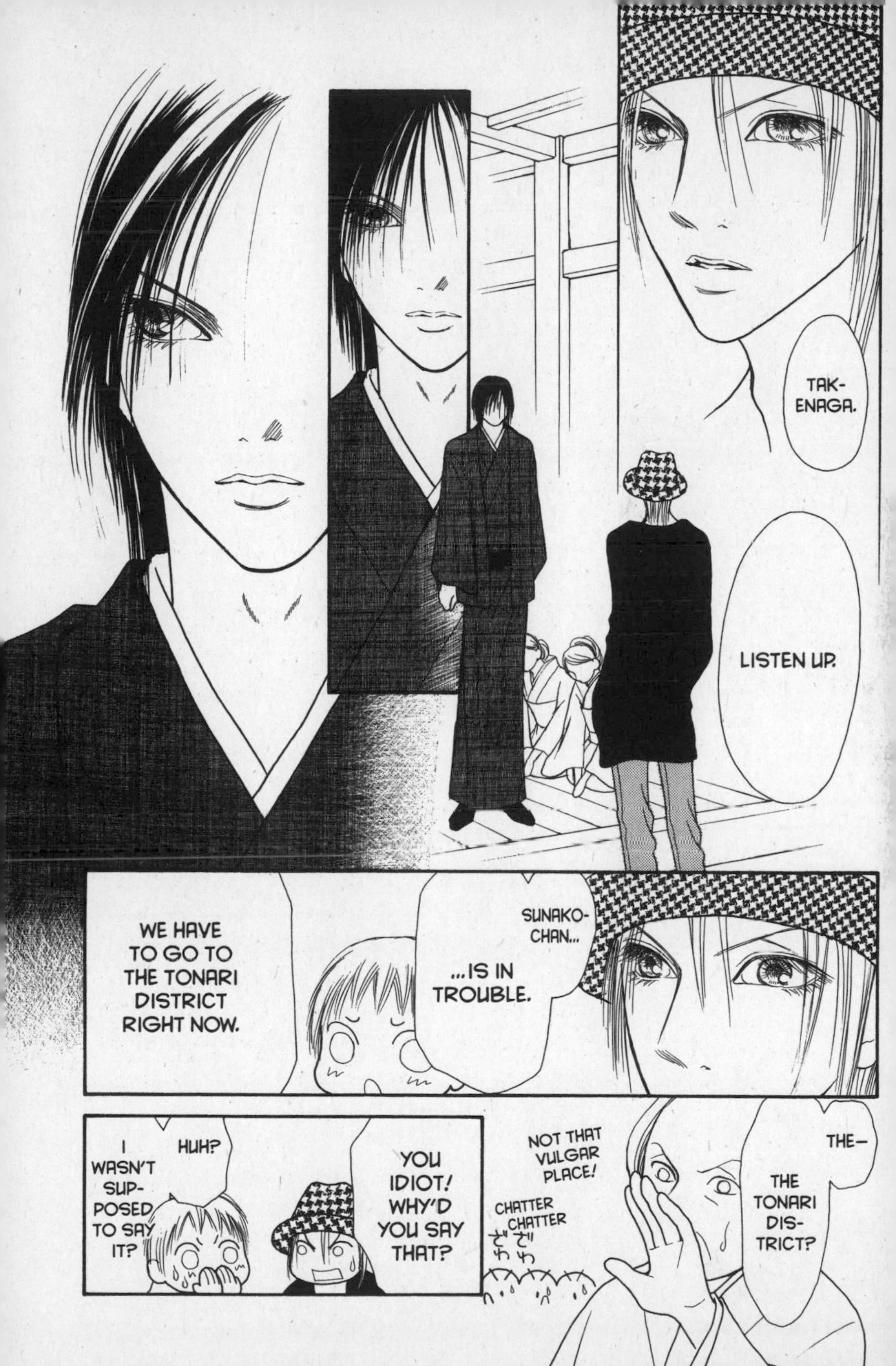
TAK-ENAGA.
LISTEN UP.
SUNAKO-CHAN...
...IS IN TROUBLE.
WE HAVE TO GO TO THE TONARI DISTRICT RIGHT NOW.
THE—
THE TONARI DIS-TRICT?
NOT THAT VULGAR PLACE!
CHATTER CHATTER
YOU IDIOT! WHY'D YOU SAY THAT?
HUH?
I WASN'T SUP-POSED TO SAY IT?

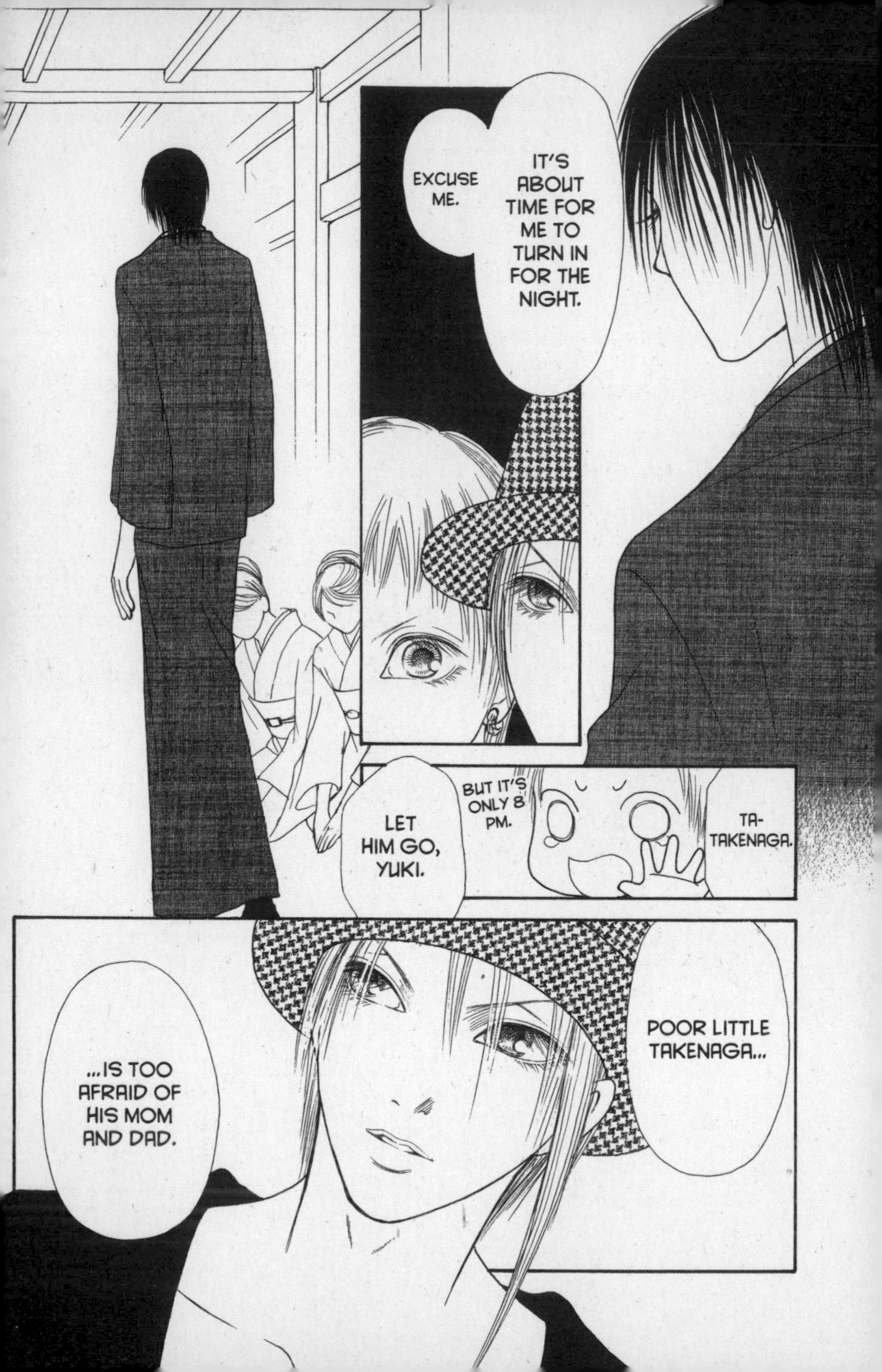
IT'S ABOUT TIME FOR ME TO TURN IN FOR THE NIGHT.
EXCUSE ME.
TA-TAKENAGA.
BUT IT'S ONLY 8 PM.
LET HIM GO, YUKI.
POOR LITTLE TAKENAGA...
...IS TOO AFRAID OF HIS MOM AND DAD.

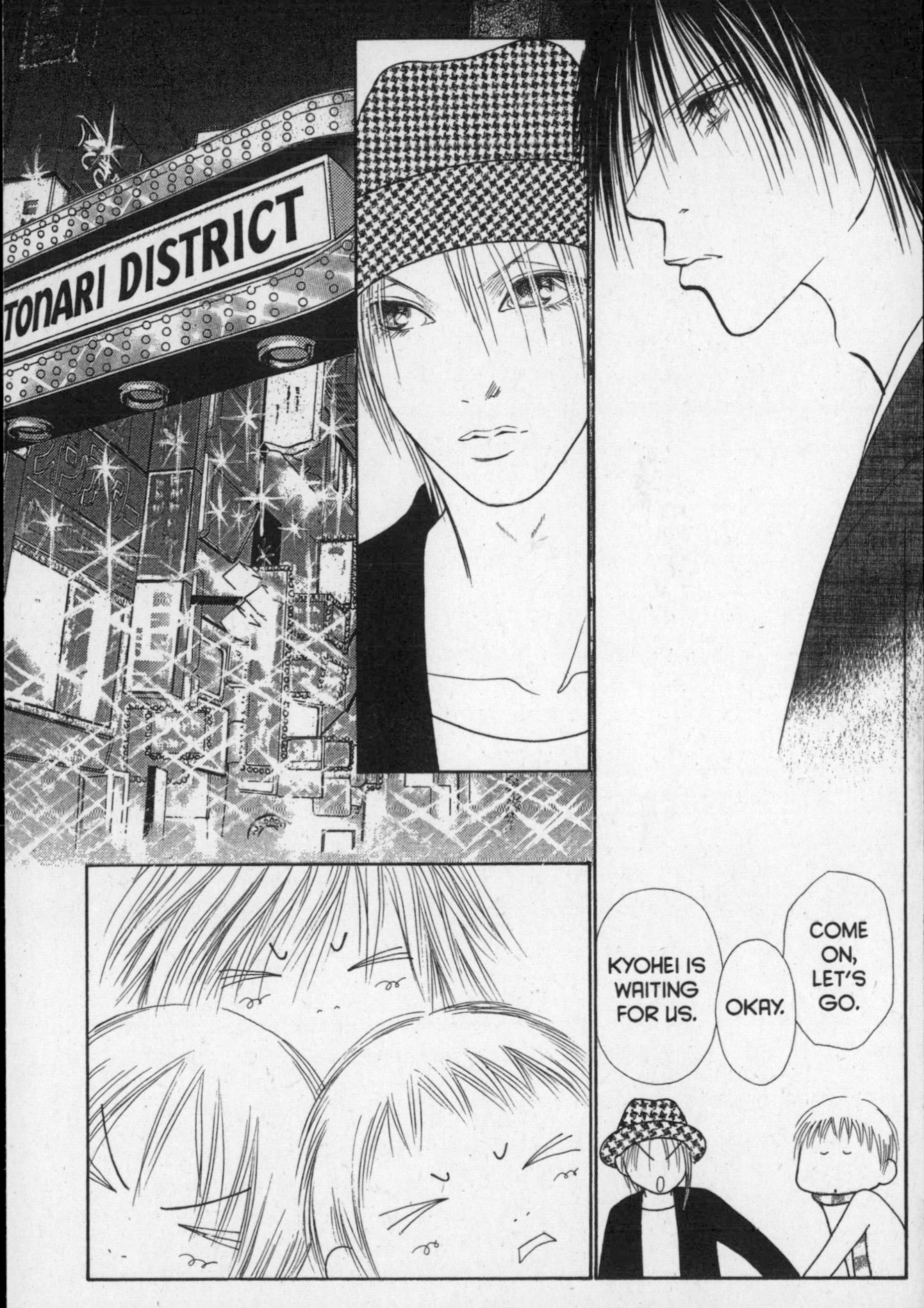
TONARI DISTRICT
COME ON, LET'S GO.
OKAY.
KYOHEI IS WAITING FOR US.

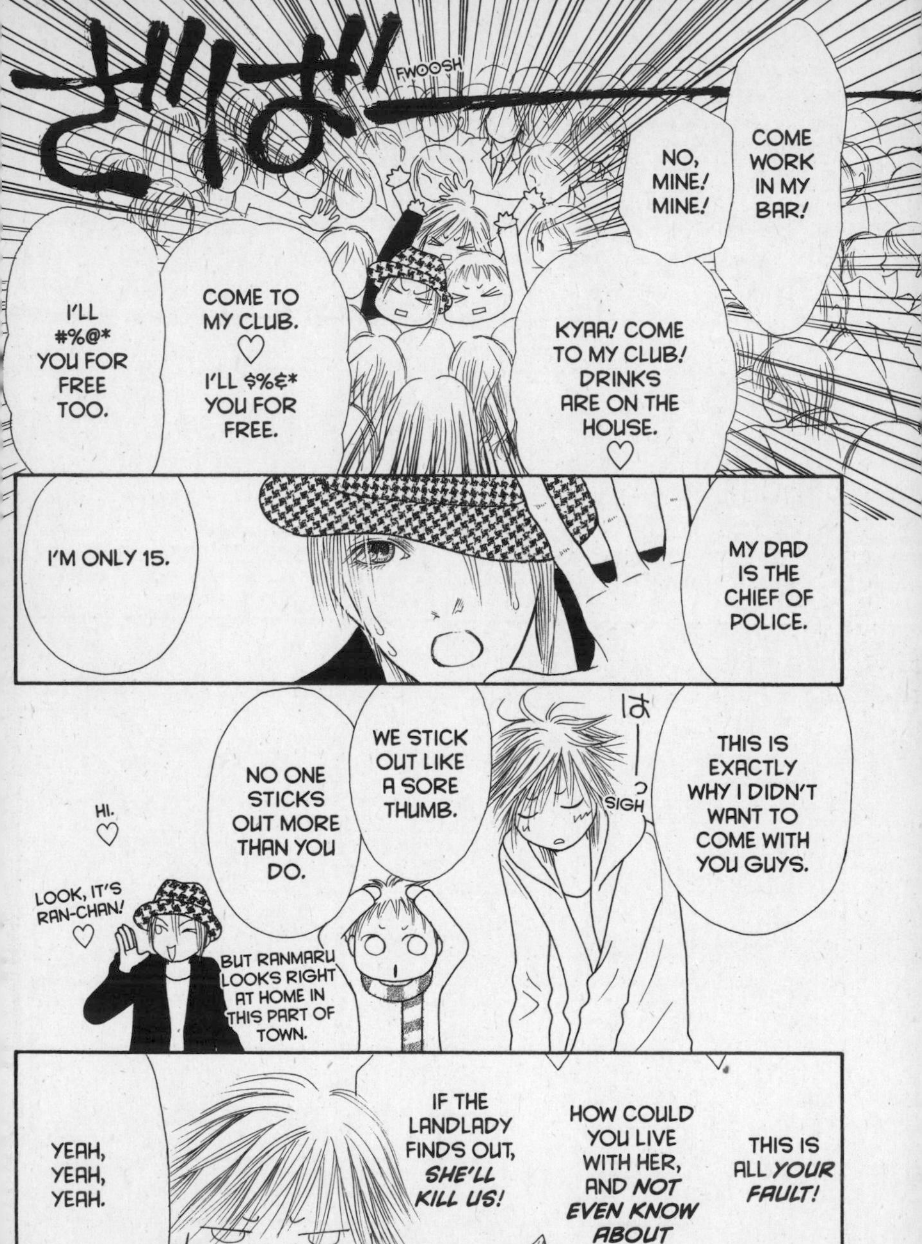
FWOOSH
COME WORK IN MY BAR!
NO, MINE! MINE!
KYAA! COME TO MY CLUB! DRINKS ARE ON THE HOUSE. ♡
COME TO MY CLUB. ♡ I'LL $%&* YOU FOR FREE.
I'LL #%@* YOU FOR FREE TOO.
MY DAD IS THE CHIEF OF POLICE.
I'M ONLY 15.
はーっ
SIGH
THIS IS EXACTLY WHY I DIDN'T WANT TO COME WITH YOU GUYS.
WE STICK OUT LIKE A SORE THUMB.
NO ONE STICKS OUT MORE THAN YOU DO.
HI. ♡
LOOK, IT'S RAN-CHAN! ♡
BUT RANMARU LOOKS RIGHT AT HOME IN THIS PART OF TOWN.
THIS IS ALL *YOUR FAULT!*
HOW COULD YOU LIVE WITH HER, AND *NOT EVEN KNOW ABOUT THIS?*
IF THE LANDLADY FINDS OUT, *SHE'LL KILL US!*
YEAH, YEAH, YEAH.

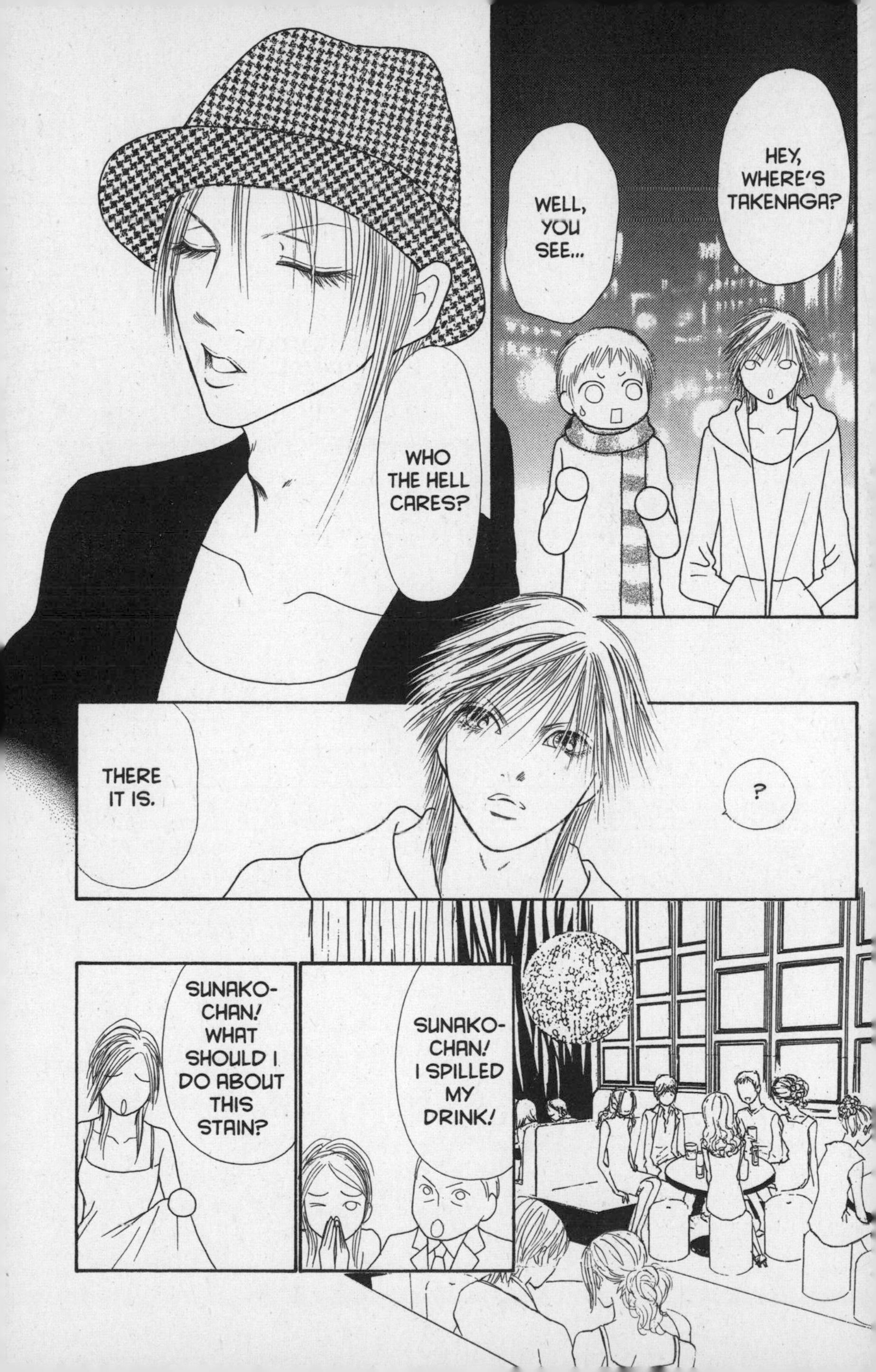
HEY, WHERE'S TAKENAGA?
WELL, YOU SEE...
WHO THE HELL CARES?
?
THERE IT IS.
SUNAKO-CHAN! I SPILLED MY DRINK!
SUNAKO-CHAN! WHAT SHOULD I DO ABOUT THIS STAIN?

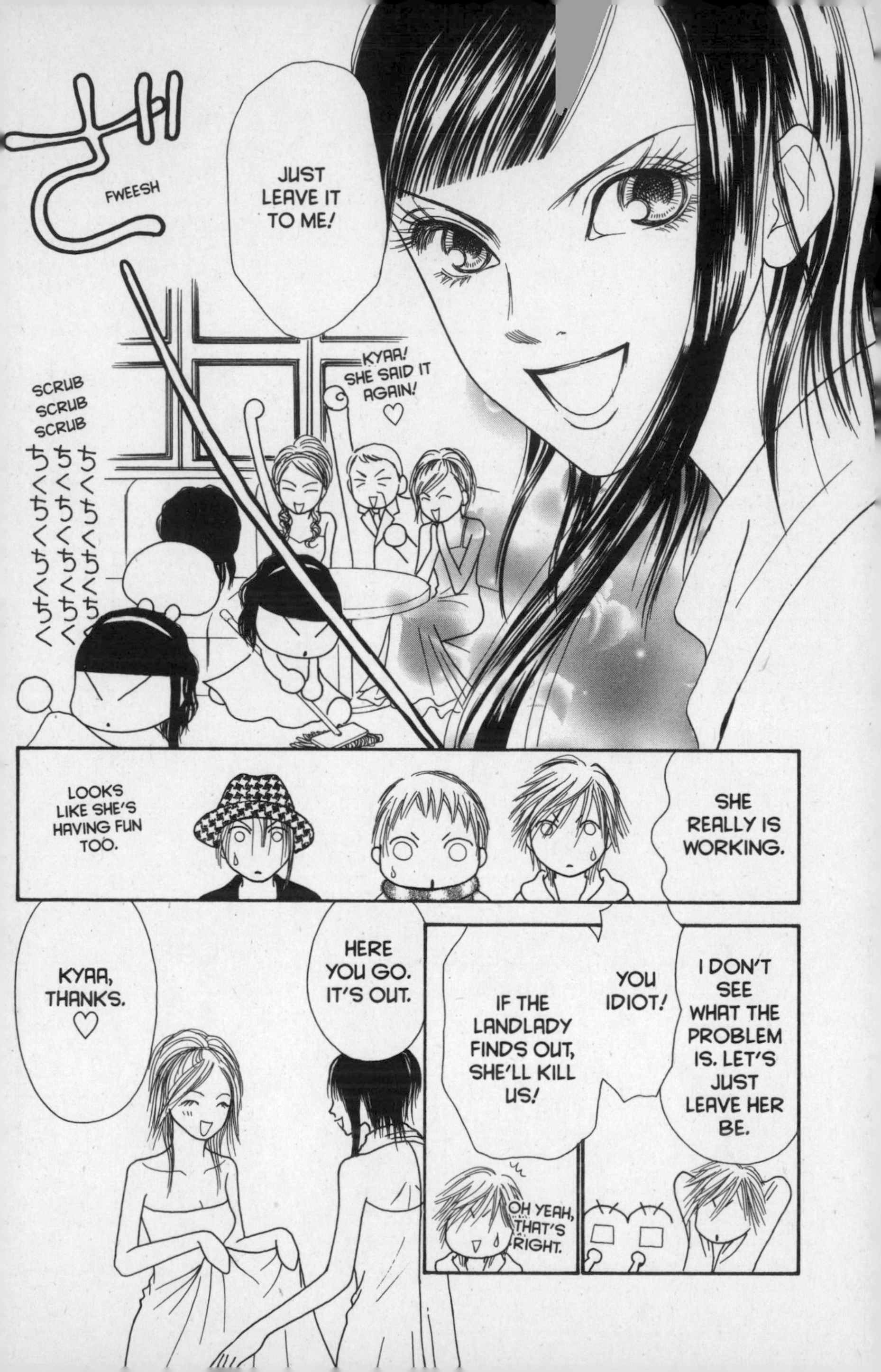
JUST LEAVE IT TO ME!
FWEESH
KYAA! SHE SAID IT AGAIN! ♡
SCRUB SCRUB SCRUB
SHE REALLY IS WORKING.
LOOKS LIKE SHE'S HAVING FUN TOO.
I DON'T SEE WHAT THE PROBLEM IS. LET'S JUST LEAVE HER BE.
YOU IDIOT!
IF THE LANDLADY FINDS OUT, SHE'LL KILL US!
OH YEAH, THAT'S RIGHT.
HERE YOU GO. IT'S OUT.
KYAA, THANKS. ♡

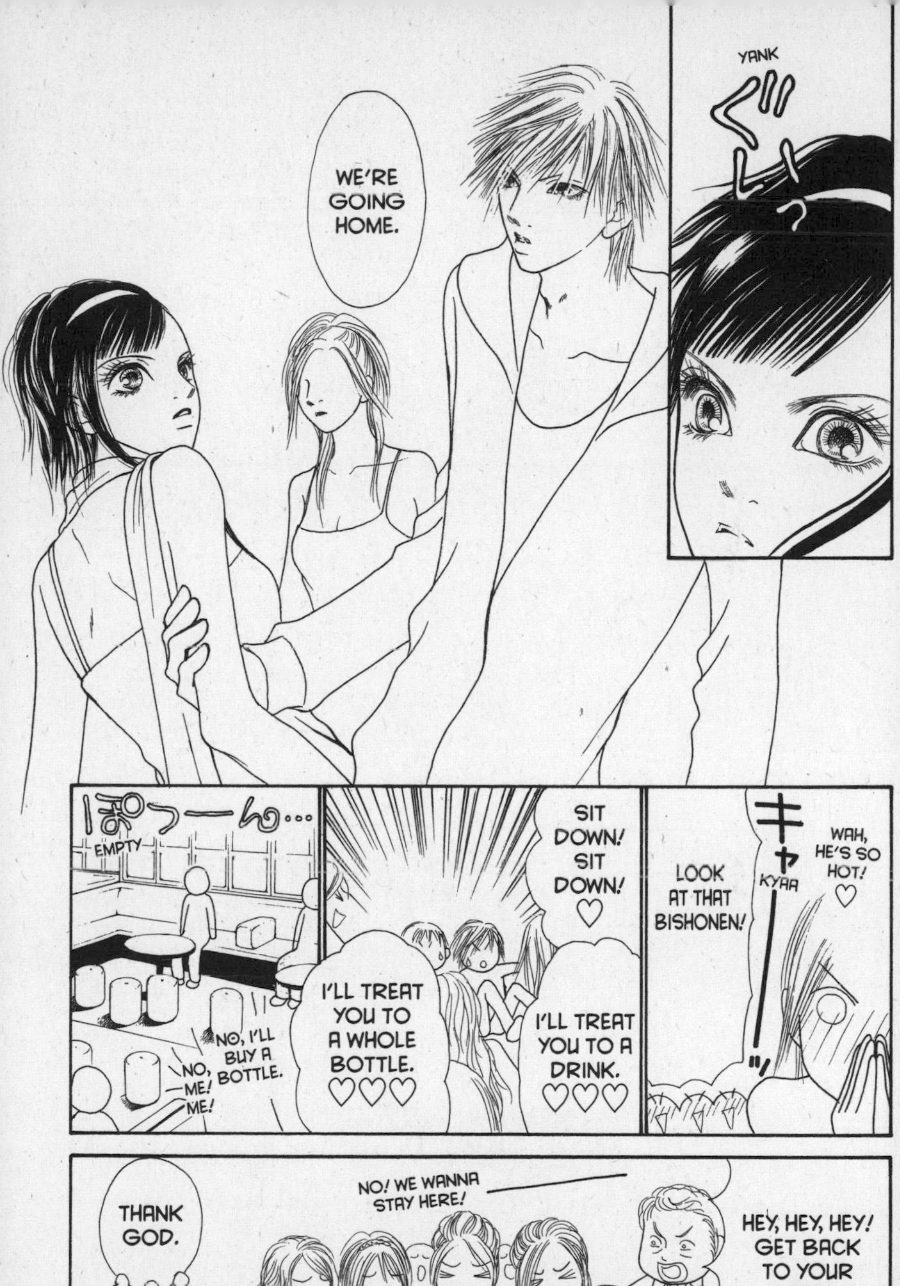
YANK
ぐいっ
WE'RE GOING HOME.
キャー
KYAA
WAH, HE'S SO HOT! ♡
LOOK AT THAT BISHONEN!
SIT DOWN! SIT DOWN! ♡
I'LL TREAT YOU TO A DRINK. ♡♡♡
I'LL TREAT YOU TO A WHOLE BOTTLE. ♡♡♡
ぽつーん…
EMPTY
NO, I'LL BUY A BOTTLE.
NO, ME! ME!
HEY, HEY, HEY! GET BACK TO YOUR SEATS!
NO! WE WANNA STAY HERE!
THANK GOD.

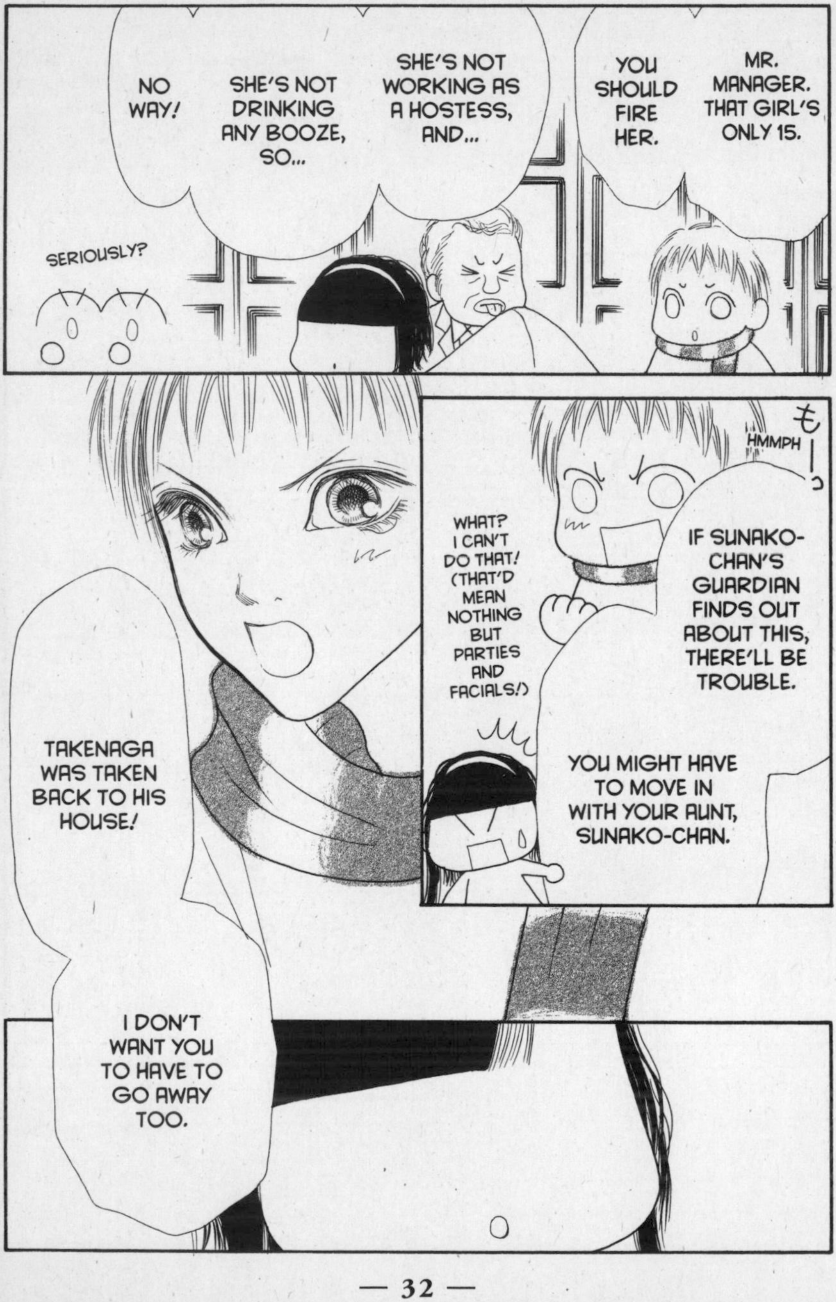
MR. MANAGER. THAT GIRL'S ONLY 15.
YOU SHOULD FIRE HER.
SHE'S NOT WORKING AS A HOSTESS, AND...
SHE'S NOT DRINKING ANY BOOZE, SO...
NO WAY!
SERIOUSLY?
もーっ
HMMPH
IF SUNAKO-CHAN'S GUARDIAN FINDS OUT ABOUT THIS, THERE'LL BE TROUBLE.
WHAT? I CAN'T DO THAT! (THAT'D MEAN NOTHING BUT PARTIES AND FACIALS!)
YOU MIGHT HAVE TO MOVE IN WITH YOUR AUNT, SUNAKO-CHAN.
TAKENAGA WAS TAKEN BACK TO HIS HOUSE!
I DON'T WANT YOU TO HAVE TO GO AWAY TOO.

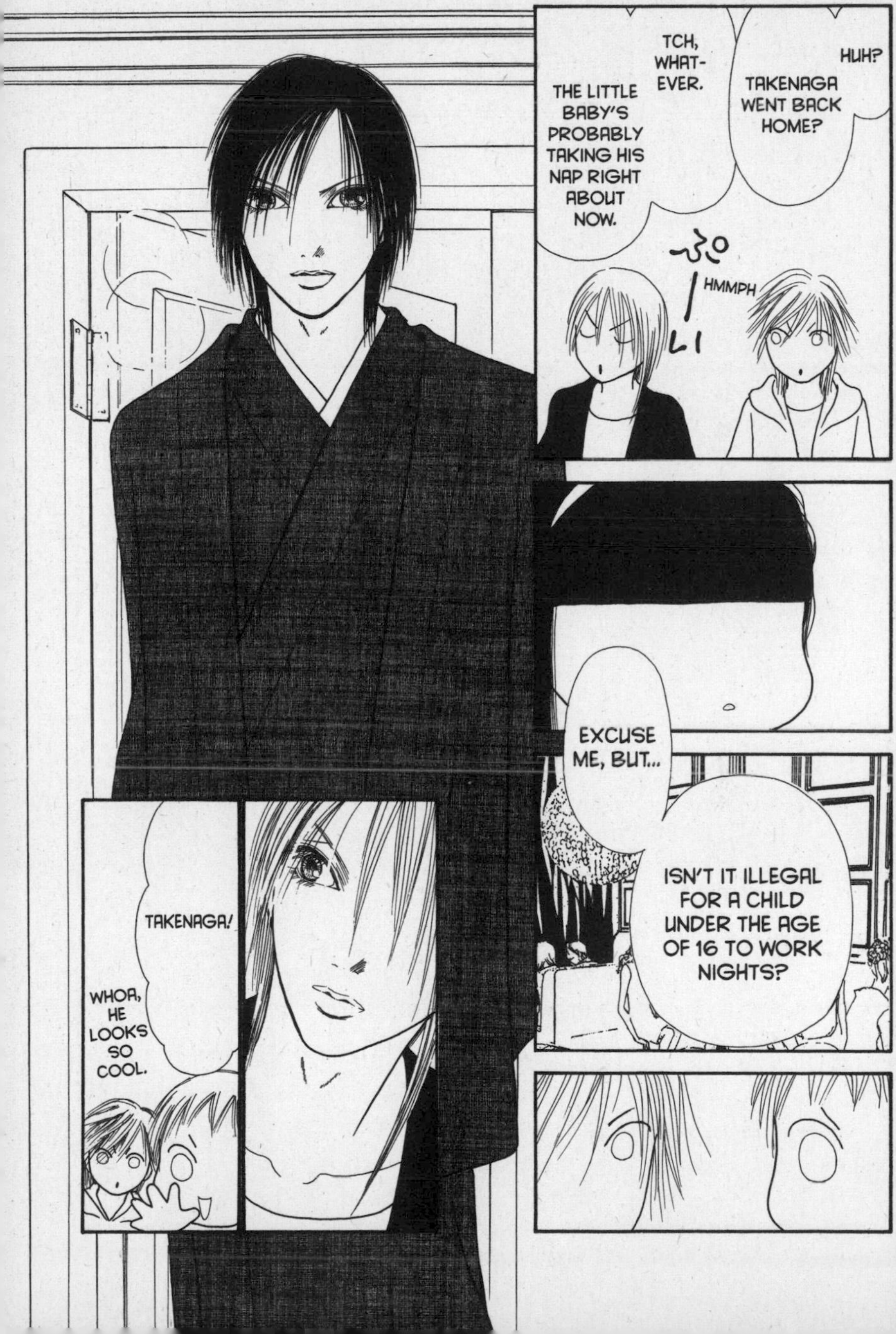
HUH?
TAKENAGA WENT BACK HOME?
TCH, WHAT-EVER.
THE LITTLE BABY'S PROBABLY TAKING HIS NAP RIGHT ABOUT NOW.
HMMPH
EXCUSE ME, BUT...
ISN'T IT ILLEGAL FOR A CHILD UNDER THE AGE OF 16 TO WORK NIGHTS?
TAKENAGA!
WHOA, HE LOOKS SO COOL.

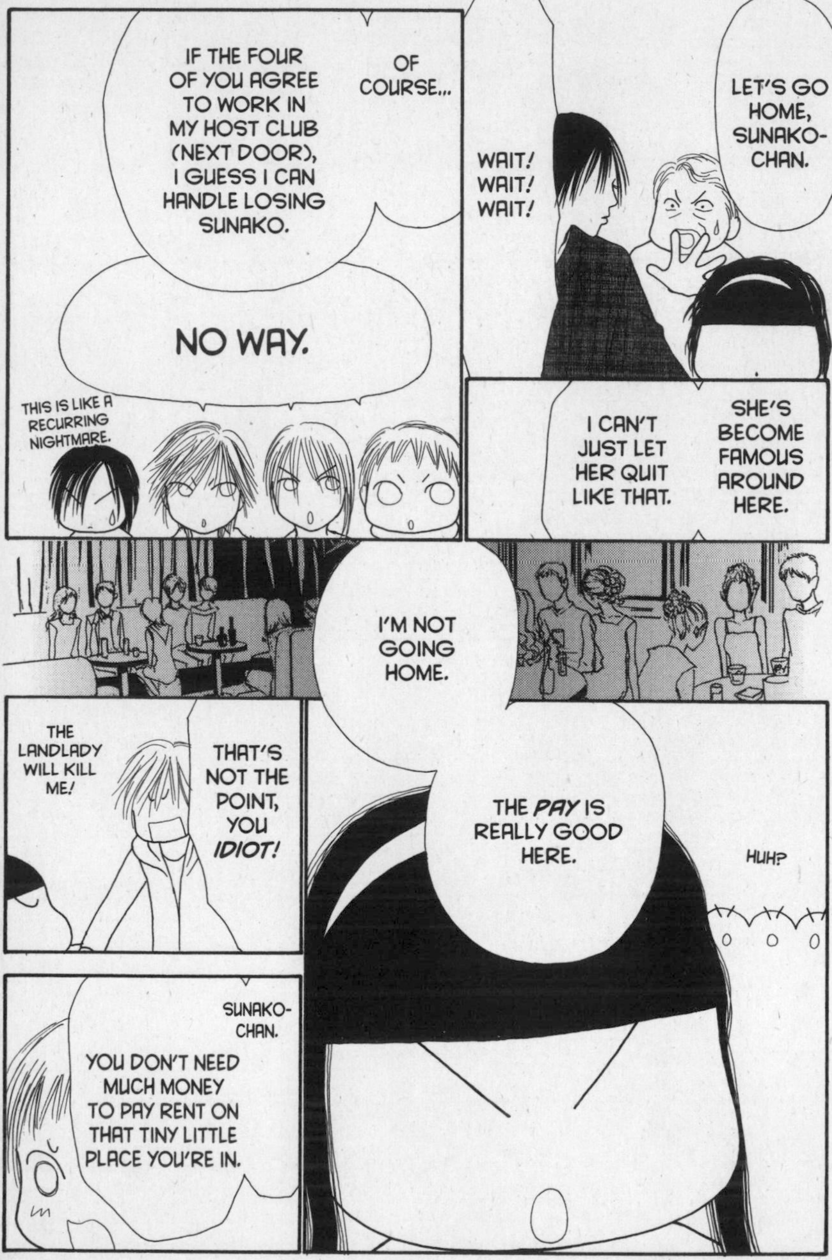
LET'S GO HOME, SUNAKO-CHAN.
WAIT! WAIT! WAIT!
SHE'S BECOME FAMOUS AROUND HERE.
I CAN'T JUST LET HER QUIT LIKE THAT.
OF COURSE...
IF THE FOUR OF YOU AGREE TO WORK IN MY HOST CLUB (NEXT DOOR), I GUESS I CAN HANDLE LOSING SUNAKO.
NO WAY.
THIS IS LIKE A RECURRING NIGHTMARE.
I'M NOT GOING HOME.
HUH?
THE *PAY* IS REALLY GOOD HERE.
THAT'S NOT THE POINT, YOU *IDIOT!*
THE LANDLADY WILL KILL ME!
SUNAKO-CHAN.
YOU DON'T NEED MUCH MONEY TO PAY RENT ON THAT TINY LITTLE PLACE YOU'RE IN.

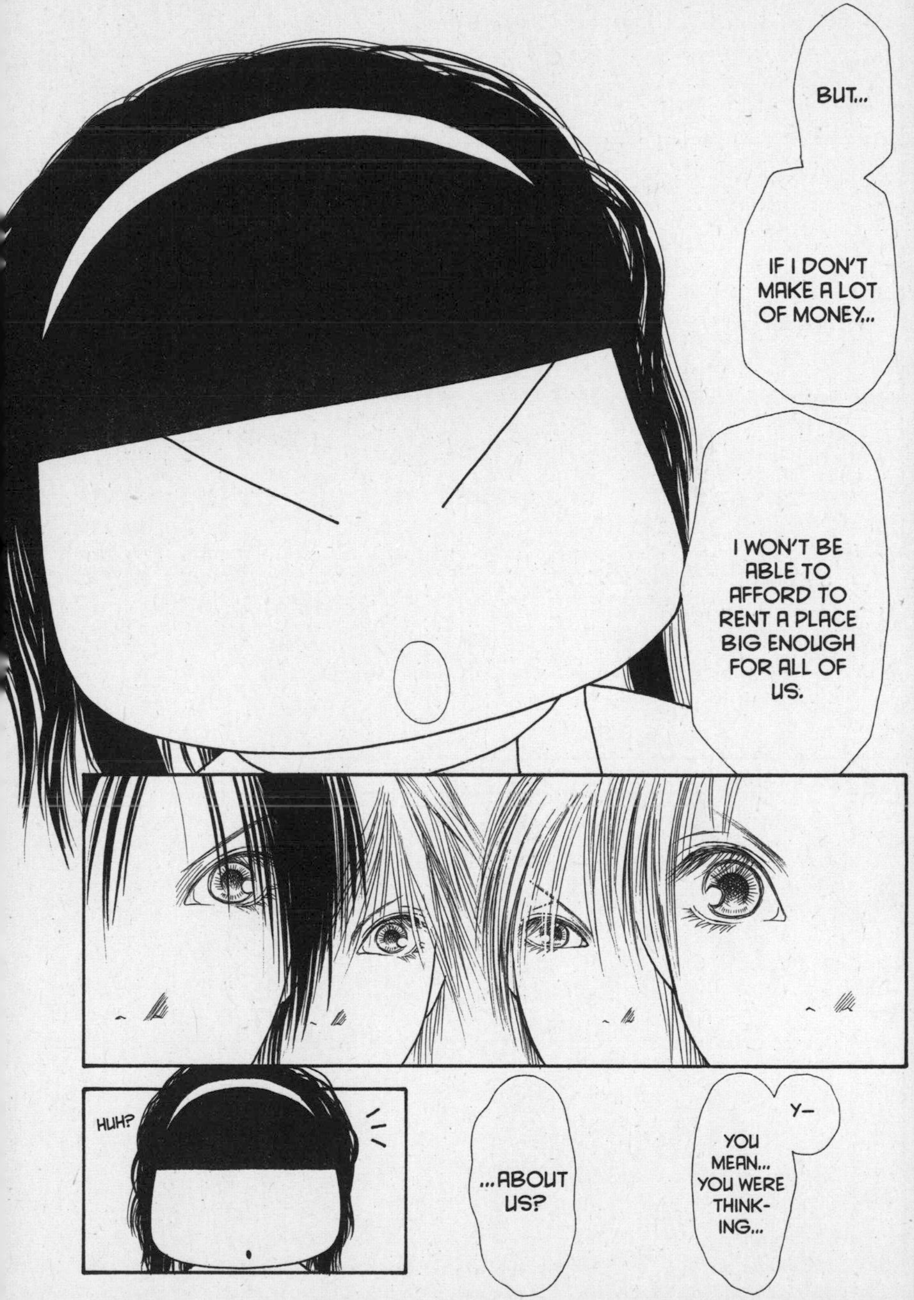
BUT...
IF I DON'T MAKE A LOT OF MONEY...
I WON'T BE ABLE TO AFFORD TO RENT A PLACE BIG ENOUGH FOR ALL OF US.
Y—
YOU MEAN... YOU WERE THINK-ING...
...ABOUT US?
HUH?

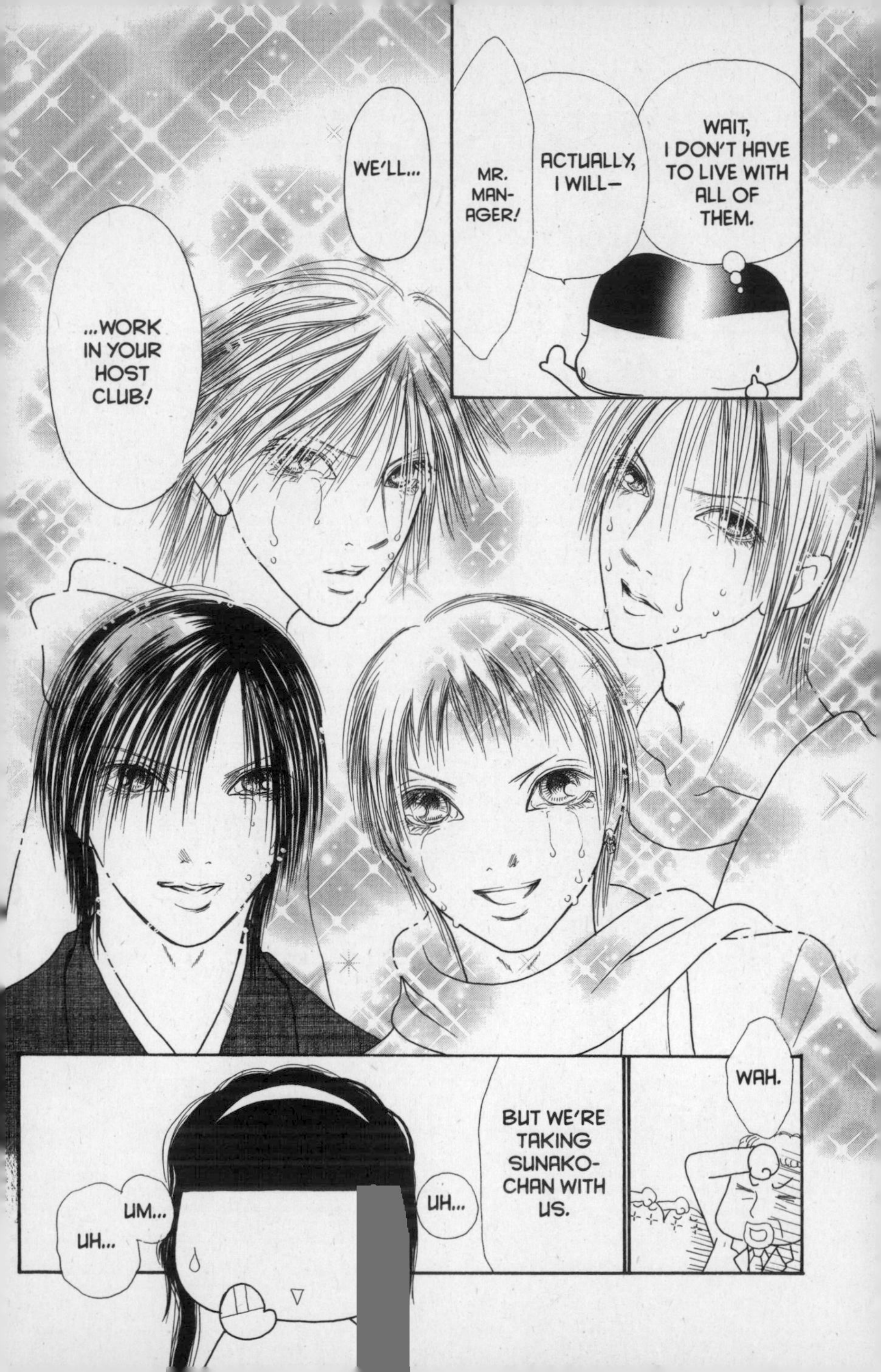
WAIT, I DON'T HAVE TO LIVE WITH ALL OF THEM.
ACTUALLY, I WILL—
MR. MAN-AGER!
WE'LL...
...WORK IN YOUR HOST CLUB!
WAH.
BUT WE'RE TAKING SUNAKO-CHAN WITH US.
UH...
UM...
UH...

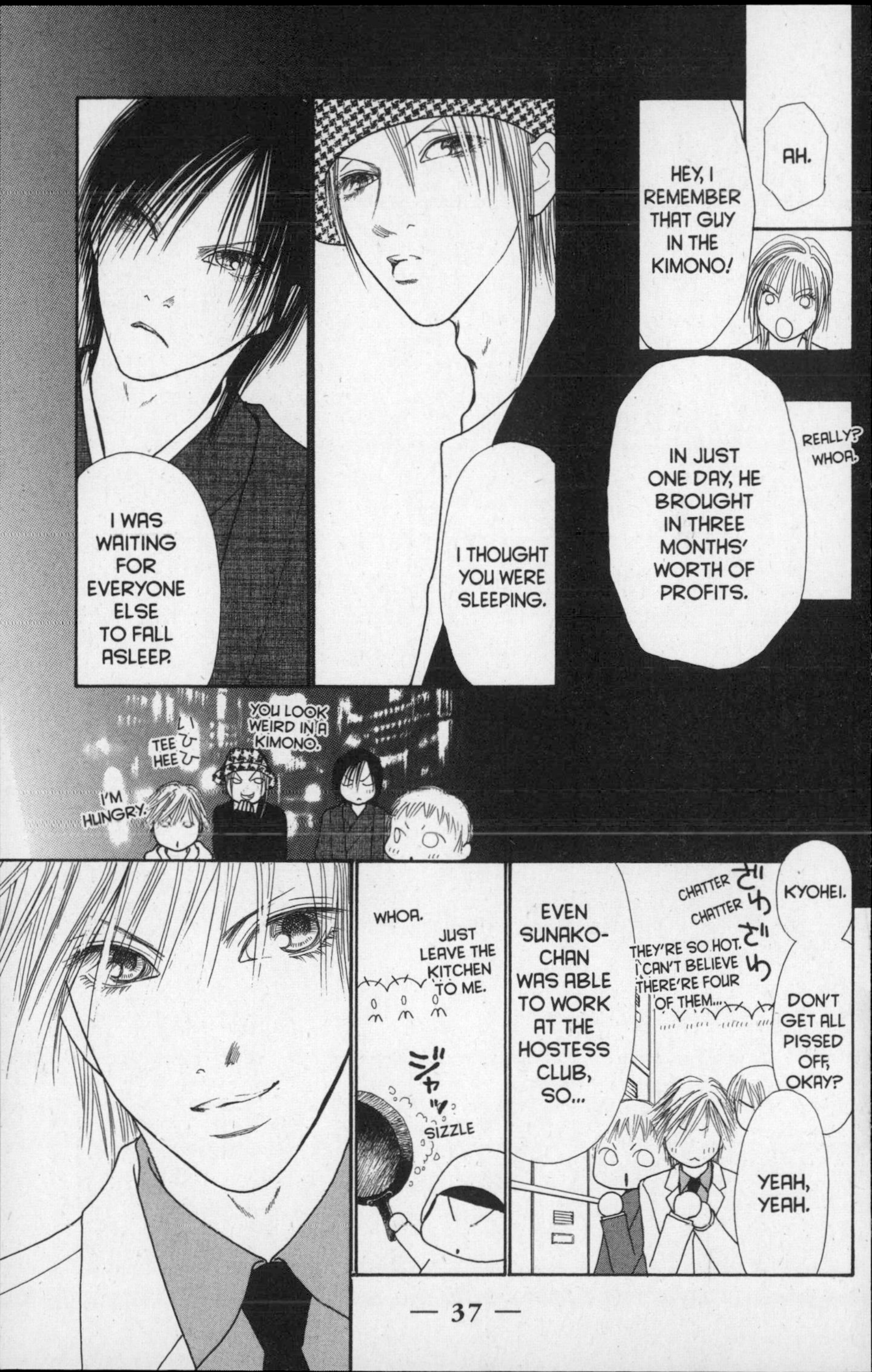
AH.
HEY, I REMEMBER THAT GUY IN THE KIMONO!
IN JUST ONE DAY, HE BROUGHT IN THREE MONTHS' WORTH OF PROFITS.
REALLY? WHOA.
I THOUGHT YOU WERE SLEEPING.
I WAS WAITING FOR EVERYONE ELSE TO FALL ASLEEP.
YOU LOOK WEIRD IN A KIMONO.
いひひ
TEE HEE
I'M HUNGRY.
KYOHEI.
ざわざわ
CHATTER CHATTER
THEY'RE SO HOT. I CAN'T BELIEVE THERE'RE FOUR OF THEM...
DON'T GET ALL PISSED OFF, OKAY?
EVEN SUNAKO-CHAN WAS ABLE TO WORK AT THE HOSTESS CLUB, SO...
YEAH, YEAH.
WHOA.
JUST LEAVE THE KITCHEN TO ME.
ジャッ
SIZZLE

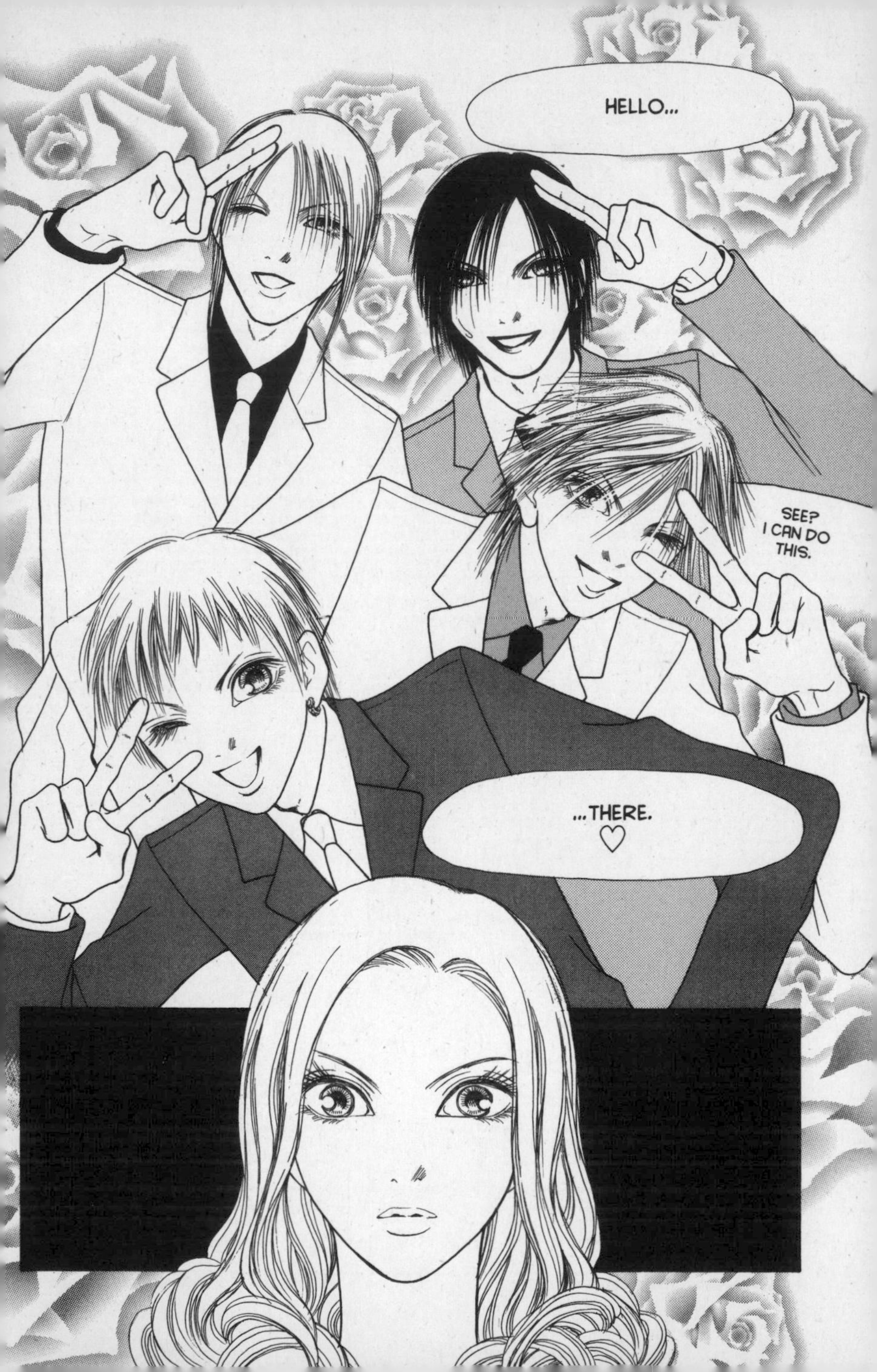
HELLO...
SEE? I CAN DO THIS.
...THERE. ♡

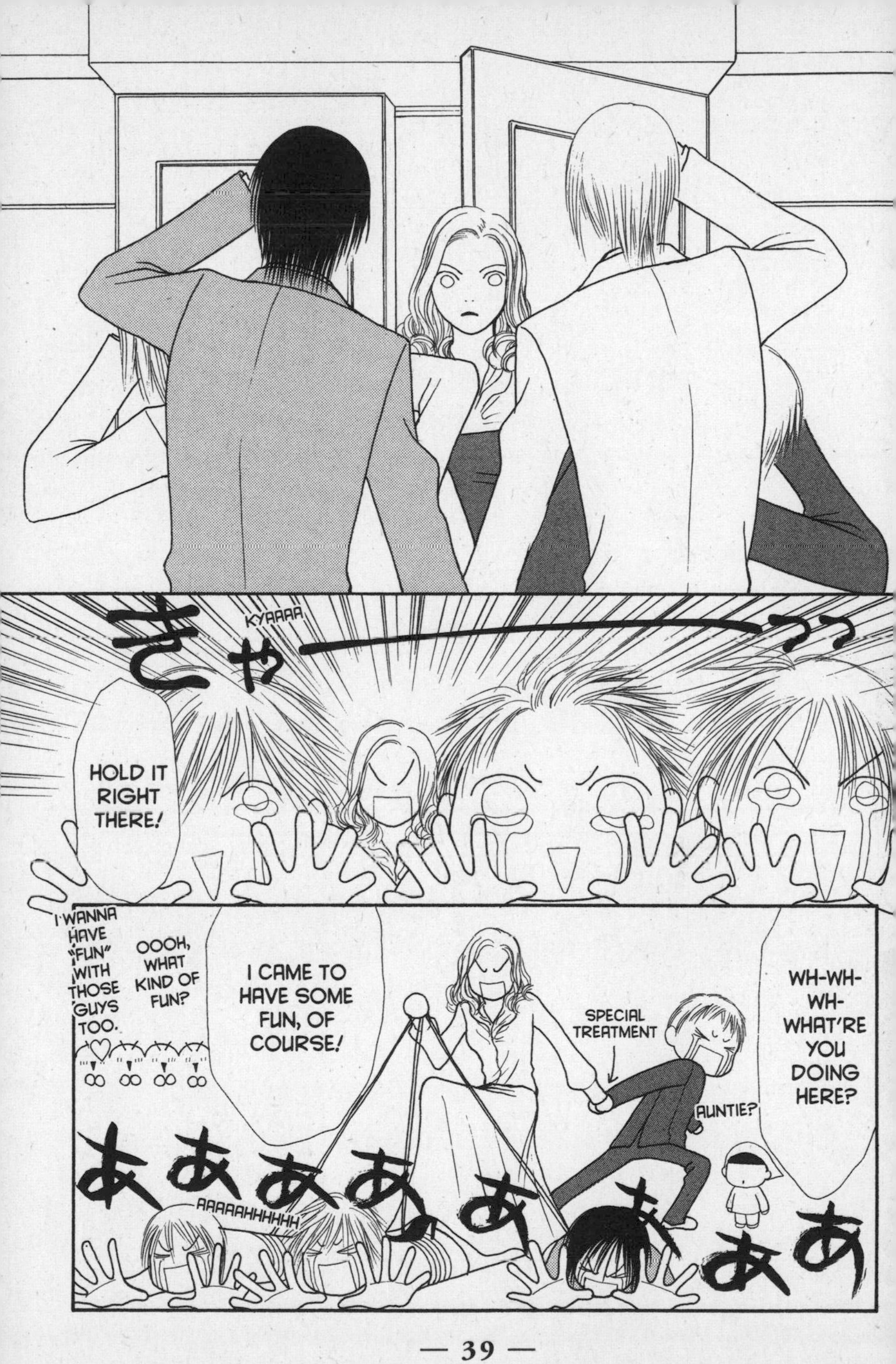
きゃーっっ
KYAAAA
HOLD IT RIGHT THERE!
WH-WH-WH-WHAT'RE YOU DOING HERE?
AUNTIE?
SPECIAL TREATMENT
I CAME TO HAVE SOME FUN, OF COURSE!
OOOH, WHAT KIND OF FUN?
I WANNA HAVE "FUN" WITH THOSE GUYS TOO.
ああああああああ
AAAAAHHHHHH

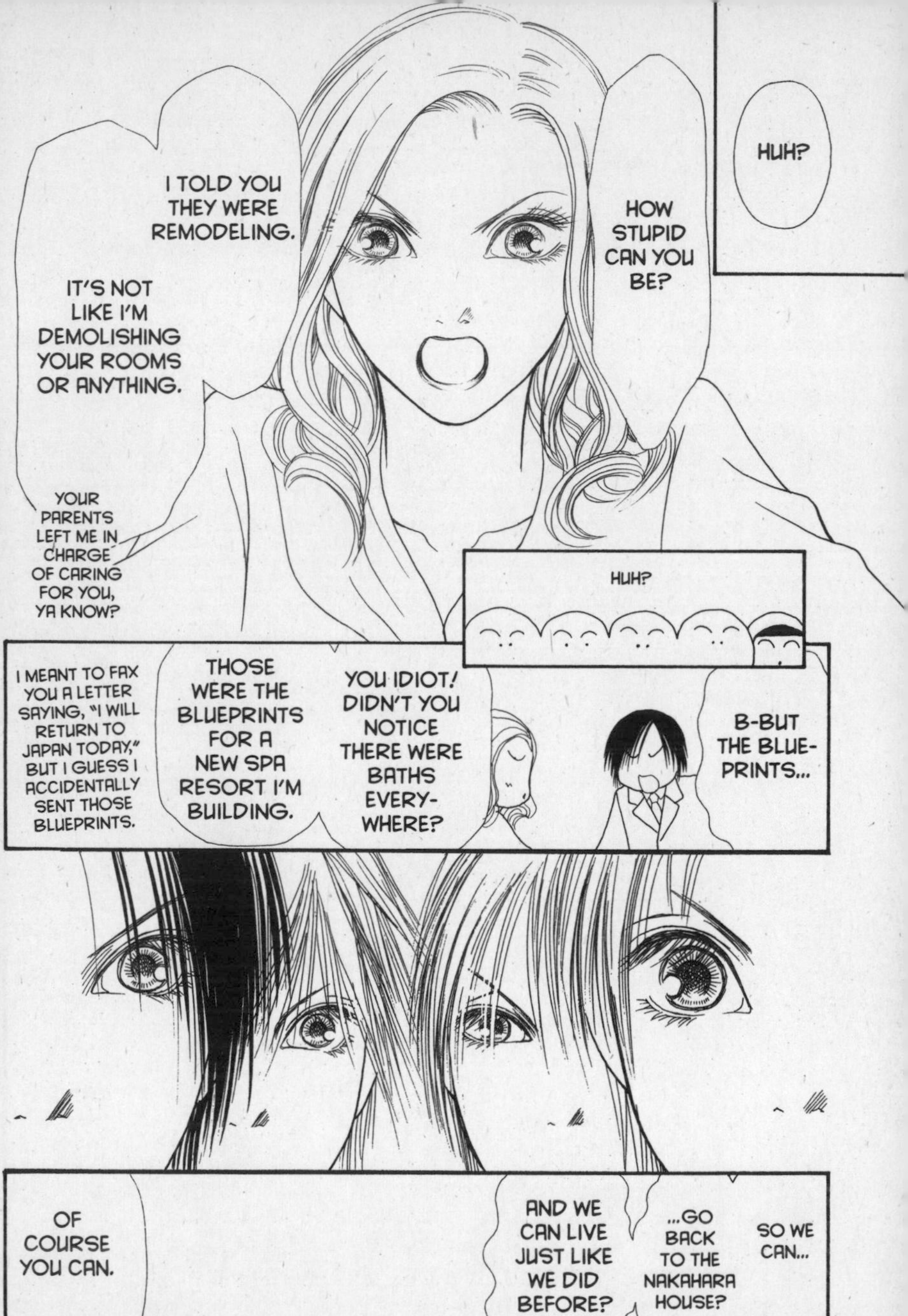
HUH?
HOW STUPID CAN YOU BE?
I TOLD YOU THEY WERE REMODELING.
IT'S NOT LIKE I'M DEMOLISHING YOUR ROOMS OR ANYTHING.
YOUR PARENTS LEFT ME IN CHARGE OF CARING FOR YOU, YA KNOW?
HUH?
B-BUT THE BLUE-PRINTS...
YOU IDIOT! DIDN'T YOU NOTICE THERE WERE BATHS EVERY-WHERE?
THOSE WERE THE BLUEPRINTS FOR A NEW SPA RESORT I'M BUILDING.
I MEANT TO FAX YOU A LETTER SAYING, "I WILL RETURN TO JAPAN TODAY," BUT I GUESS I ACCIDENTALLY SENT THOSE BLUEPRINTS.
SO WE CAN...
...GO BACK TO THE NAKAHARA HOUSE?
AND WE CAN LIVE JUST LIKE WE DID BEFORE?
OF COURSE YOU CAN.

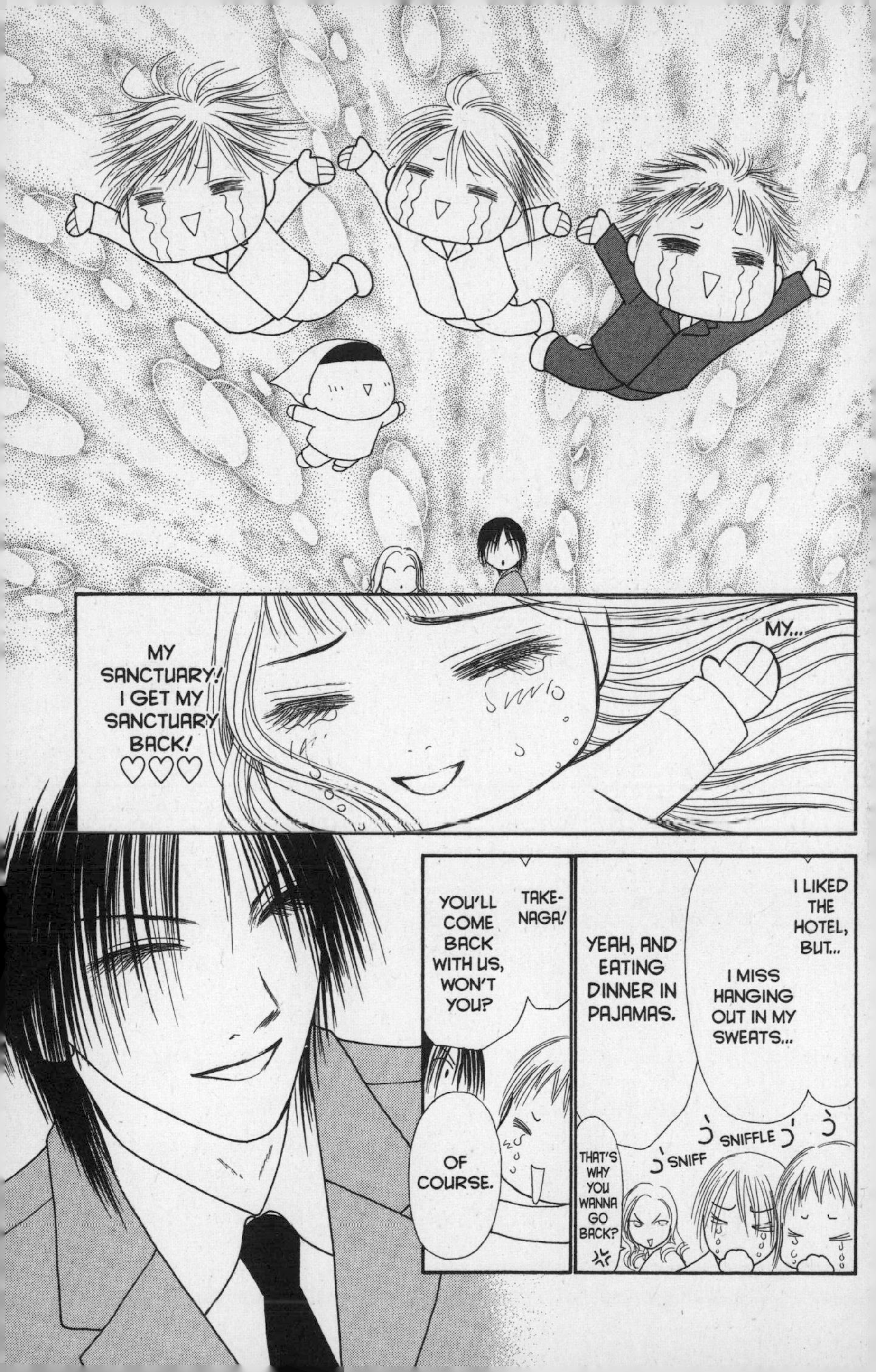
MY...
MY SANCTUARY! I GET MY SANCTUARY BACK! ♡♡♡
I LIKED THE HOTEL, BUT...
I MISS HANGING OUT IN MY SWEATS...
YEAH, AND EATING DINNER IN PAJAMAS.
SNIFFLE
SNIFF
THAT'S WHY YOU WANNA GO BACK?
TAKE-NAGA!
YOU'LL COME BACK WITH US, WON'T YOU?
OF COURSE.

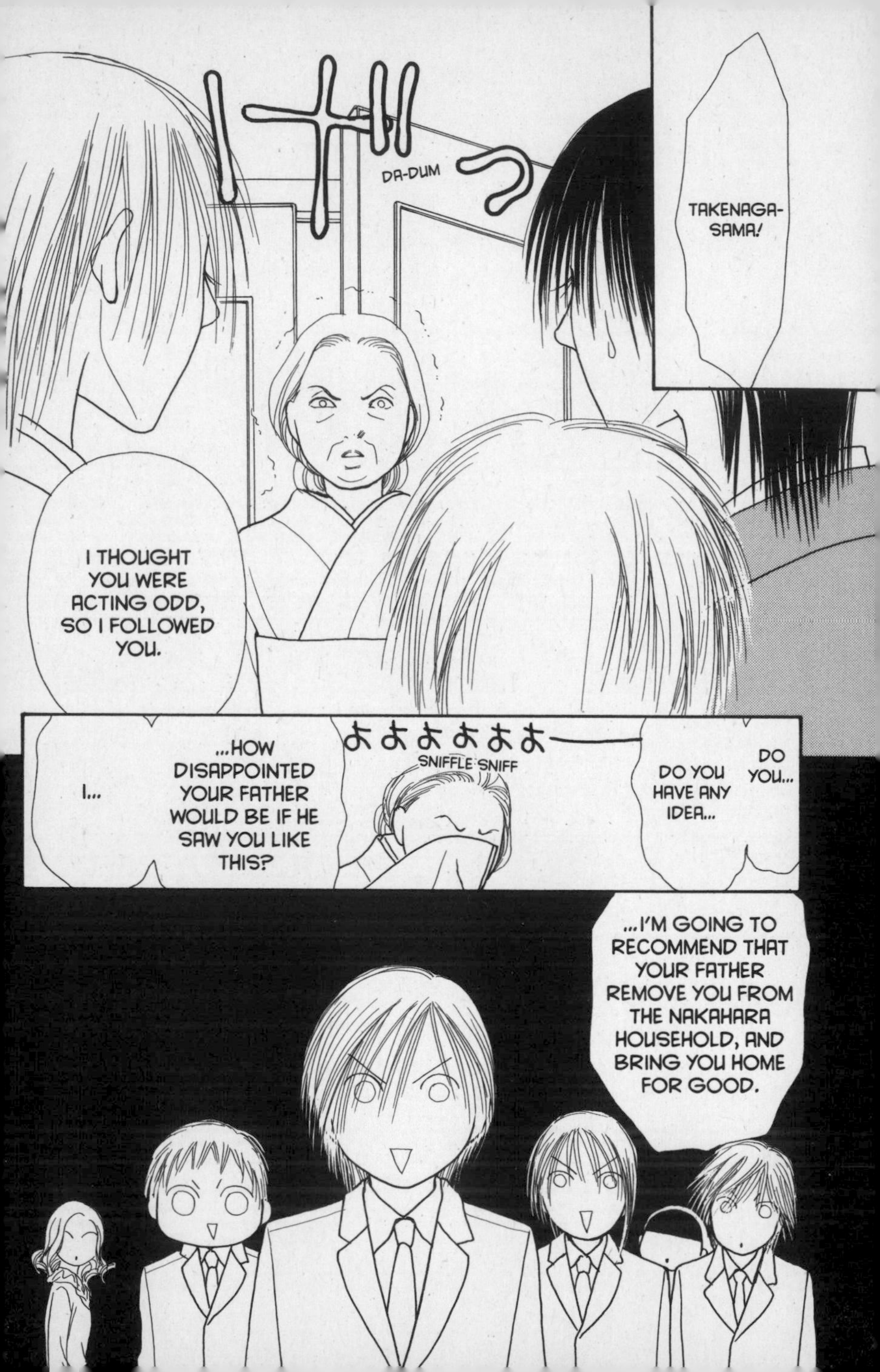
TAKENAGA-SAMA!
DA-DUM
I THOUGHT YOU WERE ACTING ODD, SO I FOLLOWED YOU.
DO YOU...
DO YOU HAVE ANY IDEA...
よよよよよよ—
SNIFFLE SNIFF
...HOW DISAPPOINTED YOUR FATHER WOULD BE IF HE SAW YOU LIKE THIS?
I...
...I'M GOING TO RECOMMEND THAT YOUR FATHER REMOVE YOU FROM THE NAKAHARA HOUSEHOLD, AND BRING YOU HOME FOR GOOD.

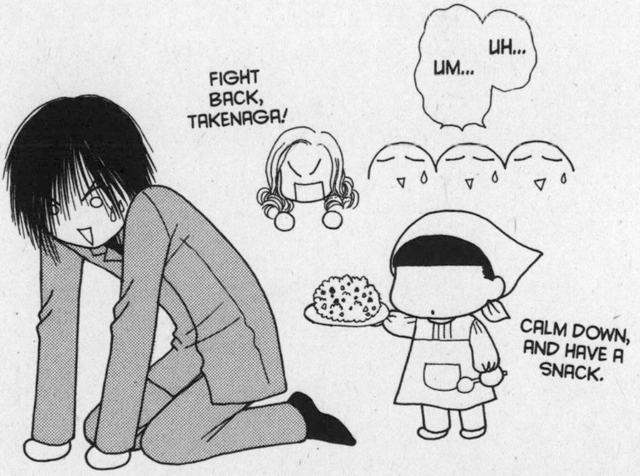
UH...
UM...
FIGHT BACK, TAKENAGA!
CALM DOWN, AND HAVE A SNACK.

Chapter 72

THE PRIDE OF TAKENAGA

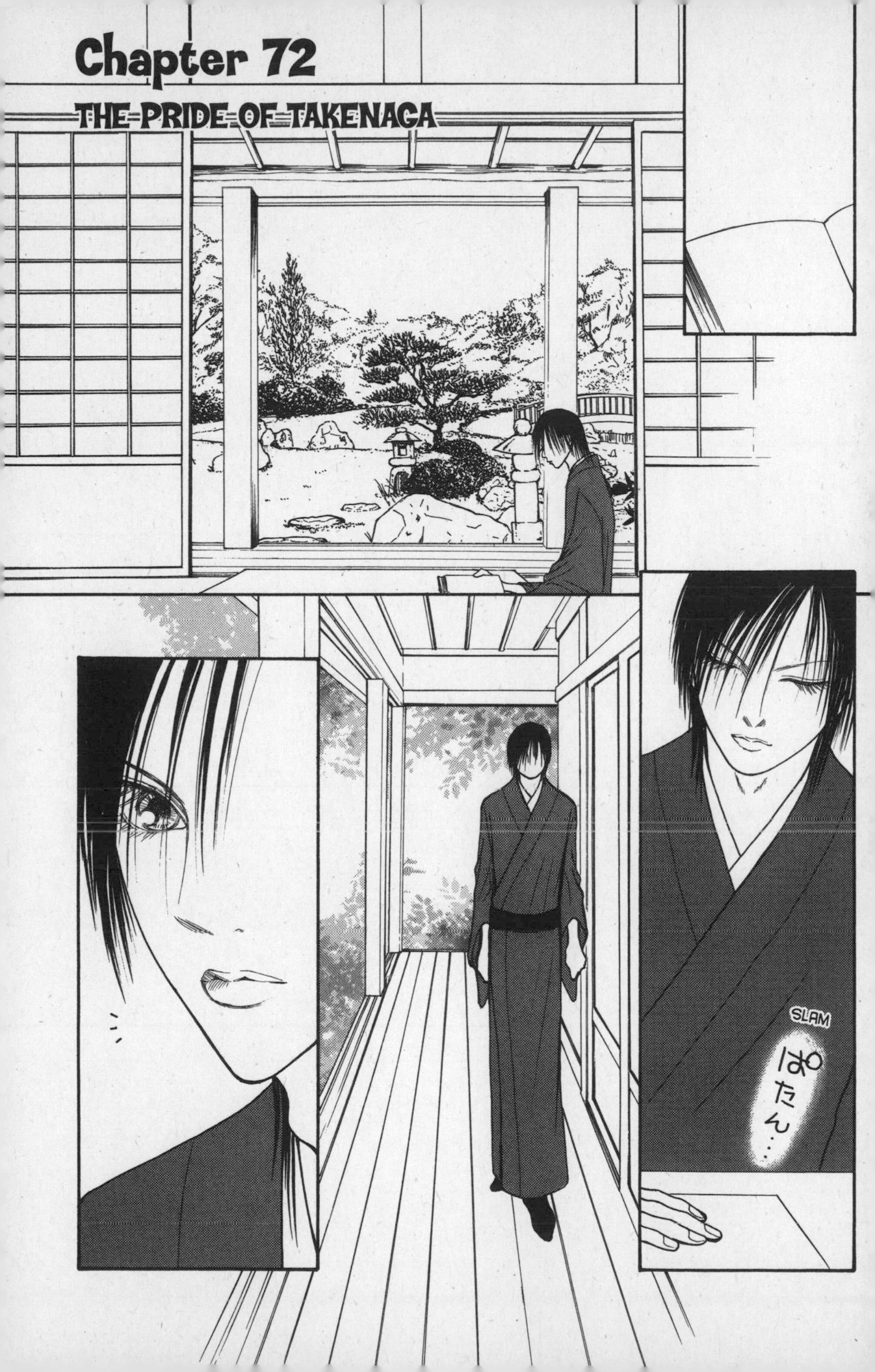
SLAM
ぱたん…

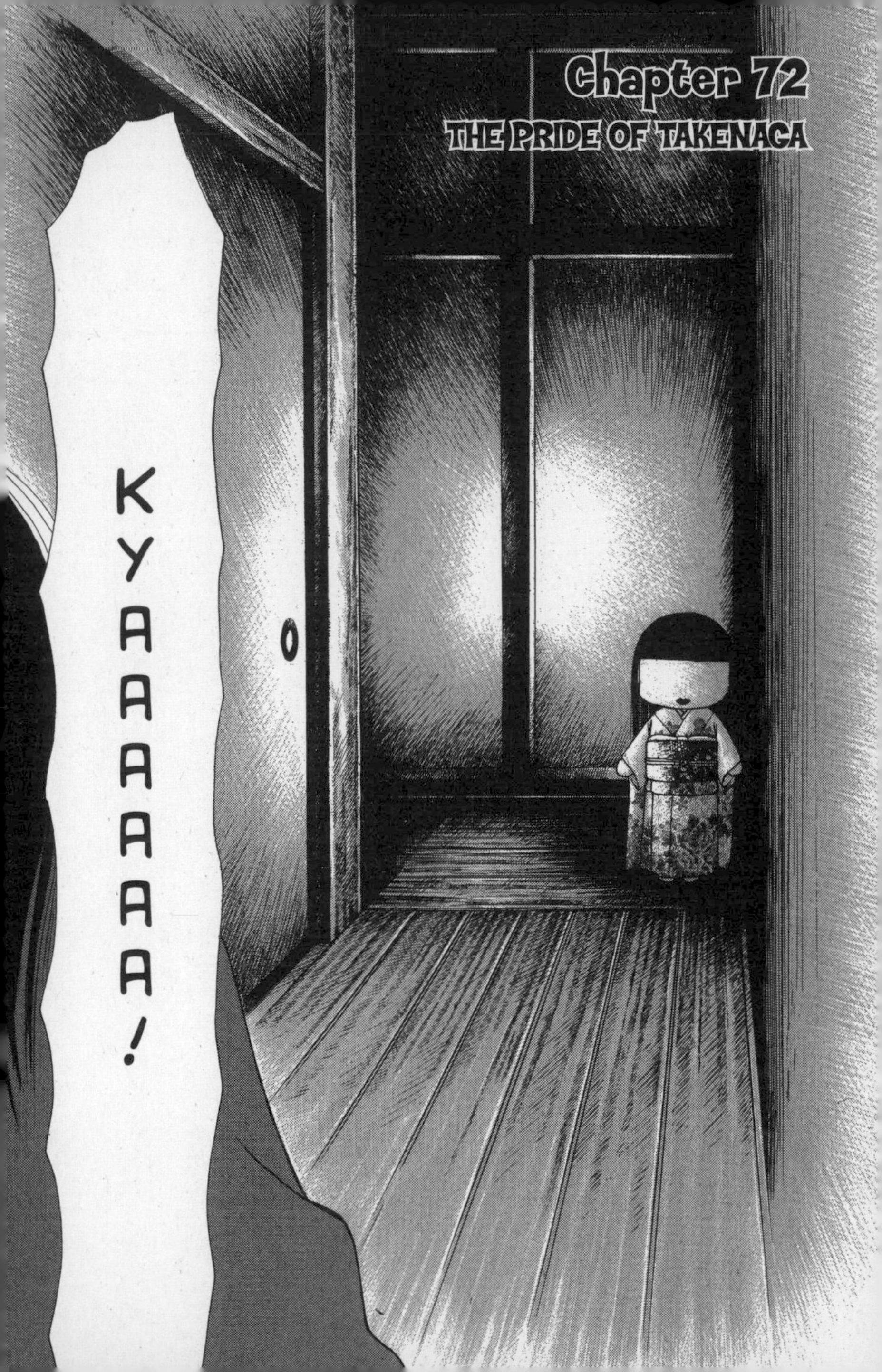
Chapter 72
THE PRIDE OF TAKENAGA
KYAAAAAA!

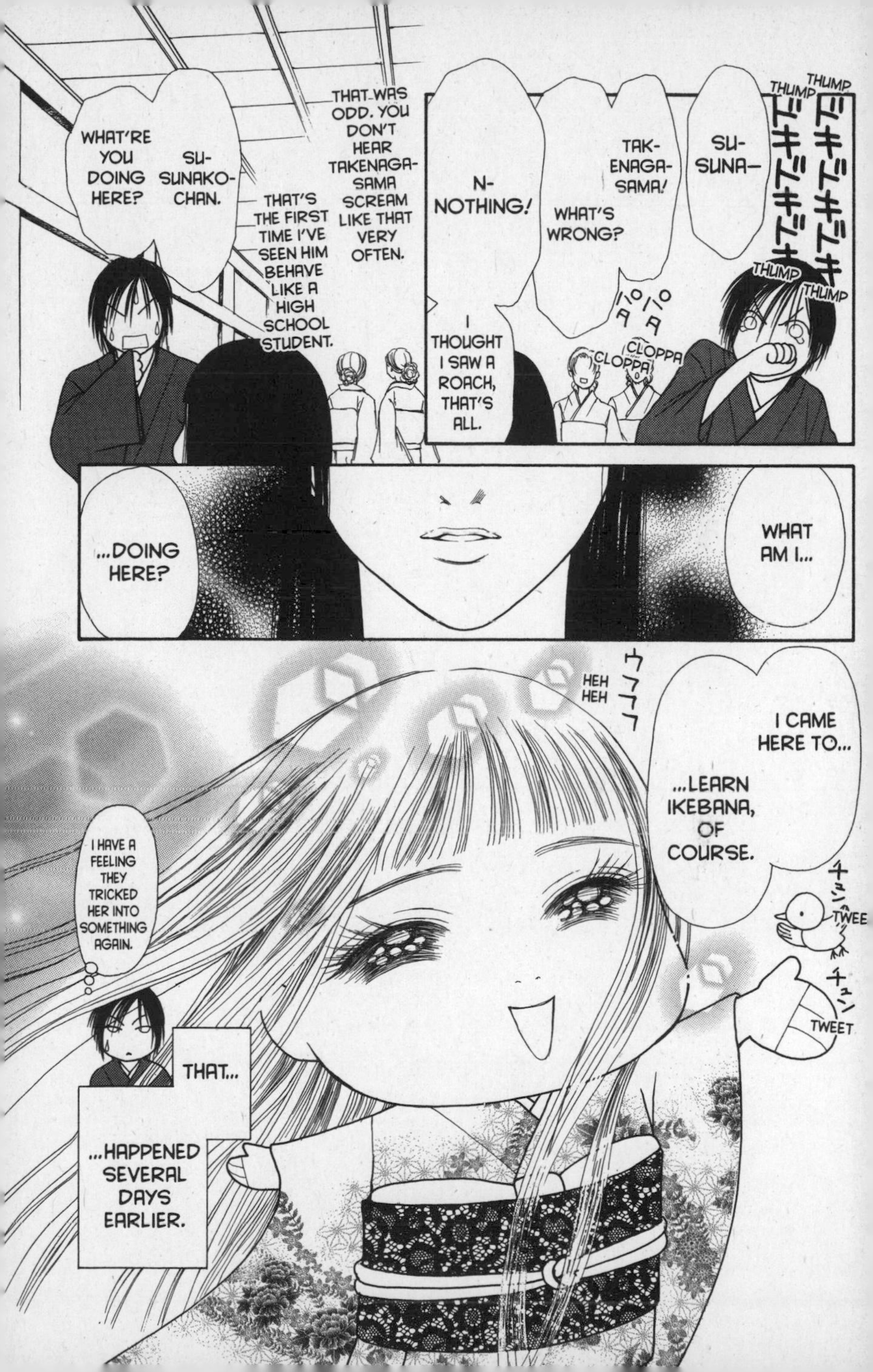
ドキドキ
THUMP THUMP
ドキドキ
THUMP THUMP
SU-SUNA—
TAK-ENAGA-SAMA!
WHAT'S WRONG?
パタパタ
CLOPPA CLOPPA
N-NOTHING!
I THOUGHT I SAW A ROACH, THAT'S ALL.
THAT WAS ODD. YOU DON'T HEAR TAKENAGA-SAMA SCREAM LIKE THAT VERY OFTEN.
THAT'S THE FIRST TIME I'VE SEEN HIM BEHAVE LIKE A HIGH SCHOOL STUDENT.
SU-SUNAKO-CHAN.
WHAT'RE YOU DOING HERE?
WHAT AM I...
...DOING HERE?
ウフフフ
HEH HEH
I CAME HERE TO...
...LEARN IKEBANA, OF COURSE.
チュン
TWEE
チュン
TWEET
I HAVE A FEELING THEY TRICKED HER INTO SOMETHING AGAIN.
THAT...
...HAPPENED SEVERAL DAYS EARLIER.

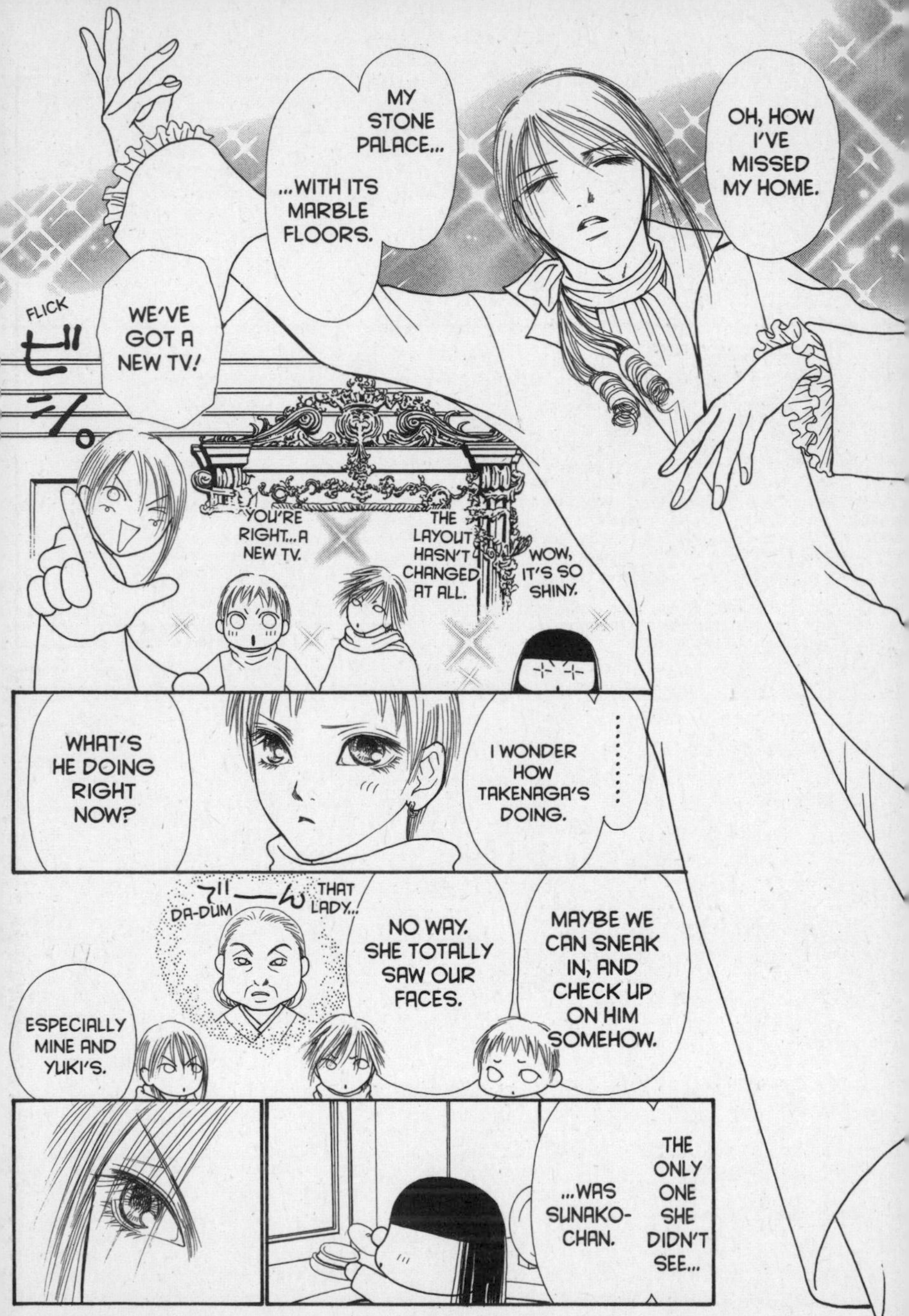
OH, HOW I'VE MISSED MY HOME.
MY STONE PALACE...
...WITH ITS MARBLE FLOORS.
WE'VE GOT A NEW TV!
FLICK
WOW, IT'S SO SHINY.
THE LAYOUT HASN'T CHANGED AT ALL.
YOU'RE RIGHT...A NEW TV.
......
I WONDER HOW TAKENAGA'S DOING.
WHAT'S HE DOING RIGHT NOW?
MAYBE WE CAN SNEAK IN, AND CHECK UP ON HIM SOMEHOW.
NO WAY. SHE TOTALLY SAW OUR FACES.
THAT LADY...
DA-DUM
ESPECIALLY MINE AND YUKI'S.
THE ONLY ONE SHE DIDN'T SEE...
...WAS SUNAKO-CHAN.

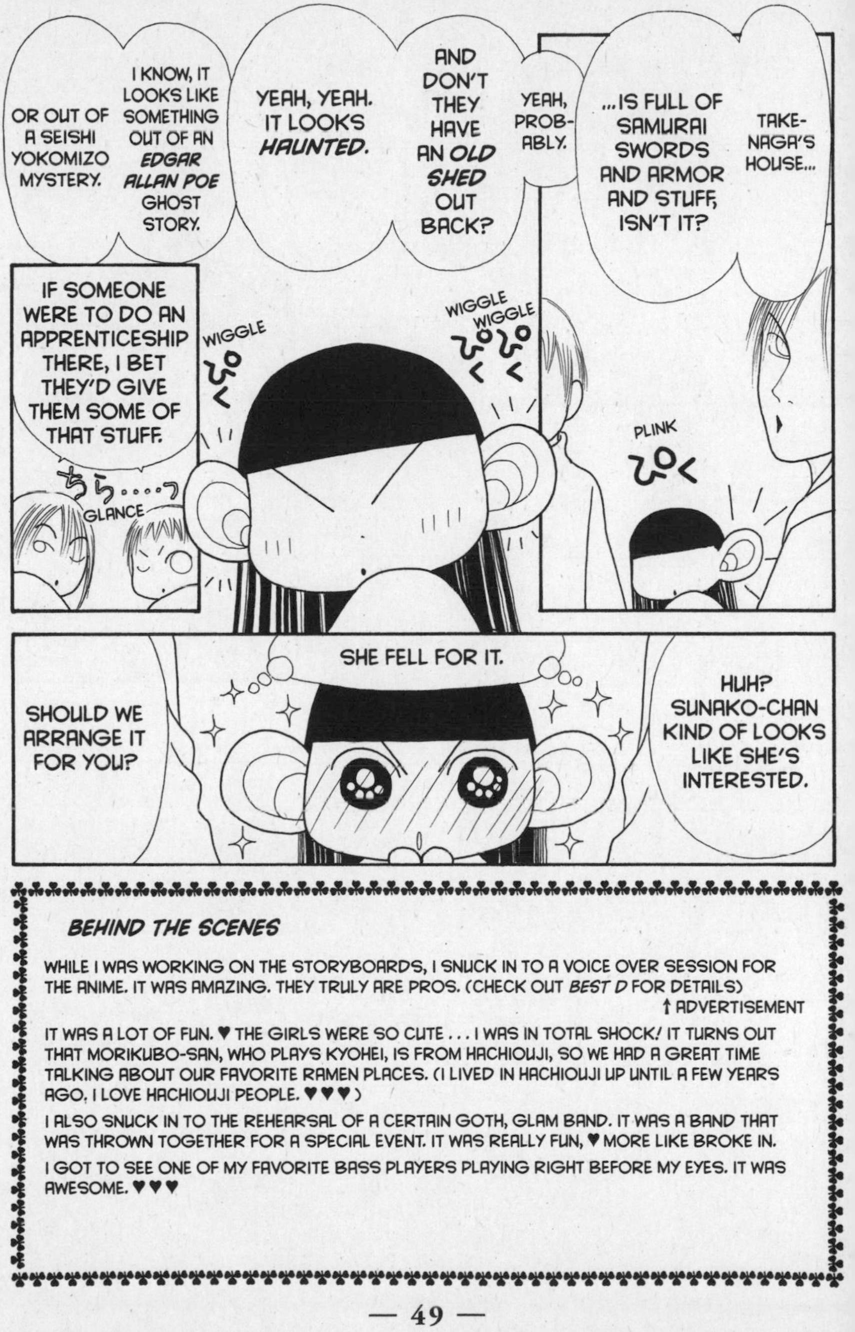
TAKE-NAGA'S HOUSE...
...IS FULL OF SAMURAI SWORDS AND ARMOR AND STUFF, ISN'T IT?
YEAH, PROBABLY.
AND DON'T THEY HAVE AN *OLD SHED* OUT BACK?
YEAH, YEAH. IT LOOKS *HAUNTED*.
I KNOW, IT LOOKS LIKE SOMETHING OUT OF AN *EDGAR ALLAN POE* GHOST STORY.
OR OUT OF A SEISHI YOKOMIZO MYSTERY.
PLINK
WIGGLE WIGGLE
WIGGLE
IF SOMEONE WERE TO DO AN APPRENTICESHIP THERE, I BET THEY'D GIVE THEM SOME OF THAT STUFF.
GLANCE
HUH? SUNAKO-CHAN KIND OF LOOKS LIKE SHE'S INTERESTED.
SHE FELL FOR IT.
SHOULD WE ARRANGE IT FOR YOU?

BEHIND THE SCENES

WHILE I WAS WORKING ON THE STORYBOARDS, I SNUCK IN TO A VOICE OVER SESSION FOR THE ANIME. IT WAS AMAZING. THEY TRULY ARE PROS. (CHECK OUT *BEST D* FOR DETAILS)

↑ ADVERTISEMENT

IT WAS A LOT OF FUN. ♥ THE GIRLS WERE SO CUTE . . . I WAS IN TOTAL SHOCK! IT TURNS OUT THAT MORIKUBO-SAN, WHO PLAYS KYOHEI, IS FROM HACHIOUJI, SO WE HAD A GREAT TIME TALKING ABOUT OUR FAVORITE RAMEN PLACES. (I LIVED IN HACHIOUJI UP UNTIL A FEW YEARS AGO. I LOVE HACHIOUJI PEOPLE. ♥♥♥)

I ALSO SNUCK IN TO THE REHEARSAL OF A CERTAIN GOTH, GLAM BAND. IT WAS A BAND THAT WAS THROWN TOGETHER FOR A SPECIAL EVENT. IT WAS REALLY FUN, ♥ MORE LIKE BROKE IN.

I GOT TO SEE ONE OF MY FAVORITE BASS PLAYERS PLAYING RIGHT BEFORE MY EYES. IT WAS AWESOME. ♥♥♥

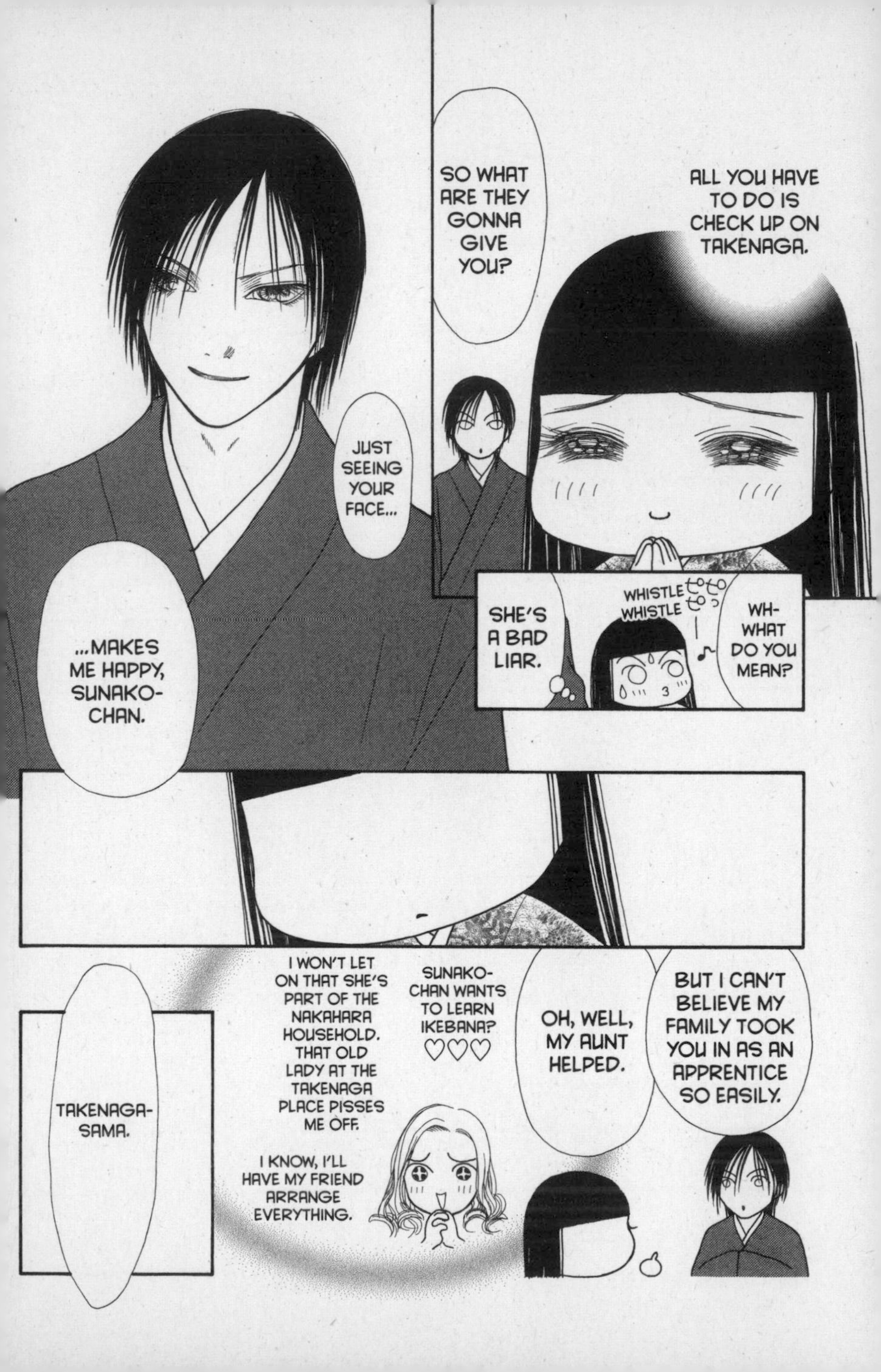
ALL YOU HAVE TO DO IS CHECK UP ON TAKENAGA.
SO WHAT ARE THEY GONNA GIVE YOU?
WH- WHAT DO YOU MEAN?
WHISTLE WHISTLE
SHE'S A BAD LIAR.
JUST SEEING YOUR FACE...
...MAKES ME HAPPY, SUNAKO-CHAN.
BUT I CAN'T BELIEVE MY FAMILY TOOK YOU IN AS AN APPRENTICE SO EASILY.
OH, WELL, MY AUNT HELPED.
SUNAKO-CHAN WANTS TO LEARN IKEBANA? ♡♡♡
I WON'T LET ON THAT SHE'S PART OF THE NAKAHARA HOUSEHOLD. THAT OLD LADY AT THE TAKENAGA PLACE PISSES ME OFF.
I KNOW, I'LL HAVE MY FRIEND ARRANGE EVERYTHING.
TAKENAGA-SAMA.

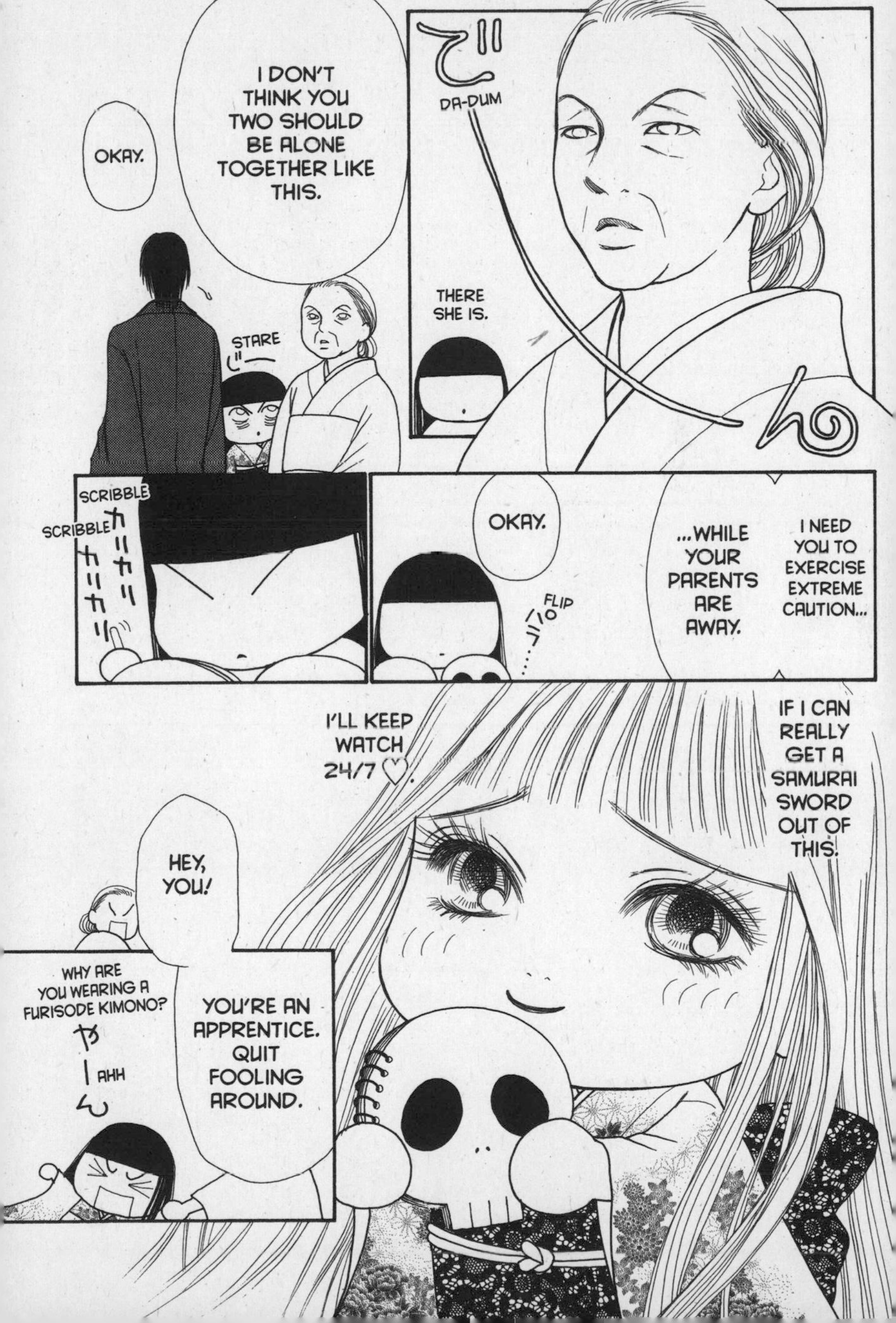
DA-DUM
THERE SHE IS.
I DON'T THINK YOU TWO SHOULD BE ALONE TOGETHER LIKE THIS.
STARE
OKAY.
I NEED YOU TO EXERCISE EXTREME CAUTION...
...WHILE YOUR PARENTS ARE AWAY.
OKAY.
FLIP
SCRIBBLE
SCRIBBLE
IF I CAN REALLY GET A SAMURAI SWORD OUT OF THIS.
I'LL KEEP WATCH 24/7 ♡.
HEY, YOU!
YOU'RE AN APPRENTICE. QUIT FOOLING AROUND.
WHY ARE YOU WEARING A FURISODE KIMONO?
AHH

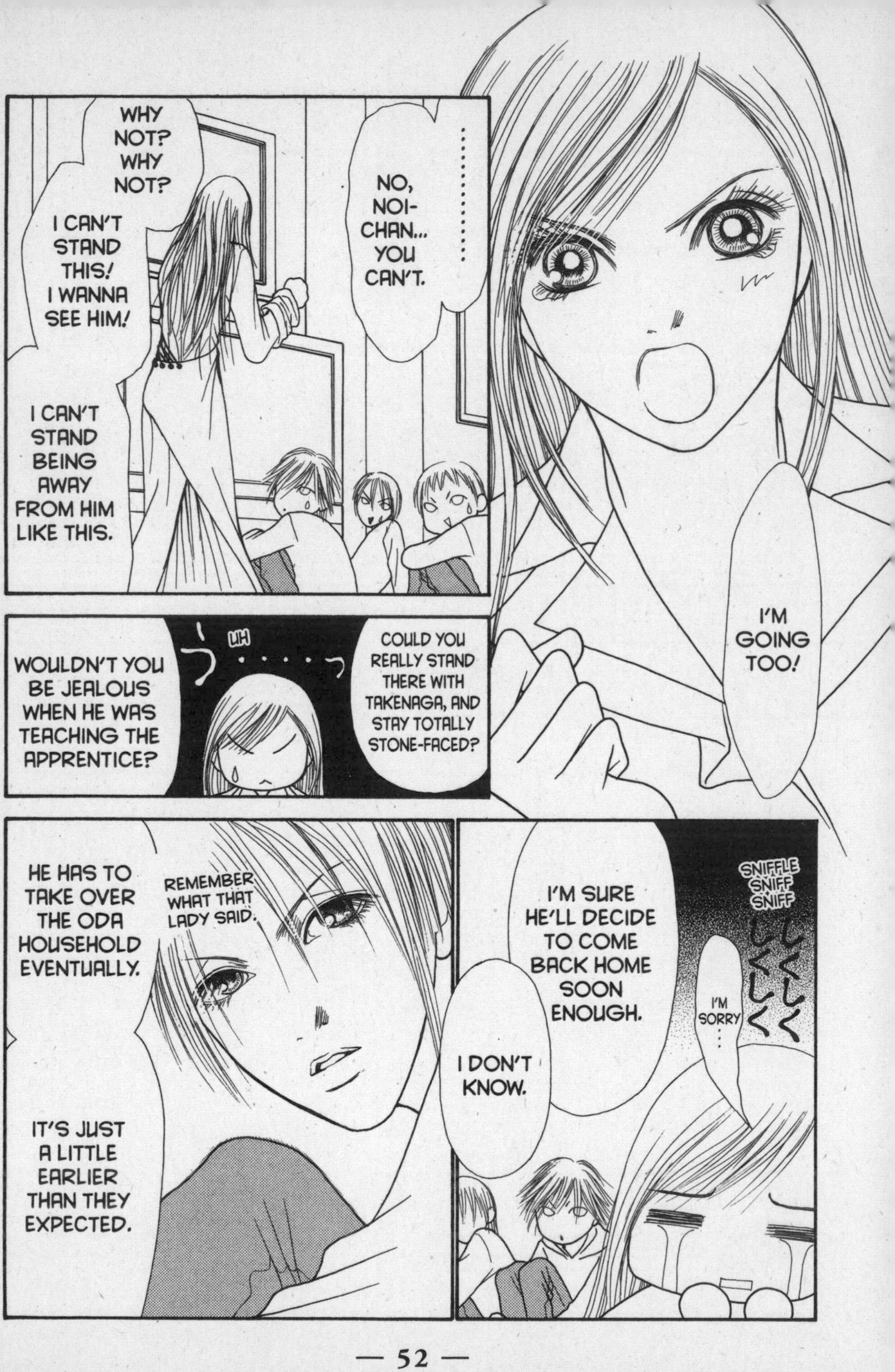
I'M GOING TOO!
......
NO, NOI-CHAN... YOU CAN'T.
WHY NOT? WHY NOT?
I CAN'T STAND THIS! I WANNA SEE HIM!
I CAN'T STAND BEING AWAY FROM HIM LIKE THIS.
COULD YOU REALLY STAND THERE WITH TAKENAGA, AND STAY TOTALLY STONE-FACED?
UH
WOULDN'T YOU BE JEALOUS WHEN HE WAS TEACHING THE APPRENTICE?
SNIFFLE SNIFF SNIFF
I'M SORRY...
I'M SURE HE'LL DECIDE TO COME BACK HOME SOON ENOUGH.
I DON'T KNOW.
REMEMBER WHAT THAT LADY SAID.
HE HAS TO TAKE OVER THE ODA HOUSEHOLD EVENTUALLY.
IT'S JUST A LITTLE EARLIER THAN THEY EXPECTED.

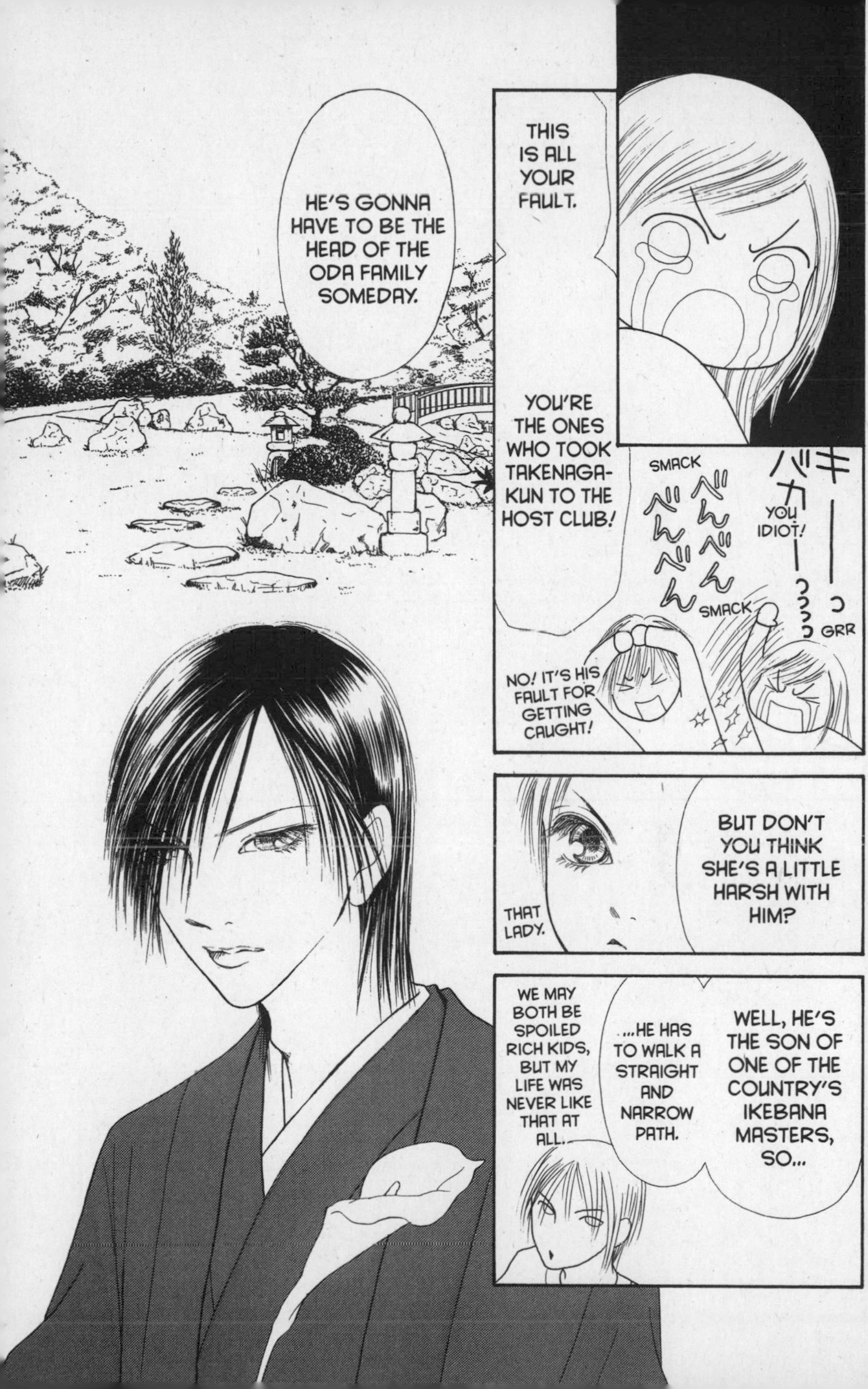
THIS IS ALL YOUR FAULT.
YOU'RE THE ONES WHO TOOK TAKENAGA-KUN TO THE HOST CLUB!
SMACK
べんべん
べんべん
SMACK
キーーっ
バカーっっっ
YOU IDIOT!
GRR
NO! IT'S HIS FAULT FOR GETTING CAUGHT!
BUT DON'T YOU THINK SHE'S A LITTLE HARSH WITH HIM?
THAT LADY.
WELL, HE'S THE SON OF ONE OF THE COUNTRY'S IKEBANA MASTERS, SO...
...HE HAS TO WALK A STRAIGHT AND NARROW PATH.
WE MAY BOTH BE SPOILED RICH KIDS, BUT MY LIFE WAS NEVER LIKE THAT AT ALL.
HE'S GONNA HAVE TO BE THE HEAD OF THE ODA FAMILY SOMEDAY.

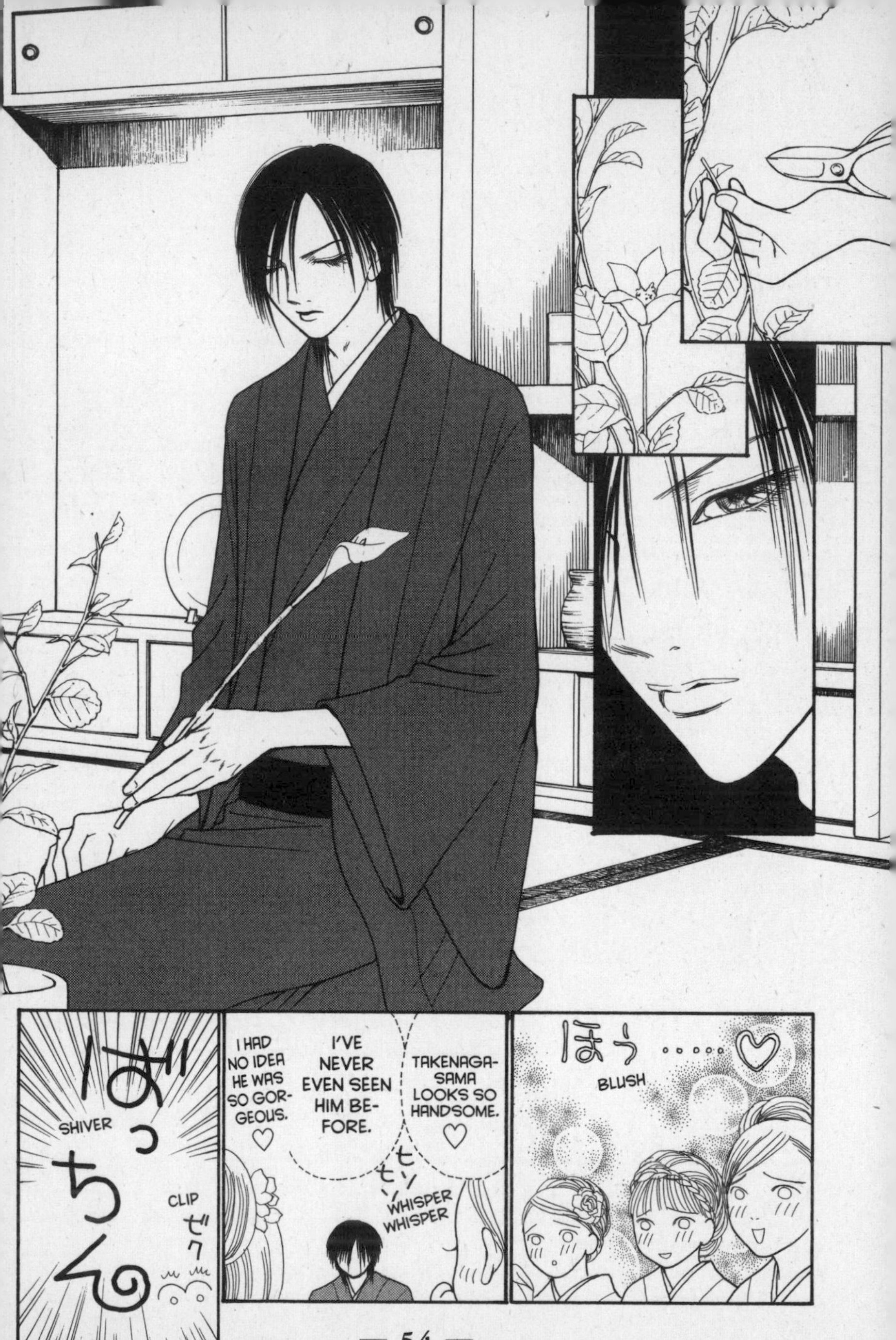
ほぅ……♡
BLUSH
TAKENAGA-SAMA LOOKS SO HANDSOME. ♡
I'VE NEVER EVEN SEEN HIM BEFORE.
I HAD NO IDEA HE WAS SO GORGEOUS. ♡
ヒソヒソ
WHISPER WHISPER
ぱっちん
SHIVER
ゾク
CLIP

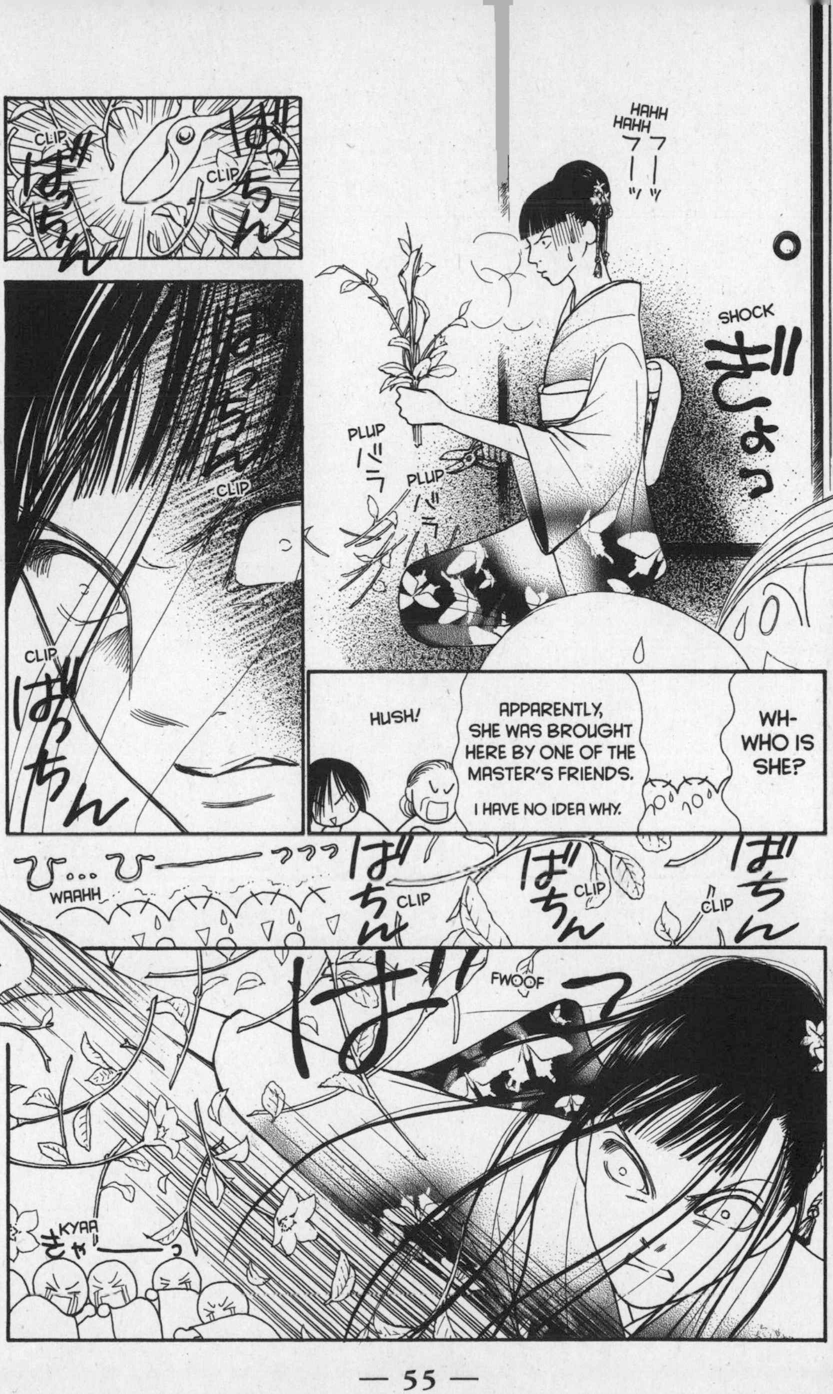
HAHH
HAHH
フーッ
フーッ
PLUP
バラ
PLUP
バラ
SHOCK
ぎょっ
WH-
WHO IS
SHE?
APPARENTLY,
SHE WAS BROUGHT
HERE BY ONE OF THE
MASTER'S FRIENDS.
I HAVE NO IDEA WHY.
HUSH!
CLIP
ばっちん
CLIP
ばっちん
ばっちん
CLIP
CLIP
ばっちん
ばちん
CLIP
ばちん
CLIP
ばちん
CLIP
ひ…ひーーっっっ
WAAHH
FWOOF
ばっ
KYAA
きゃーっ

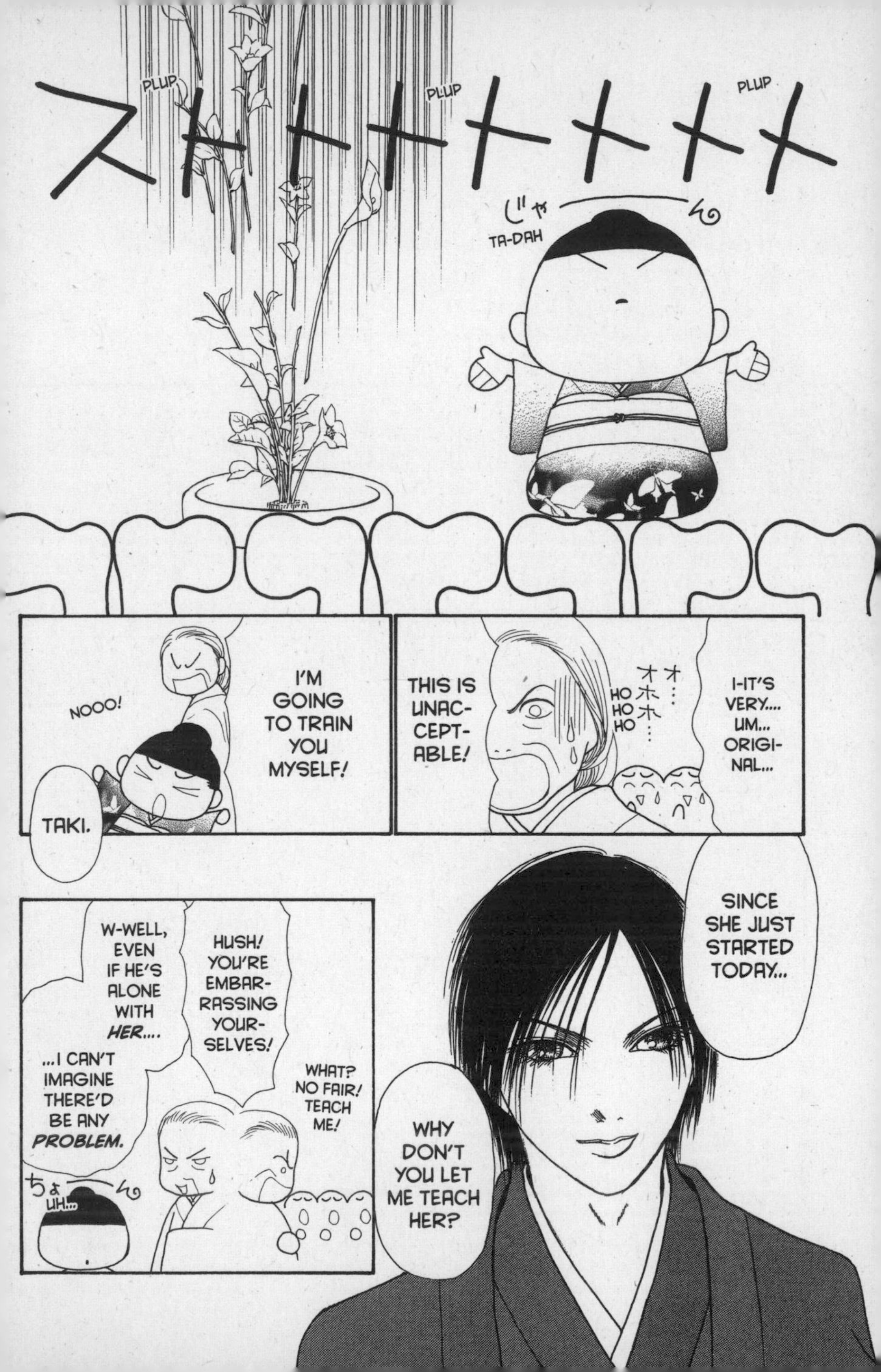
ストトトトトトト
PLUP
PLUP
PLUP
じゃーーん
TA-DAH
I-IT'S VERY.... UM... ORIGINAL...
オ…オホホ…
HO HO HO
THIS IS UNACCEPTABLE!
I'M GOING TO TRAIN YOU MYSELF!
NOOO!
TAKI.
SINCE SHE JUST STARTED TODAY...
WHY DON'T YOU LET ME TEACH HER?
HUSH! YOU'RE EMBARRASSING YOURSELVES!
W-WELL, EVEN IF HE'S ALONE WITH *HER*....
...I CAN'T IMAGINE THERE'D BE ANY *PROBLEM*.
WHAT? NO FAIR! TEACH ME!
ちょーーん
UH...

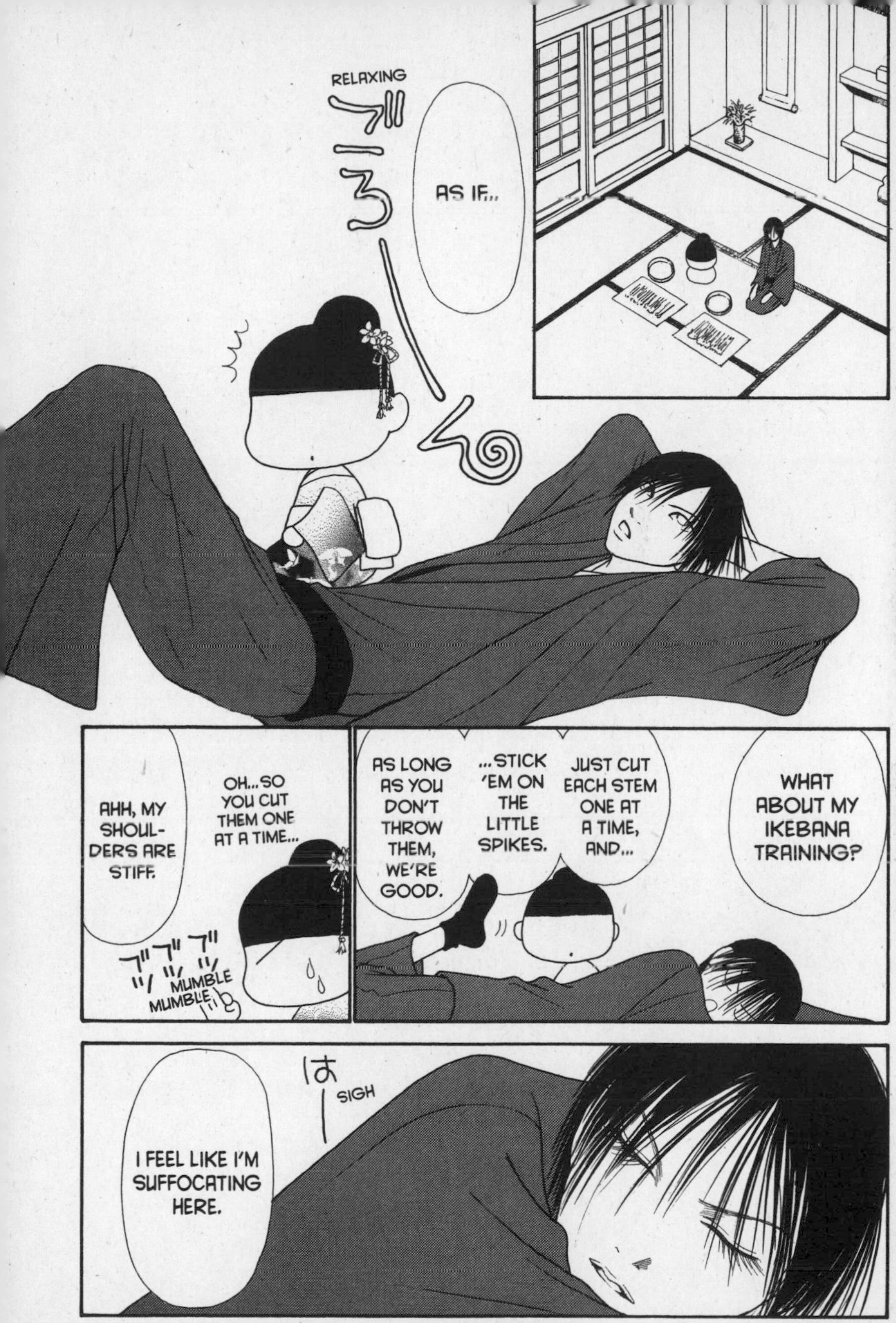
AS IF...
RELAXING
WHAT ABOUT MY IKEBANA TRAINING?
JUST CUT EACH STEM ONE AT A TIME, AND...
...STICK 'EM ON THE LITTLE SPIKES.
AS LONG AS YOU DON'T THROW THEM, WE'RE GOOD.
OH...SO YOU CUT THEM ONE AT A TIME...
AHH, MY SHOULDERS ARE STIFF.
MUMBLE MUMBLE
SIGH
I FEEL LIKE I'M SUFFOCATING HERE.

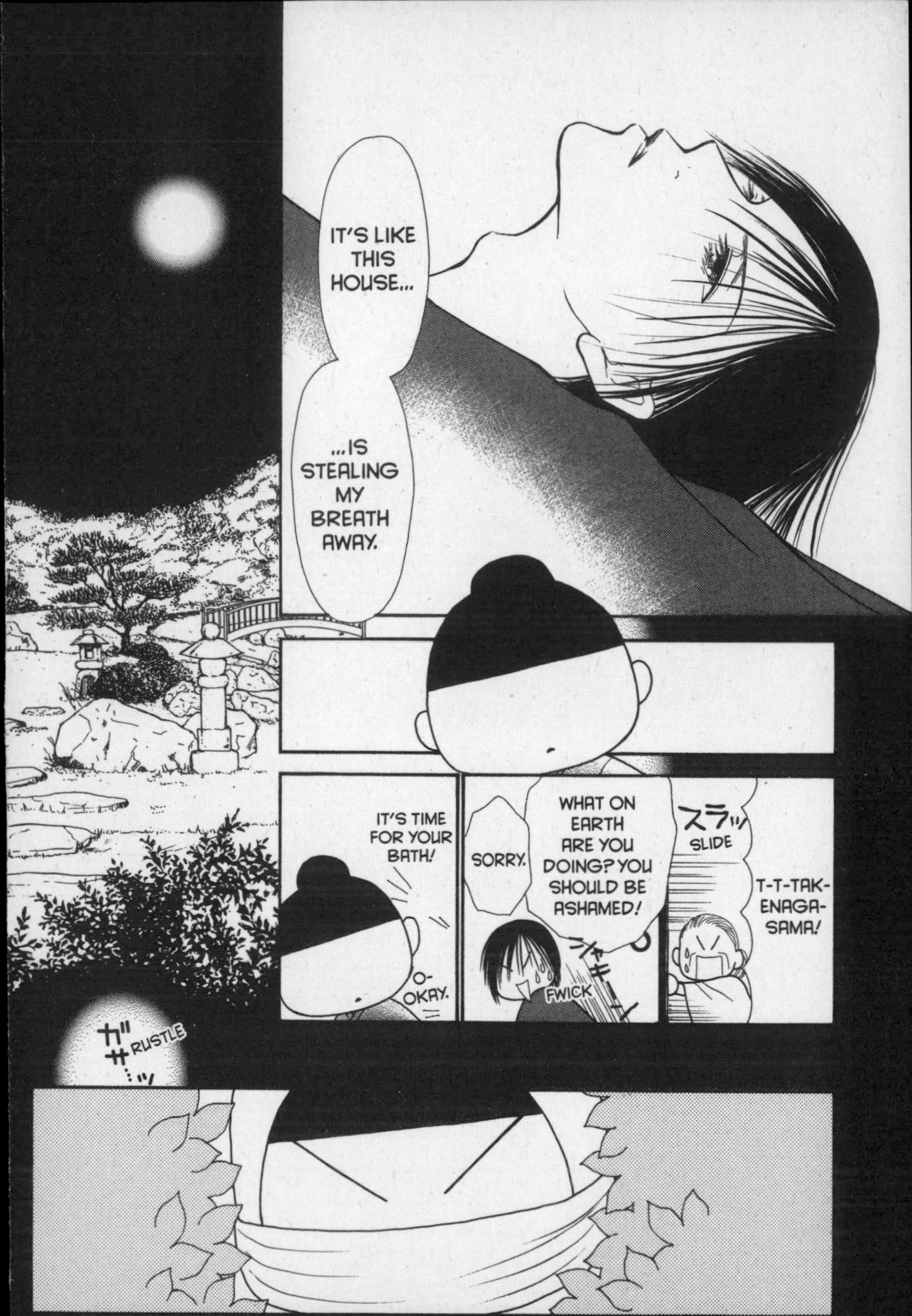
IT'S LIKE THIS HOUSE...
...IS STEALING MY BREATH AWAY.
スラッ
SLIDE
T-T-TAK-ENAGA-SAMA!
WHAT ON EARTH ARE YOU DOING? YOU SHOULD BE ASHAMED!
SORRY.
FWICK
IT'S TIME FOR YOUR BATH!
O-OKAY.
ガサ…ッ
RUSTLE

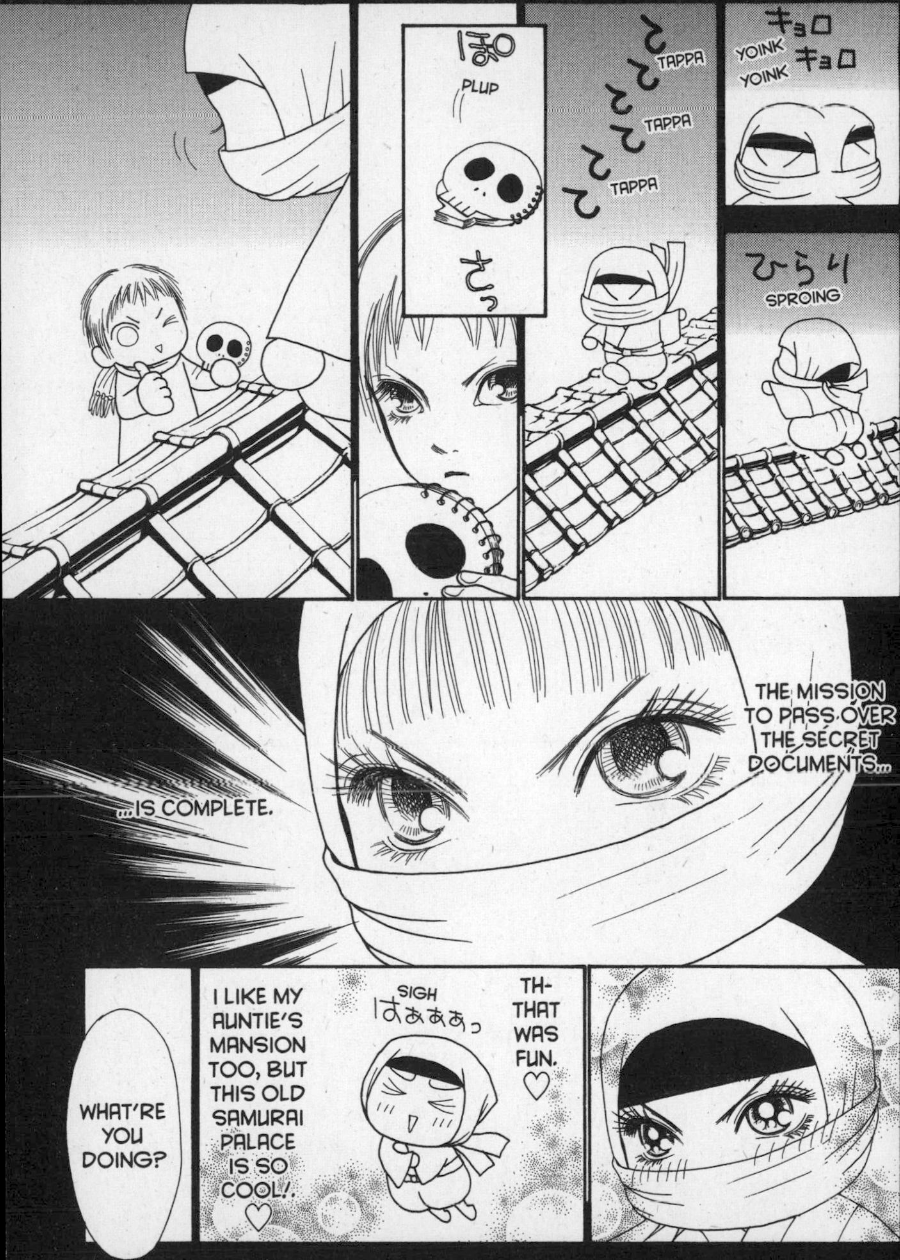
キョロ YOINK
キョロ YOINK
ひらり SPROING
てててててて TAPPA TAPPA TAPPA
PLUP
さっ
THE MISSION TO PASS OVER THE SECRET DOCUMENTS...
...IS COMPLETE.
TH-THAT WAS FUN. ♡
SIGH はあああっ
I LIKE MY AUNTIE'S MANSION TOO, BUT THIS OLD SAMURAI PALACE IS SO COOL!. ♡
WHAT'RE YOU DOING?

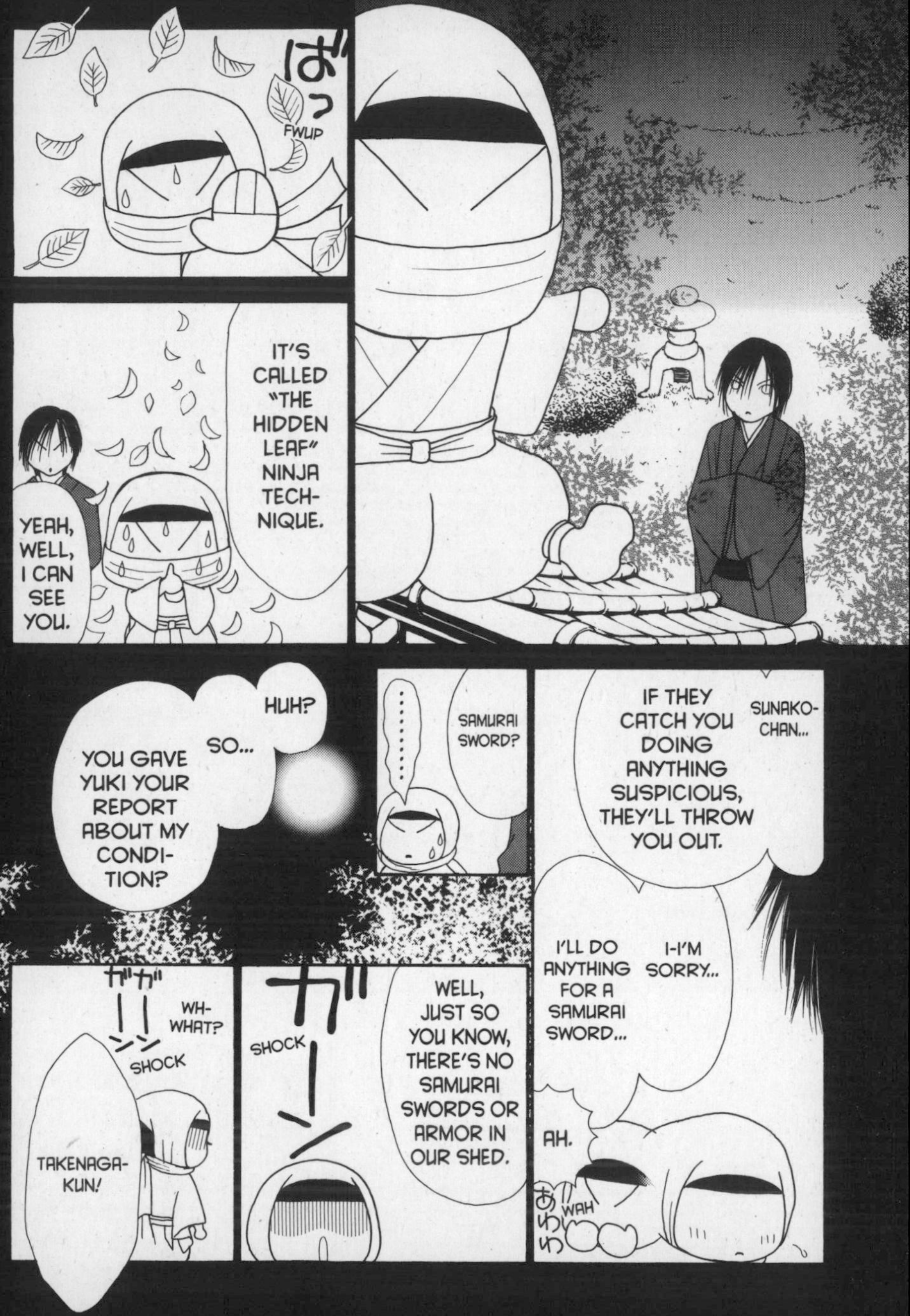
ばっ
FWUP
IT'S CALLED "THE HIDDEN LEAF" NINJA TECHNIQUE.
YEAH, WELL, I CAN SEE YOU.
SUNAKO-CHAN...
IF THEY CATCH YOU DOING ANYTHING SUSPICIOUS, THEY'LL THROW YOU OUT.
I-I'M SORRY...
I'LL DO ANYTHING FOR A SAMURAI SWORD...
AH.
あわわ
WAH
SAMURAI SWORD?
......
HUH?
SO...
YOU GAVE YUKI YOUR REPORT ABOUT MY CONDITION?
WELL, JUST SO YOU KNOW, THERE'S NO SAMURAI SWORDS OR ARMOR IN OUR SHED.
ガーン
SHOCK
ガガーン
SHOCK
WH-WHAT?
TAKENAGA-KUN!

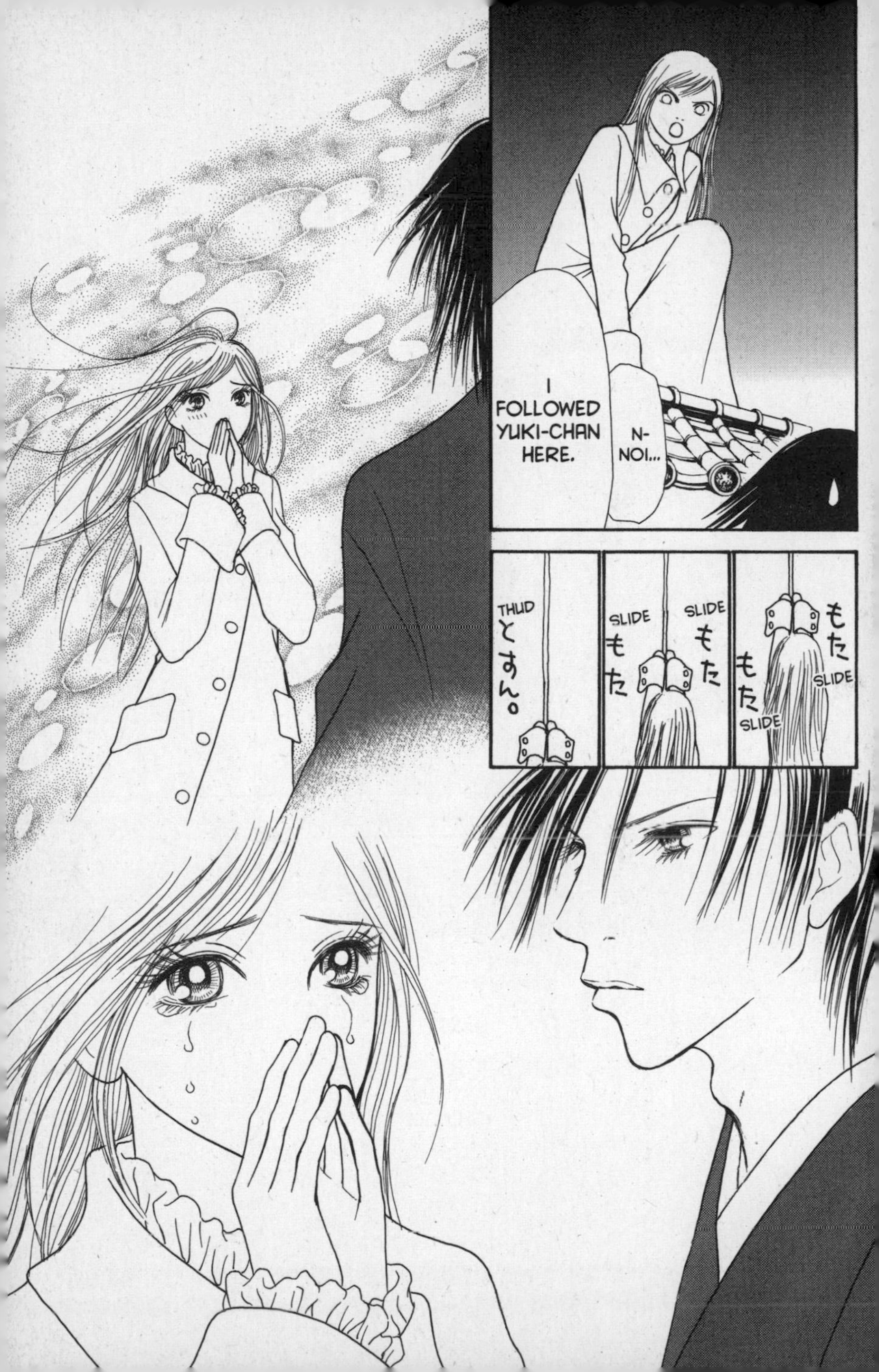
N-NOI...
I FOLLOWED YUKI-CHAN HERE.
もた
SLIDE
もた
SLIDE
SLIDE
もた
SLIDE
もた
THUD
とすん。

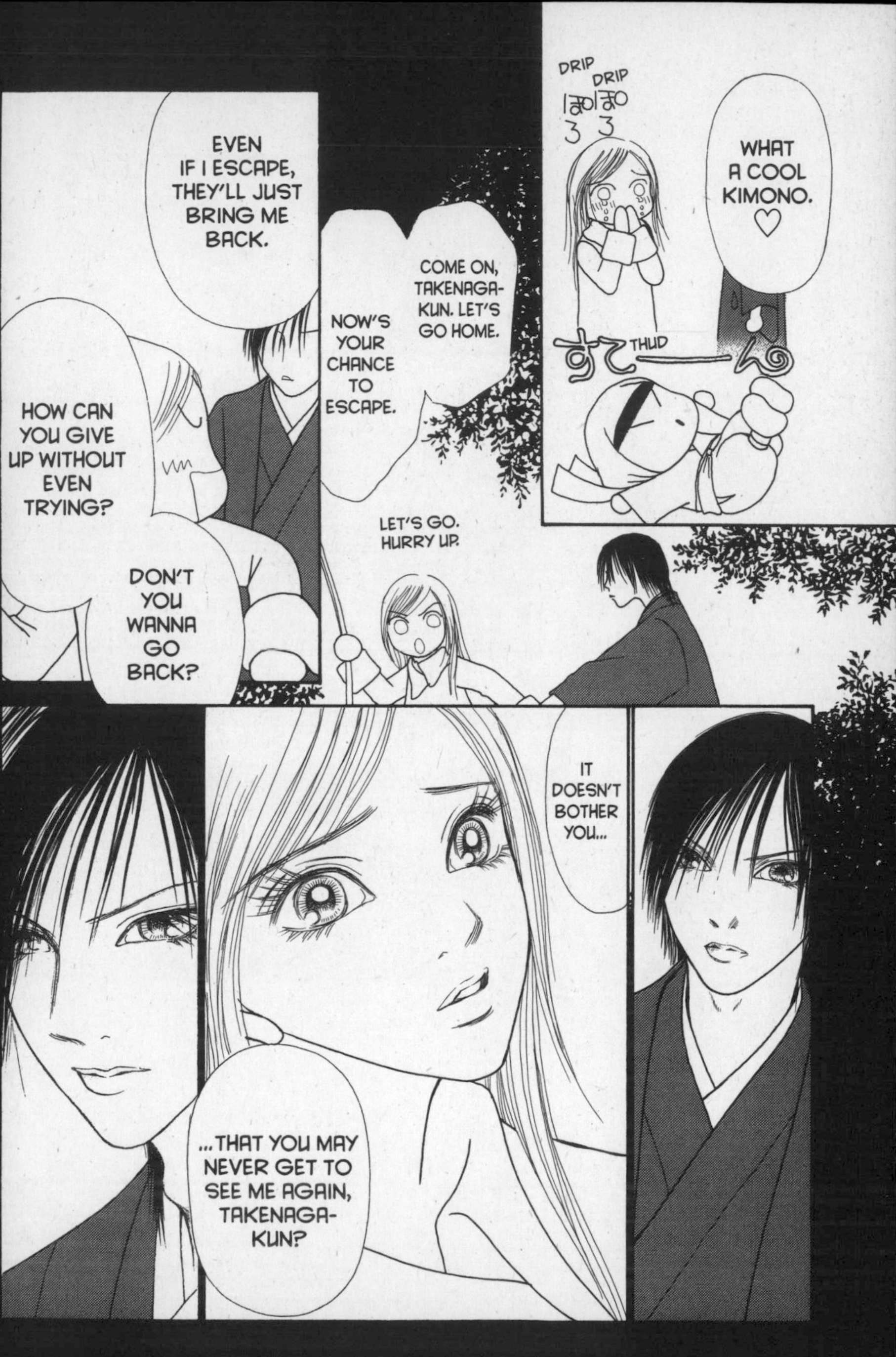
DRIP DRIP
ほろほろ
WHAT A COOL KIMONO. ♡
THUD
すてーん
COME ON, TAKENAGA-KUN. LET'S GO HOME.
NOW'S YOUR CHANCE TO ESCAPE.
LET'S GO. HURRY UP.
EVEN IF I ESCAPE, THEY'LL JUST BRING ME BACK.
HOW CAN YOU GIVE UP WITHOUT EVEN TRYING?
DON'T YOU WANNA GO BACK?
IT DOESN'T BOTHER YOU...
...THAT YOU MAY NEVER GET TO SEE ME AGAIN, TAKENAGA-KUN?

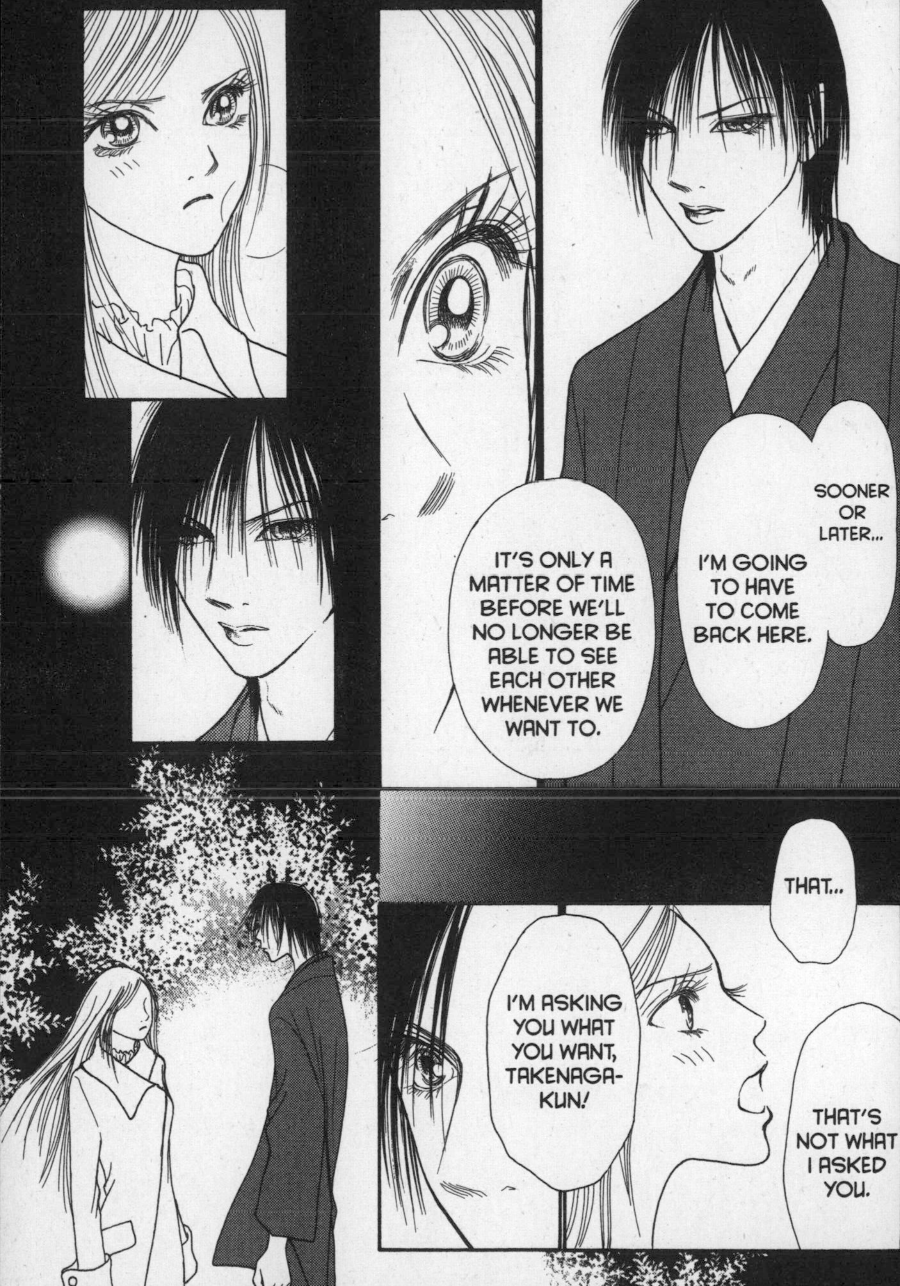
SOONER OR LATER...
I'M GOING TO HAVE TO COME BACK HERE.
IT'S ONLY A MATTER OF TIME BEFORE WE'LL NO LONGER BE ABLE TO SEE EACH OTHER WHENEVER WE WANT TO.
THAT...
THAT'S NOT WHAT I ASKED YOU.
I'M ASKING YOU WHAT YOU WANT, TAKENAGA-KUN!

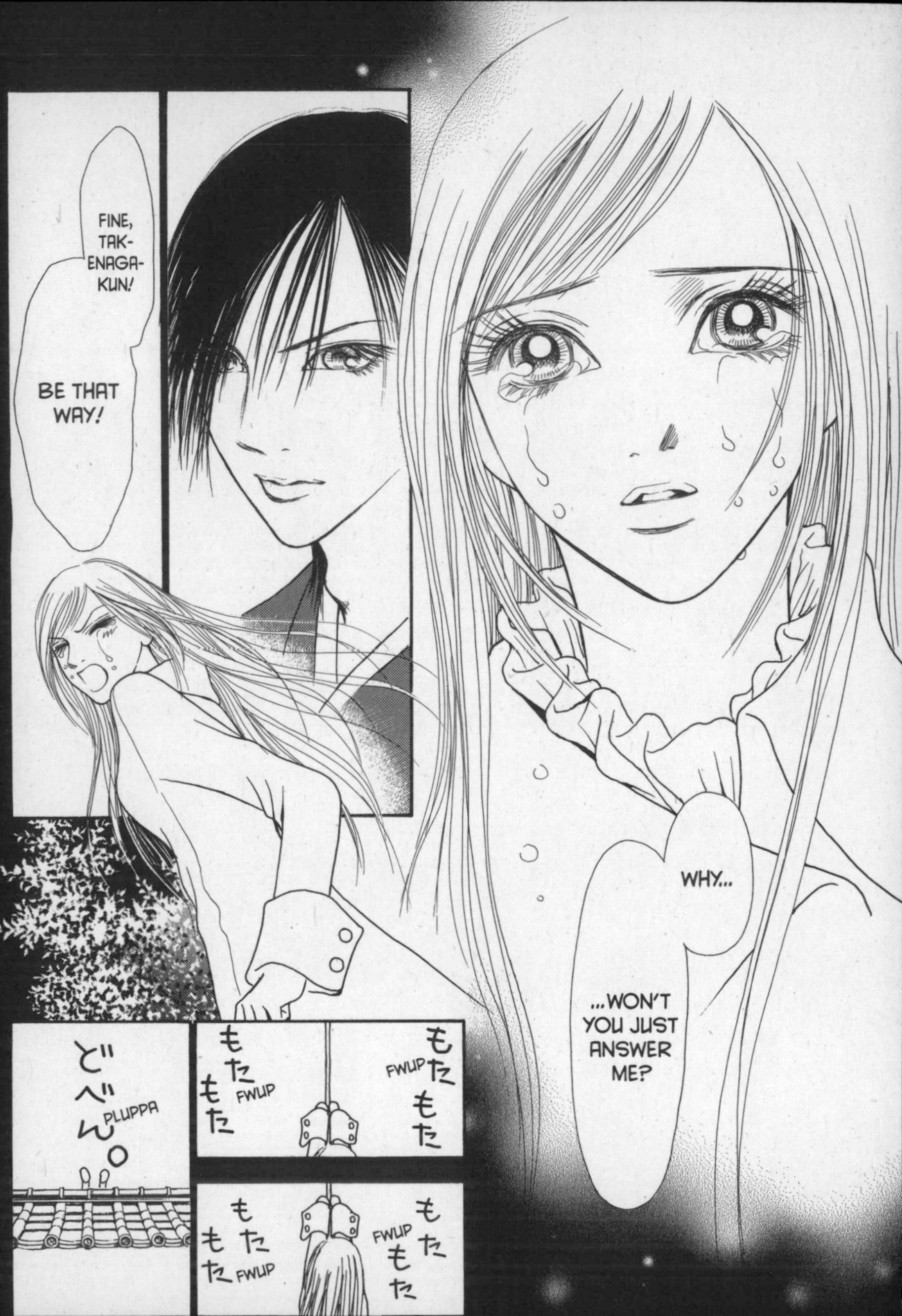
WHY...
...WON'T YOU JUST ANSWER ME?
FINE, TAK-ENAGA-KUN!
BE THAT WAY!
もたもた FWUP
もたもた FWUP
もたもた FWUP
もたもた FWUP
どべん。 PLUPPA

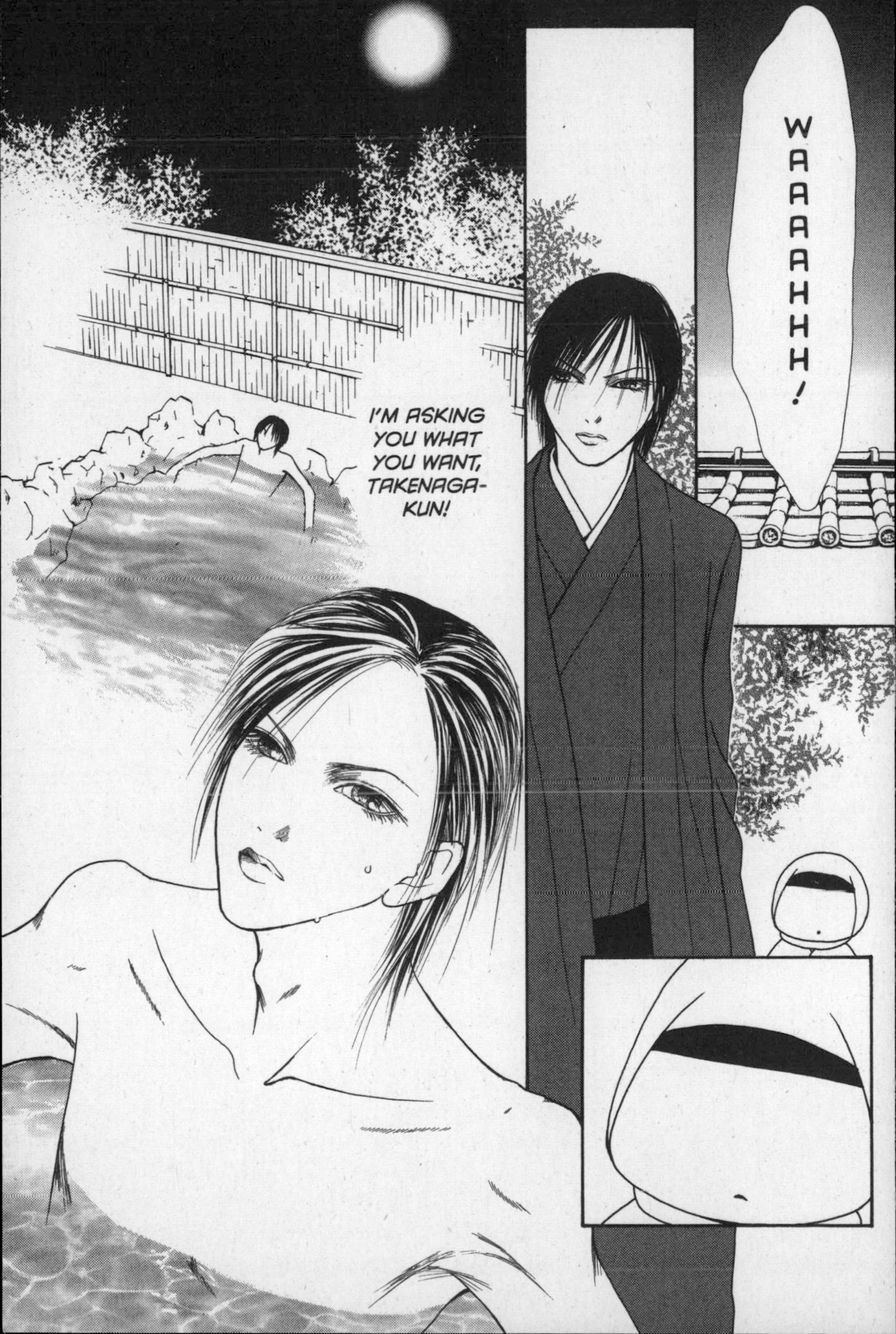
WAAAAAHHH!
I'M ASKING YOU WHAT YOU WANT, TAKENAGA-KUN!

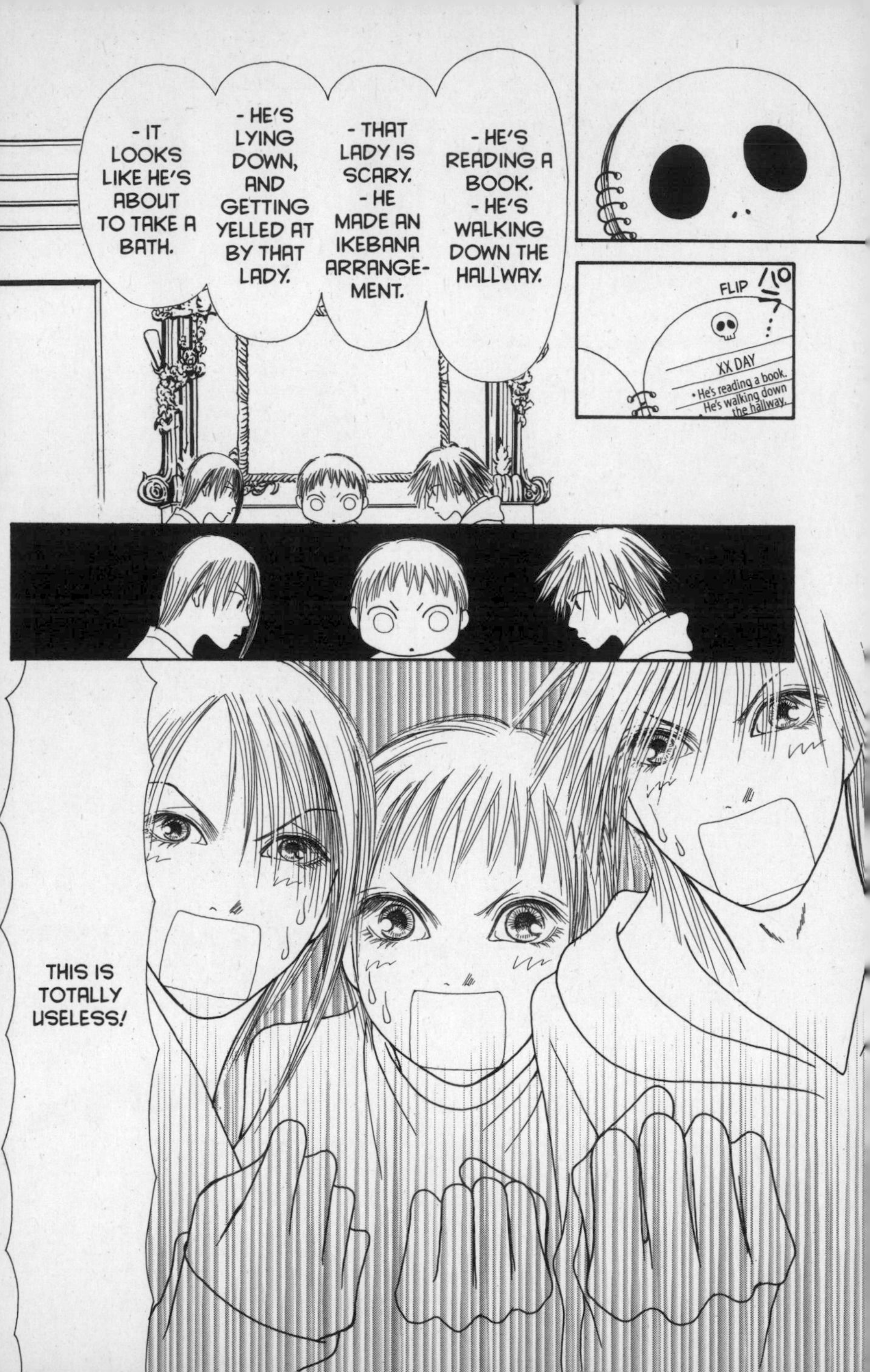
FLIP
XX DAY
• He's reading a book.
• He's walking down the hallway.
- HE'S READING A BOOK. - HE'S WALKING DOWN THE HALLWAY.
- THAT LADY IS SCARY. - HE MADE AN IKEBANA ARRANGEMENT.
- HE'S LYING DOWN, AND GETTING YELLED AT BY THAT LADY.
- IT LOOKS LIKE HE'S ABOUT TO TAKE A BATH.
THIS IS TOTALLY USELESS!

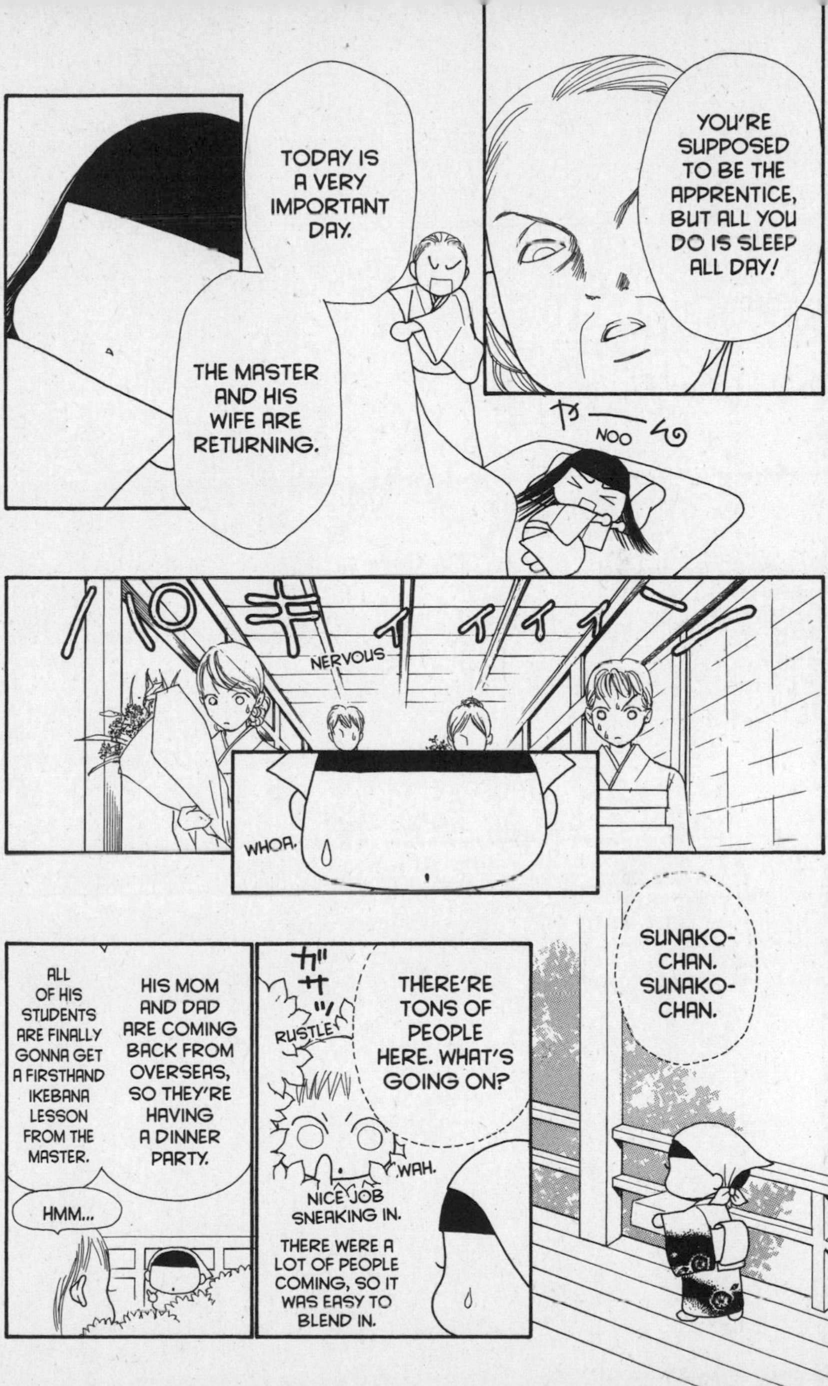
YOU'RE SUPPOSED TO BE THE APPRENTICE, BUT ALL YOU DO IS SLEEP ALL DAY!
NOO
TODAY IS A VERY IMPORTANT DAY.
THE MASTER AND HIS WIFE ARE RETURNING.
NERVOUS
WHOA.
SUNAKO-CHAN. SUNAKO-CHAN.
RUSTLE
THERE'RE TONS OF PEOPLE HERE. WHAT'S GOING ON?
WAH.
NICE JOB SNEAKING IN.
THERE WERE A LOT OF PEOPLE COMING, SO IT WAS EASY TO BLEND IN.
HIS MOM AND DAD ARE COMING BACK FROM OVERSEAS, SO THEY'RE HAVING A DINNER PARTY.
ALL OF HIS STUDENTS ARE FINALLY GONNA GET A FIRSTHAND IKEBANA LESSON FROM THE MASTER.
HMM...

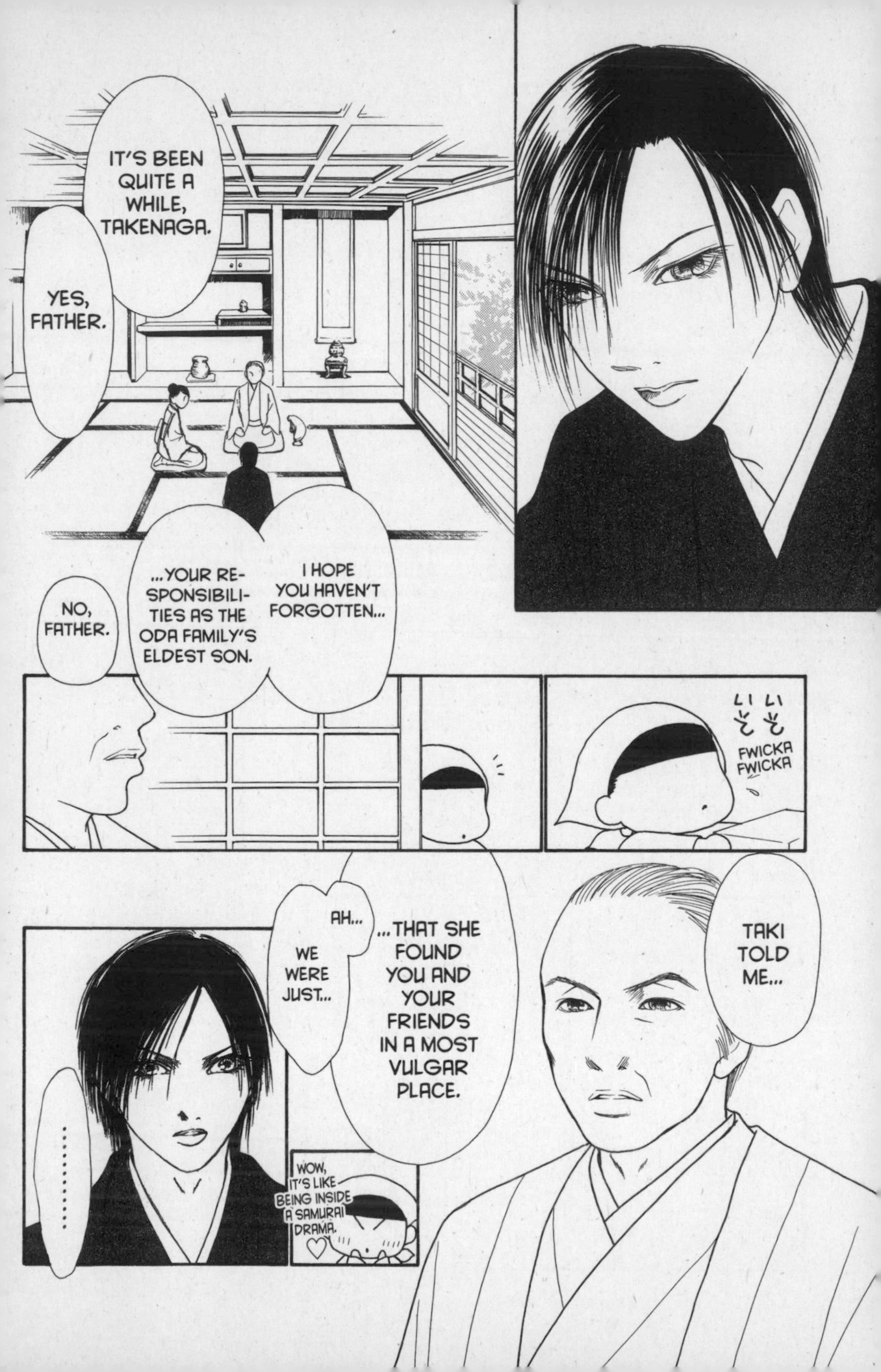
IT'S BEEN QUITE A WHILE, TAKENAGA.
YES, FATHER.
I HOPE YOU HAVEN'T FORGOTTEN...
...YOUR RE-SPONSIBILI-TIES AS THE ODA FAMILY'S ELDEST SON.
NO, FATHER.
いそいそ
FWICKA FWICKA
TAKI TOLD ME...
...THAT SHE FOUND YOU AND YOUR FRIENDS IN A MOST VULGAR PLACE.
AH...
WE WERE JUST...
WOW, IT'S LIKE BEING INSIDE A SAMURAI DRAMA.
....

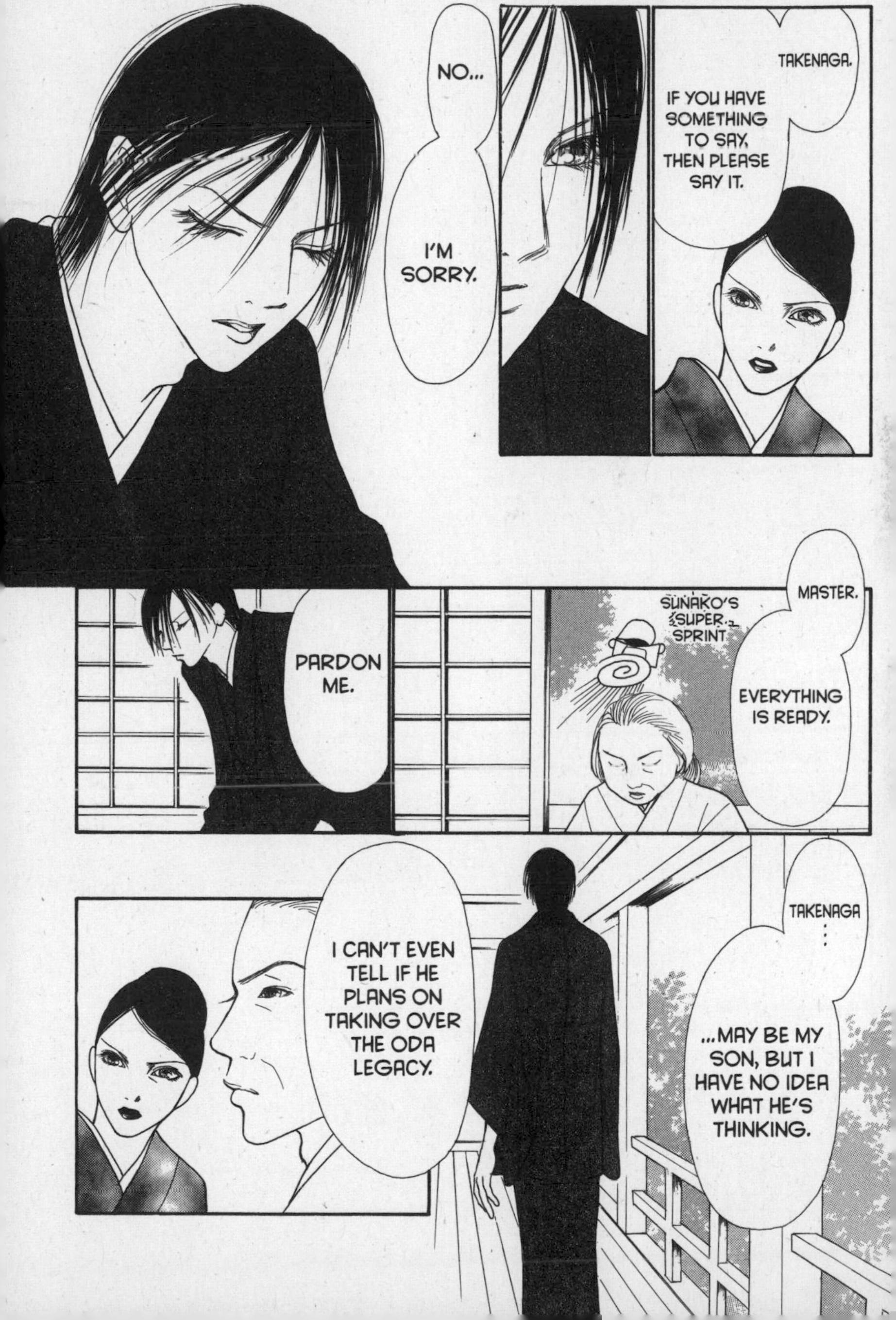
TAKENAGA.
IF YOU HAVE SOMETHING TO SAY, THEN PLEASE SAY IT.
NO...
I'M SORRY.
MASTER.
EVERYTHING IS READY.
SUNAKO'S SUPER SPRINT
PARDON ME.
TAKENAGA...
...MAY BE MY SON, BUT I HAVE NO IDEA WHAT HE'S THINKING.
I CAN'T EVEN TELL IF HE PLANS ON TAKING OVER THE ODA LEGACY.

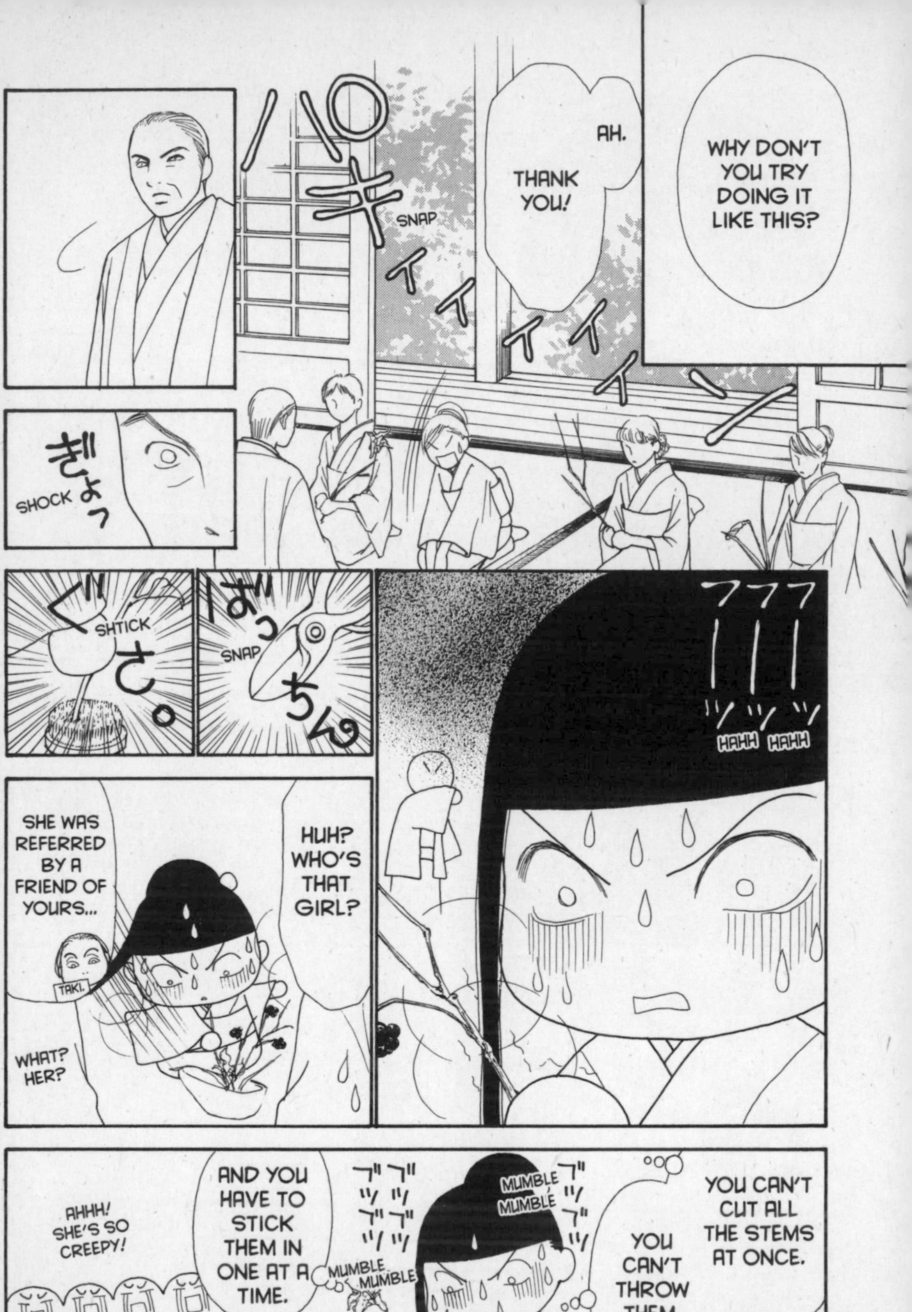
WHY DON'T YOU TRY DOING IT LIKE THIS?
AH.
THANK YOU!
SNAP
SHOCK
HAHH HAHH
SNAP
SHTICK
HUH? WHO'S THAT GIRL?
SHE WAS REFERRED BY A FRIEND OF YOURS...
TAKI.
WHAT? HER?
YOU CAN'T CUT ALL THE STEMS AT ONCE.
YOU CAN'T THROW THEM.
MUMBLE MUMBLE
AND YOU HAVE TO STICK THEM IN ONE AT A TIME.
MUMBLE MUMBLE
AHHH! SHE'S SO CREEPY!

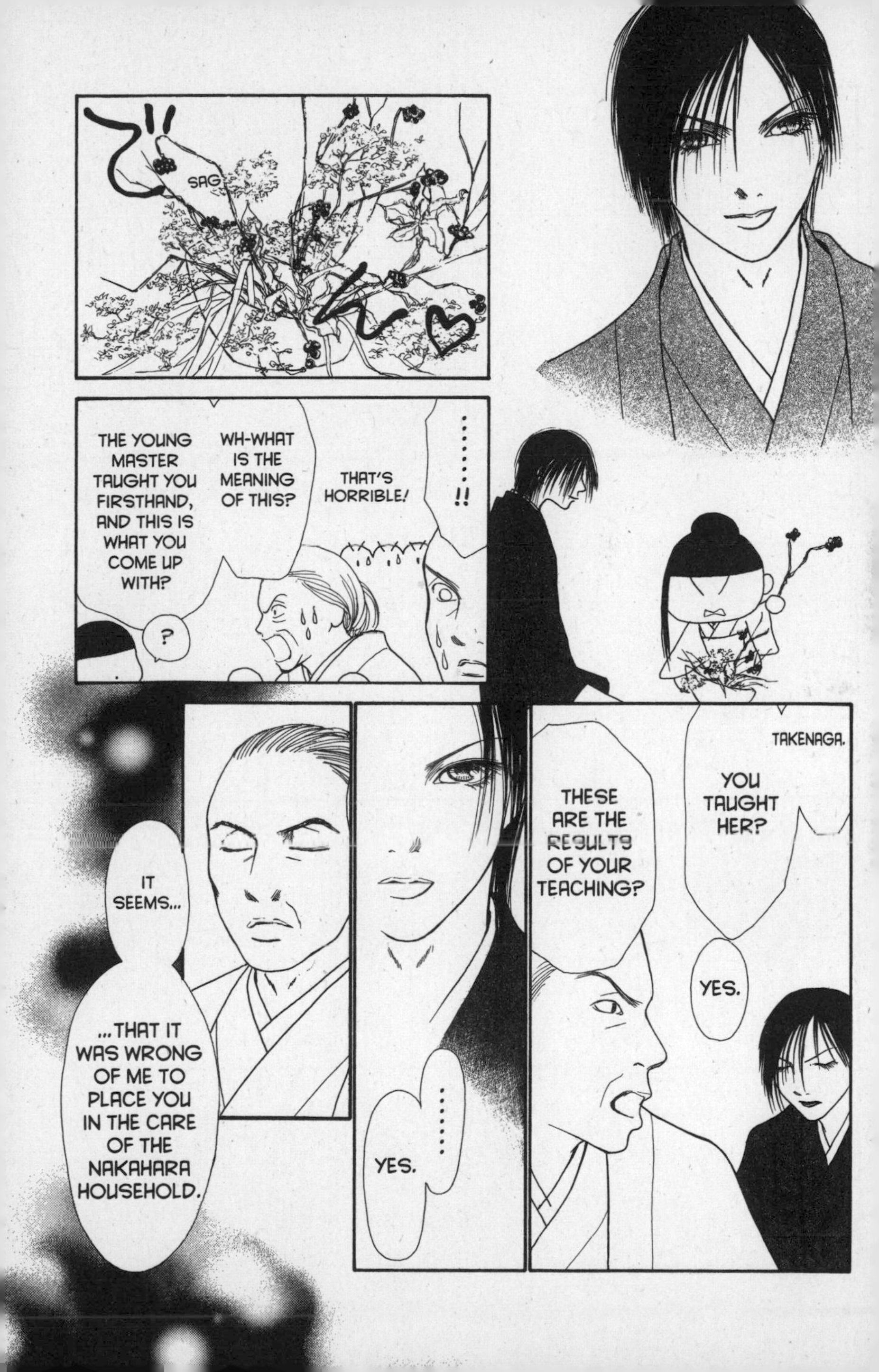
SAG
......!!
THAT'S HORRIBLE!
WH-WHAT IS THE MEANING OF THIS?
THE YOUNG MASTER TAUGHT YOU FIRSTHAND, AND THIS IS WHAT YOU COME UP WITH?
?
TAKENAGA.
YOU TAUGHT HER?
THESE ARE THE RESULTS OF YOUR TEACHING?
YES.
...... YES.
IT SEEMS...
...THAT IT WAS WRONG OF ME TO PLACE YOU IN THE CARE OF THE NAKAHARA HOUSEHOLD.

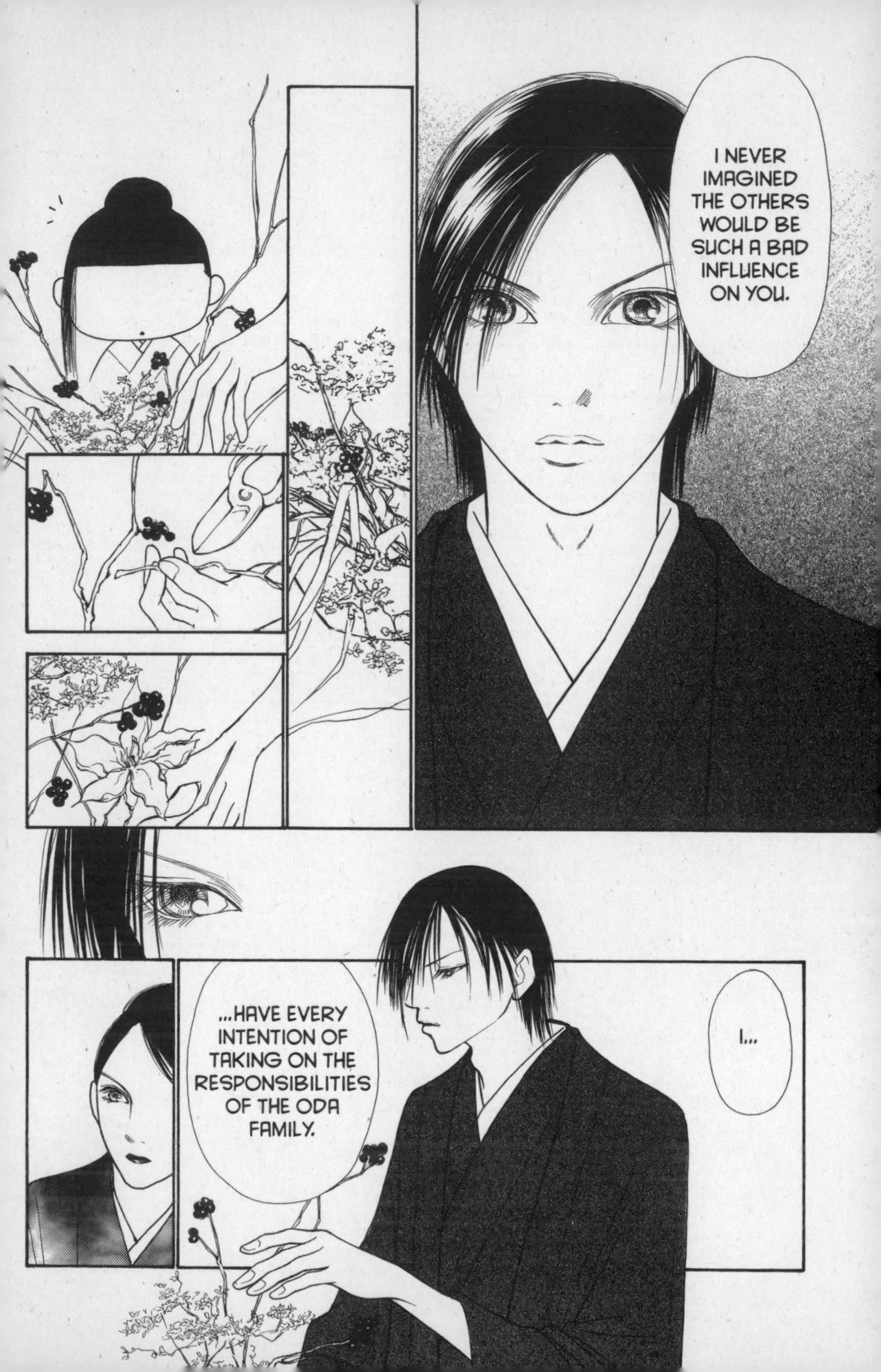
I NEVER IMAGINED THE OTHERS WOULD BE SUCH A BAD INFLUENCE ON YOU.
I...
...HAVE EVERY INTENTION OF TAKING ON THE RESPONSIBILITIES OF THE ODA FAMILY.

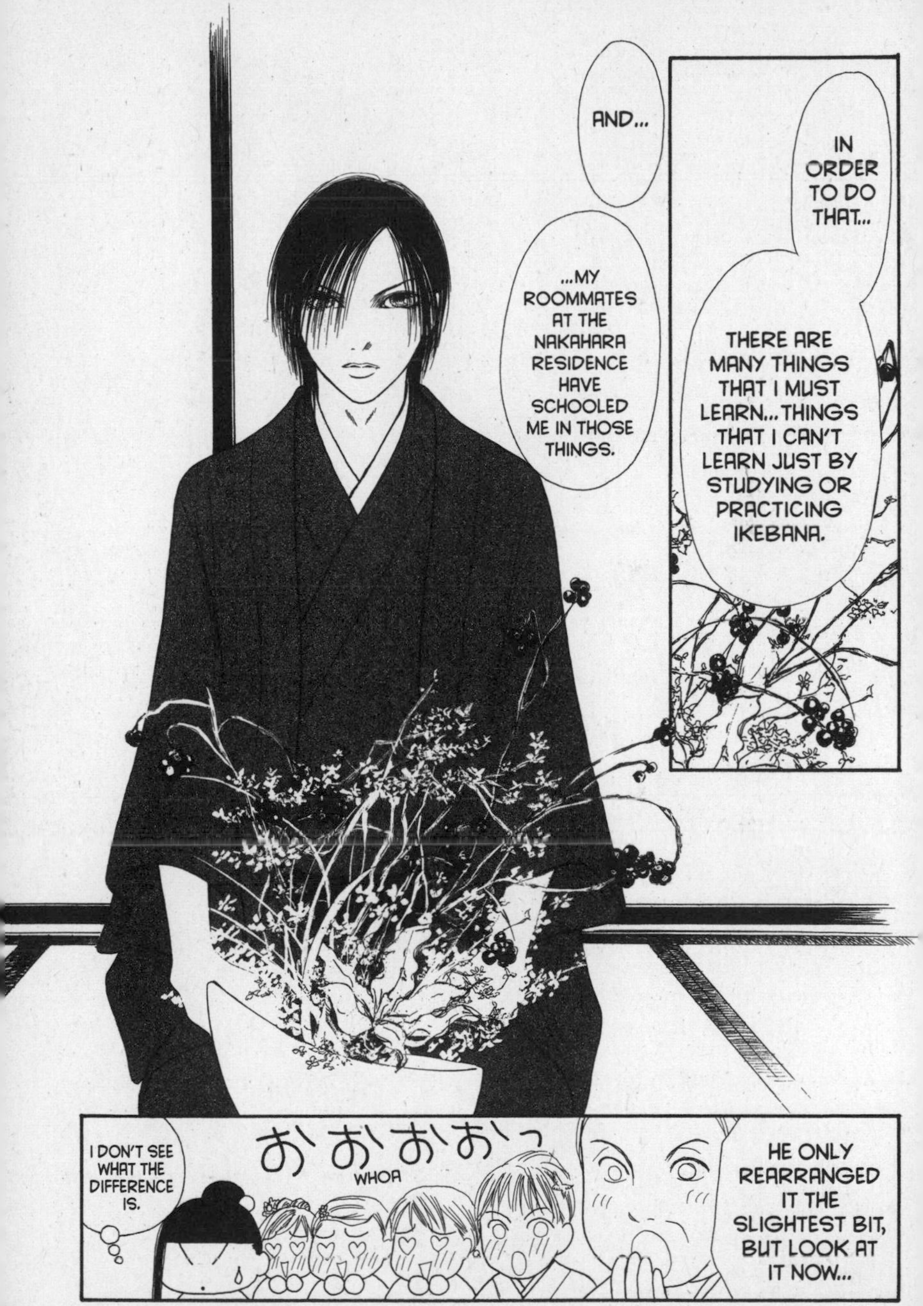
IN ORDER TO DO THAT...
THERE ARE MANY THINGS THAT I MUST LEARN...THINGS THAT I CAN'T LEARN JUST BY STUDYING OR PRACTICING IKEBANA.
AND...
...MY ROOMMATES AT THE NAKAHARA RESIDENCE HAVE SCHOOLED ME IN THOSE THINGS.
HE ONLY REARRANGED IT THE SLIGHTEST BIT, BUT LOOK AT IT NOW...
おおおおっ
WHOA
I DON'T SEE WHAT THE DIFFERENCE IS.

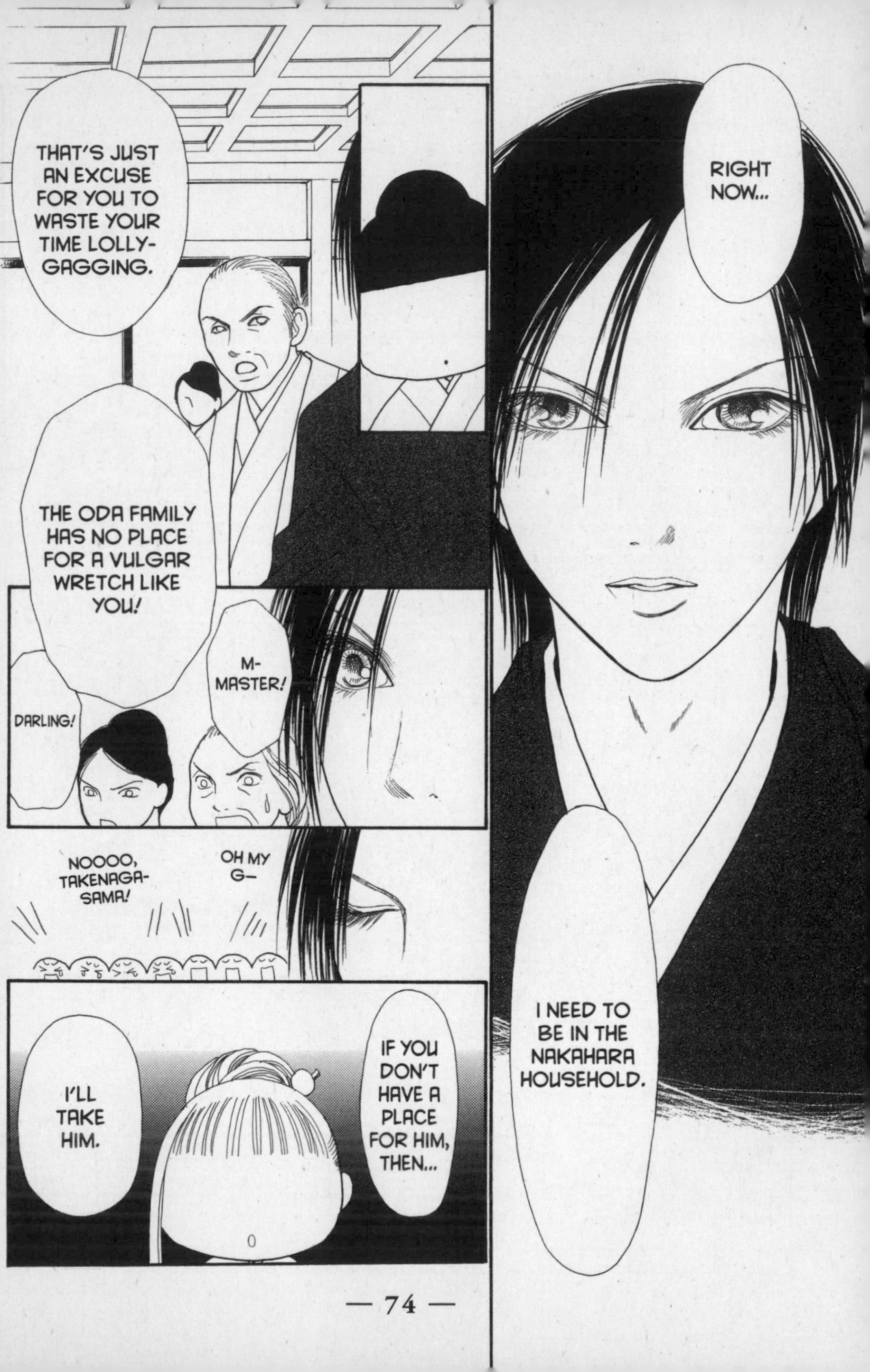
RIGHT NOW...
I NEED TO BE IN THE NAKAHARA HOUSEHOLD.
THAT'S JUST AN EXCUSE FOR YOU TO WASTE YOUR TIME LOLLY-GAGGING.
THE ODA FAMILY HAS NO PLACE FOR A VULGAR WRETCH LIKE YOU!
M-MASTER!
DARLING!
OH MY G—
NOOOO, TAKENAGA-SAMA!
IF YOU DON'T HAVE A PLACE FOR HIM, THEN...
I'LL TAKE HIM.

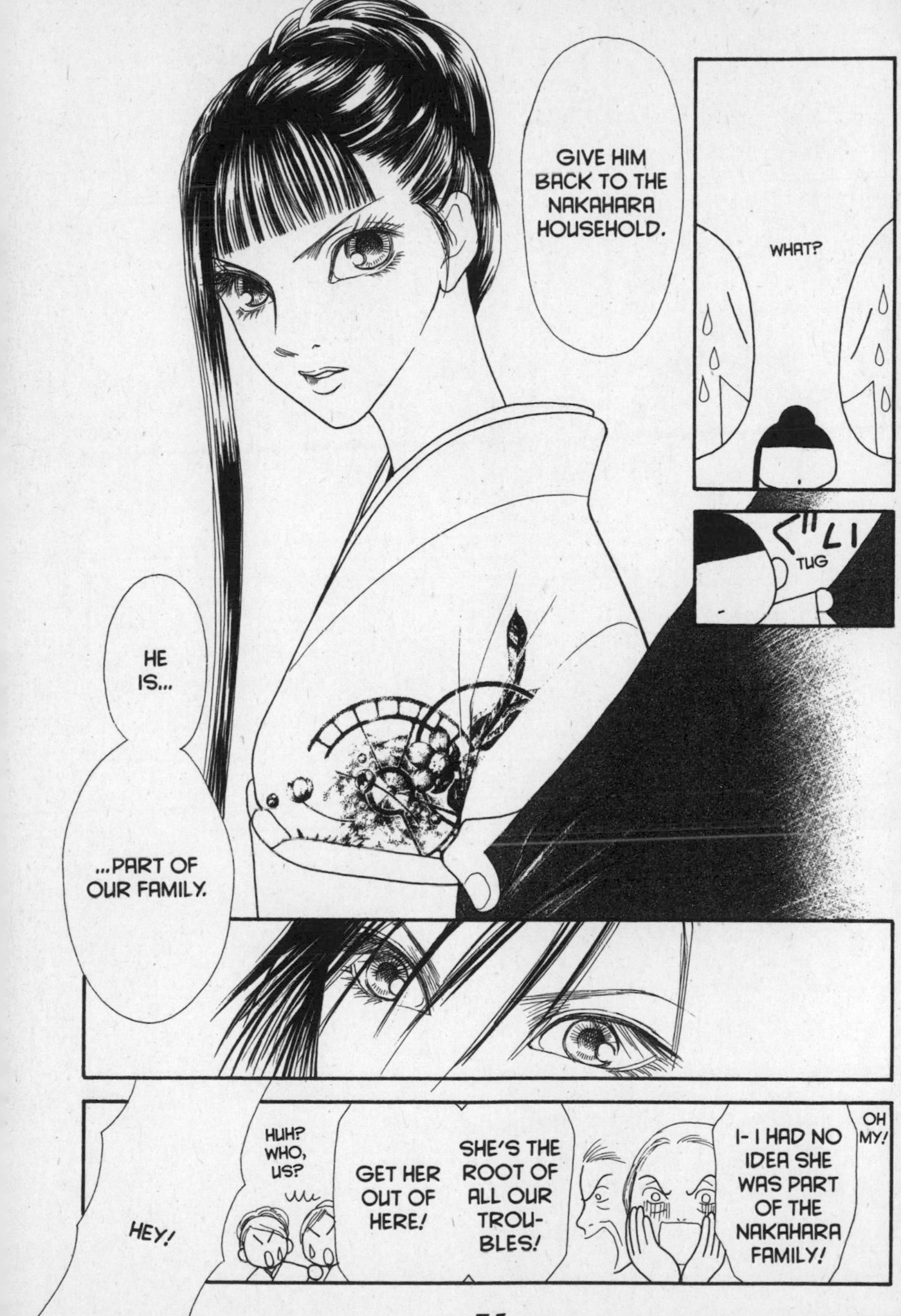
WHAT?
くい
TUG
GIVE HIM BACK TO THE NAKAHARA HOUSEHOLD.
HE IS...
...PART OF OUR FAMILY.
OH MY!
I- I HAD NO IDEA SHE WAS PART OF THE NAKAHARA FAMILY!
SHE'S THE ROOT OF ALL OUR TROU-BLES!
GET HER OUT OF HERE!
HUH? WHO, US?
HEY!

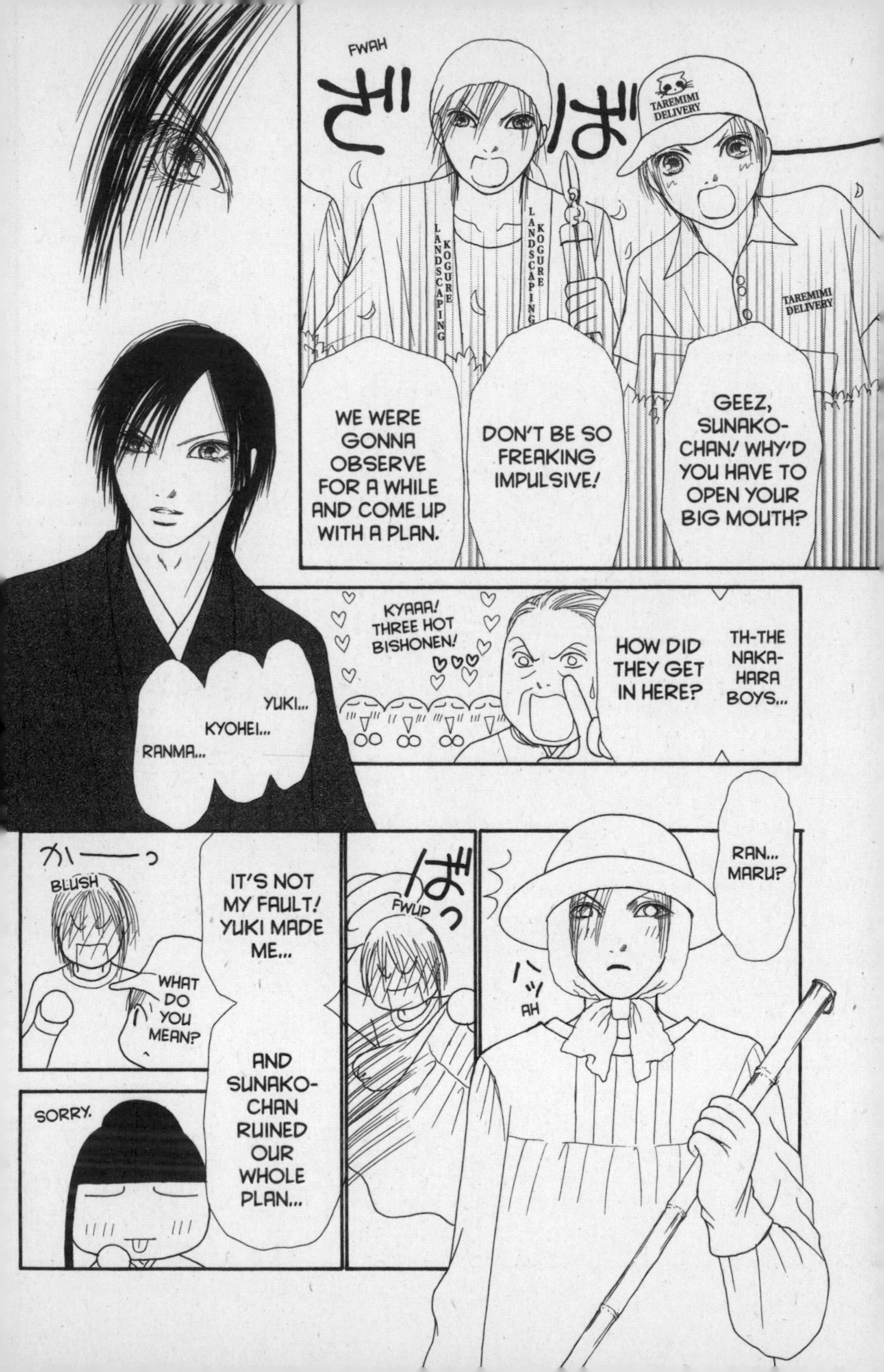
ざば
FWAH
TAREMIMI DELIVERY
LANDSCAPING KOGURE
GEEZ, SUNAKO-CHAN! WHY'D YOU HAVE TO OPEN YOUR BIG MOUTH?
DON'T BE SO FREAKING IMPULSIVE!
WE WERE GONNA OBSERVE FOR A WHILE AND COME UP WITH A PLAN.
TH-THE NAKA-HARA BOYS...
HOW DID THEY GET IN HERE?
KYAAA! THREE HOT BISHONEN!
YUKI...
KYOHEI...
RANMA...
RAN... MARU?
ハッ
AH
ぼっ
FWUP
IT'S NOT MY FAULT! YUKI MADE ME...
AND SUNAKO-CHAN RUINED OUR WHOLE PLAN...
かーっ
BLUSH
WHAT DO YOU MEAN?
SORRY.

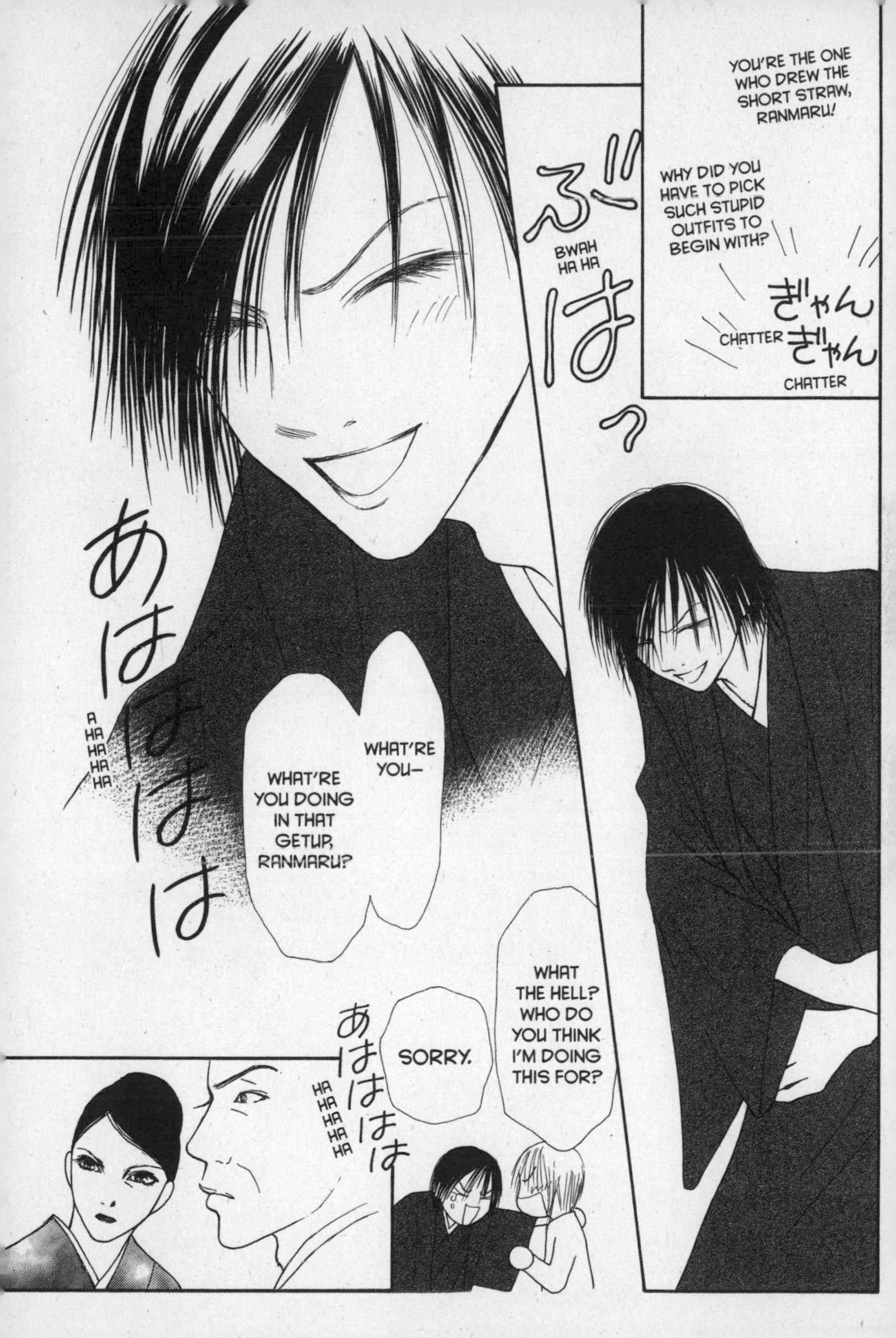
YOU'RE THE ONE WHO DREW THE SHORT STRAW, RANMARU!
WHY DID YOU HAVE TO PICK SUCH STUPID OUTFITS TO BEGIN WITH?
ぎゃんぎゃん
CHATTER CHATTER
ぶはっ
BWAH HA HA
WHAT'RE YOU—
WHAT'RE YOU DOING IN THAT GETUP, RANMARU?
あははは
A HA HA HA HA
WHAT THE HELL? WHO DO YOU THINK I'M DOING THIS FOR?
SORRY.
あははは
HA HA HA HA HA

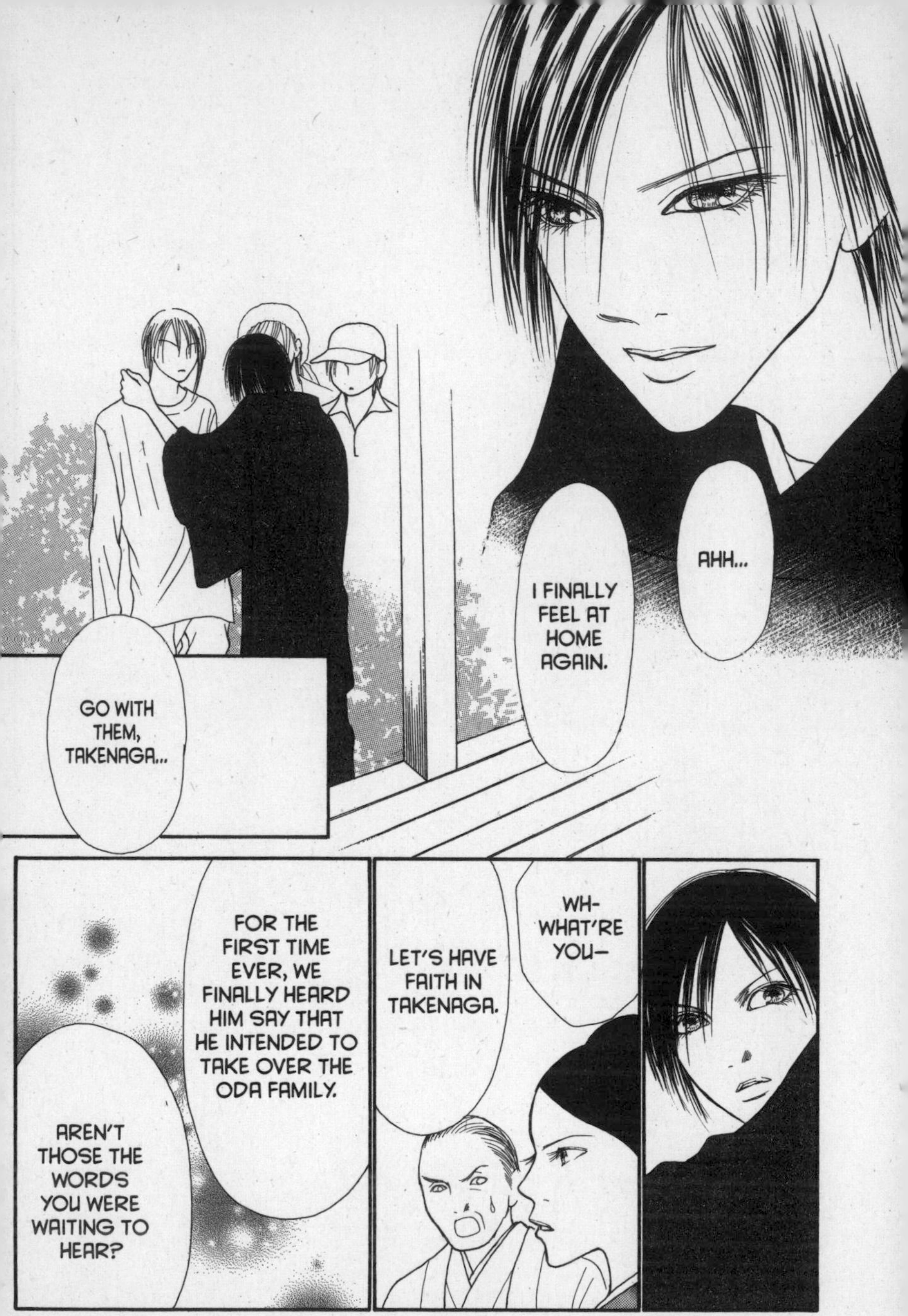
AHH...
I FINALLY FEEL AT HOME AGAIN.
GO WITH THEM, TAKENAGA...
WH-WHAT'RE YOU—
LET'S HAVE FAITH IN TAKENAGA.
FOR THE FIRST TIME EVER, WE FINALLY HEARD HIM SAY THAT HE INTENDED TO TAKE OVER THE ODA FAMILY.
AREN'T THOSE THE WORDS YOU WERE WAITING TO HEAR?

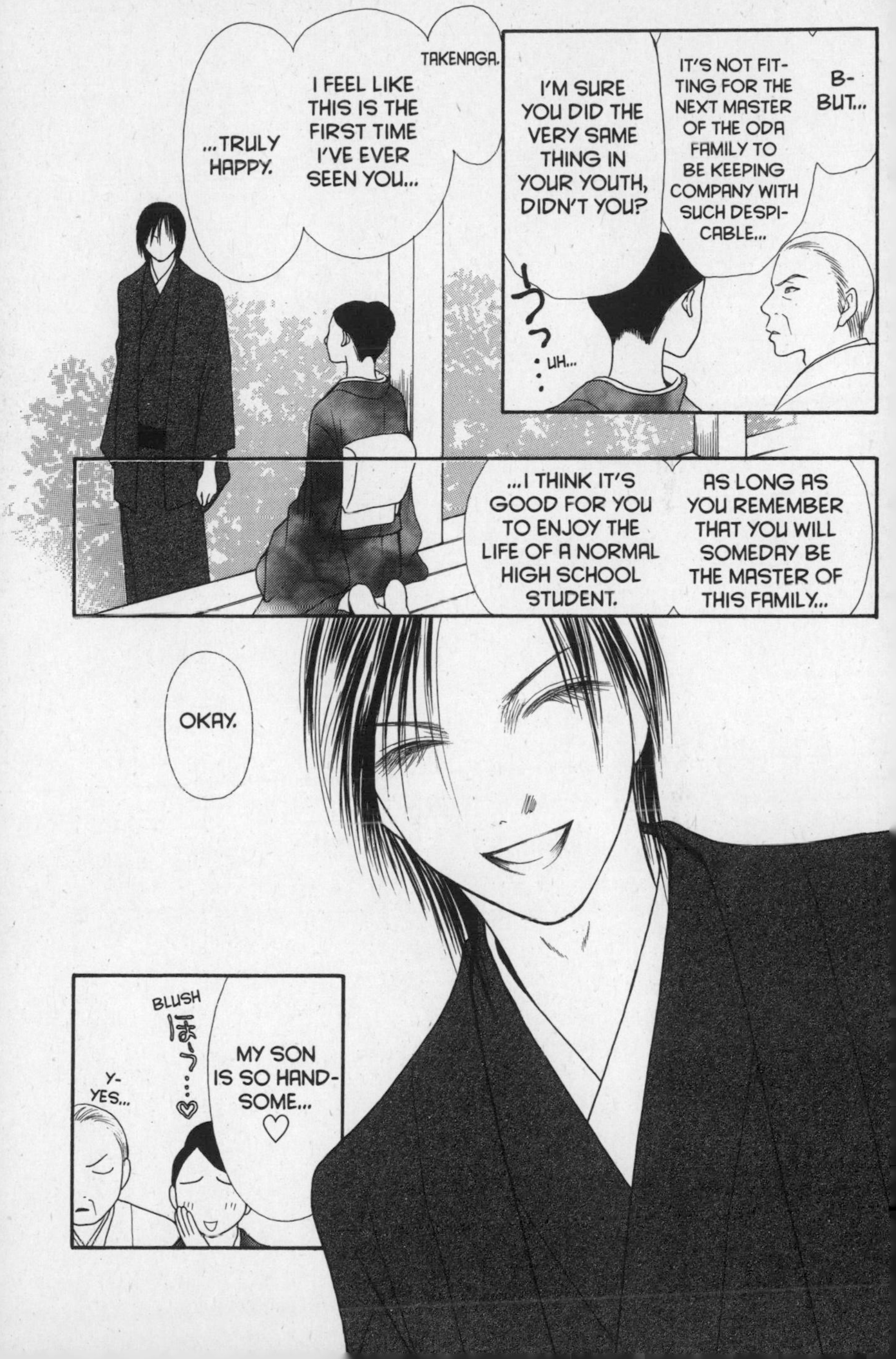
B-BUT...
IT'S NOT FITTING FOR THE NEXT MASTER OF THE ODA FAMILY TO BE KEEPING COMPANY WITH SUCH DESPICABLE...
I'M SURE YOU DID THE VERY SAME THING IN YOUR YOUTH, DIDN'T YOU?
うっ…
UH...
TAKENAGA.
I FEEL LIKE THIS IS THE FIRST TIME I'VE EVER SEEN YOU...
...TRULY HAPPY.
AS LONG AS YOU REMEMBER THAT YOU WILL SOMEDAY BE THE MASTER OF THIS FAMILY...
...I THINK IT'S GOOD FOR YOU TO ENJOY THE LIFE OF A NORMAL HIGH SCHOOL STUDENT.
OKAY.
MY SON IS SO HANDSOME... ♡
ほっ…♡
BLUSH
Y-YES...

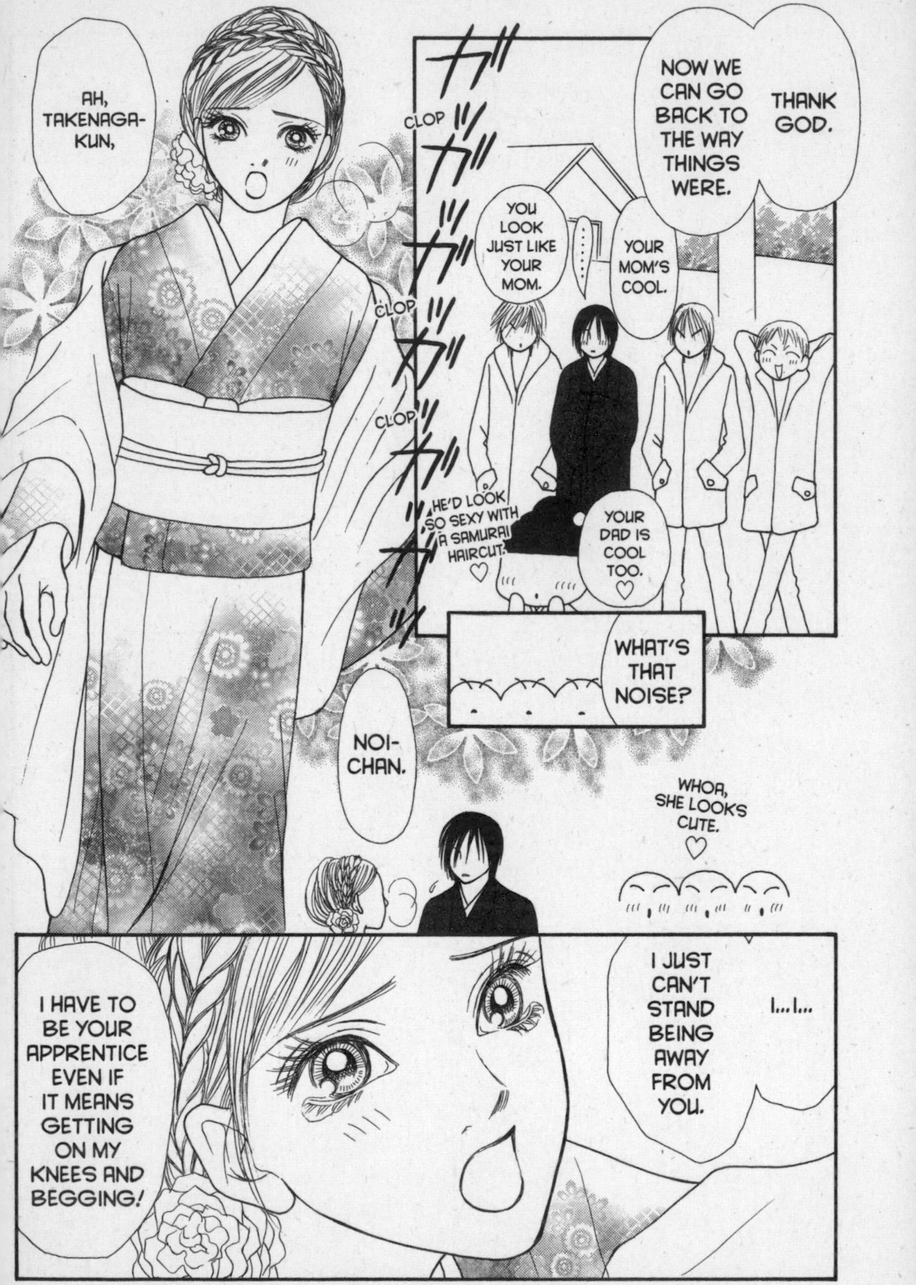
THANK GOD.
NOW WE CAN GO BACK TO THE WAY THINGS WERE.
YOUR MOM'S COOL.
...
YOU LOOK JUST LIKE YOUR MOM.
CLOP
CLOP
CLOP
YOUR DAD IS COOL TOO. ♡
HE'D LOOK SO SEXY WITH A SAMURAI HAIRCUT. ♡
WHAT'S THAT NOISE?
WHOA, SHE LOOKS CUTE. ♡
AH, TAKENAGA-KUN,
NOI-CHAN.
I...I...
I JUST CAN'T STAND BEING AWAY FROM YOU.
I HAVE TO BE YOUR APPRENTICE EVEN IF IT MEANS GETTING ON MY KNEES AND BEGGING!

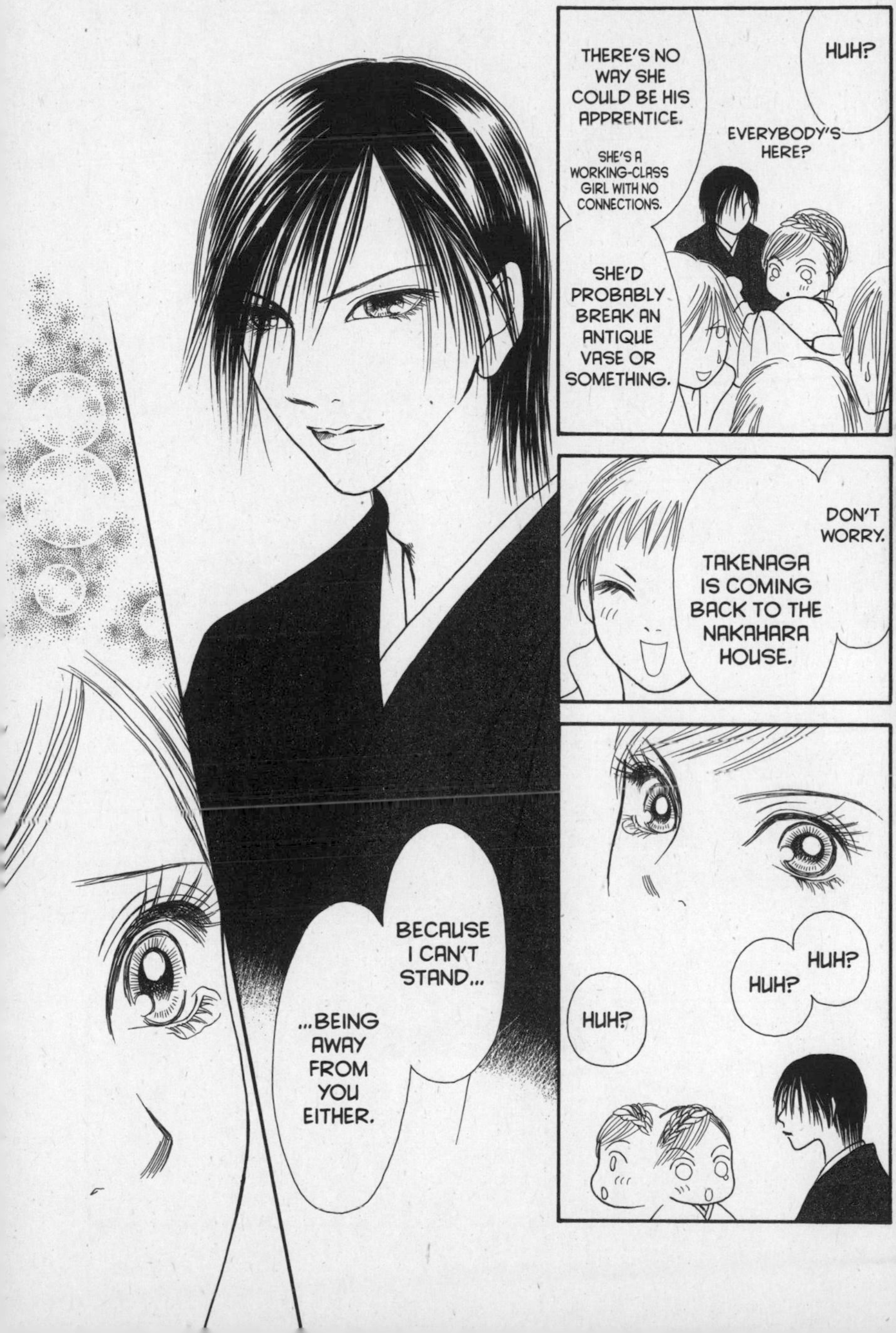
HUH?
EVERYBODY'S HERE?
THERE'S NO WAY SHE COULD BE HIS APPRENTICE.
SHE'S A WORKING-CLASS GIRL WITH NO CONNECTIONS.
SHE'D PROBABLY BREAK AN ANTIQUE VASE OR SOMETHING.
DON'T WORRY.
TAKENAGA IS COMING BACK TO THE NAKAHARA HOUSE.
HUH?
HUH?
HUH?
BECAUSE I CAN'T STAND...
...BEING AWAY FROM YOU EITHER.

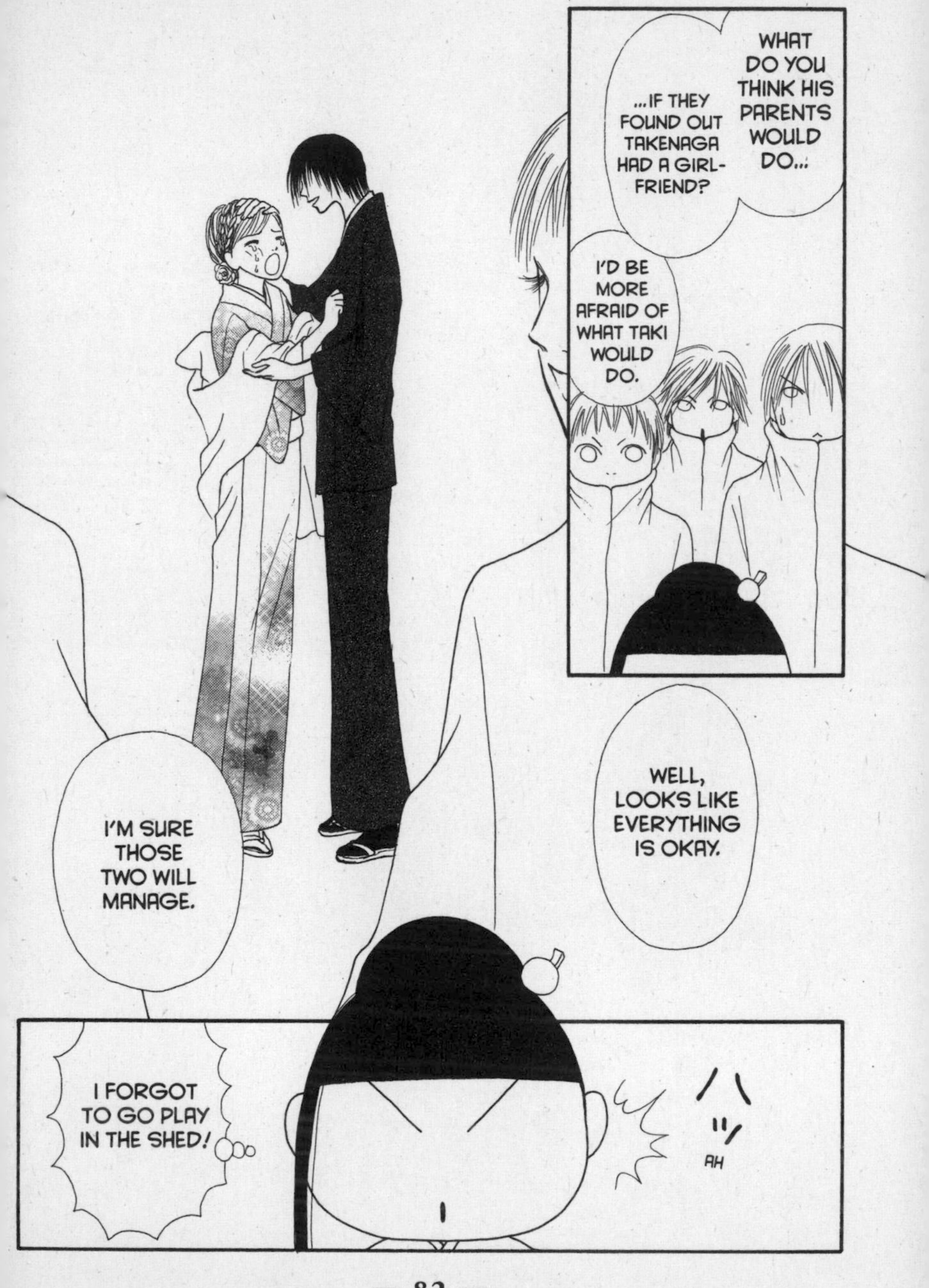
WHAT DO YOU THINK HIS PARENTS WOULD DO...
...IF THEY FOUND OUT TAKENAGA HAD A GIRL-FRIEND?
I'D BE MORE AFRAID OF WHAT TAKI WOULD DO.
WELL, LOOKS LIKE EVERYTHING IS OKAY.
I'M SURE THOSE TWO WILL MANAGE.
AH
I FORGOT TO GO PLAY IN THE SHED!

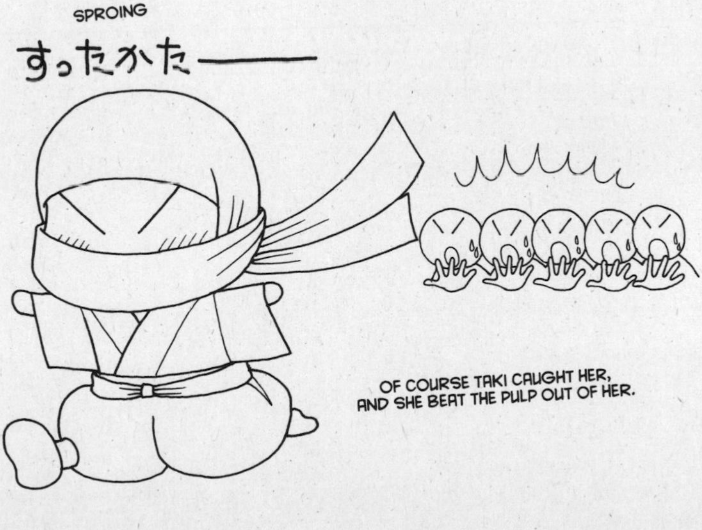
SPROING
すったかたーーー
OF COURSE TAKI CAUGHT HER,
AND SHE BEAT THE PULP OUT OF HER.

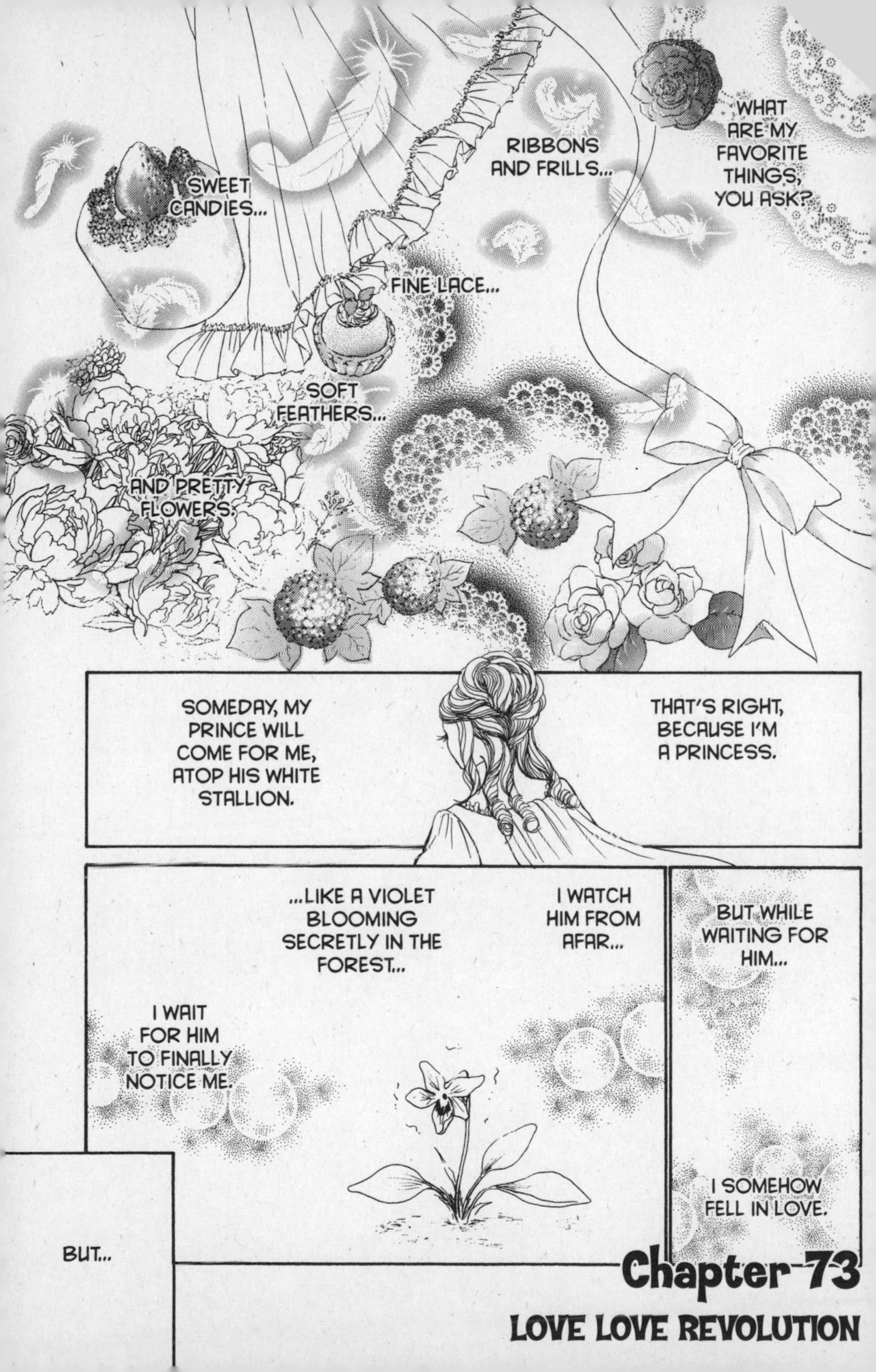
WHAT ARE MY FAVORITE THINGS, YOU ASK?
RIBBONS AND FRILLS...
SWEET CANDIES...
FINE LACE...
SOFT FEATHERS...
AND PRETTY FLOWERS.
THAT'S RIGHT, BECAUSE I'M A PRINCESS.
SOMEDAY, MY PRINCE WILL COME FOR ME, ATOP HIS WHITE STALLION.
BUT WHILE WAITING FOR HIM...
I SOMEHOW FELL IN LOVE.
I WATCH HIM FROM AFAR...
...LIKE A VIOLET BLOOMING SECRETLY IN THE FOREST...
I WAIT FOR HIM TO FINALLY NOTICE ME.
BUT...
Chapter 73
LOVE LOVE REVOLUTION

Chapter 73
LOVE LOVE REVOLUTION

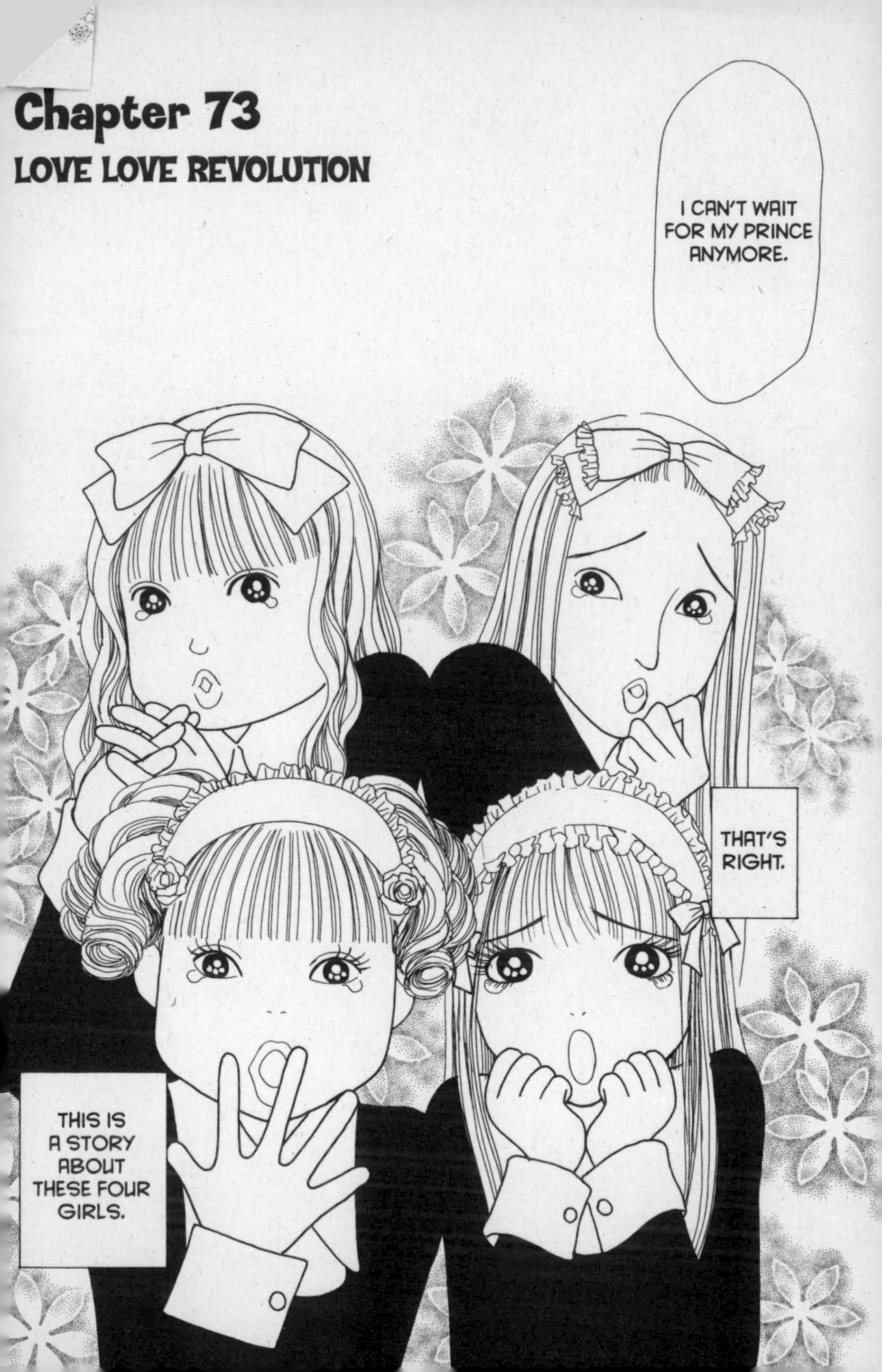
I CAN'T WAIT FOR MY PRINCE ANYMORE.
THAT'S RIGHT.
THIS IS A STORY ABOUT THESE FOUR GIRLS.

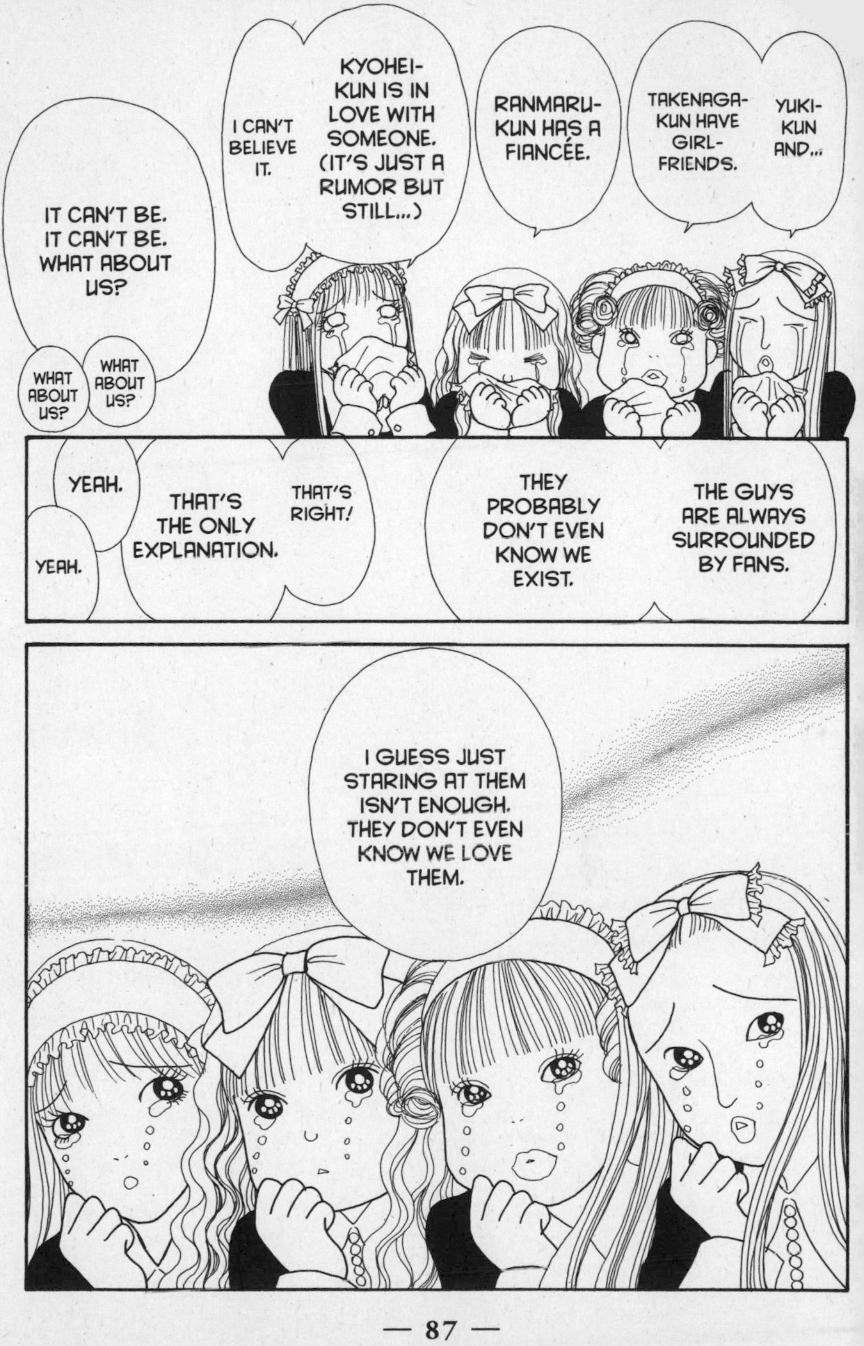
YUKI-KUN AND...
TAKENAGA-KUN HAVE GIRL-FRIENDS.
RANMARU-KUN HAS A FIANCÉE.
KYOHEI-KUN IS IN LOVE WITH SOMEONE. (IT'S JUST A RUMOR BUT STILL...)
I CAN'T BELIEVE IT.
IT CAN'T BE. IT CAN'T BE. WHAT ABOUT US?
WHAT ABOUT US?
WHAT ABOUT US?
THE GUYS ARE ALWAYS SURROUNDED BY FANS.
THEY PROBABLY DON'T EVEN KNOW WE EXIST.
THAT'S RIGHT!
THAT'S THE ONLY EXPLANATION.
YEAH.
YEAH.
I GUESS JUST STARING AT THEM ISN'T ENOUGH. THEY DON'T EVEN KNOW WE LOVE THEM.

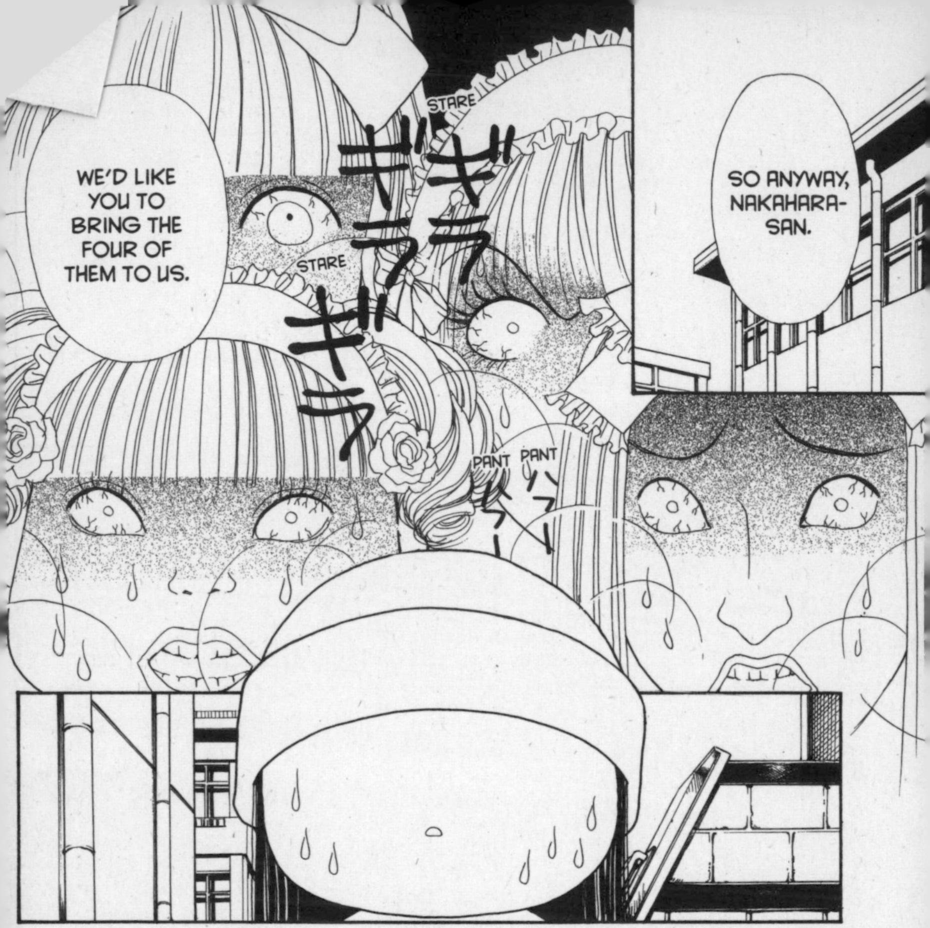
SO ANYWAY, NAKAHARA-SAN.
WE'D LIKE YOU TO BRING THE FOUR OF THEM TO US.
STARE
STARE
PANT PANT

BEHIND THE SCENES

I WROTE THIS STORY IN DECEMBER. OUR YEAR-END SCHEDULE IS REALLY TIGHT, AND THE DEADLINES ARE QUICK!

THAT'S WHY I MISSED THE KIYOHARU CONCERT! WAAAAHHH... I WAS SO SAD I COULDN'T EVEN LISTEN TO HIS CD. SNIFFLE SNIFF SNIFF

A FEW DAYS AFTER I FINISHED THE STORYBOARDS, I WENT TO THE BUCK-TICK CONCERT. WOW. THEY HAVE REAL PRESENCE. THEY'RE SO COOL. ♥ FOR NEW YEAR'S, I WENT TO THE MERRY CONCERT. ♥ THEY PLAYED A LOT OF MY FAVORITE SONGS... SONGS THAT THEY USUALLY DON'T PLAY LIVE. I WAS SO HAPPY. ♥ ♥ ♥ MERRY IS SO COOL. ♥ ♥ ♥

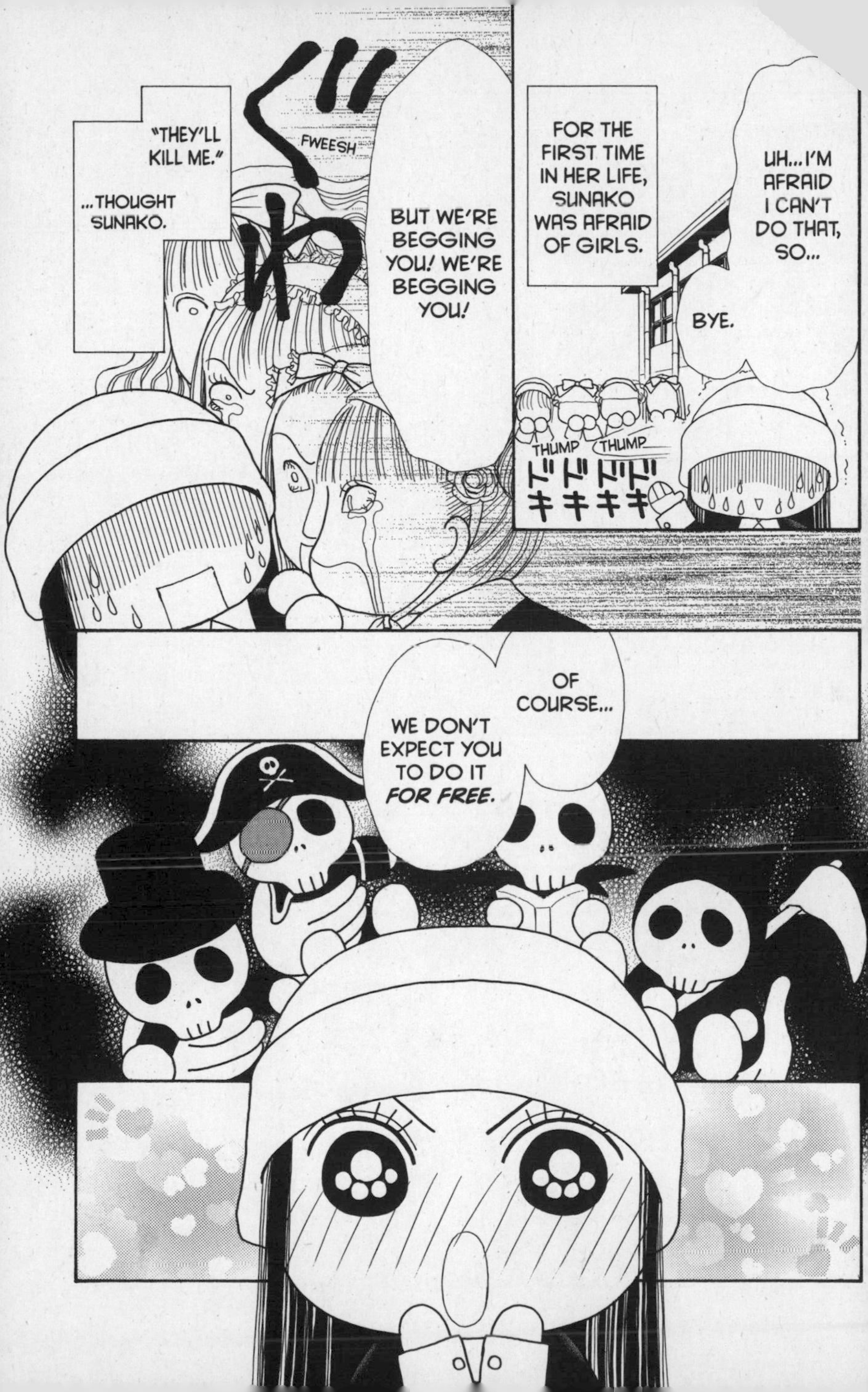
FOR THE FIRST TIME IN HER LIFE, SUNAKO WAS AFRAID OF GIRLS.
UH...I'M AFRAID I CAN'T DO THAT, SO...
BYE.
THUMP THUMP
ドドドド
キキキキ
BUT WE'RE BEGGING YOU! WE'RE BEGGING YOU!
ぐわ
FWEESH
"THEY'LL KILL ME."
...THOUGHT SUNAKO.
OF COURSE...
WE DON'T EXPECT YOU TO DO IT *FOR FREE.*

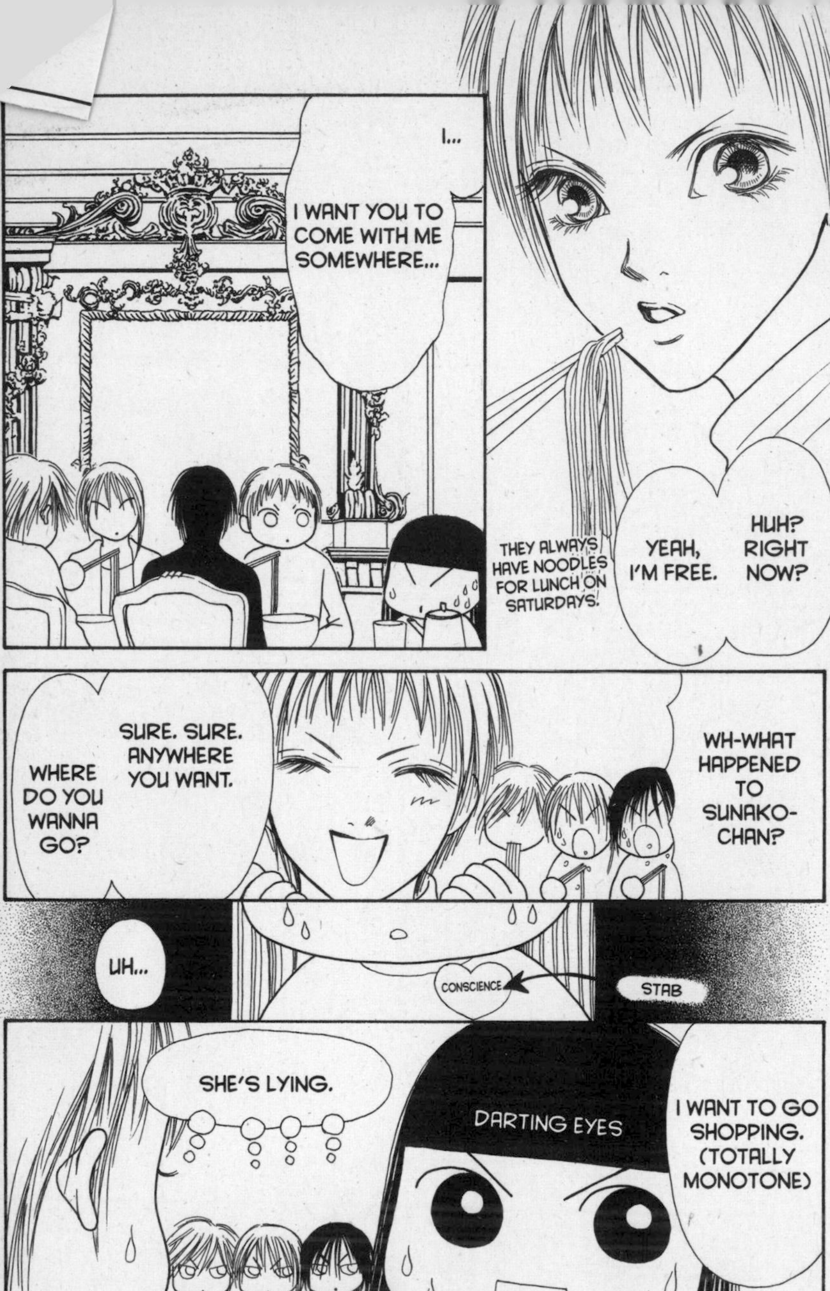
I...
I WANT YOU TO COME WITH ME SOMEWHERE...
HUH? RIGHT NOW?
YEAH, I'M FREE.
THEY ALWAYS HAVE NOODLES FOR LUNCH ON SATURDAYS.
WH-WHAT HAPPENED TO SUNAKO-CHAN?
SURE. SURE. ANYWHERE YOU WANT.
WHERE DO YOU WANNA GO?
STAB
CONSCIENCE
UH...
I WANT TO GO SHOPPING. (TOTALLY MONOTONE)
DARTING EYES
SHE'S LYING.

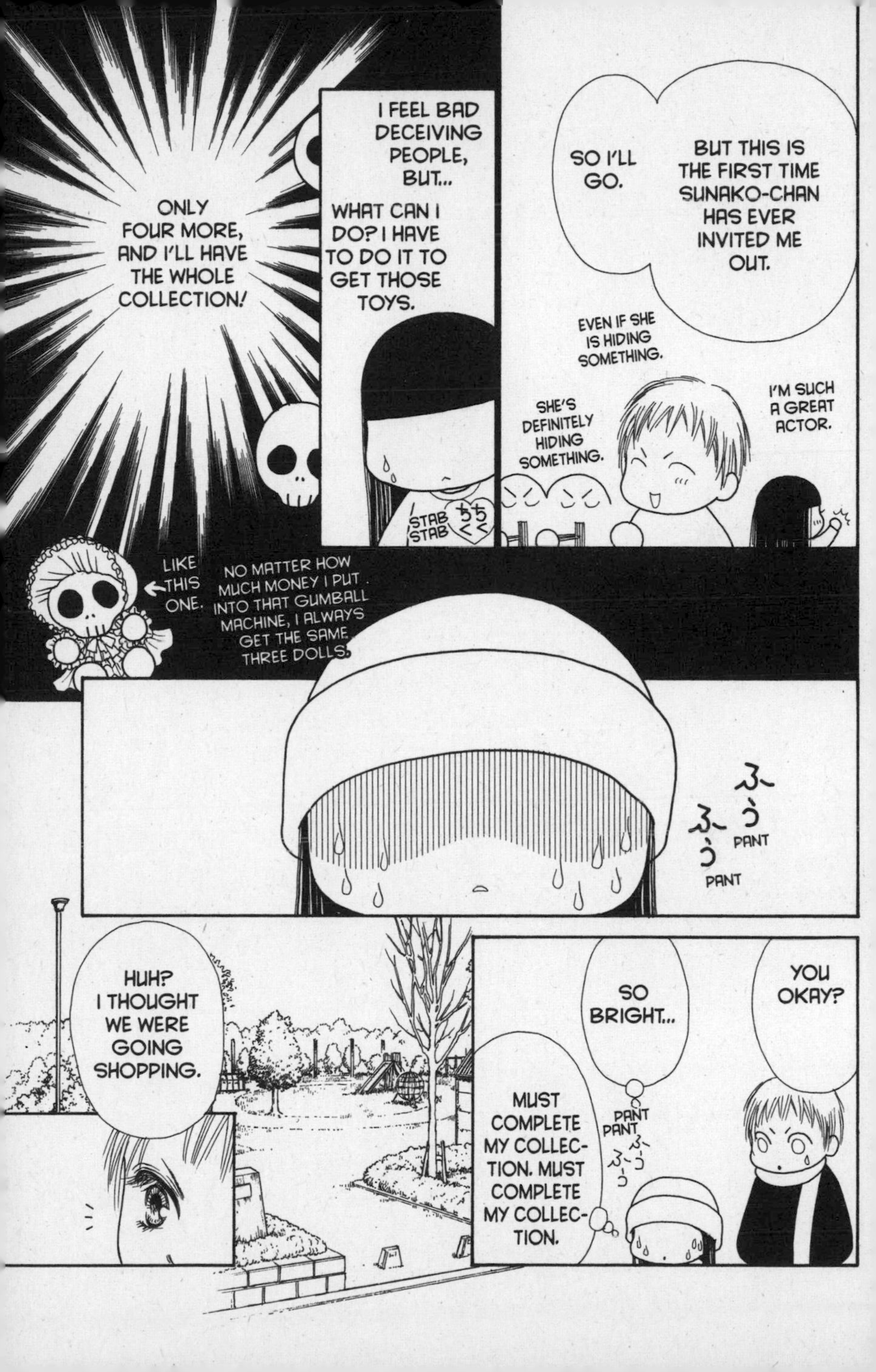
BUT THIS IS THE FIRST TIME SUNAKO-CHAN HAS EVER INVITED ME OUT.
SO I'LL GO.
EVEN IF SHE IS HIDING SOMETHING.
I'M SUCH A GREAT ACTOR.
SHE'S DEFINITELY HIDING SOMETHING.
I FEEL BAD DECEIVING PEOPLE, BUT...
WHAT CAN I DO? I HAVE TO DO IT TO GET THOSE TOYS.
ちくちく
STAB STAB
ONLY FOUR MORE, AND I'LL HAVE THE WHOLE COLLECTION!
NO MATTER HOW MUCH MONEY I PUT INTO THAT GUMBALL MACHINE, I ALWAYS GET THE SAME THREE DOLLS.
LIKE THIS ONE.
ふーう PANT
ふーう PANT
YOU OKAY?
SO BRIGHT...
PANT PANT
MUST COMPLETE MY COLLEC-TION. MUST COMPLETE MY COLLEC-TION.
HUH? I THOUGHT WE WERE GOING SHOPPING.

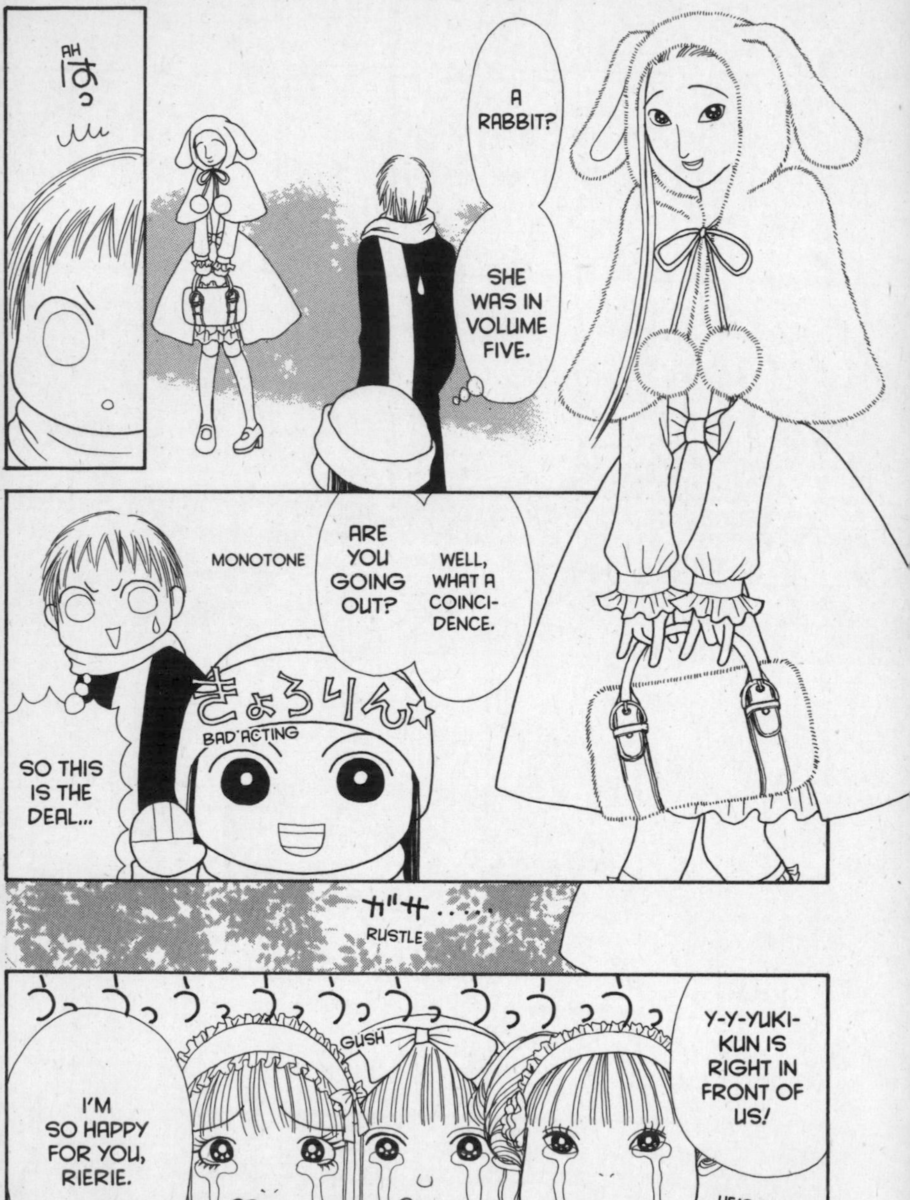

A RABBIT?
SHE WAS IN VOLUME FIVE.
はっ
AH
WELL, WHAT A COINCIDENCE.
ARE YOU GOING OUT?
MONOTONE
きょろりん☆
BAD ACTING
SO THIS IS THE DEAL...
ガサ……
RUSTLE
Y-Y-YUKI-KUN IS RIGHT IN FRONT OF US!
HE'S CUTE. HE'S SO CUTE.
うっうっうっうっうっうっうっうっうっうっ
GUSH
I'M SO HAPPY FOR YOU, RIERIE.

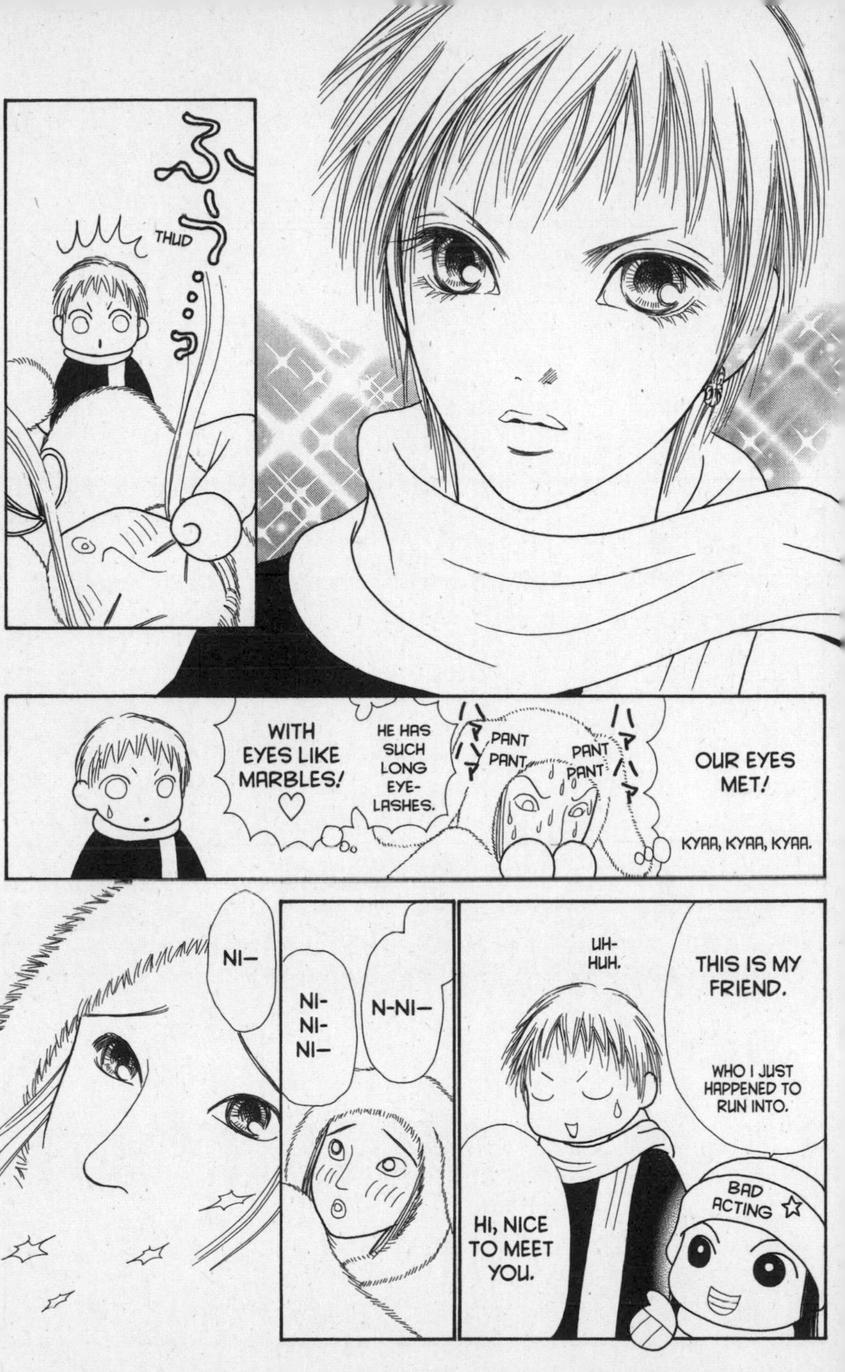
THUD
OUR EYES MET!
KYAA, KYAA, KYAA.
PANT PANT
PANT PANT
HE HAS SUCH LONG EYE-LASHES.
WITH EYES LIKE MARBLES! ♡
THIS IS MY FRIEND.
WHO I JUST HAPPENED TO RUN INTO.
UH-HUH.
BAD ACTING ☆
HI, NICE TO MEET YOU.
N-NI—
NI- NI- NI—
NI—

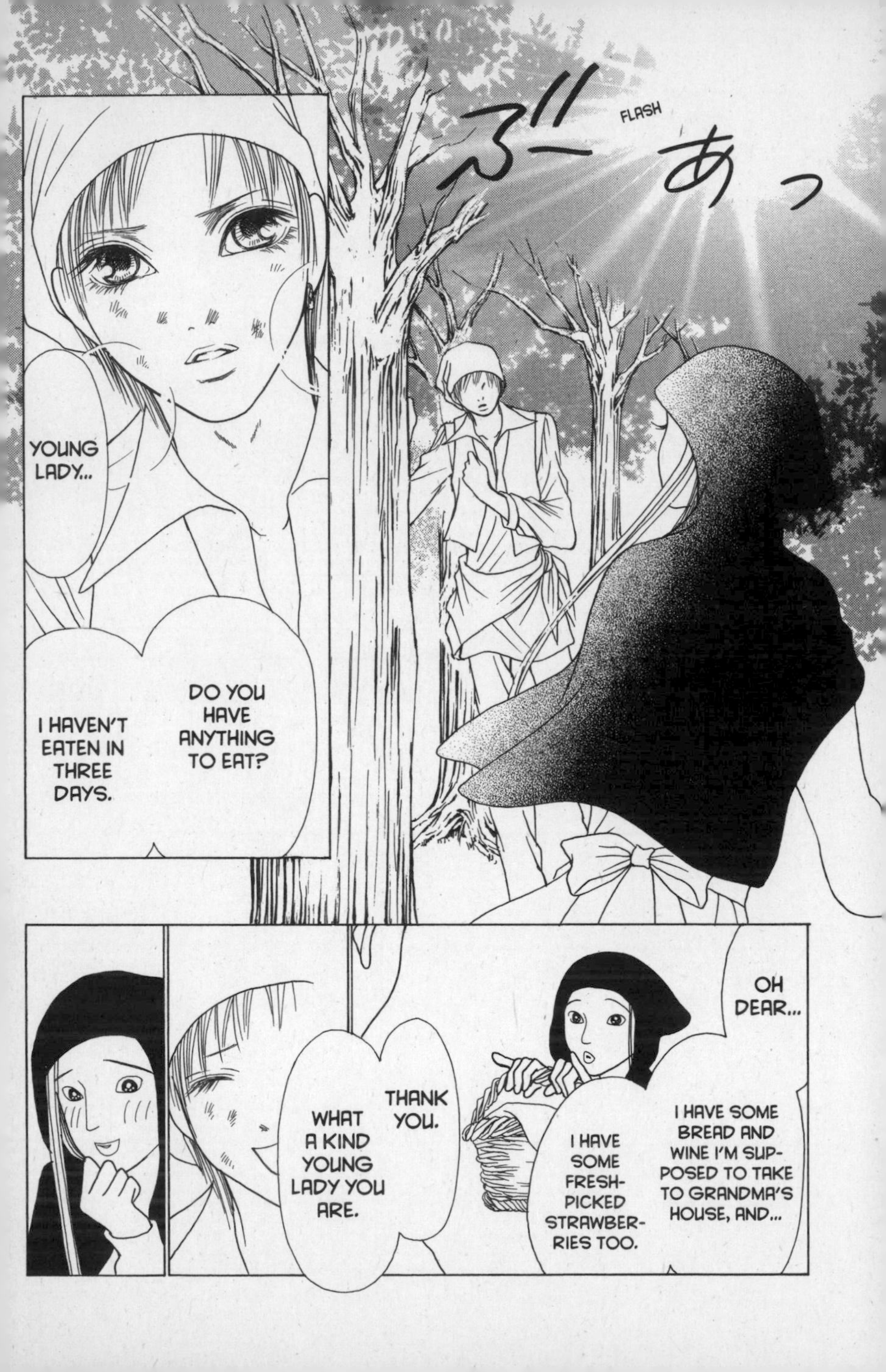
ぶあっ
FLASH
YOUNG LADY...
DO YOU HAVE ANYTHING TO EAT?
I HAVEN'T EATEN IN THREE DAYS.
OH DEAR...
I HAVE SOME BREAD AND WINE I'M SUP-POSED TO TAKE TO GRANDMA'S HOUSE, AND...
I HAVE SOME FRESH-PICKED STRAWBER-RIES TOO.
THANK YOU.
WHAT A KIND YOUNG LADY YOU ARE.

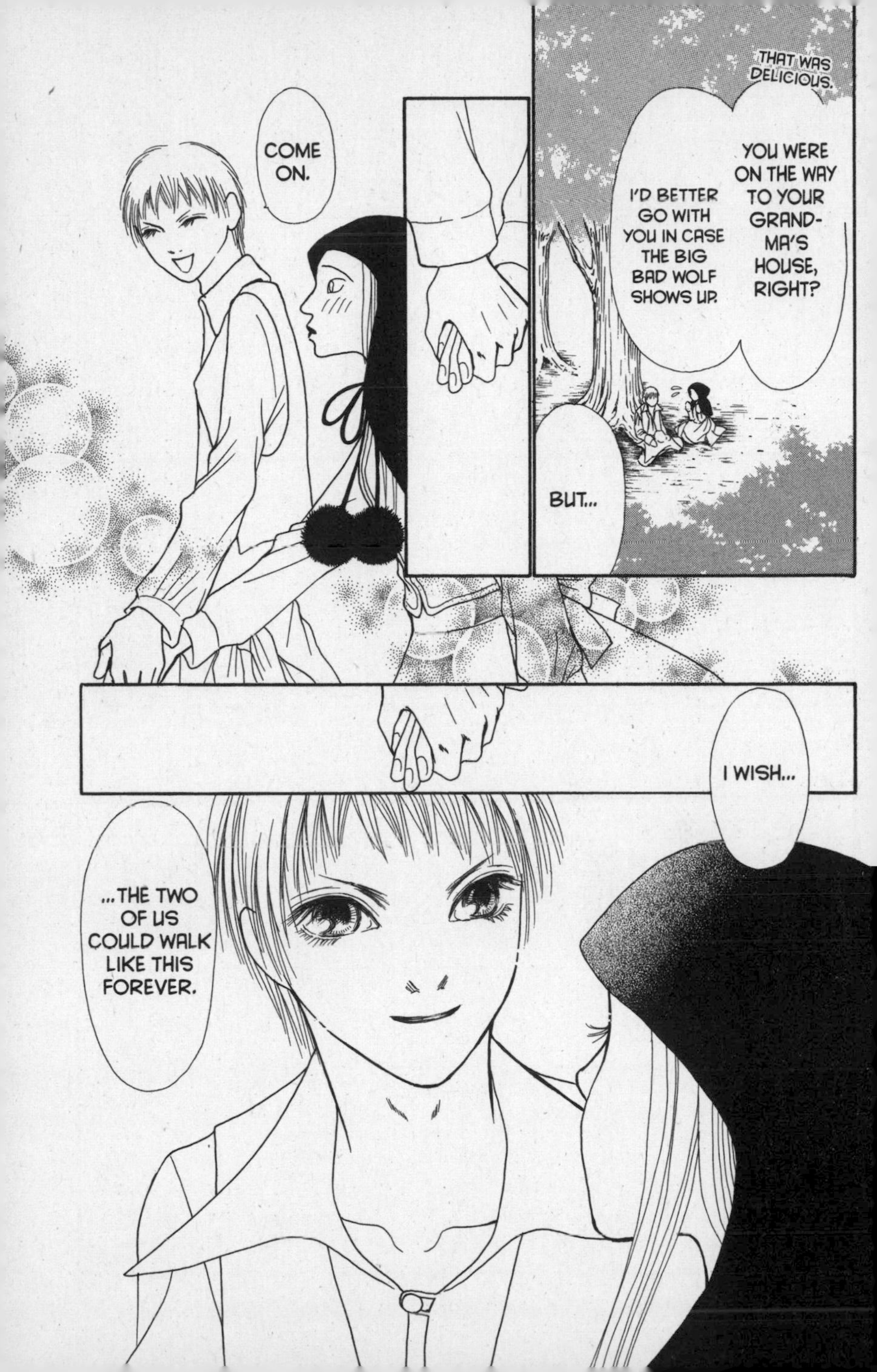
THAT WAS DELICIOUS.
YOU WERE ON THE WAY TO YOUR GRAND-MA'S HOUSE, RIGHT?
I'D BETTER GO WITH YOU IN CASE THE BIG BAD WOLF SHOWS UP.
BUT...
COME ON.
I WISH...
...THE TWO OF US COULD WALK LIKE THIS FOREVER.

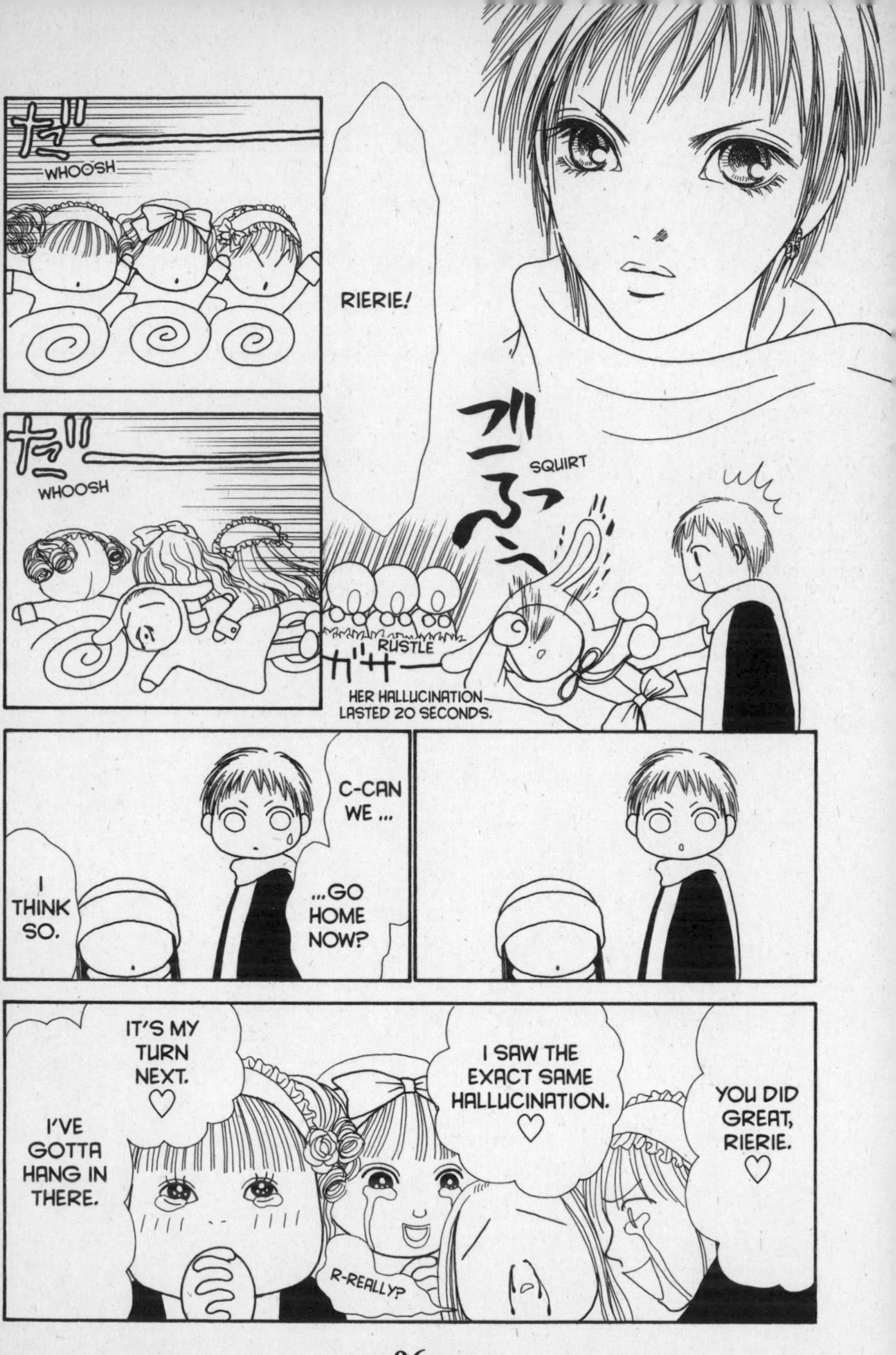
RIERIE!
SQUIRT
RUSTLE
HER HALLUCINATION LASTED 20 SECONDS.
WHOOSH
WHOOSH
C-CAN WE ...
...GO HOME NOW?
I THINK SO.
YOU DID GREAT, RIERIE. ♡
I SAW THE EXACT SAME HALLUCINATION. ♡
IT'S MY TURN NEXT. ♡
I'VE GOTTA HANG IN THERE.
R-REALLY?

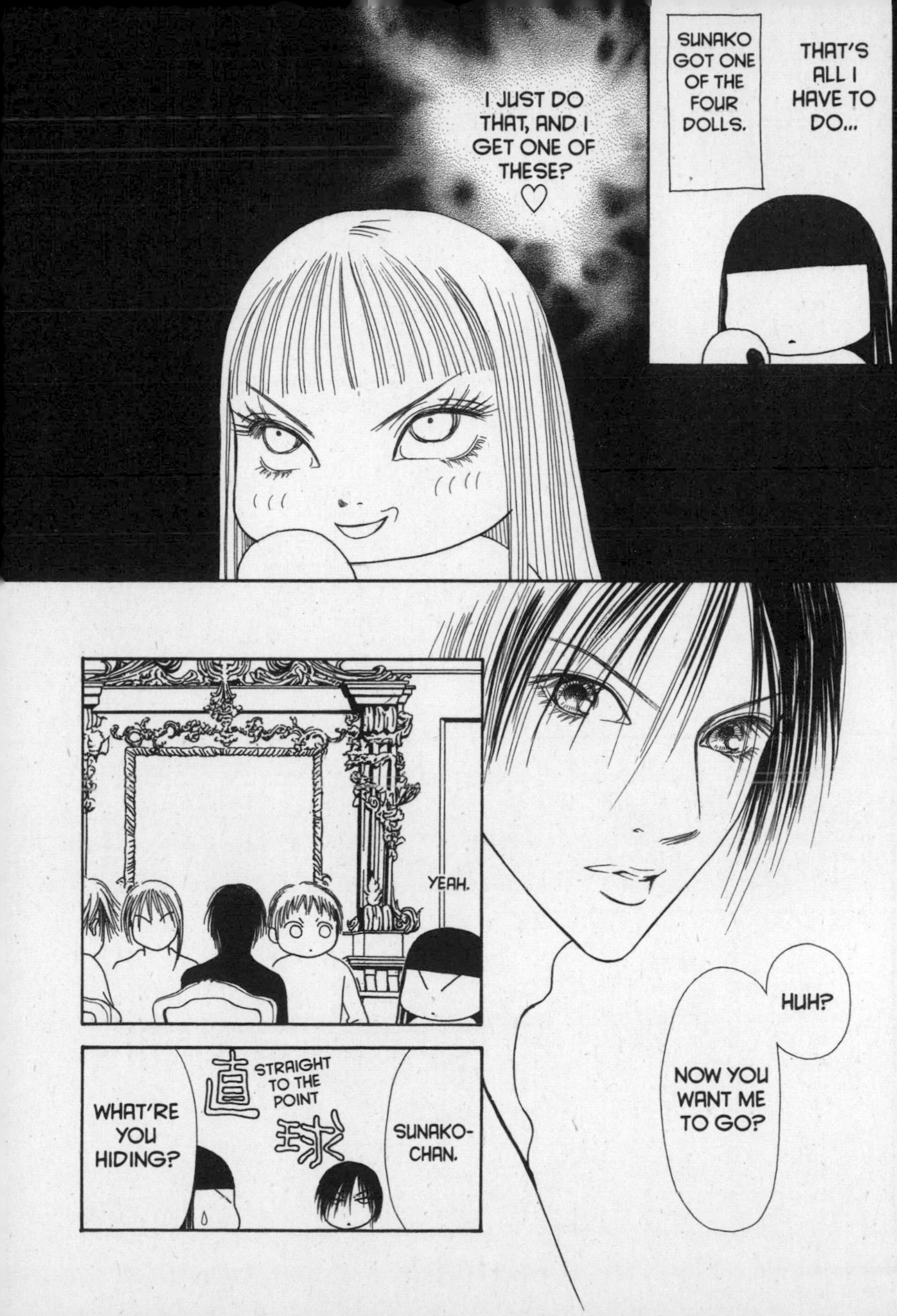
THAT'S ALL I HAVE TO DO...
SUNAKO GOT ONE OF THE FOUR DOLLS.
I JUST DO THAT, AND I GET ONE OF THESE? ♡
YEAH.
HUH?
NOW YOU WANT ME TO GO?
SUNAKO-CHAN.
直球
STRAIGHT TO THE POINT
WHAT'RE YOU HIDING?

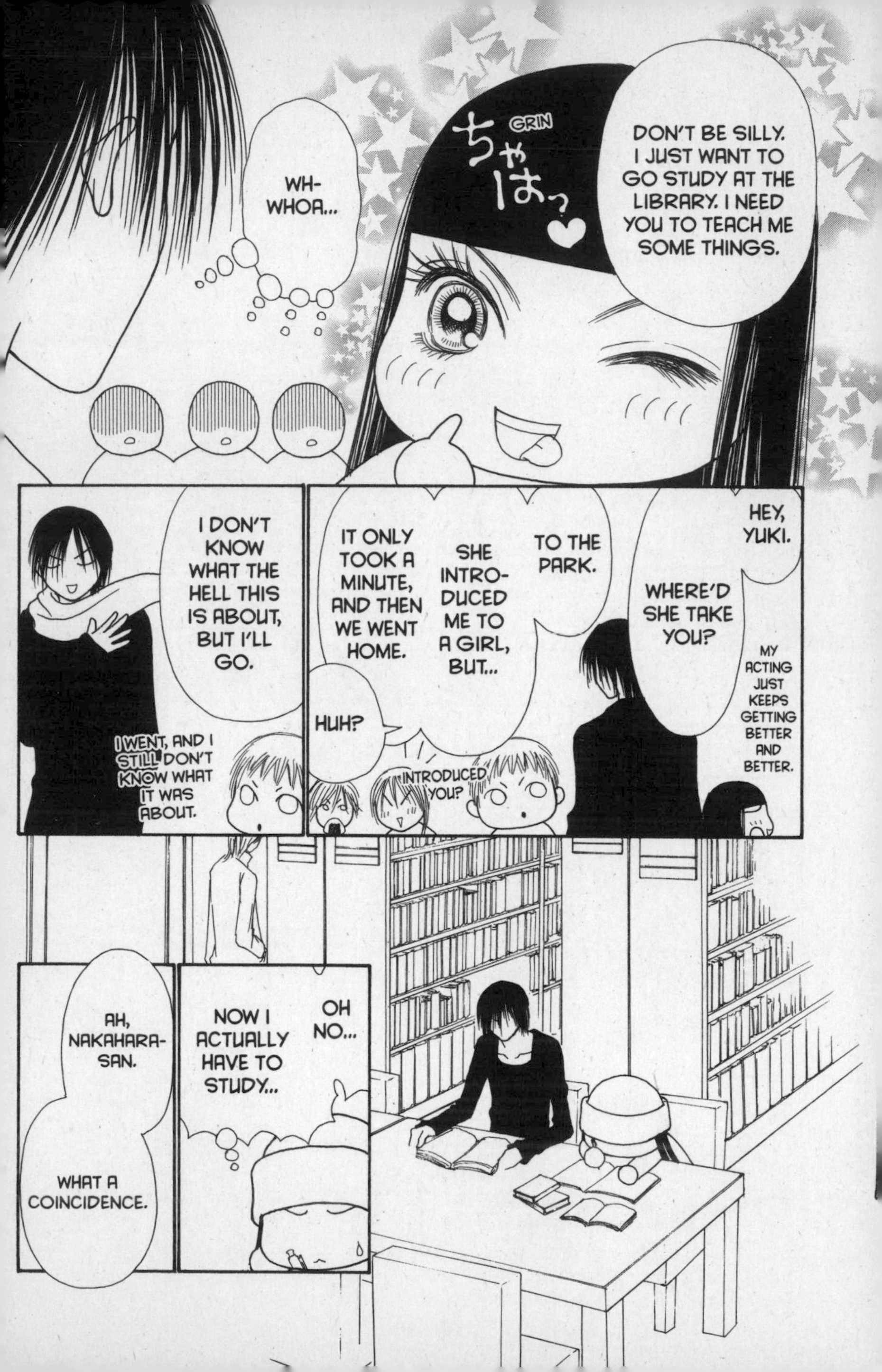
DON'T BE SILLY. I JUST WANT TO GO STUDY AT THE LIBRARY. I NEED YOU TO TEACH ME SOME THINGS.
ちゃはっ
GRIN
WH- WHOA...
HEY, YUKI.
WHERE'D SHE TAKE YOU?
MY ACTING JUST KEEPS GETTING BETTER AND BETTER.
TO THE PARK.
SHE INTRODUCED ME TO A GIRL, BUT...
IT ONLY TOOK A MINUTE, AND THEN WE WENT HOME.
INTRODUCED YOU?
HUH?
I DON'T KNOW WHAT THE HELL THIS IS ABOUT, BUT I'LL GO.
I WENT, AND I STILL DON'T KNOW WHAT IT WAS ABOUT.
OH NO...
NOW I ACTUALLY HAVE TO STUDY...
AH, NAKAHARA-SAN.
WHAT A COINCIDENCE.

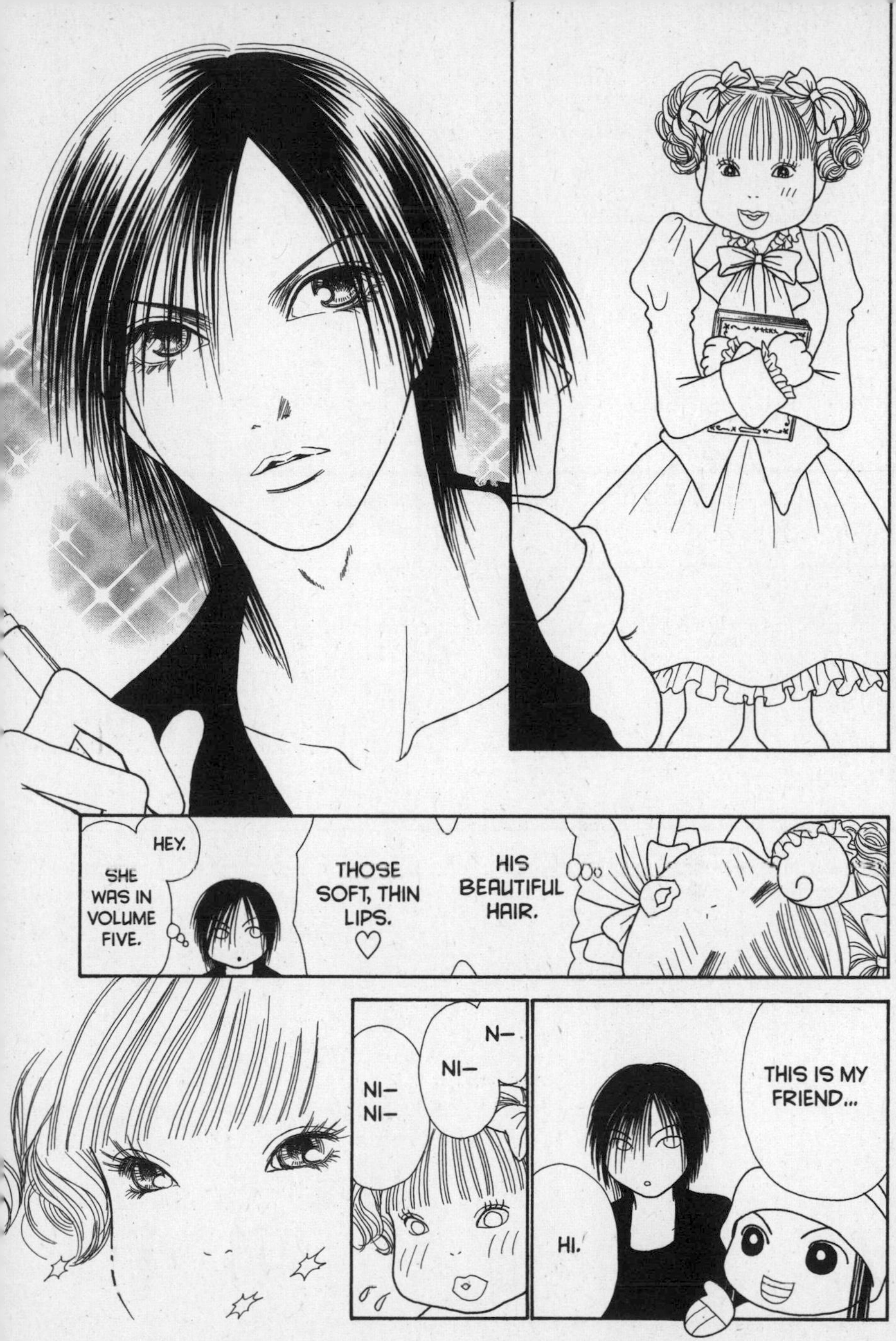
HIS BEAUTIFUL HAIR.
THOSE SOFT, THIN LIPS. ♡
HEY.
SHE WAS IN VOLUME FIVE.
THIS IS MY FRIEND...
HI.
N–
NI–
NI– NI–

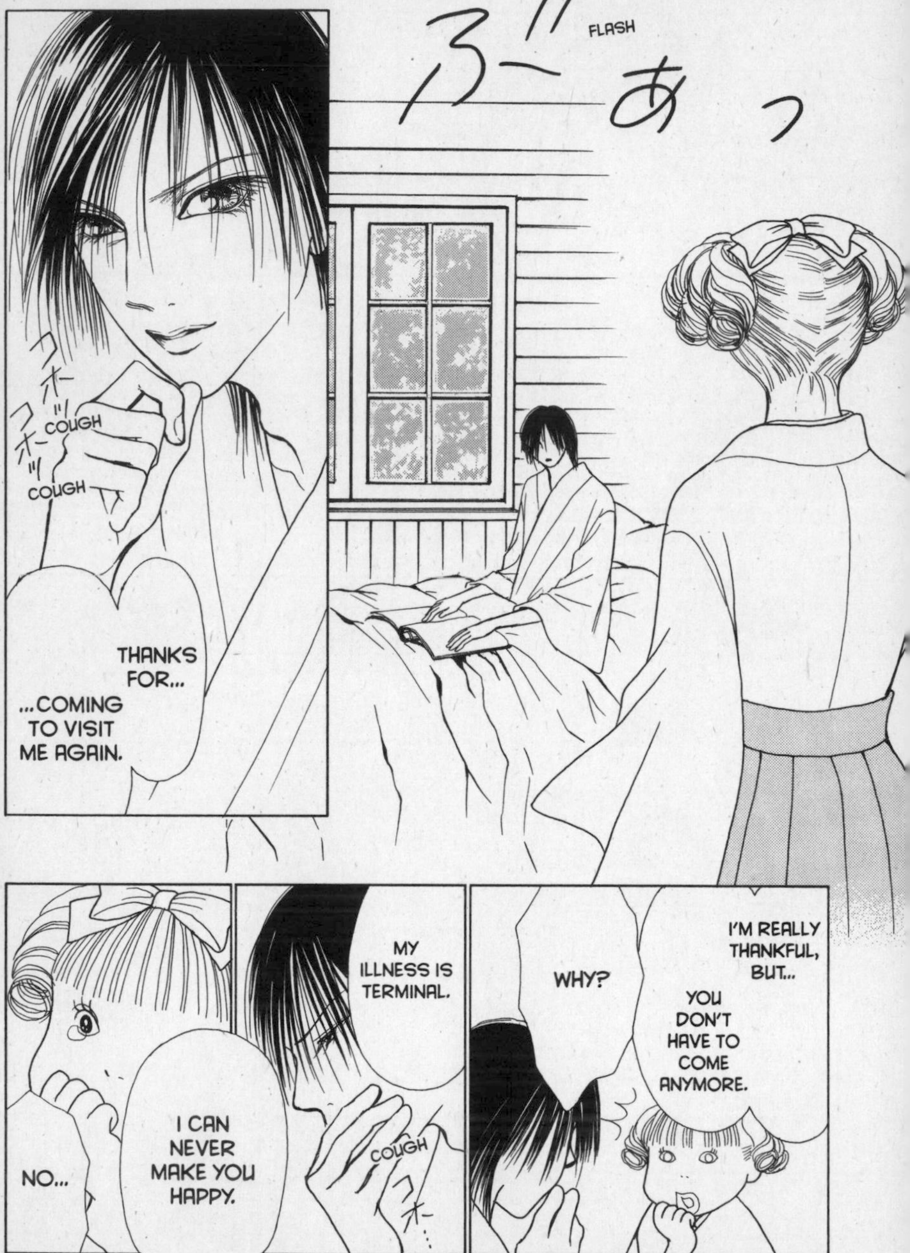
FLASH
COUGH
COUGH
THANKS FOR...
...COMING TO VISIT ME AGAIN.
I'M REALLY THANKFUL, BUT...
YOU DON'T HAVE TO COME ANYMORE.
WHY?
MY ILLNESS IS TERMINAL.
COUGH
I CAN NEVER MAKE YOU HAPPY.
NO...

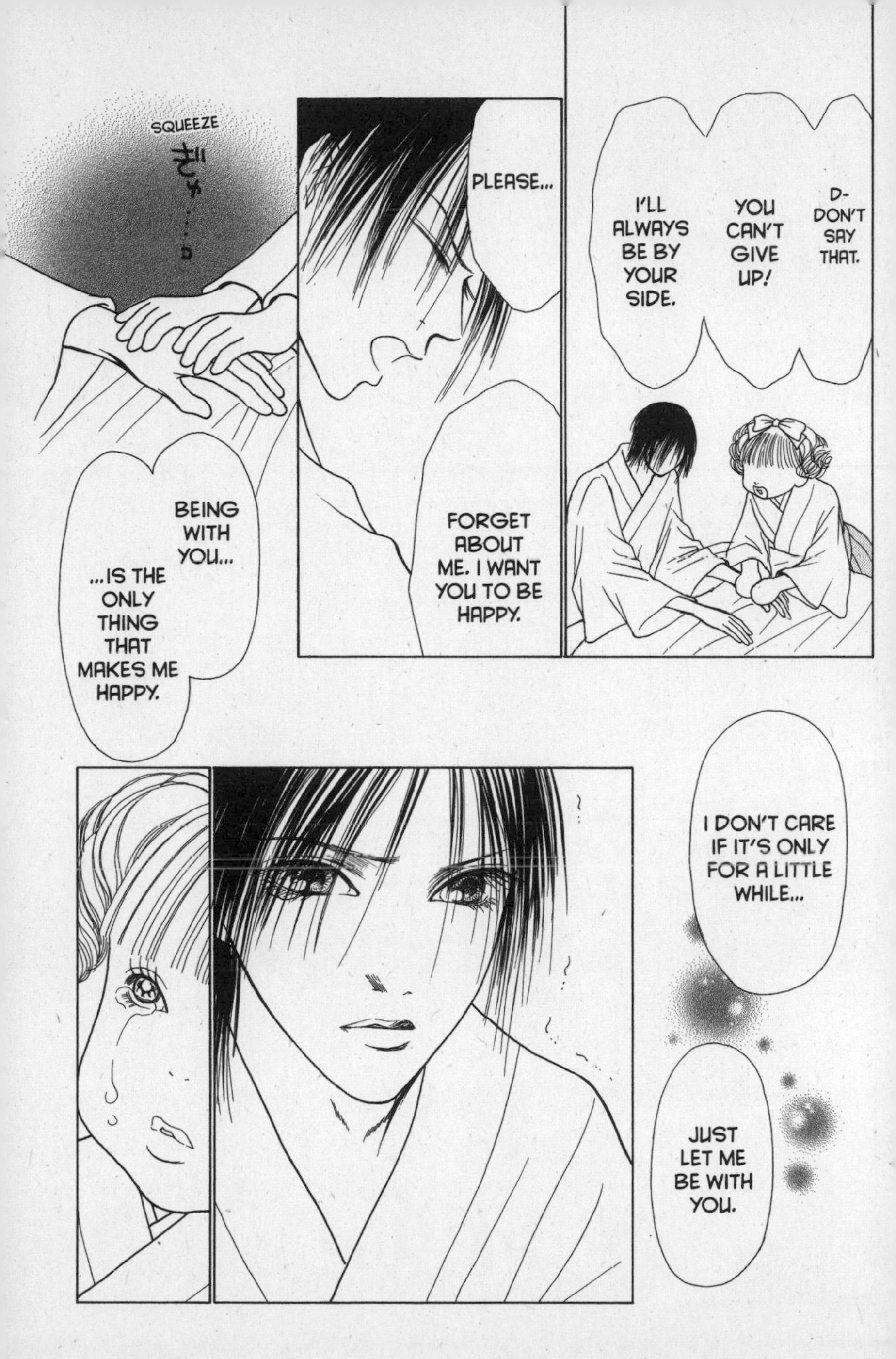
D-DON'T SAY THAT.
YOU CAN'T GIVE UP!
I'LL ALWAYS BE BY YOUR SIDE.
PLEASE...
FORGET ABOUT ME. I WANT YOU TO BE HAPPY.
SQUEEZE
BEING WITH YOU...
...IS THE ONLY THING THAT MAKES ME HAPPY.
I DON'T CARE IF IT'S ONLY FOR A LITTLE WHILE...
JUST LET ME BE WITH YOU.

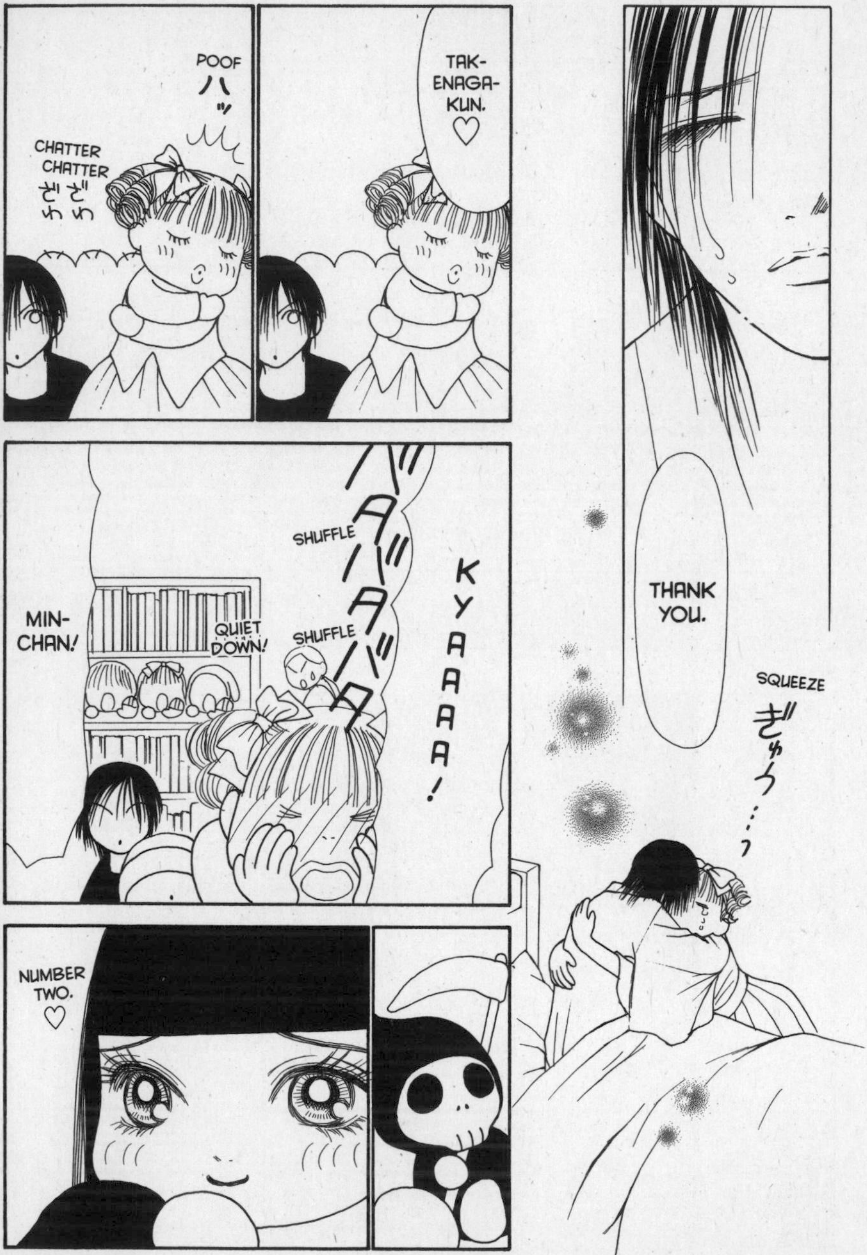
THANK YOU.
SQUEEZE
ぎゅう…っ
TAK-ENAGA-KUN. ♡
POOF
ハッ
CHATTER CHATTER
ざわざわ
KYAAAAA!
SHUFFLE
SHUFFLE
QUIET DOWN!
MIN-CHAN!
NUMBER TWO. ♡

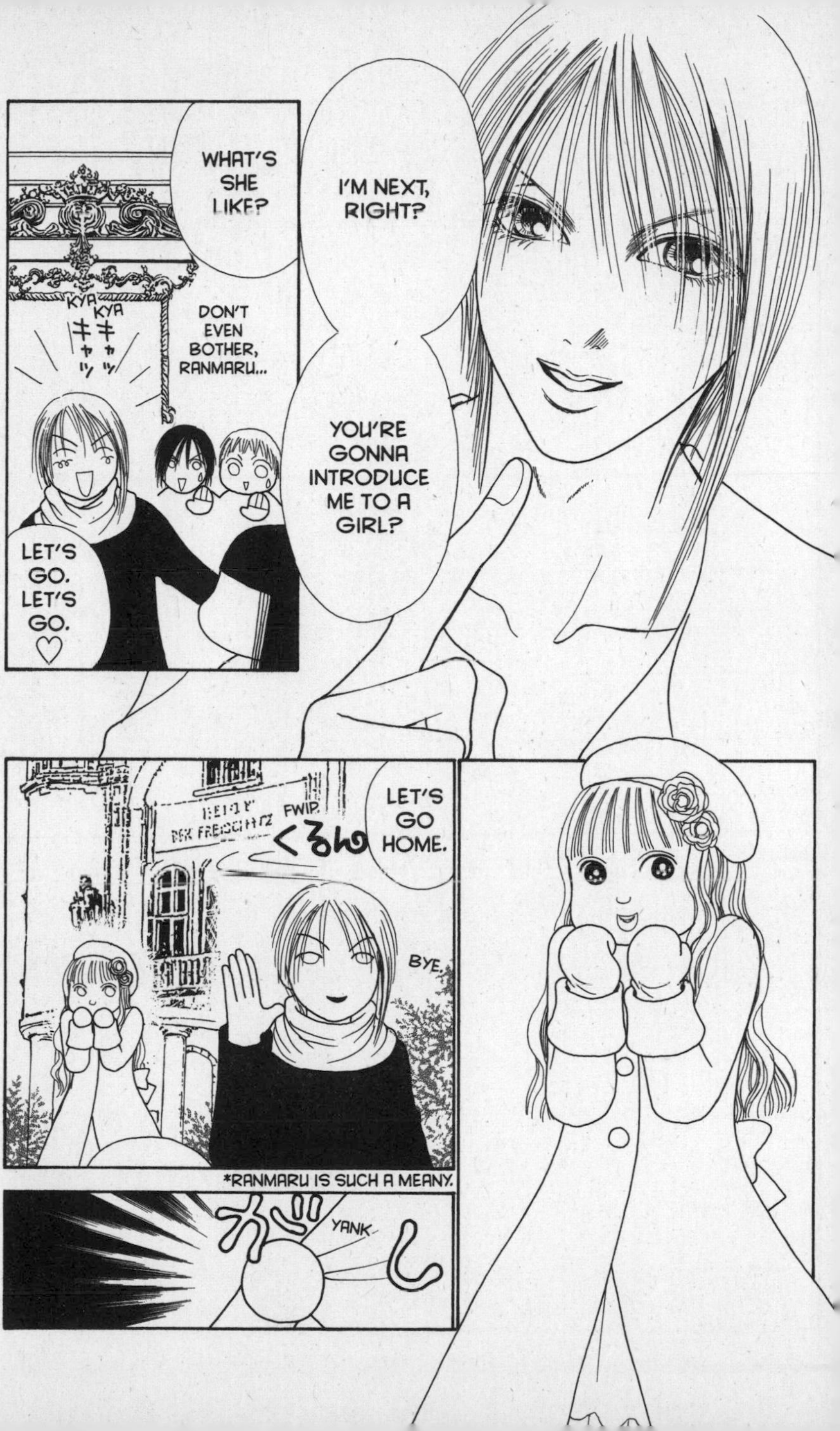
I'M NEXT, RIGHT?
YOU'RE GONNA INTRODUCE ME TO A GIRL?
WHAT'S SHE LIKE?
KYA KYA
キャッ キャッ
DON'T EVEN BOTHER, RANMARU...
LET'S GO. LET'S GO. ♡
LET'S GO HOME.
FWIP.
くるん
BYE.
*RANMARU IS SUCH A MEANY.
YANK
ガシ

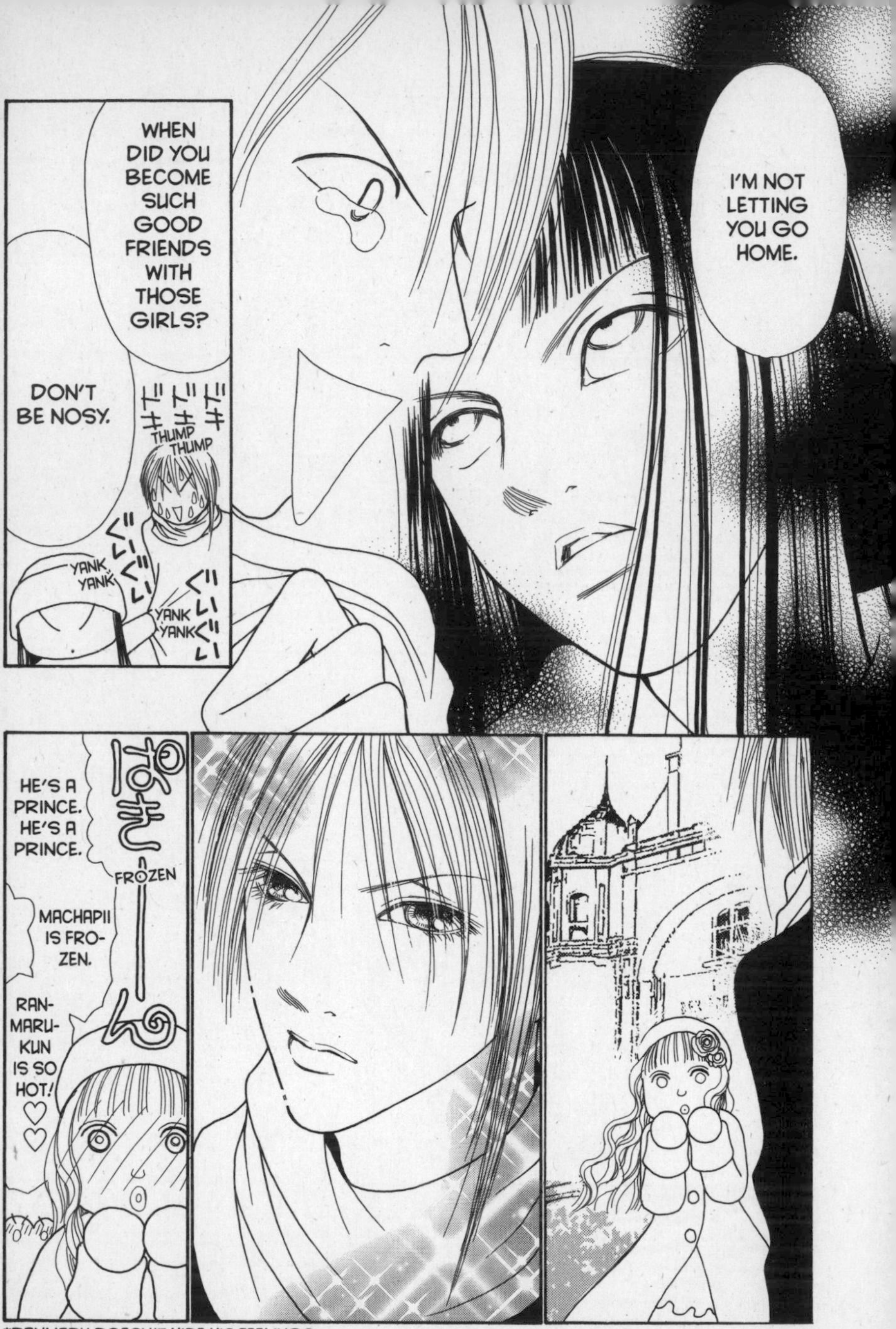
I'M NOT LETTING YOU GO HOME.
WHEN DID YOU BECOME SUCH GOOD FRIENDS WITH THOSE GIRLS?
DON'T BE NOSY.
ドキドキドキ
THUMP THUMP
ぐいぐい
YANK, YANK
ぐいぐい
YANK YANK
HE'S A PRINCE. HE'S A PRINCE.
ぱきーん
FROZEN
MACHAPII IS FRO-ZEN.
RAN-MARU-KUN IS SO HOT! ♡♡

*RANMARU DOESN'T HIDE HIS FEELINGS.

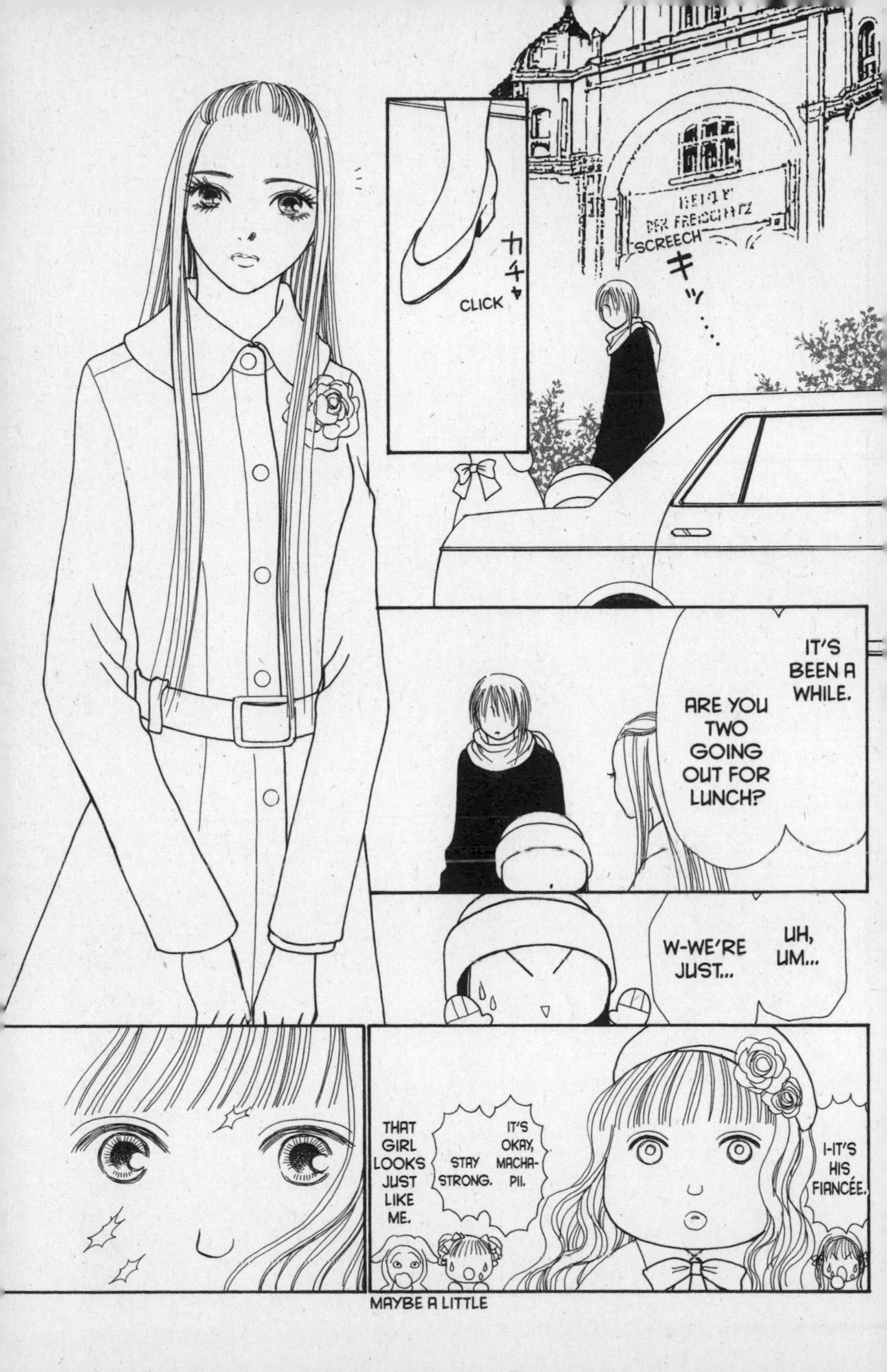
DER FREISCHÜTZ
SCREECH
キッ…
CLICK
カチャ
IT'S BEEN A WHILE.
ARE YOU TWO GOING OUT FOR LUNCH?
UH, UM...
W-WE'RE JUST...
I-IT'S HIS FIANCÉE.
IT'S OKAY, MACHA-PII.
STAY STRONG.
THAT GIRL LOOKS JUST LIKE ME.
MAYBE A LITTLE

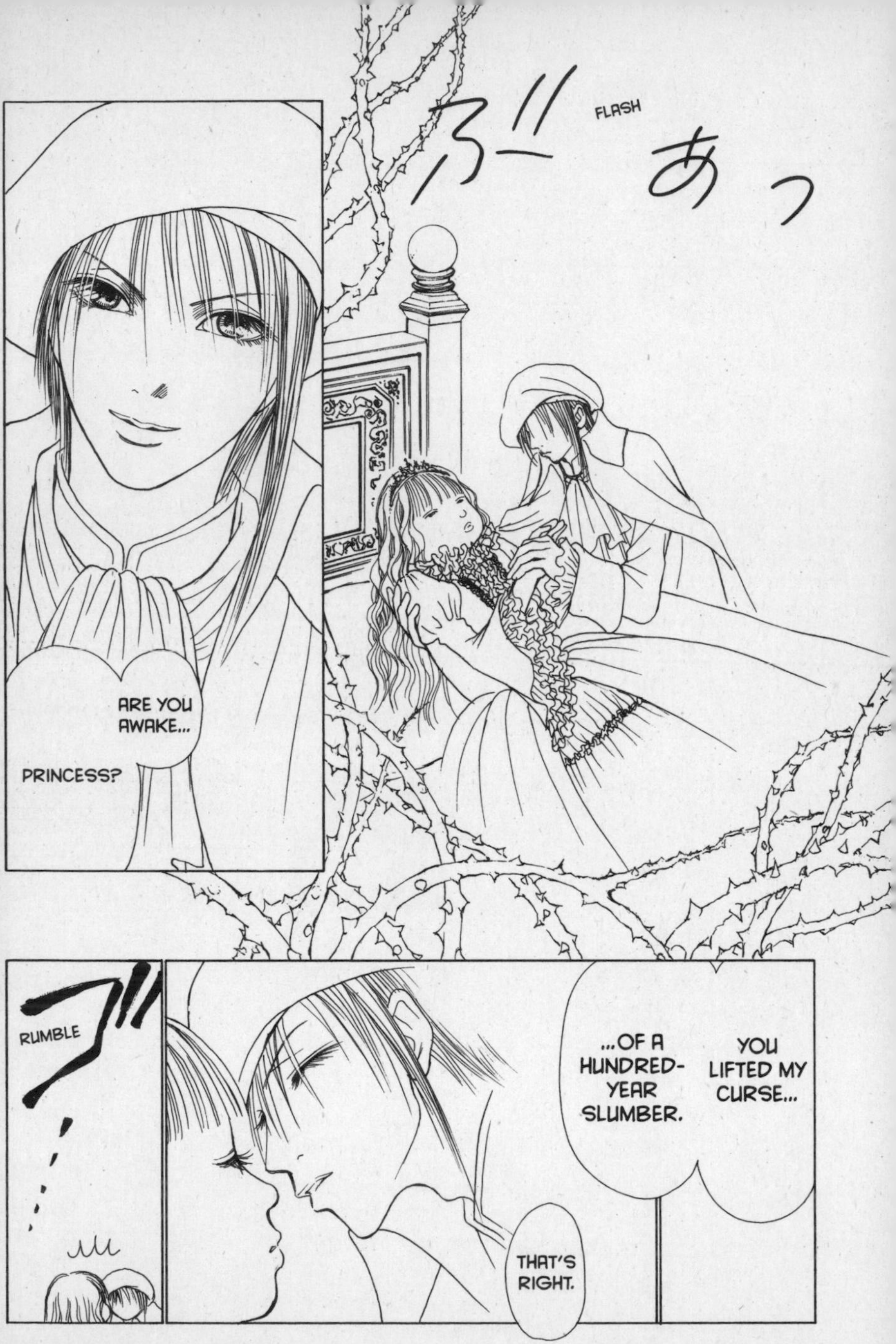
FLASH
ARE YOU AWAKE...
PRINCESS?
YOU LIFTED MY CURSE...
...OF A HUNDRED-YEAR SLUMBER.
THAT'S RIGHT.
RUMBLE

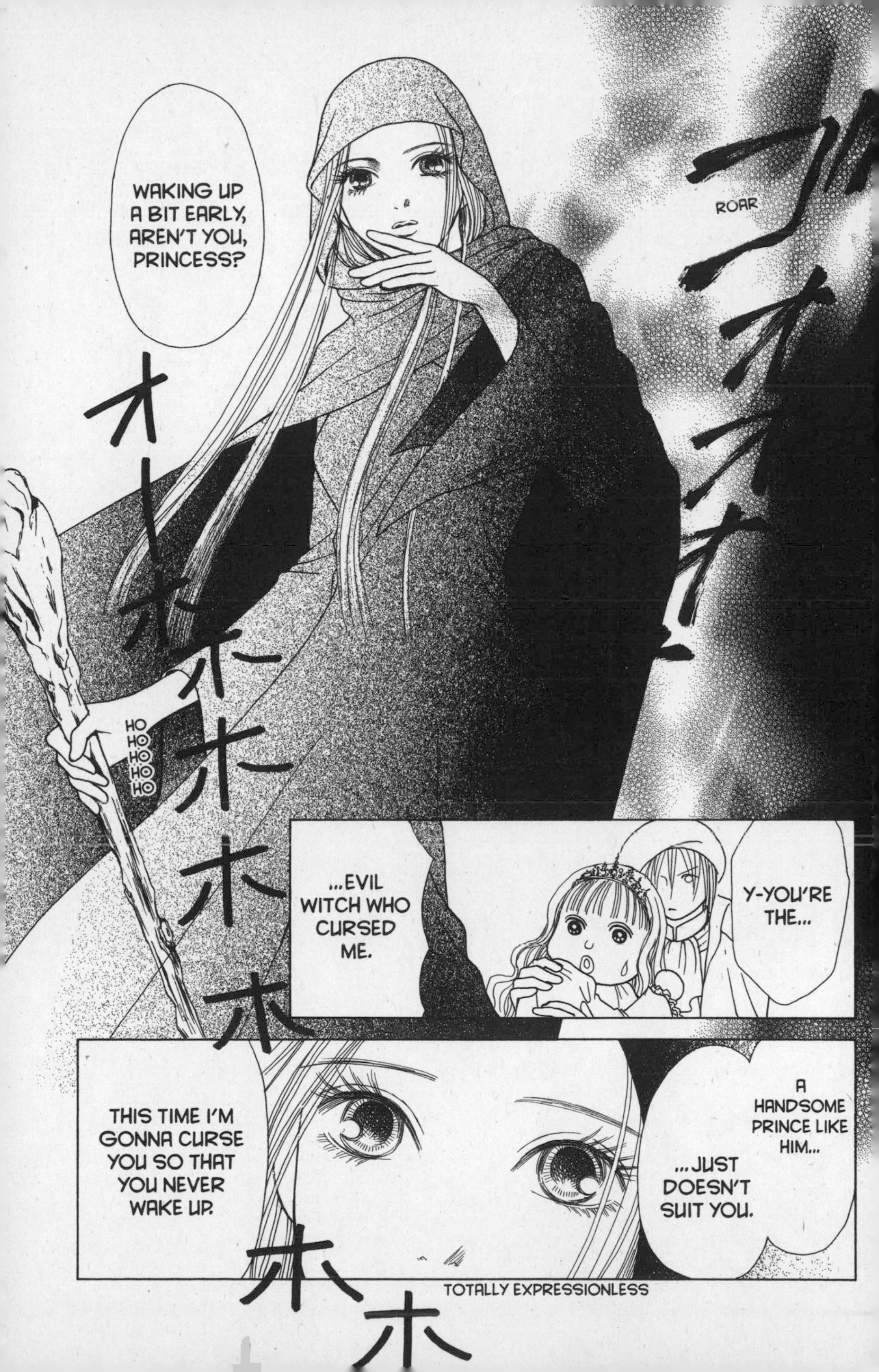
ROAR
WAKING UP A BIT EARLY, AREN'T YOU, PRINCESS?
HO HO HO HO HO
Y-YOU'RE THE...
...EVIL WITCH WHO CURSED ME.
A HANDSOME PRINCE LIKE HIM...
...JUST DOESN'T SUIT YOU.
THIS TIME I'M GONNA CURSE YOU SO THAT YOU NEVER WAKE UP.
TOTALLY EXPRESSIONLESS

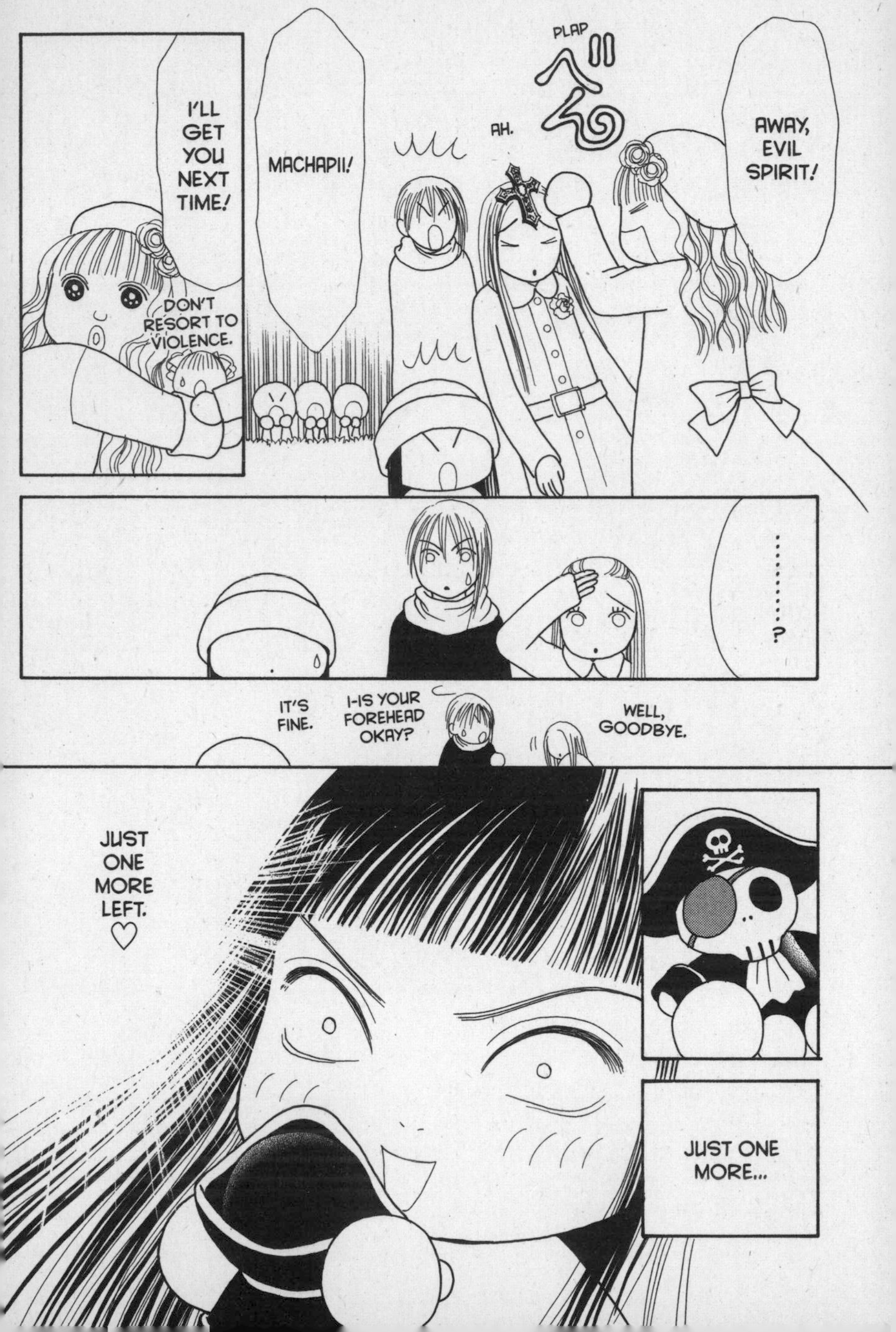
AWAY, EVIL SPIRIT!
PLAP
AH.
MACHAPII!
I'LL GET YOU NEXT TIME!
DON'T RESORT TO VIOLENCE.
......?
WELL, GOODBYE.
I-IS YOUR FOREHEAD OKAY?
IT'S FINE.
JUST ONE MORE...
JUST ONE MORE LEFT. ♡

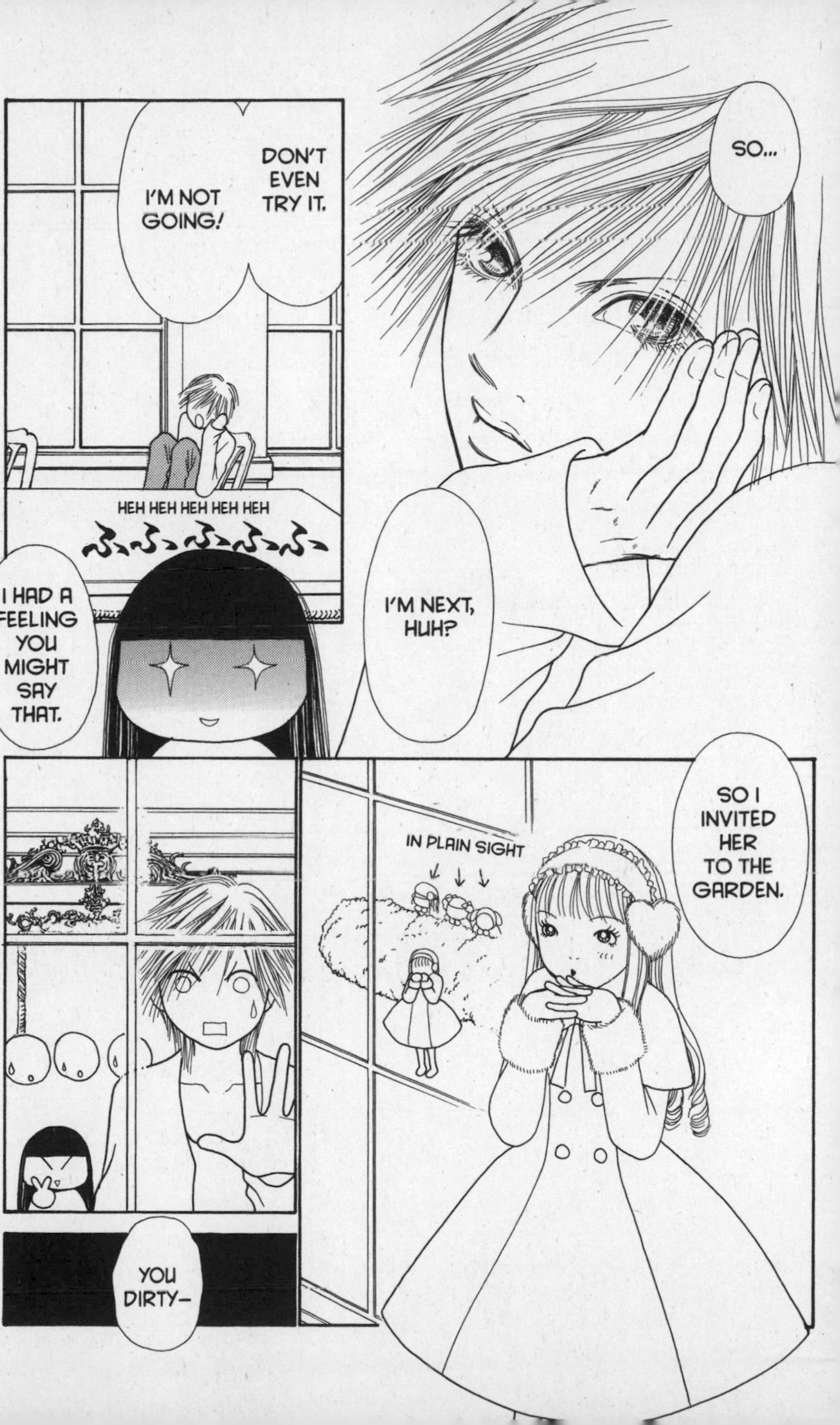
SO...
I'M NEXT, HUH?
DON'T EVEN TRY IT.
I'M NOT GOING!
HEH HEH HEH HEH HEH
ふっふっふっふっふっ
I HAD A FEELING YOU MIGHT SAY THAT.
SO I INVITED HER TO THE GARDEN.
IN PLAIN SIGHT
YOU DIRTY–

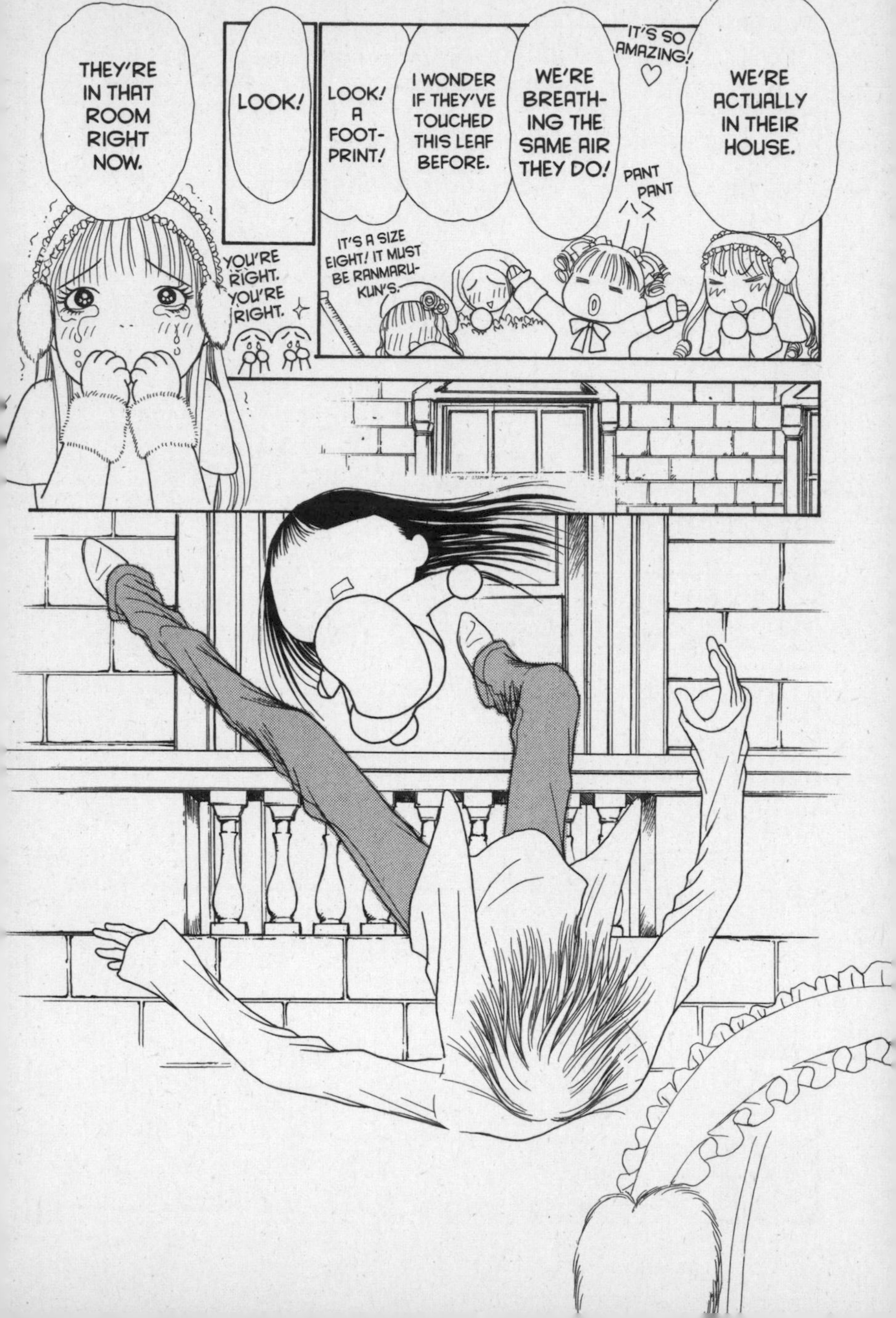
WE'RE ACTUALLY IN THEIR HOUSE.
IT'S SO AMAZING! ♡
WE'RE BREATHING THE SAME AIR THEY DO!
PANT PANT
I WONDER IF THEY'VE TOUCHED THIS LEAF BEFORE.
LOOK! A FOOTPRINT!
IT'S A SIZE EIGHT! IT MUST BE RANMARU-KUN'S.
LOOK!
YOU'RE RIGHT. YOU'RE RIGHT.
THEY'RE IN THAT ROOM RIGHT NOW.

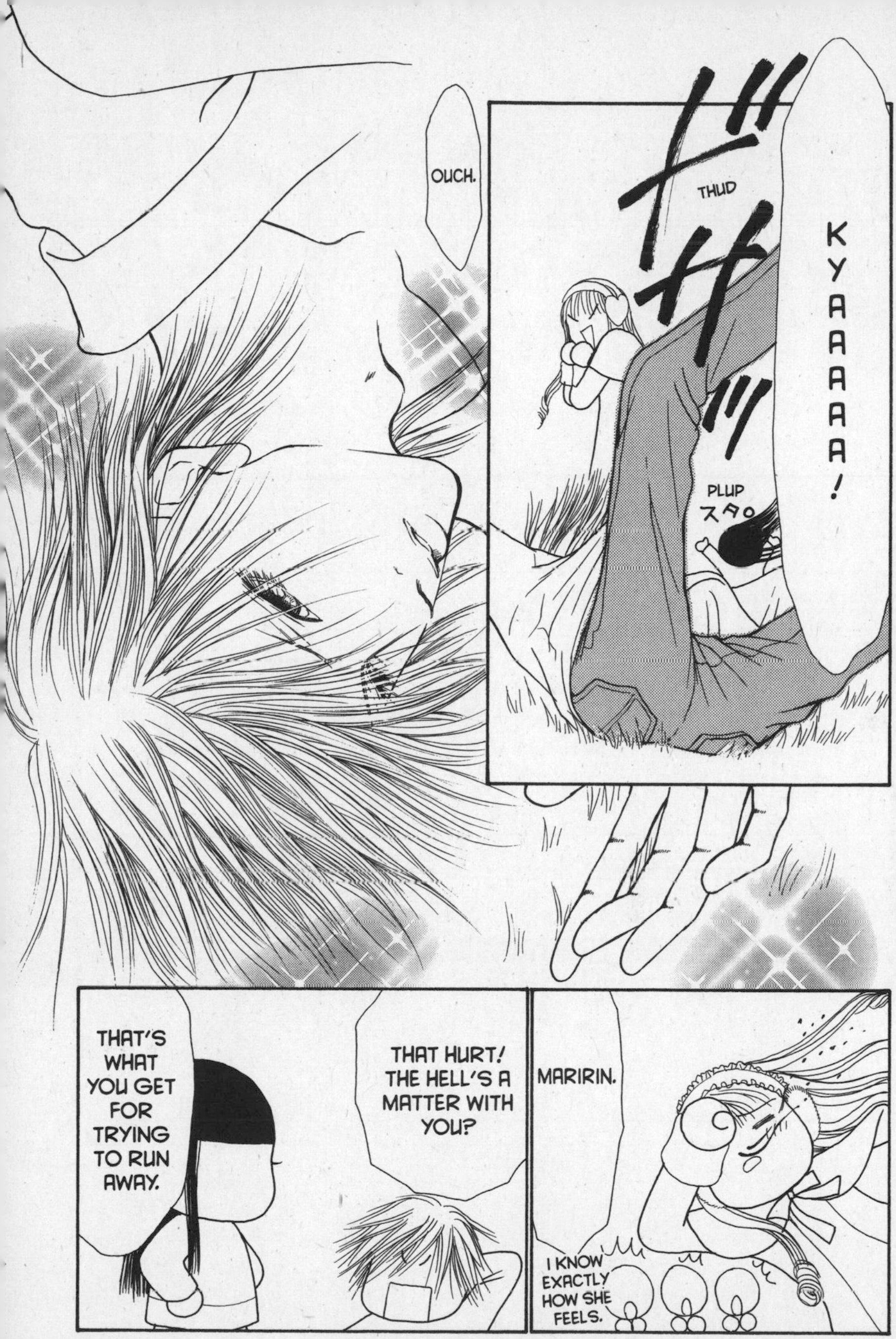
KYAAAAA!
THUD
PLUP
スタ。
OUCH.
MARIRIN.
I KNOW EXACTLY HOW SHE FEELS.
THAT HURT! THE HELL'S A MATTER WITH YOU?
THAT'S WHAT YOU GET FOR TRYING TO RUN AWAY.

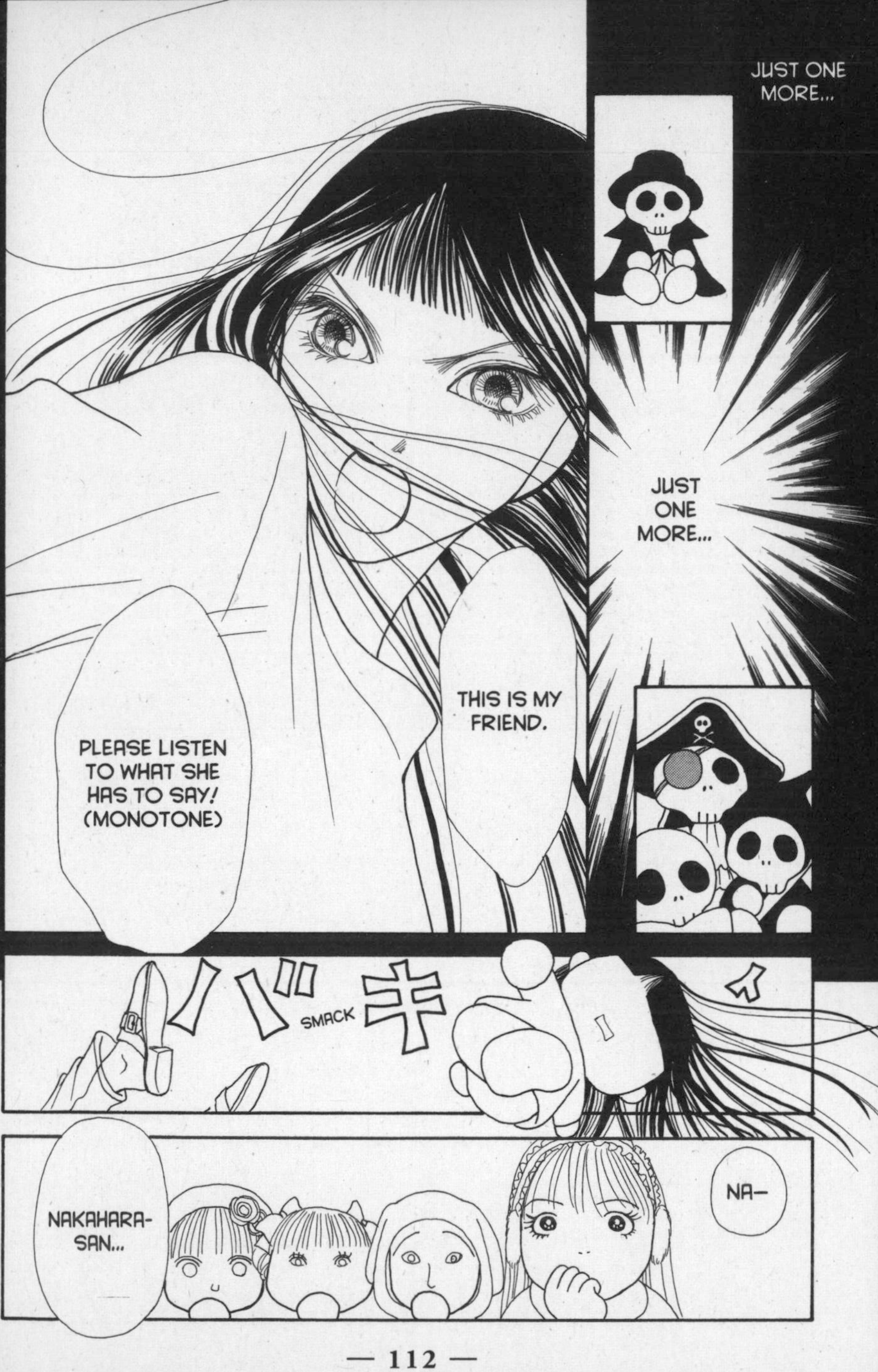
JUST ONE MORE...
JUST ONE MORE...
THIS IS MY FRIEND.
PLEASE LISTEN TO WHAT SHE HAS TO SAY! (MONOTONE)
バキーイ
SMACK
NA—
NAKAHARA-SAN...

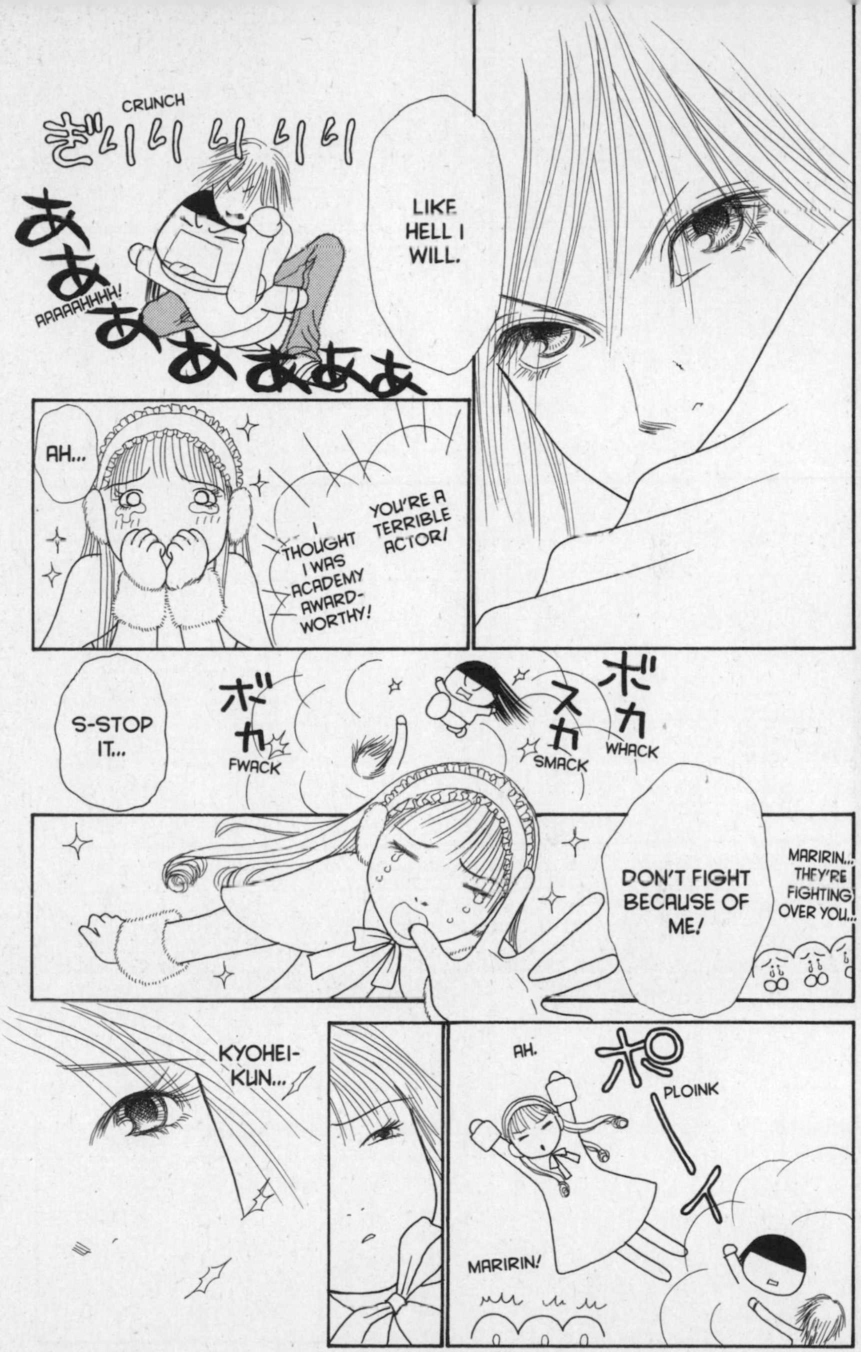
LIKE HELL I WILL.
CRUNCH
ざりりりり
ああああああ
AAAAAHHHH!
YOU'RE A TERRIBLE ACTOR!
I THOUGHT I WAS ACADEMY AWARD-WORTHY!
AH...
ボカ
WHACK
スカ
SMACK
ボカ
FWACK
S-STOP IT...
MARIRIN... THEY'RE FIGHTING OVER YOU...
DON'T FIGHT BECAUSE OF ME!
AH.
ポイ
PLOINK
MARIRIN!
KYOHEI-KUN...

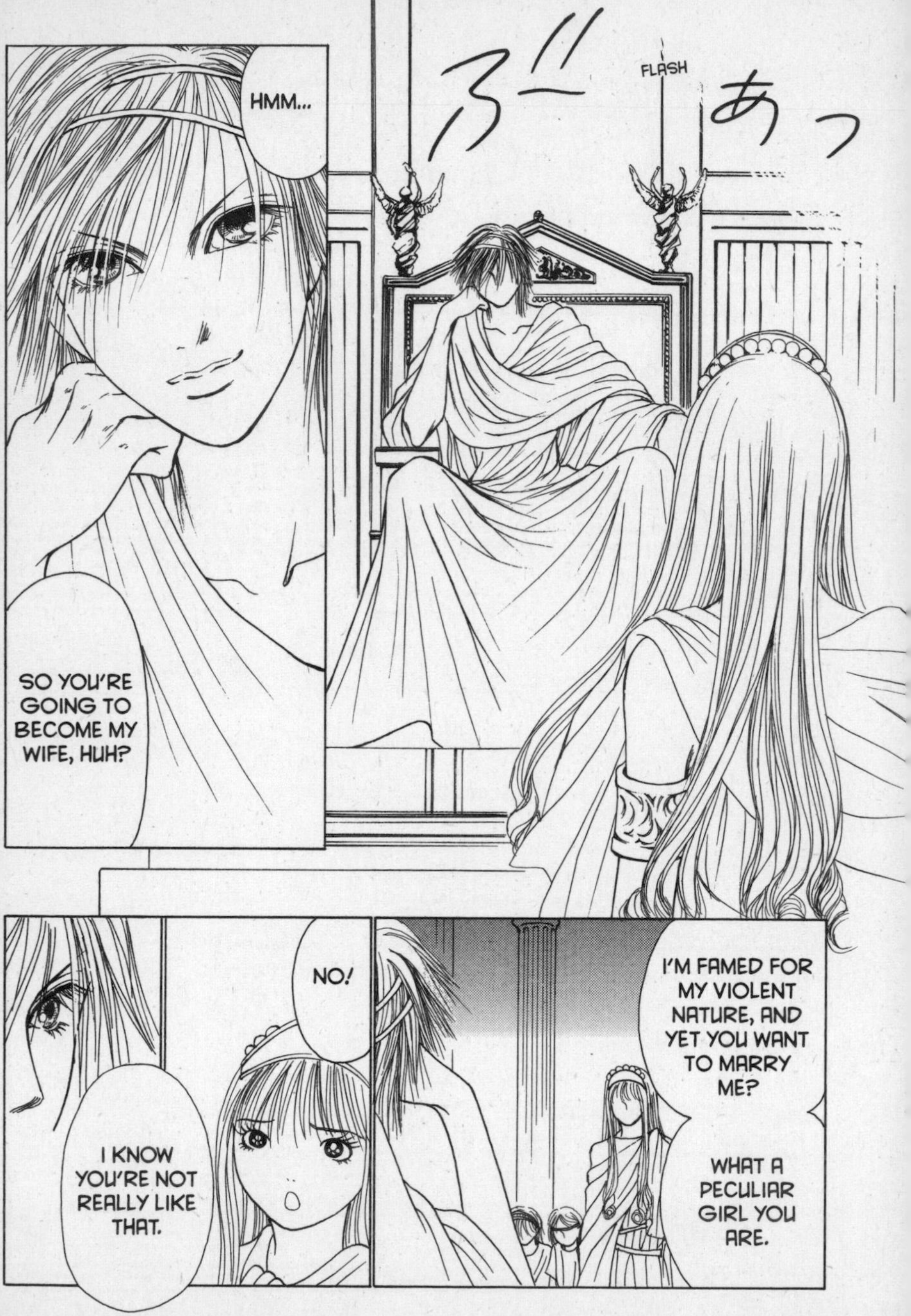
あっ
FLASH
HMM...
SO YOU'RE GOING TO BECOME MY WIFE, HUH?
I'M FAMED FOR MY VIOLENT NATURE, AND YET YOU WANT TO MARRY ME?
WHAT A PECULIAR GIRL YOU ARE.
NO!
I KNOW YOU'RE NOT REALLY LIKE THAT.

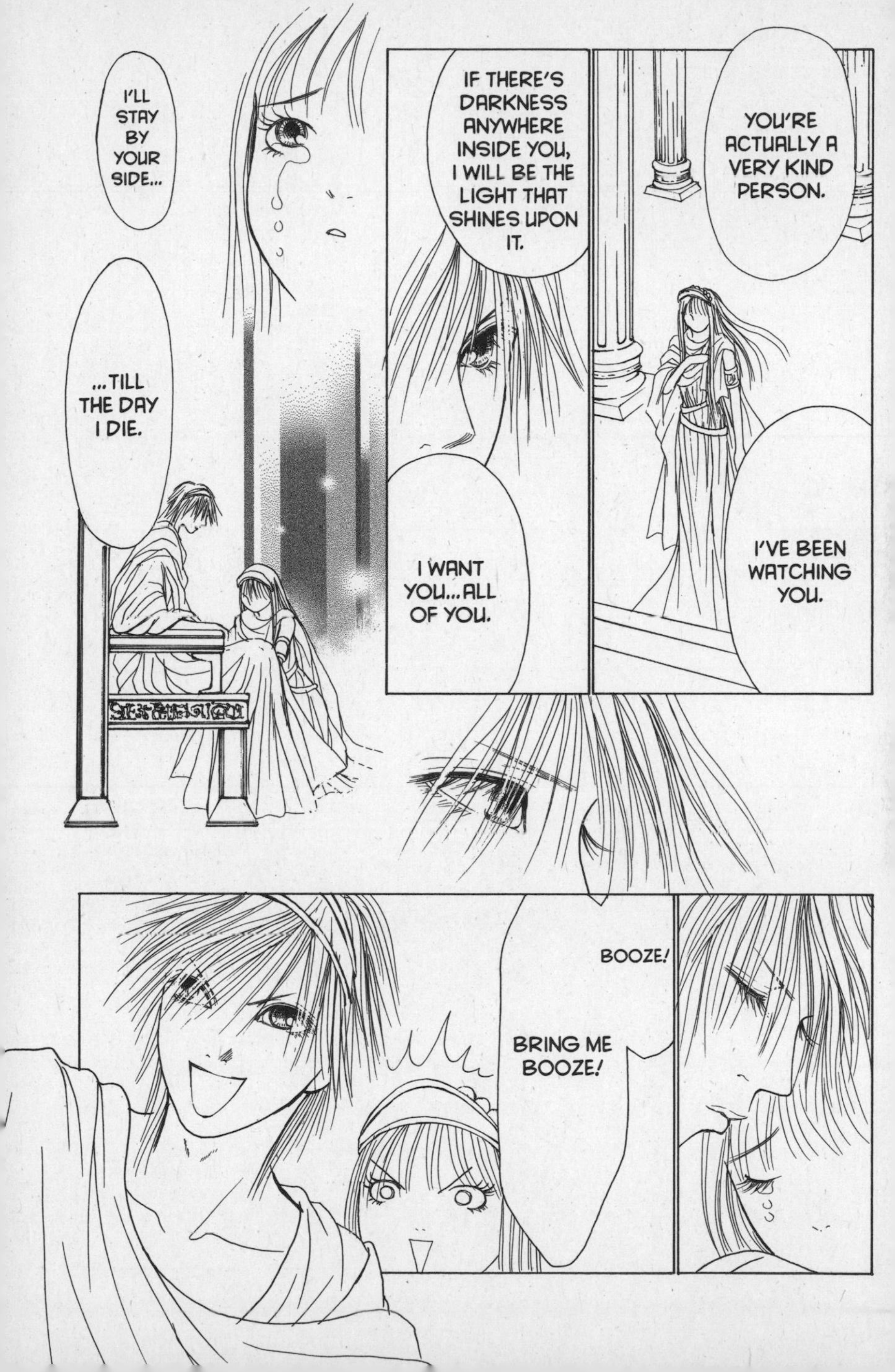
YOU'RE ACTUALLY A VERY KIND PERSON.
I'VE BEEN WATCHING YOU.
IF THERE'S DARKNESS ANYWHERE INSIDE YOU, I WILL BE THE LIGHT THAT SHINES UPON IT.
I WANT YOU...ALL OF YOU.
I'LL STAY BY YOUR SIDE...
...TILL THE DAY I DIE.
BOOZE!
BRING ME BOOZE!

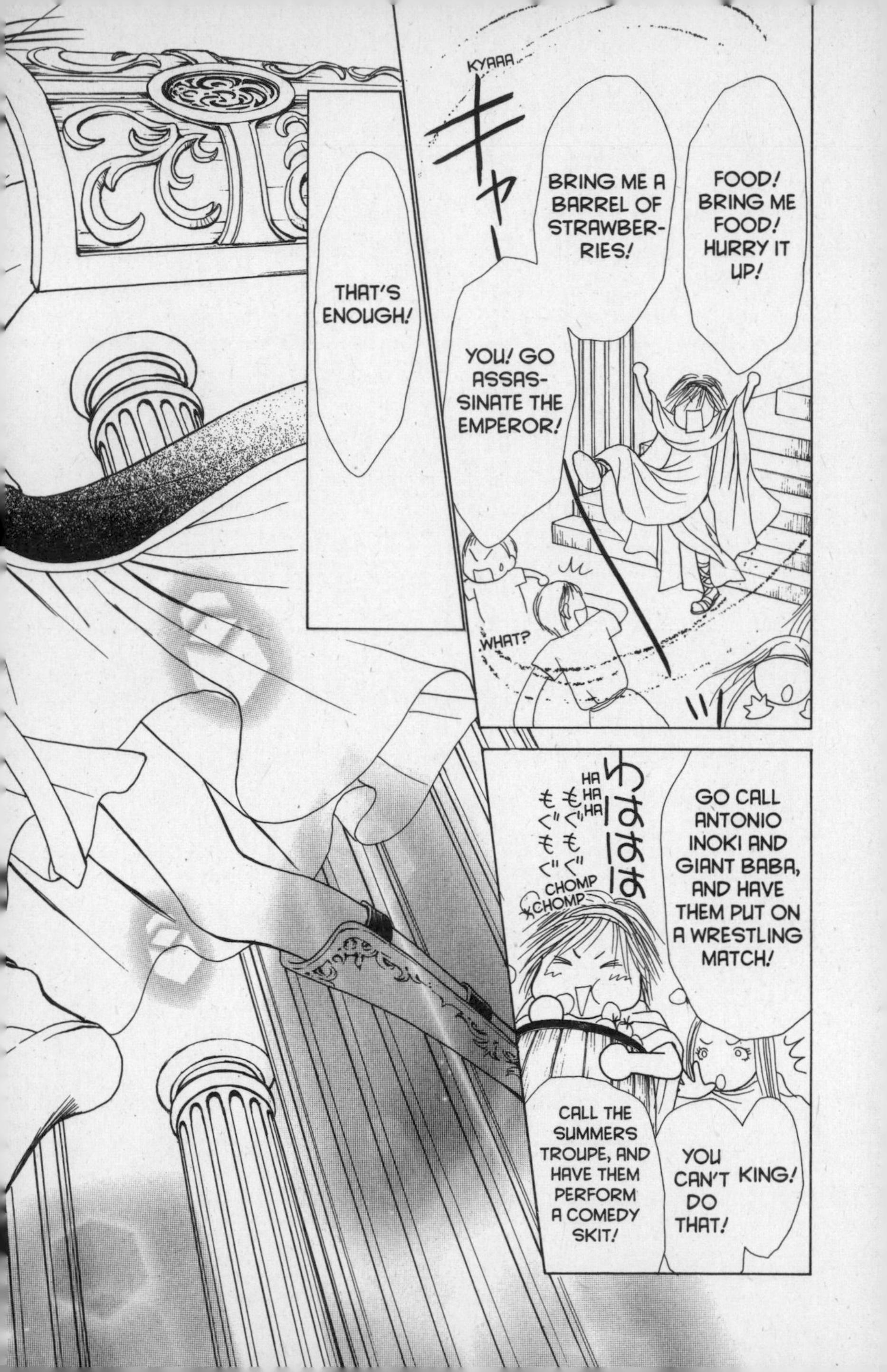

KYAAA
キャー
FOOD! BRING ME FOOD! HURRY IT UP!
BRING ME A BARREL OF STRAWBER-RIES!
YOU! GO ASSAS-SINATE THE EMPEROR!
WHAT?
GO CALL ANTONIO INOKI AND GIANT BABA, AND HAVE THEM PUT ON A WRESTLING MATCH!
わははは
HA HA HA
もぐもぐもぐもぐ
CHOMP CHOMP
KING!
YOU CAN'T DO THAT!
CALL THE SUMMERS TROUPE, AND HAVE THEM PERFORM A COMEDY SKIT!
THAT'S ENOUGH!

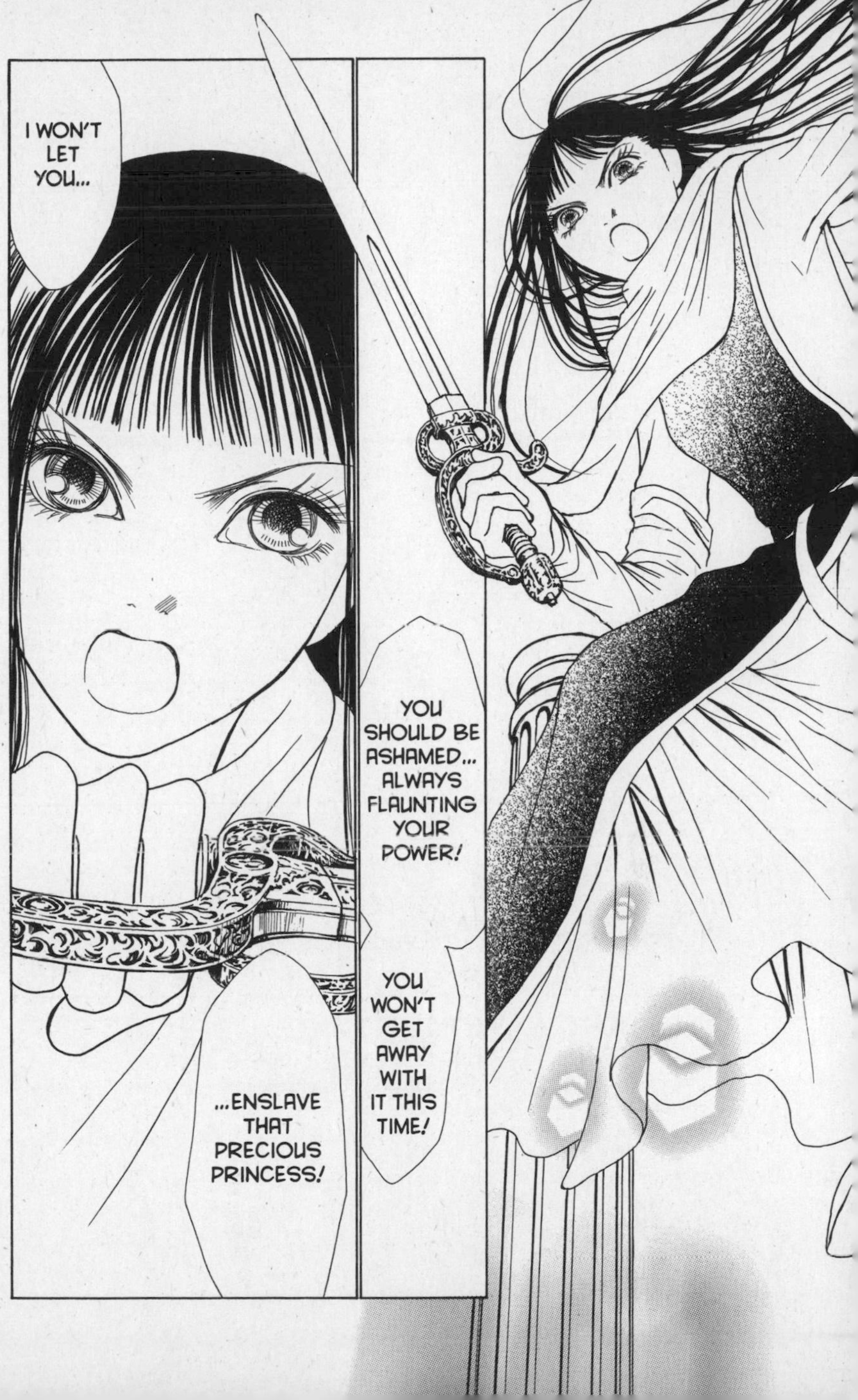
YOU SHOULD BE ASHAMED... ALWAYS FLAUNTING YOUR POWER!
YOU WON'T GET AWAY WITH IT THIS TIME!
I WON'T LET YOU...
...ENSLAVE THAT PRECIOUS PRINCESS!

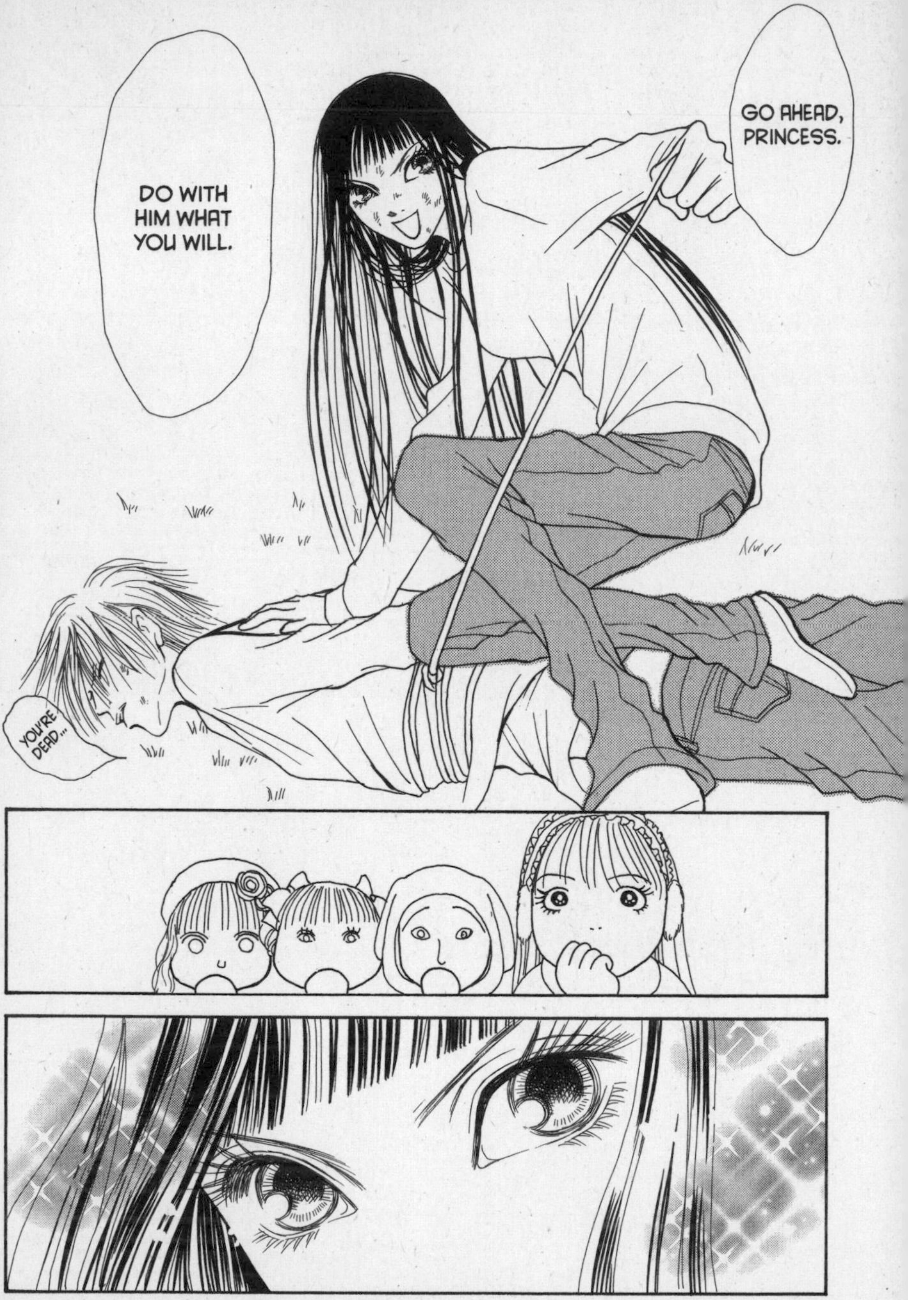
GO AHEAD, PRINCESS.
DO WITH HIM WHAT YOU WILL.
YOU'RE DEAD...

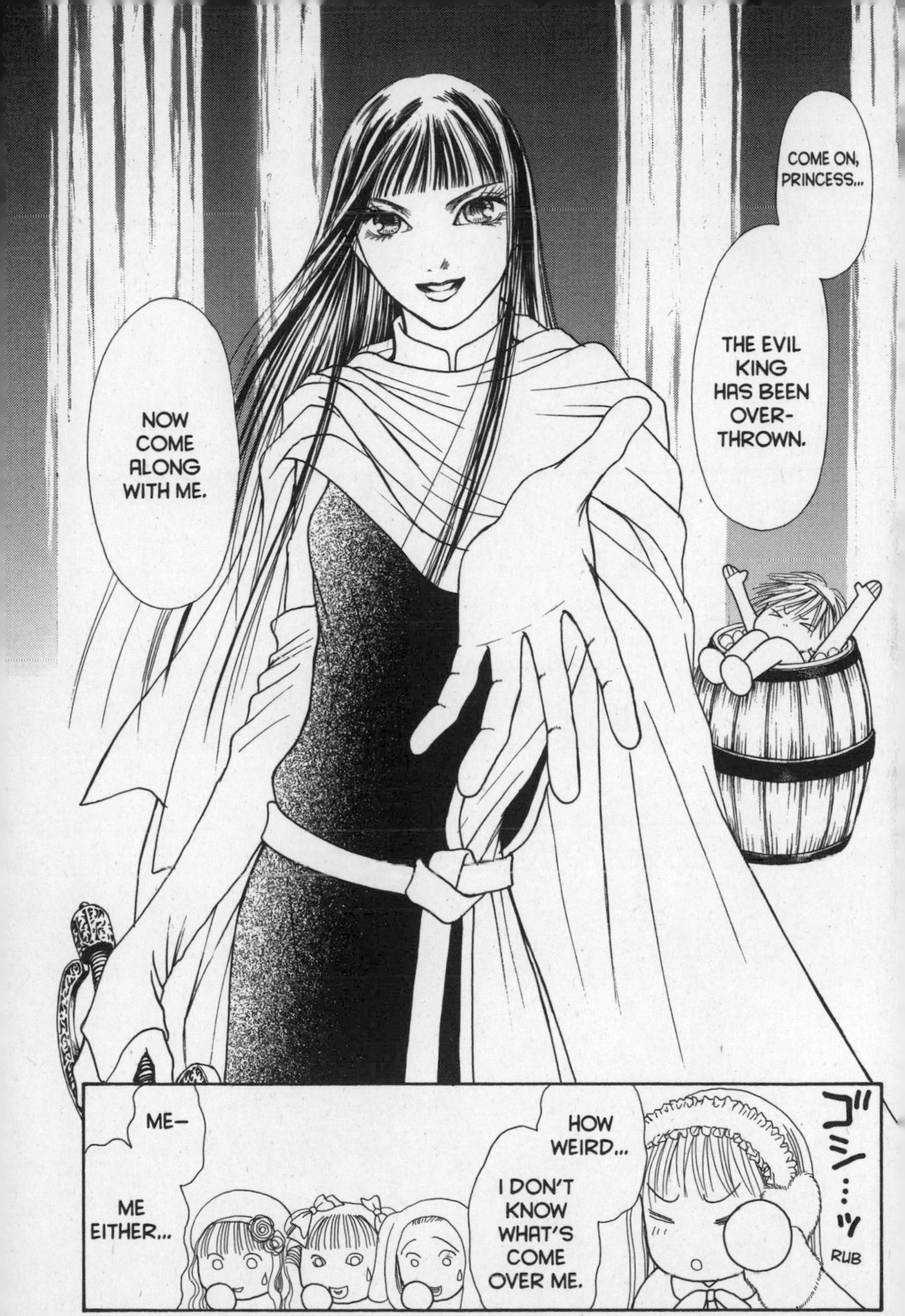
COME ON, PRINCESS...
THE EVIL KING HAS BEEN OVER-THROWN.
NOW COME ALONG WITH ME.
ゴシ…ッ
RUB
HOW WEIRD...
I DON'T KNOW WHAT'S COME OVER ME.
ME–
ME EITHER...

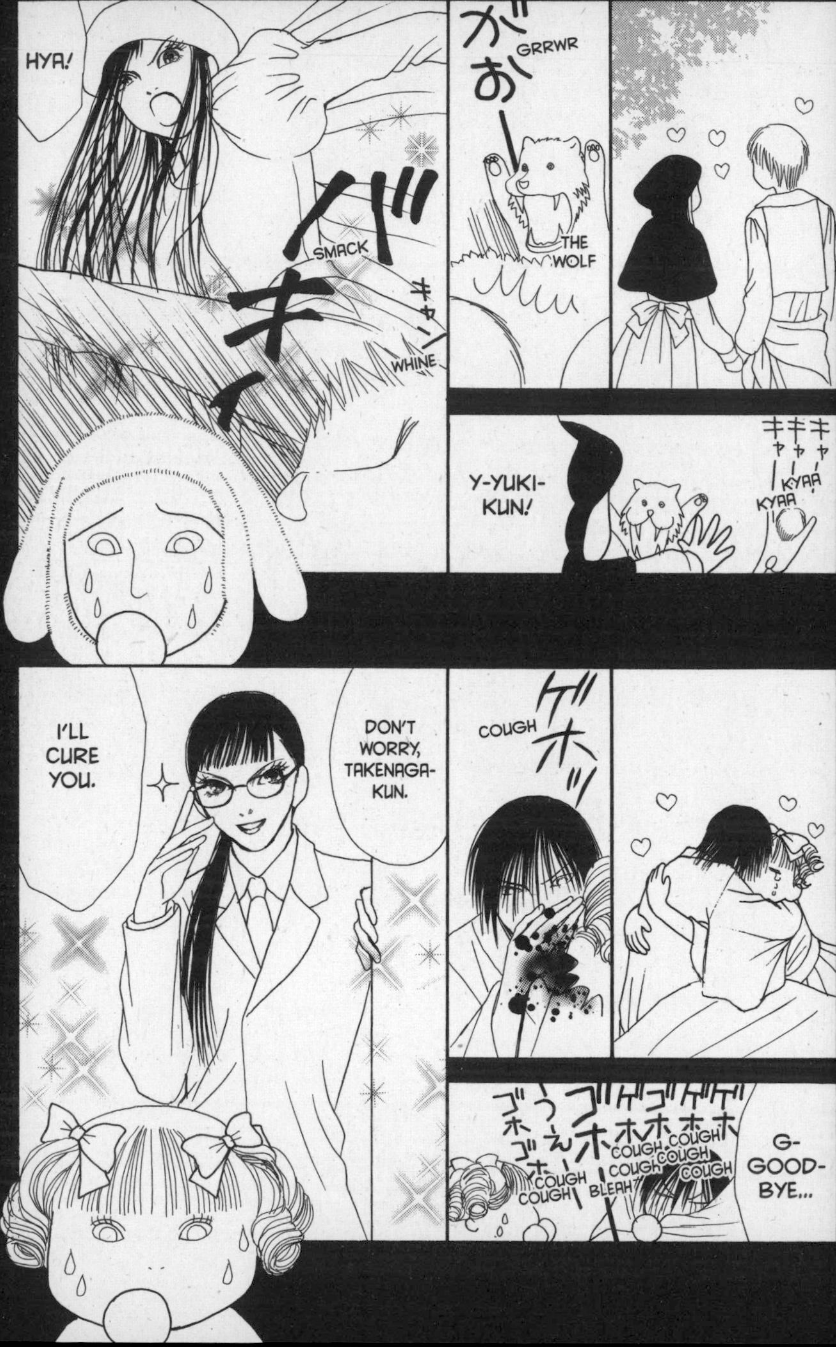
がおー
GRRWR
THE WOLF
キャーキャー
KYAA
KYAA
Y-YUKI-KUN!
HYA!
バキィ
SMACK
キャーン
WHINE
ゲホッ
COUGH
G-GOOD-BYE...
COUGH
COUGH
COUGH
COUGH
BLEAH
COUGH
COUGH
DON'T WORRY, TAKENAGA-KUN.
I'LL CURE YOU.

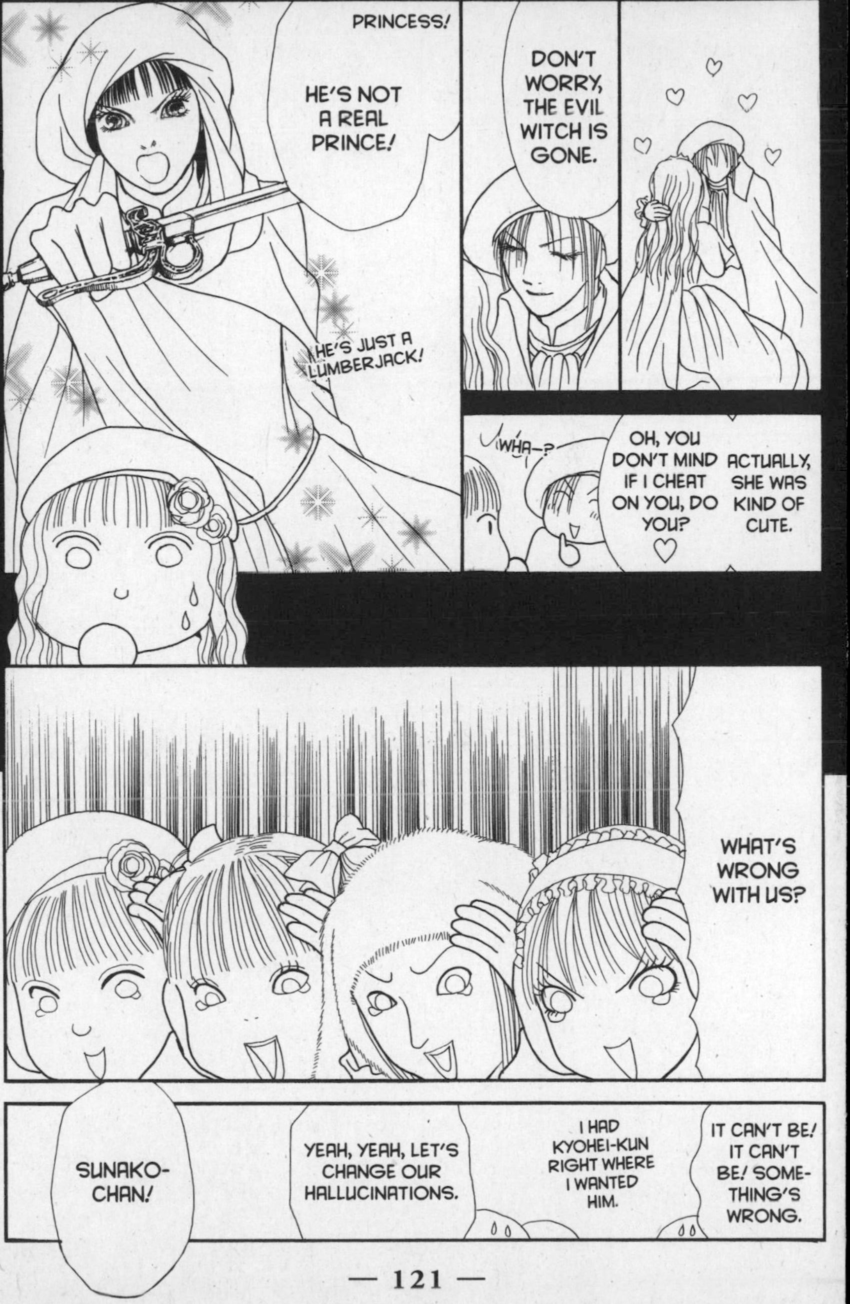
DON'T WORRY, THE EVIL WITCH IS GONE.
ACTUALLY, SHE WAS KIND OF CUTE.
OH, YOU DON'T MIND IF I CHEAT ON YOU, DO YOU?
WHA--?
PRINCESS!
HE'S NOT A REAL PRINCE!
HE'S JUST A LUMBERJACK!
WHAT'S WRONG WITH US?
IT CAN'T BE! IT CAN'T BE! SOMETHING'S WRONG.
I HAD KYOHEI-KUN RIGHT WHERE I WANTED HIM.
YEAH, YEAH, LET'S CHANGE OUR HALLUCINATIONS.
SUNAKO-CHAN!

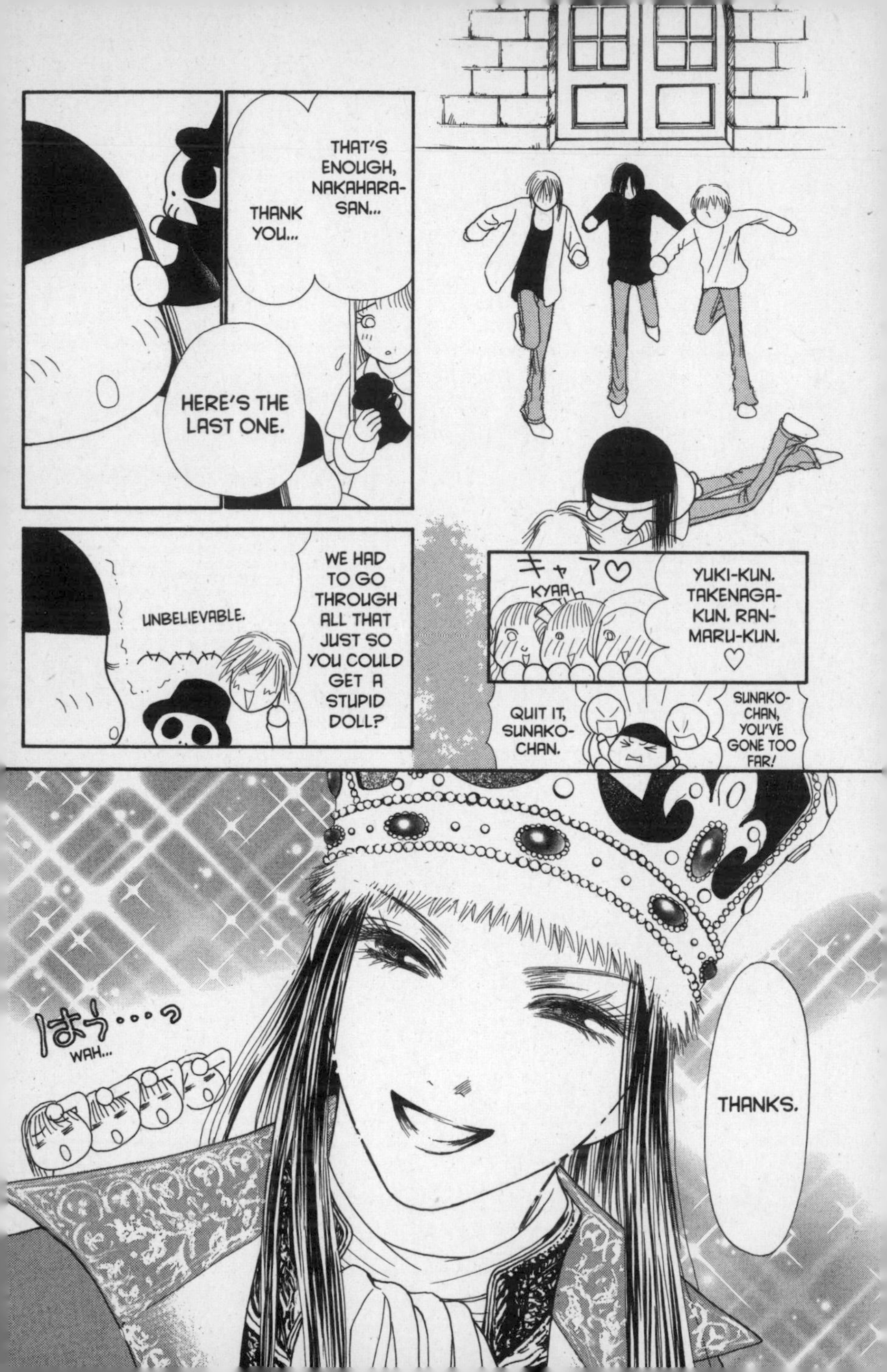

キャア♡
KYAA
YUKI-KUN. TAKENAGA-KUN. RAN-MARU-KUN. ♡
SUNAKO-CHAN, YOU'VE GONE TOO FAR!
QUIT IT, SUNAKO-CHAN.
THAT'S ENOUGH, NAKAHARA-SAN...
THANK YOU...
HERE'S THE LAST ONE.
WE HAD TO GO THROUGH ALL THAT JUST SO YOU COULD GET A STUPID DOLL?
UNBELIEVABLE.
THANKS.
はう…っ
WAH...

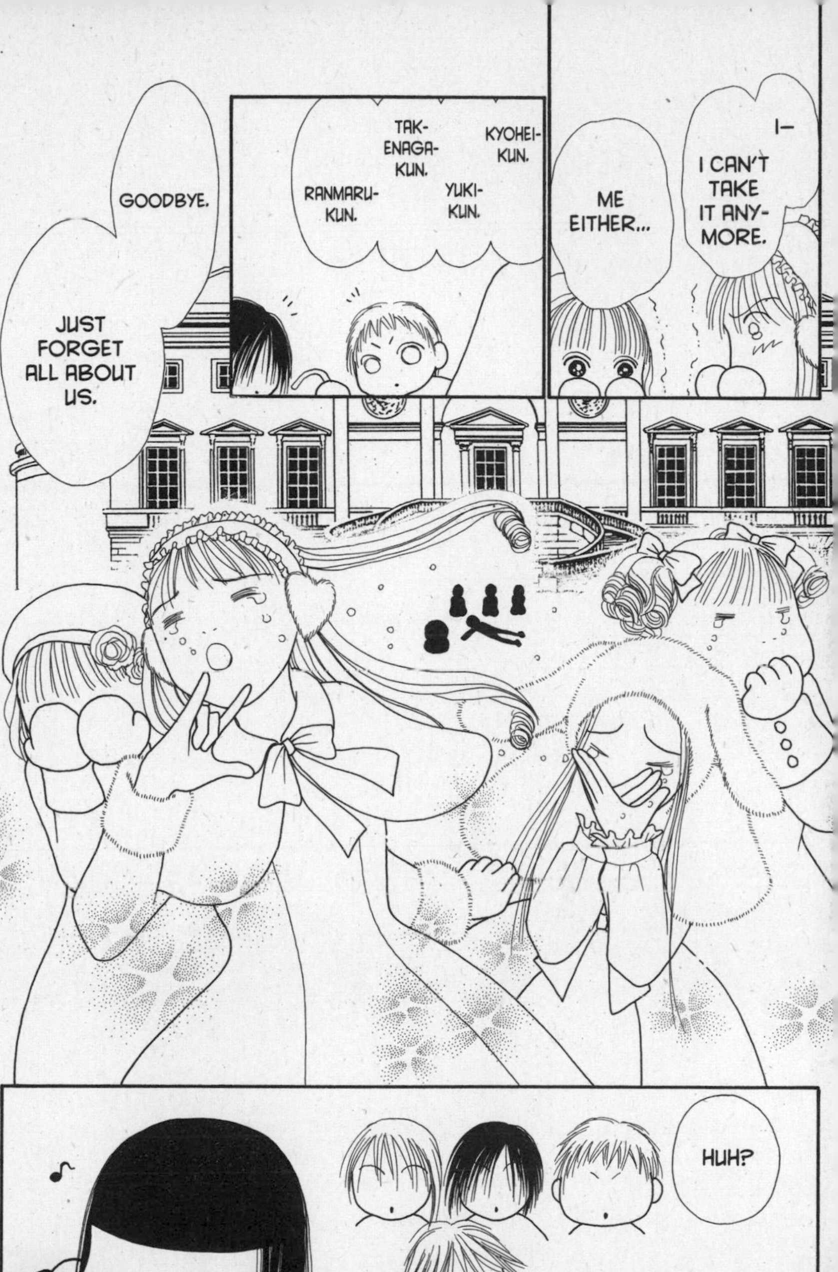
I—
I CAN'T TAKE IT ANYMORE.
ME EITHER...
KYOHEI-KUN.
TAK-ENAGA-KUN.
YUKI-KUN.
RANMARU-KUN.
GOODBYE.
JUST FORGET ALL ABOUT US.
HUH?

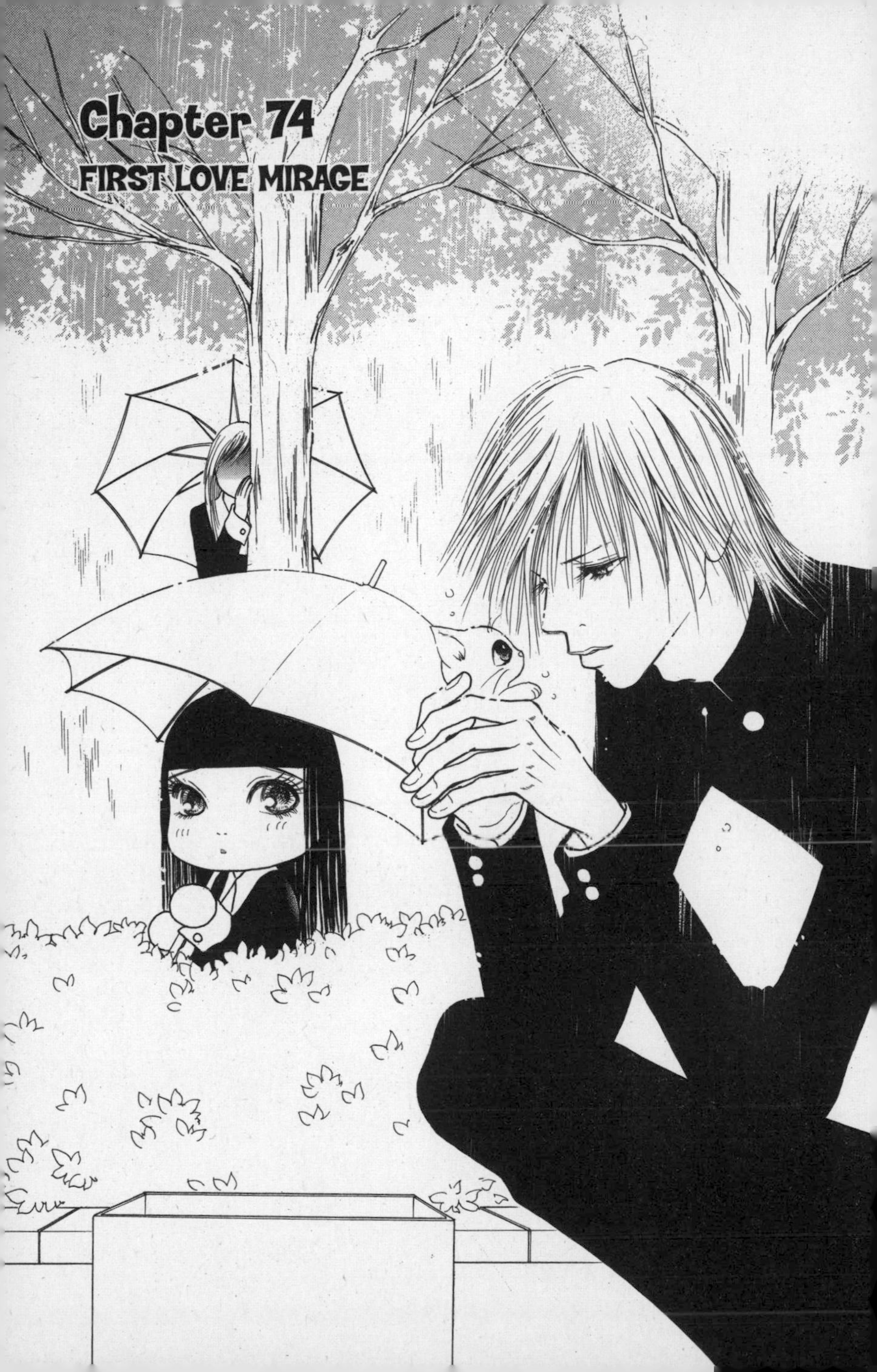
Chapter 74
FIRST LOVE MIRAGE

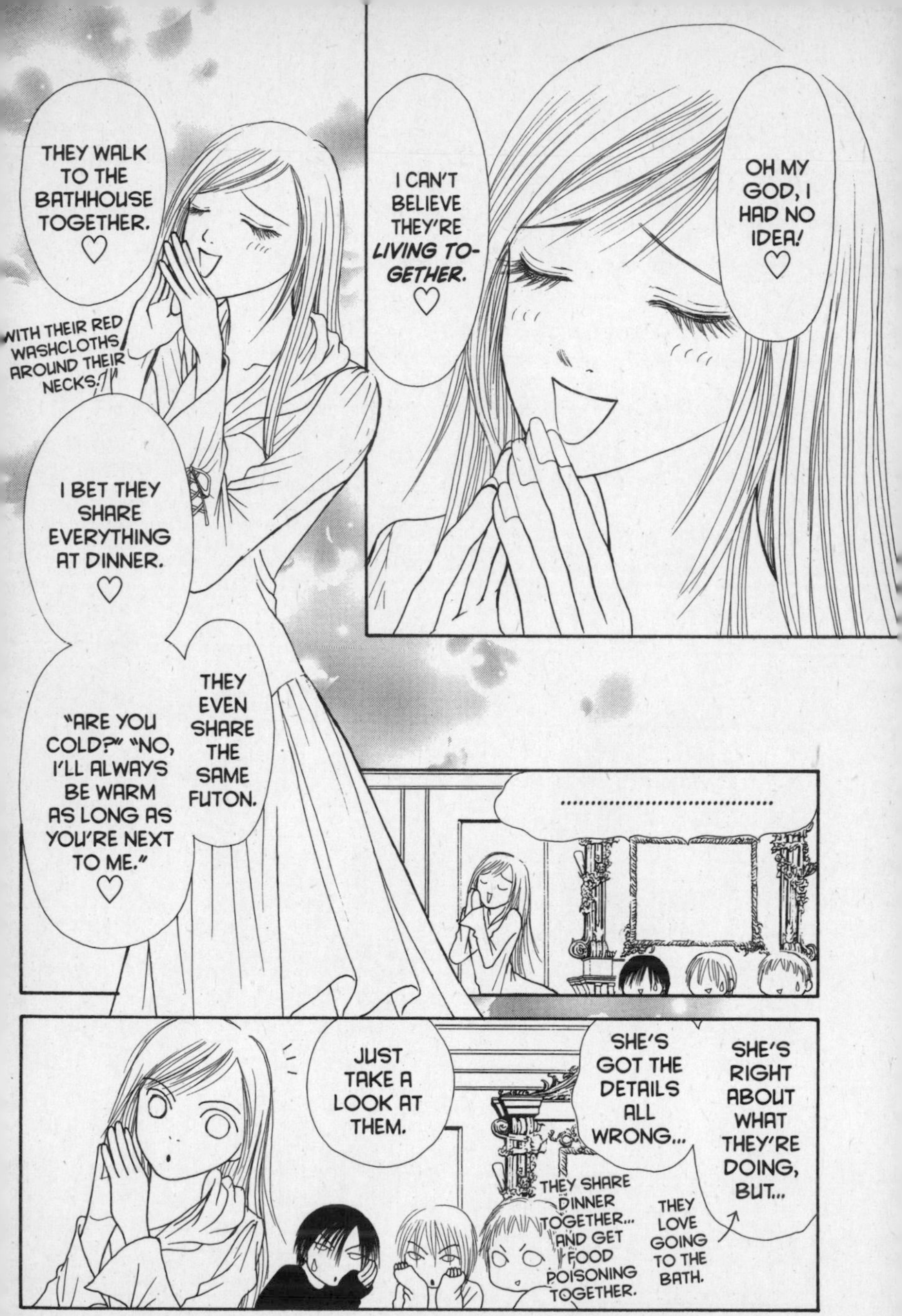
OH MY GOD, I HAD NO IDEA! ♡
I CAN'T BELIEVE THEY'RE *LIVING TOGETHER.* ♡
THEY WALK TO THE BATHHOUSE TOGETHER. ♡
WITH THEIR RED WASHCLOTHS AROUND THEIR NECKS.
I BET THEY SHARE EVERYTHING AT DINNER. ♡
THEY EVEN SHARE THE SAME FUTON.
"ARE YOU COLD?" "NO, I'LL ALWAYS BE WARM AS LONG AS YOU'RE NEXT TO ME." ♡
....
SHE'S RIGHT ABOUT WHAT THEY'RE DOING, BUT...
SHE'S GOT THE DETAILS ALL WRONG...
THEY LOVE GOING TO THE BATH.
THEY SHARE DINNER TOGETHER... AND GET FOOD POISONING TOGETHER.
JUST TAKE A LOOK AT THEM.

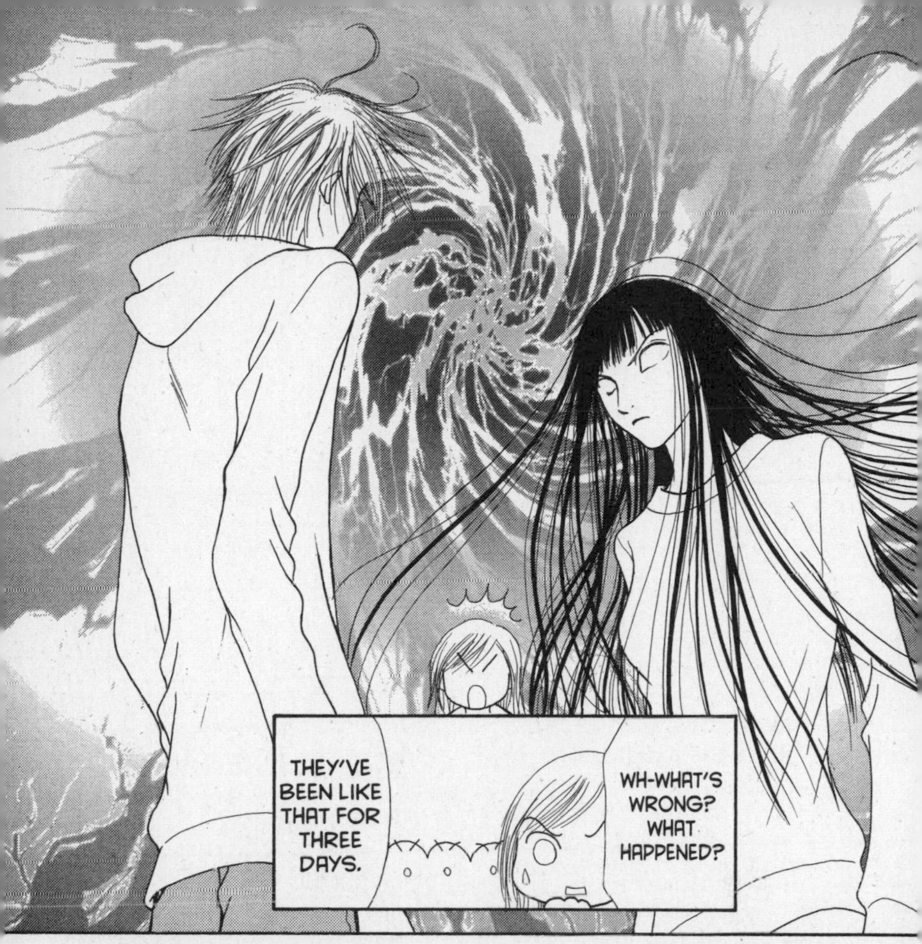
WH-WHAT'S WRONG? WHAT HAPPENED?
THEY'VE BEEN LIKE THAT FOR THREE DAYS.

BEHIND THE SCENES

EVER SINCE NEW YEAR'S DAY, BAD STUFF KEEPS HAPPENING TO ME. I WENT TO THE STORE TO GET MY FAVORITE CANDY, AND THEY WERE SOLD OUT OF IT. I WENT TO A CAFÉ, AND THEY TOOK MY FAVORITE CAKE OFF THE MENU. FOR THE FIRST TIME IN MY LIFE, I SPILLED INK ON MY COLOR STORYBOARDS (IT RUINED ALL MY PAPER, AND I HAD TO GO TO THE STORE AND BUY MORE.) AND MY BAD LUCK IS CONTINUING INTO FEBRUARY AS I WRITE THIS. I JUST HOPE THAT MY LUCK TURNS BY THE TIME THIS VOLUME IS ON THE SHELVES.

I HAD A REALLY HARD TIME WITH THIS STORY. I'M JUST SUPER, SUPER, SUPER BAD AT WRITING LOVE STORIES. BUT IT WAS FUN TRYING TO COME UP WITH A REAL SHOJO-STYLE STORY. ♥♥♥

I WENT TO A KIYOHARU CONCERT, SO I GUESS MY LUCK IS IMPROVING. ♥♥♥

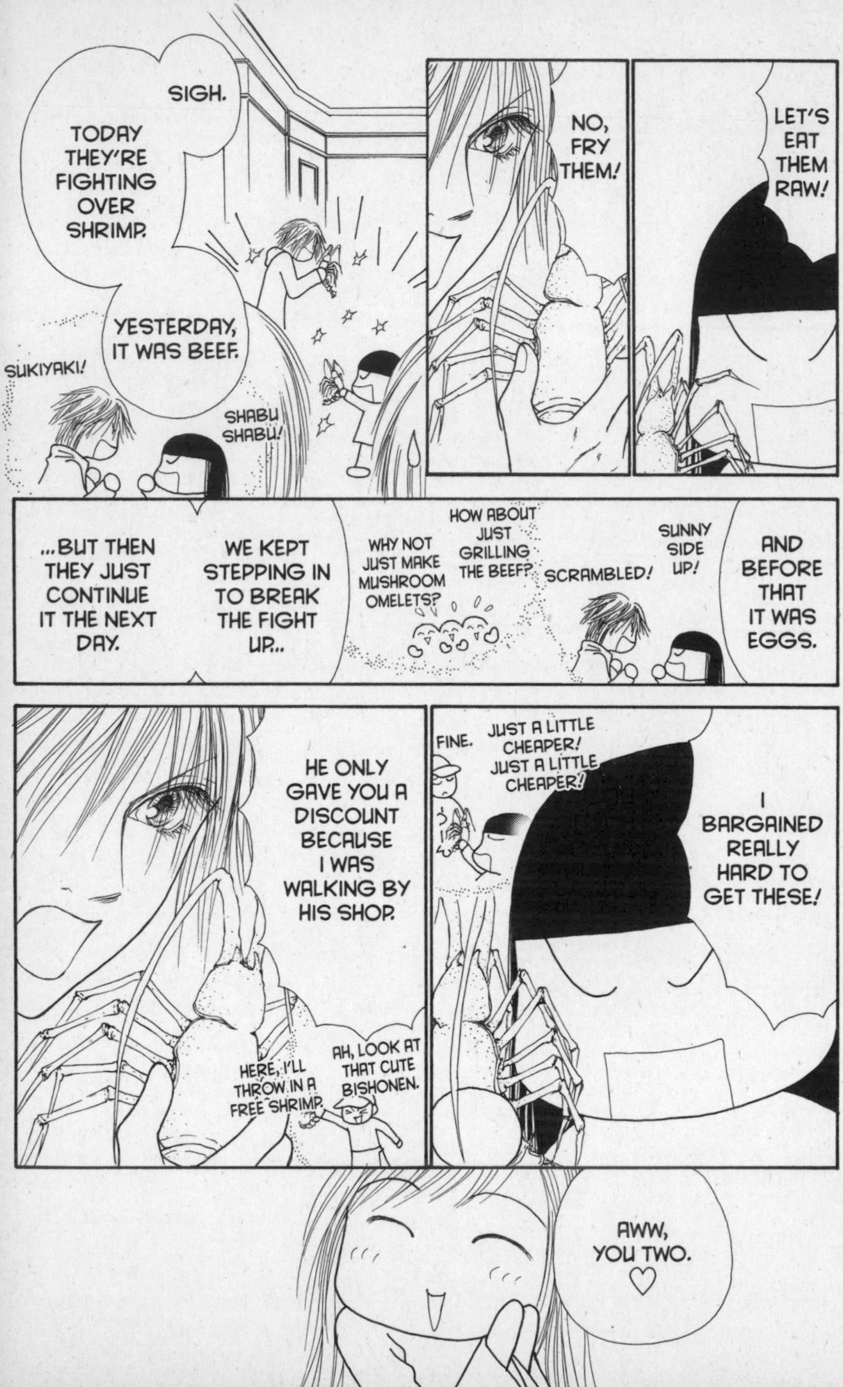
LET'S EAT THEM RAW!
NO, FRY THEM!
SIGH.
TODAY THEY'RE FIGHTING OVER SHRIMP.
YESTERDAY, IT WAS BEEF.
SHABU SHABU!
SUKIYAKI!
AND BEFORE THAT IT WAS EGGS.
SUNNY SIDE UP!
SCRAMBLED!
HOW ABOUT JUST GRILLING THE BEEF?
WHY NOT JUST MAKE MUSHROOM OMELETS?
WE KEPT STEPPING IN TO BREAK THE FIGHT UP...
...BUT THEN THEY JUST CONTINUE IT THE NEXT DAY.
I BARGAINED REALLY HARD TO GET THESE!
JUST A LITTLE CHEAPER! JUST A LITTLE CHEAPER!
FINE.
HE ONLY GAVE YOU A DISCOUNT BECAUSE I WAS WALKING BY HIS SHOP.
AH, LOOK AT THAT CUTE BISHONEN.
HERE, I'LL THROW IN A FREE SHRIMP.
AWW, YOU TWO. ♡

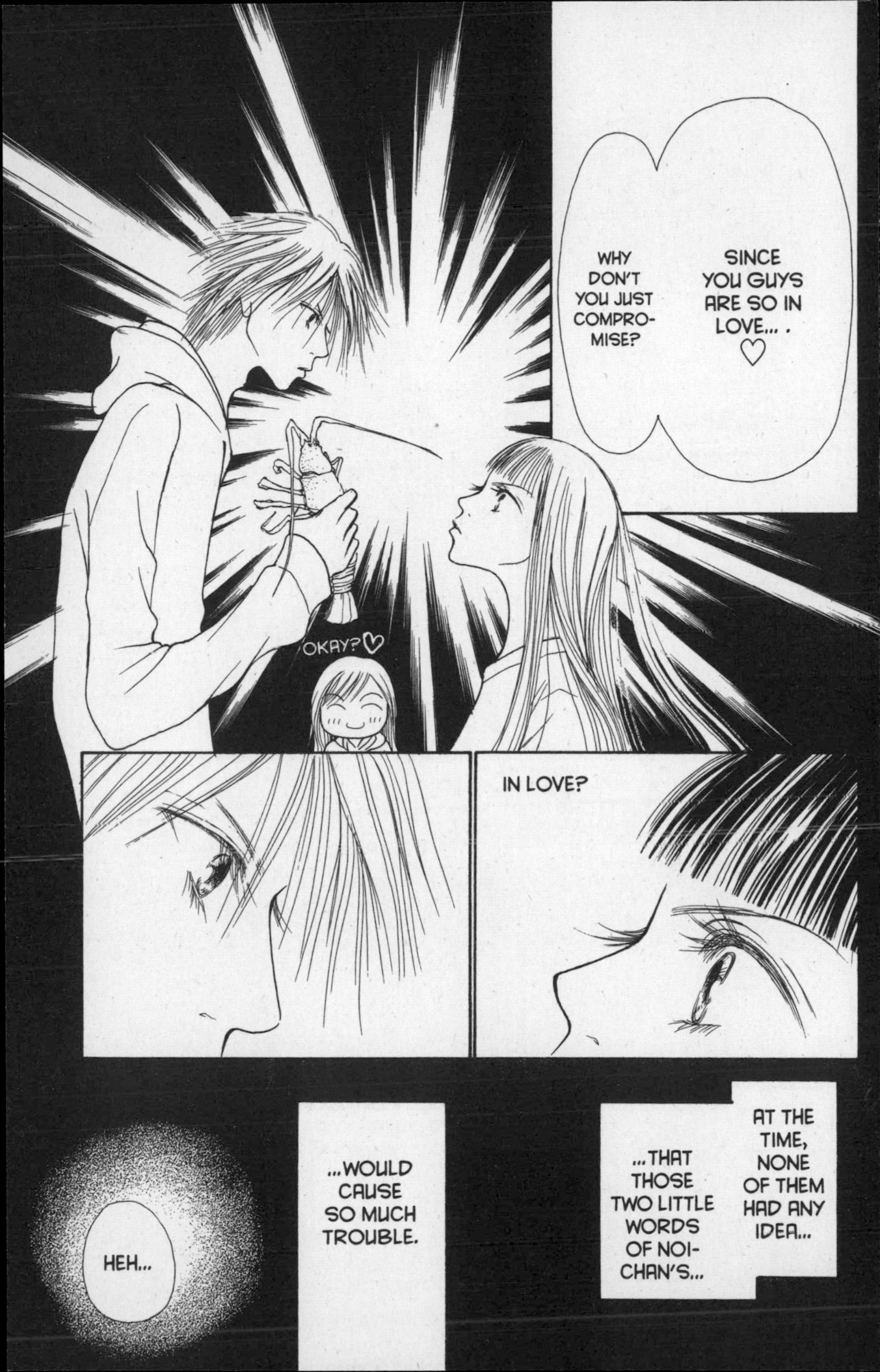
SINCE YOU GUYS ARE SO IN LOVE... . ♡
WHY DON'T YOU JUST COMPROMISE?
OKAY? ♡
IN LOVE?
AT THE TIME, NONE OF THEM HAD ANY IDEA...
...THAT THOSE TWO LITTLE WORDS OF NOI-CHAN'S...
...WOULD CAUSE SO MUCH TROUBLE.
HEH...

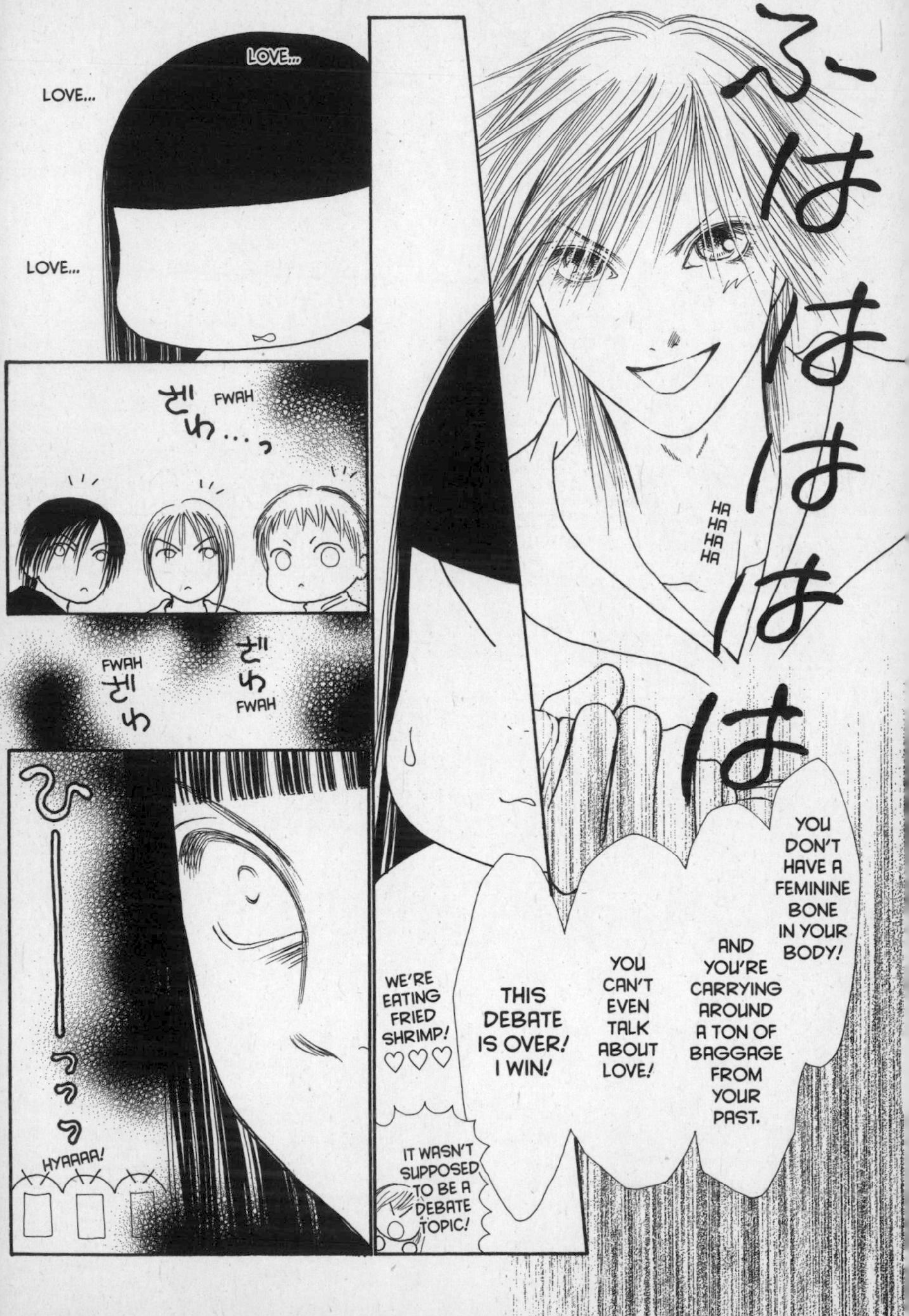
ふははははは
HA HA HA HA
YOU DON'T HAVE A FEMININE BONE IN YOUR BODY!
AND YOU'RE CARRYING AROUND A TON OF BAGGAGE FROM YOUR PAST.
YOU CAN'T EVEN TALK ABOUT LOVE!
THIS DEBATE IS OVER! I WIN!
WE'RE EATING FRIED SHRIMP! ♡♡♡
IT WASN'T SUPPOSED TO BE A DEBATE TOPIC!
LOVE...
LOVE...
LOVE...
ざわ…っ
FWAH
ざわ
FWAH
ざわ
FWAH
ひーーっっ
HYAAAA!

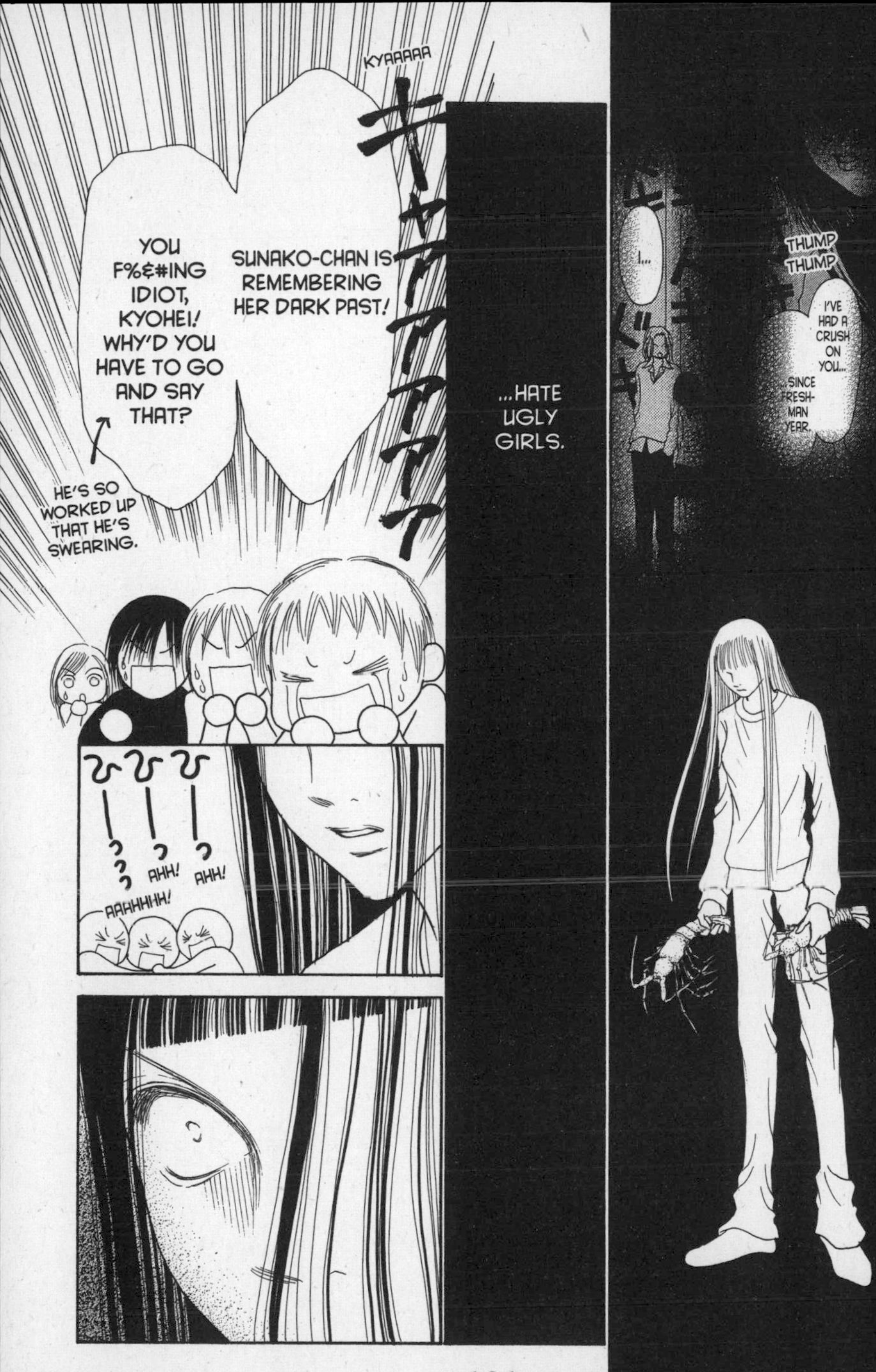
I...
THUMP THUMP
I'VE HAD A CRUSH ON YOU...
...SINCE FRESHMAN YEAR.
...HATE UGLY GIRLS.
KYAAAAA
SUNAKO-CHAN IS REMEMBERING HER DARK PAST!
YOU F%&#ING IDIOT, KYOHEI! WHY'D YOU HAVE TO GO AND SAY THAT?
HE'S SO WORKED UP THAT HE'S SWEARING.
AHH!
AHH!
AAAHHHH!

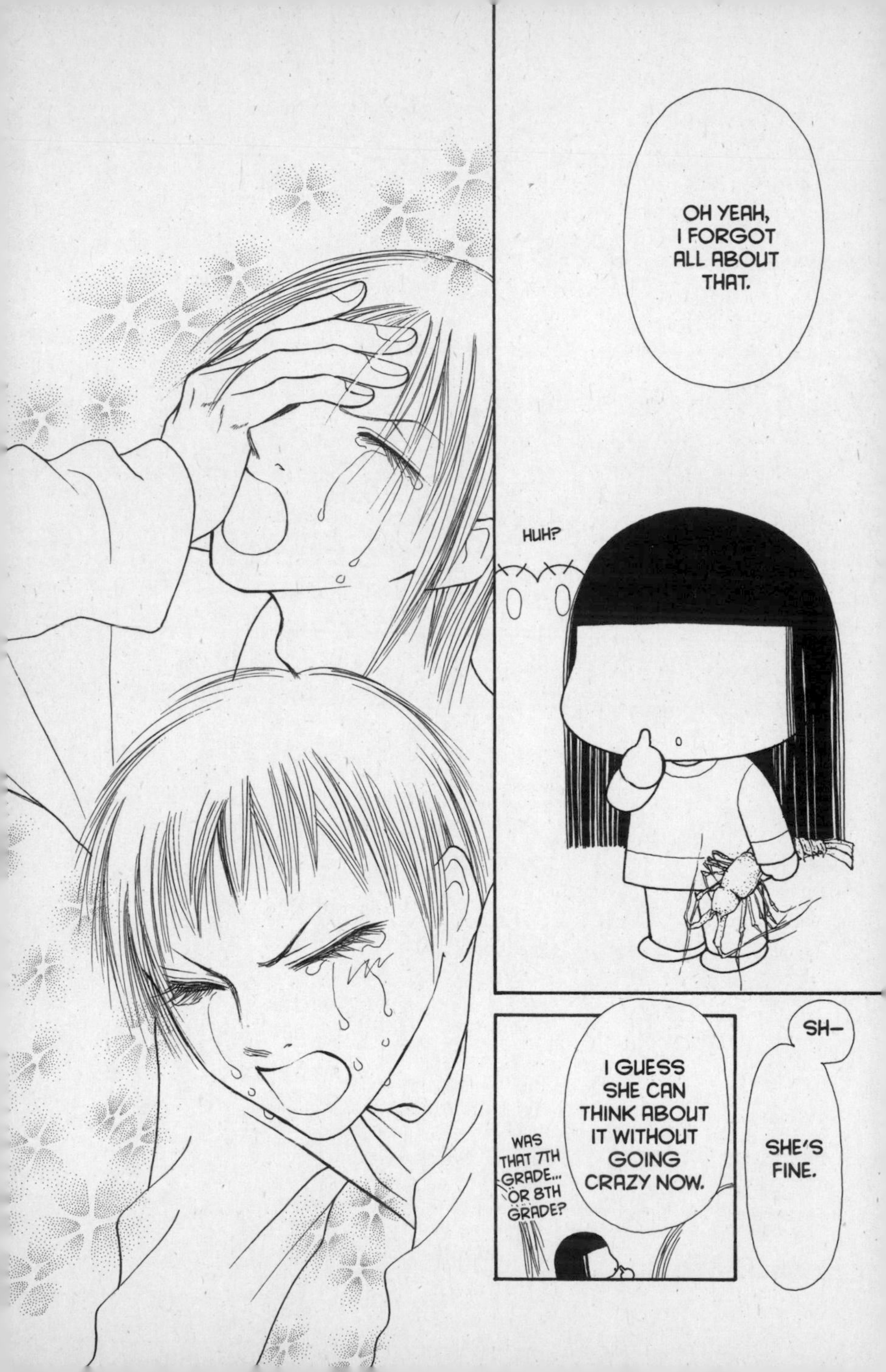
OH YEAH, I FORGOT ALL ABOUT THAT.
HUH?
SH-
SHE'S FINE.
I GUESS SHE CAN THINK ABOUT IT WITHOUT GOING CRAZY NOW.
WAS THAT 7TH GRADE... OR 8TH GRADE?

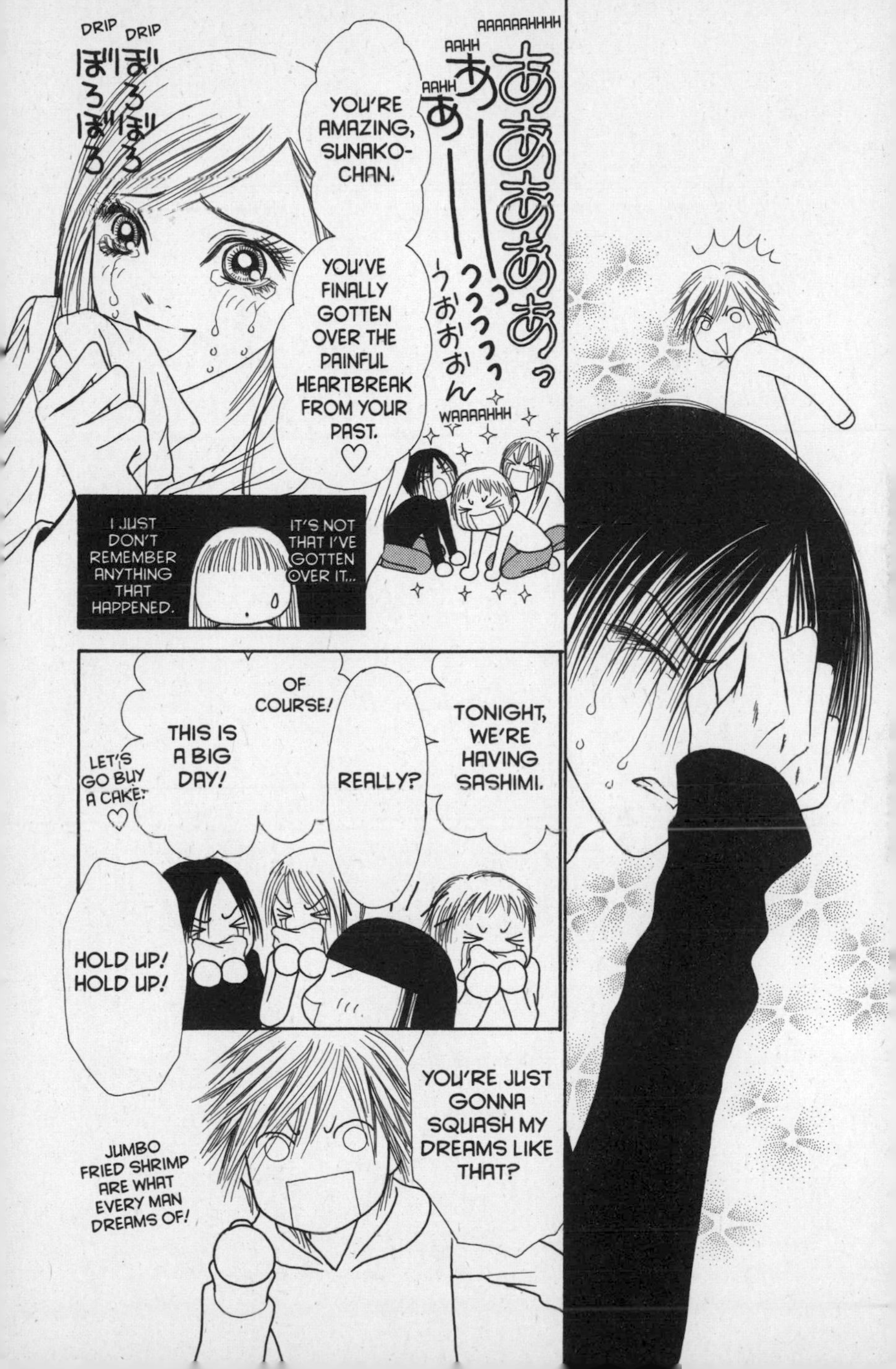
AAAAAAAHHHH
あああぁっ
AAHH
あーーっっっっっ
AAHH
あーー
うおおおん
WAAAAHHH
YOU'RE AMAZING, SUNAKO-CHAN.
YOU'VE FINALLY GOTTEN OVER THE PAINFUL HEARTBREAK FROM YOUR PAST. ♡
DRIP DRIP
ぽろぽろ ぽろぽろ
IT'S NOT THAT I'VE GOTTEN OVER IT...
I JUST DON'T REMEMBER ANYTHING THAT HAPPENED.
TONIGHT, WE'RE HAVING SASHIMI.
REALLY?
OF COURSE!
THIS IS A BIG DAY!
LET'S GO BUY A CAKE! ♡
HOLD UP! HOLD UP!
YOU'RE JUST GONNA SQUASH MY DREAMS LIKE THAT?
JUMBO FRIED SHRIMP ARE WHAT EVERY MAN DREAMS OF!

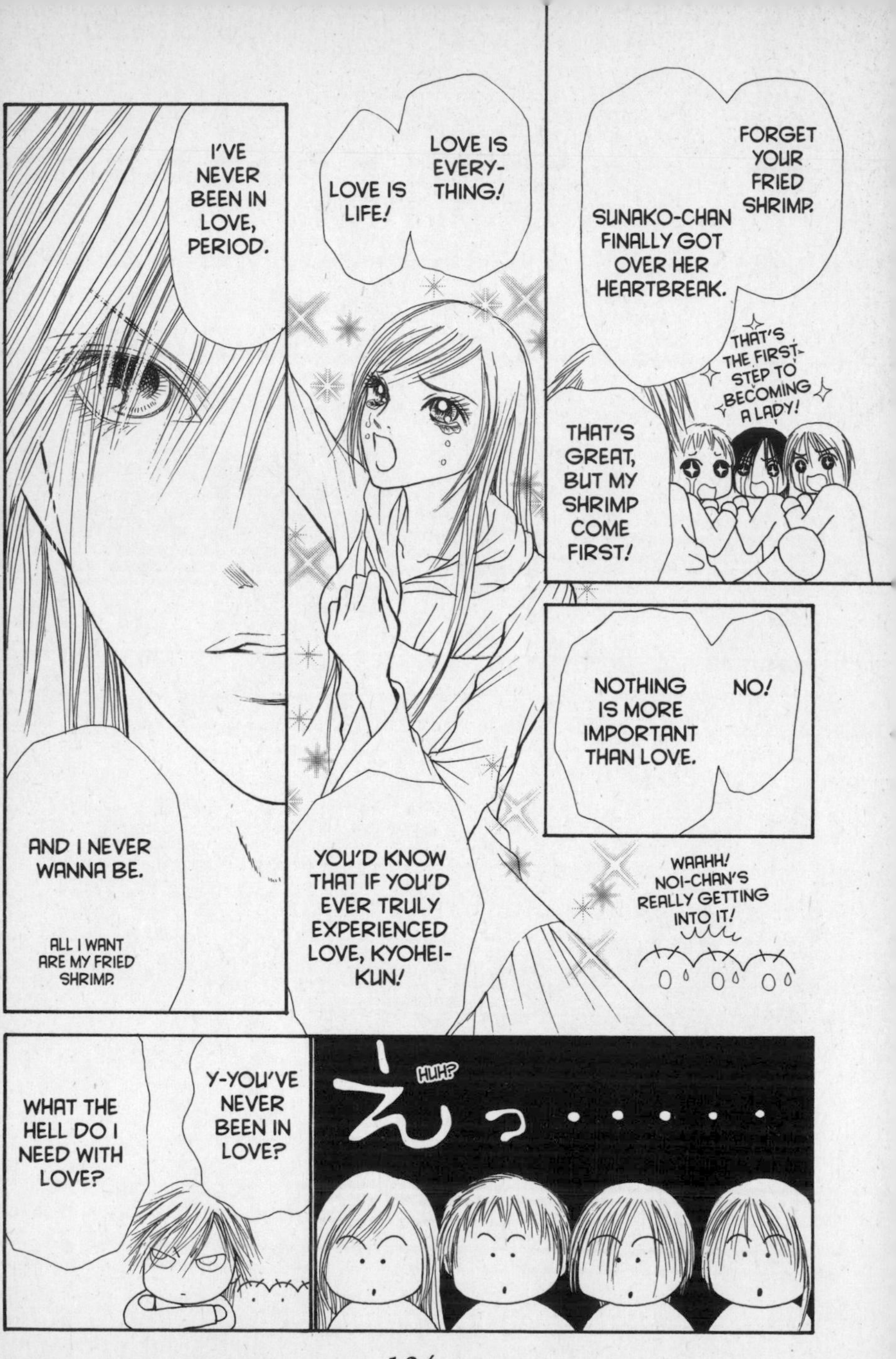
FORGET YOUR FRIED SHRIMP.
SUNAKO-CHAN FINALLY GOT OVER HER HEARTBREAK.
THAT'S THE FIRST STEP TO BECOMING A LADY!
THAT'S GREAT, BUT MY SHRIMP COME FIRST!
NO!
NOTHING IS MORE IMPORTANT THAN LOVE.
WAAHH! NOI-CHAN'S REALLY GETTING INTO IT!
LOVE IS EVERY-THING!
LOVE IS LIFE!
YOU'D KNOW THAT IF YOU'D EVER TRULY EXPERIENCED LOVE, KYOHEI-KUN!
I'VE NEVER BEEN IN LOVE, PERIOD.
AND I NEVER WANNA BE.
ALL I WANT ARE MY FRIED SHRIMP.
HUH?
えっ……
Y-YOU'VE NEVER BEEN IN LOVE?
WHAT THE HELL DO I NEED WITH LOVE?

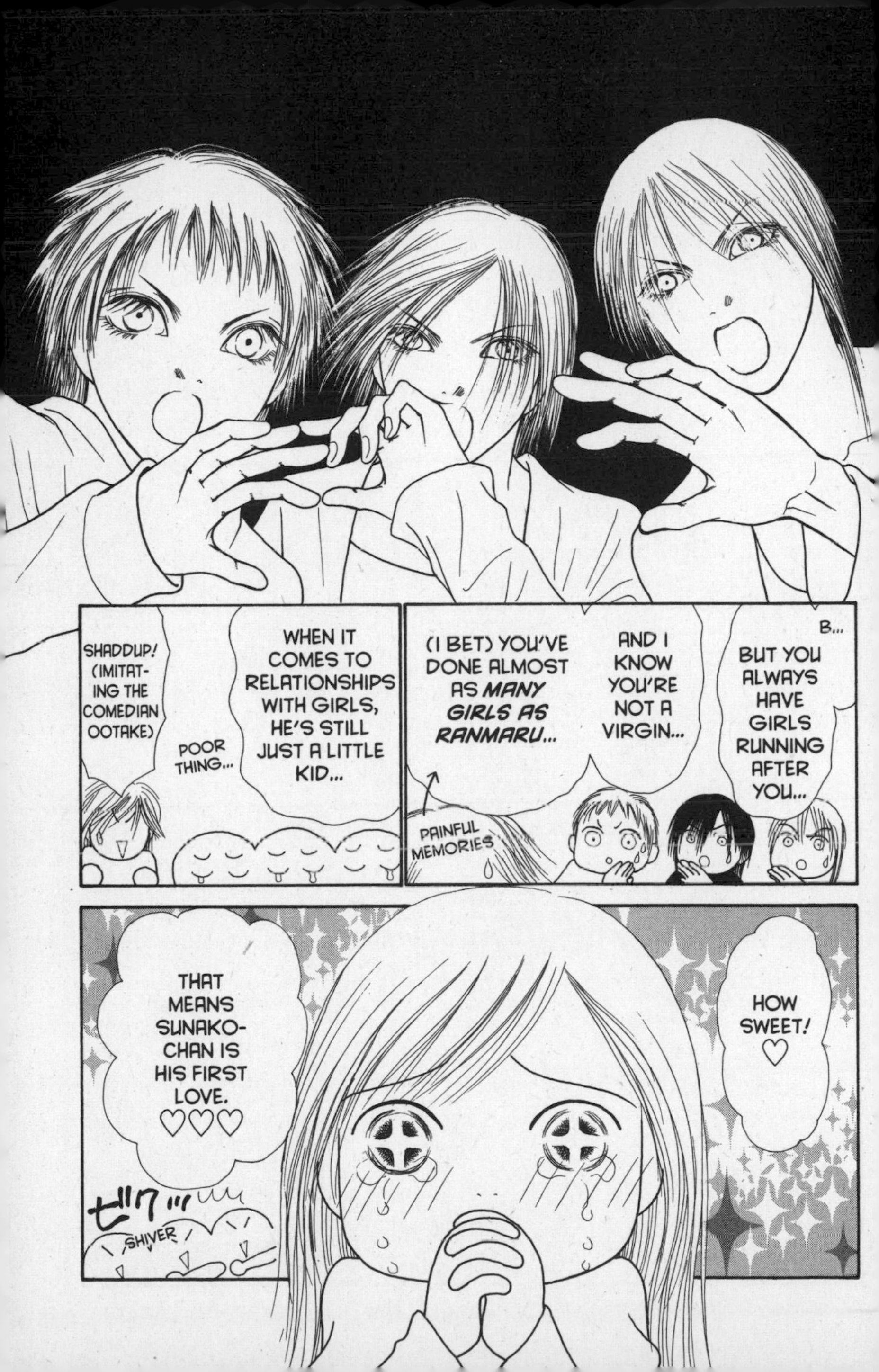
B... BUT YOU ALWAYS HAVE GIRLS RUNNING AFTER YOU...
AND I KNOW YOU'RE NOT A VIRGIN...
(I BET) YOU'VE DONE ALMOST AS *MANY GIRLS AS RANMARU*...
PAINFUL MEMORIES
WHEN IT COMES TO RELATIONSHIPS WITH GIRLS, HE'S STILL JUST A LITTLE KID...
POOR THING...
SHADDUP! (IMITATING THE COMEDIAN OOTAKE)
HOW SWEET! ♡
THAT MEANS SUNAKO-CHAN IS HIS FIRST LOVE. ♡♡♡
SHIVER

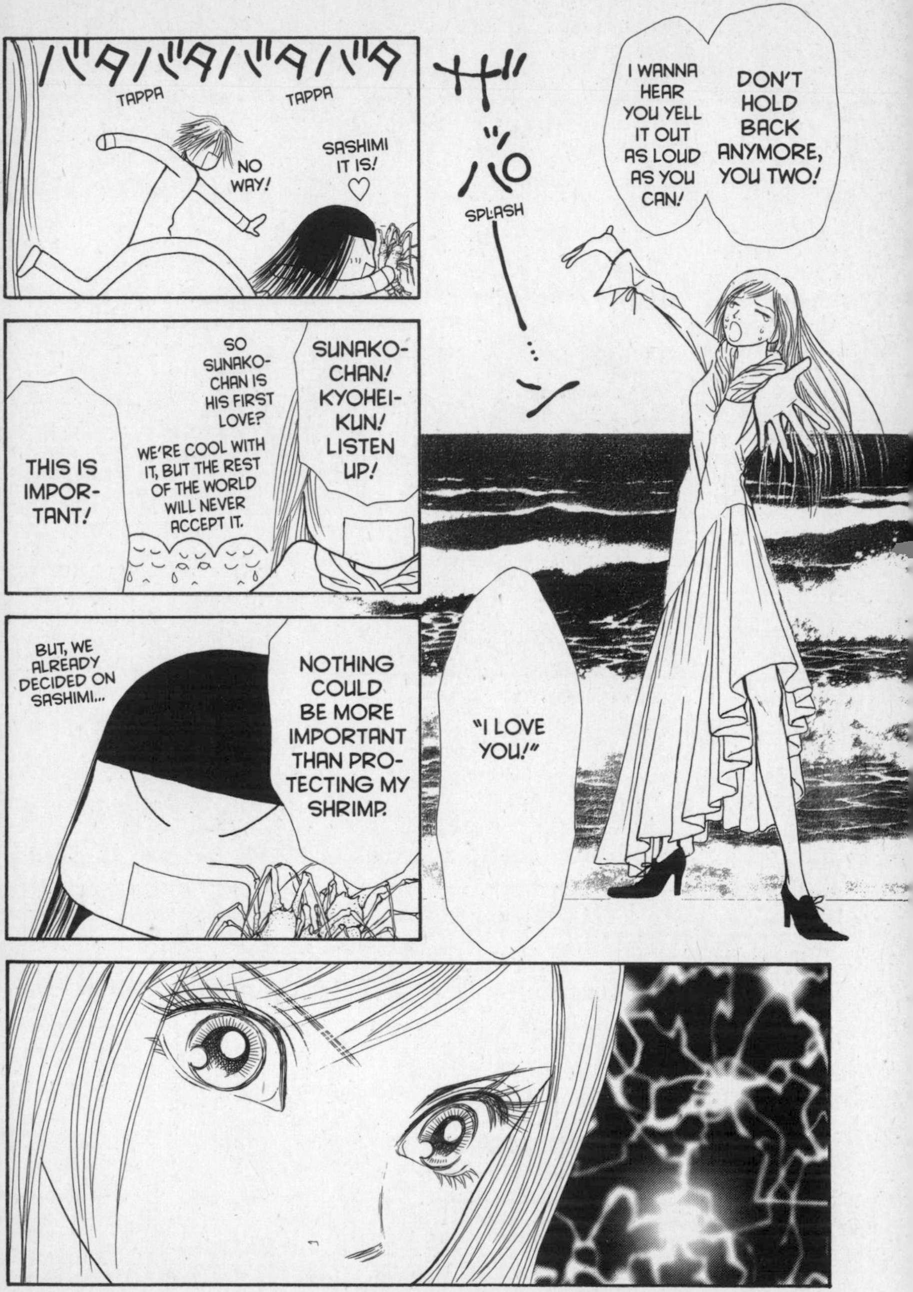
ザバ
SPLASH
DON'T HOLD BACK ANYMORE, YOU TWO!
I WANNA HEAR YOU YELL IT OUT AS LOUD AS YOU CAN!
"I LOVE YOU!"
バタバタバタバタ
TAPPA
TAPPA
SASHIMI IT IS! ♡
NO WAY!
SUNAKO-CHAN! KYOHEI-KUN! LISTEN UP!
SO SUNAKO-CHAN IS HIS FIRST LOVE?
WE'RE COOL WITH IT, BUT THE REST OF THE WORLD WILL NEVER ACCEPT IT.
THIS IS IMPORTANT!
NOTHING COULD BE MORE IMPORTANT THAN PROTECTING MY SHRIMP.
BUT, WE ALREADY DECIDED ON SASHIMI...

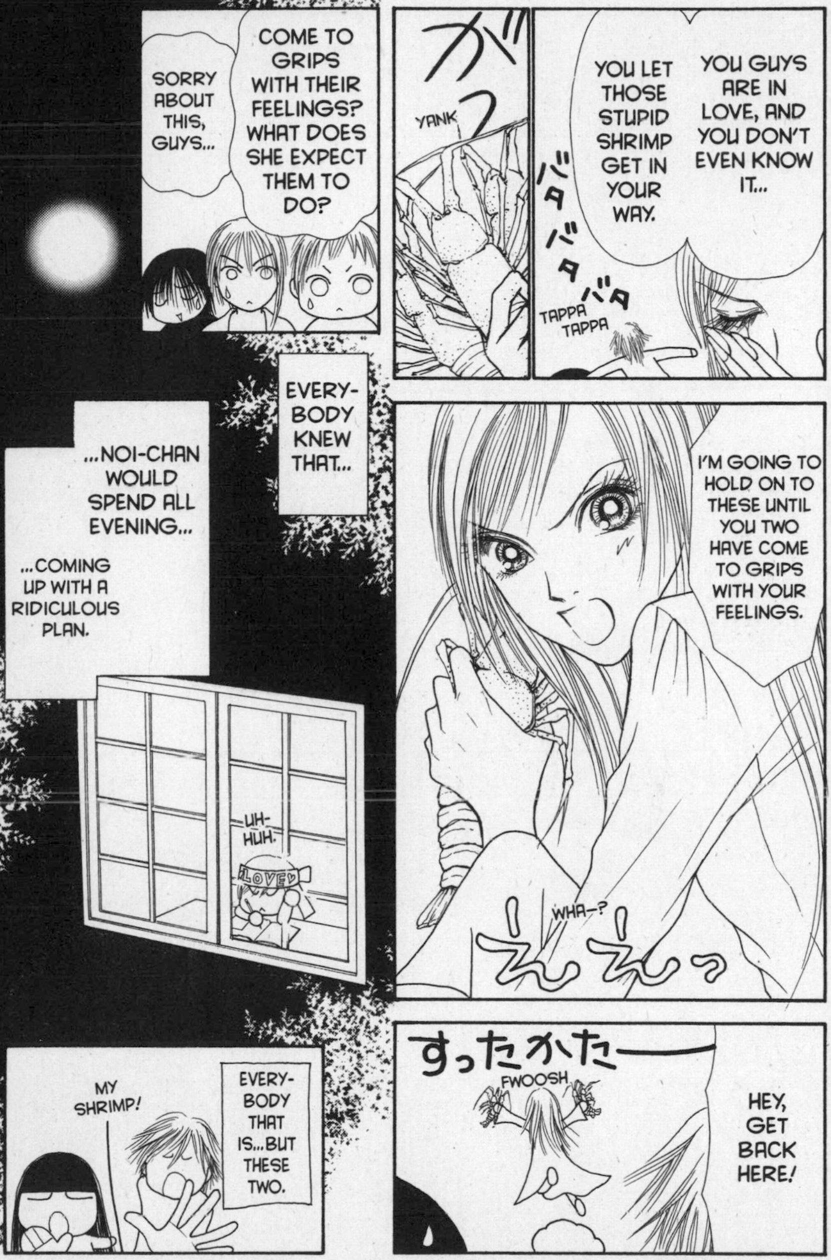
YOU GUYS ARE IN LOVE, AND YOU DON'T EVEN KNOW IT...
YOU LET THOSE STUPID SHRIMP GET IN YOUR WAY.
バタバタバタ
TAPPA TAPPA
がっ
YANK
COME TO GRIPS WITH THEIR FEELINGS? WHAT DOES SHE EXPECT THEM TO DO?
SORRY ABOUT THIS, GUYS...
I'M GOING TO HOLD ON TO THESE UNTIL YOU TWO HAVE COME TO GRIPS WITH YOUR FEELINGS.
ええっ
WHA-?
EVERY-BODY KNEW THAT...
...NOI-CHAN WOULD SPEND ALL EVENING...
...COMING UP WITH A RIDICULOUS PLAN.
UH-HUH.
LOVE
すったかたー
FWOOSH
HEY, GET BACK HERE!
EVERY-BODY THAT IS...BUT THESE TWO.
MY SHRIMP!

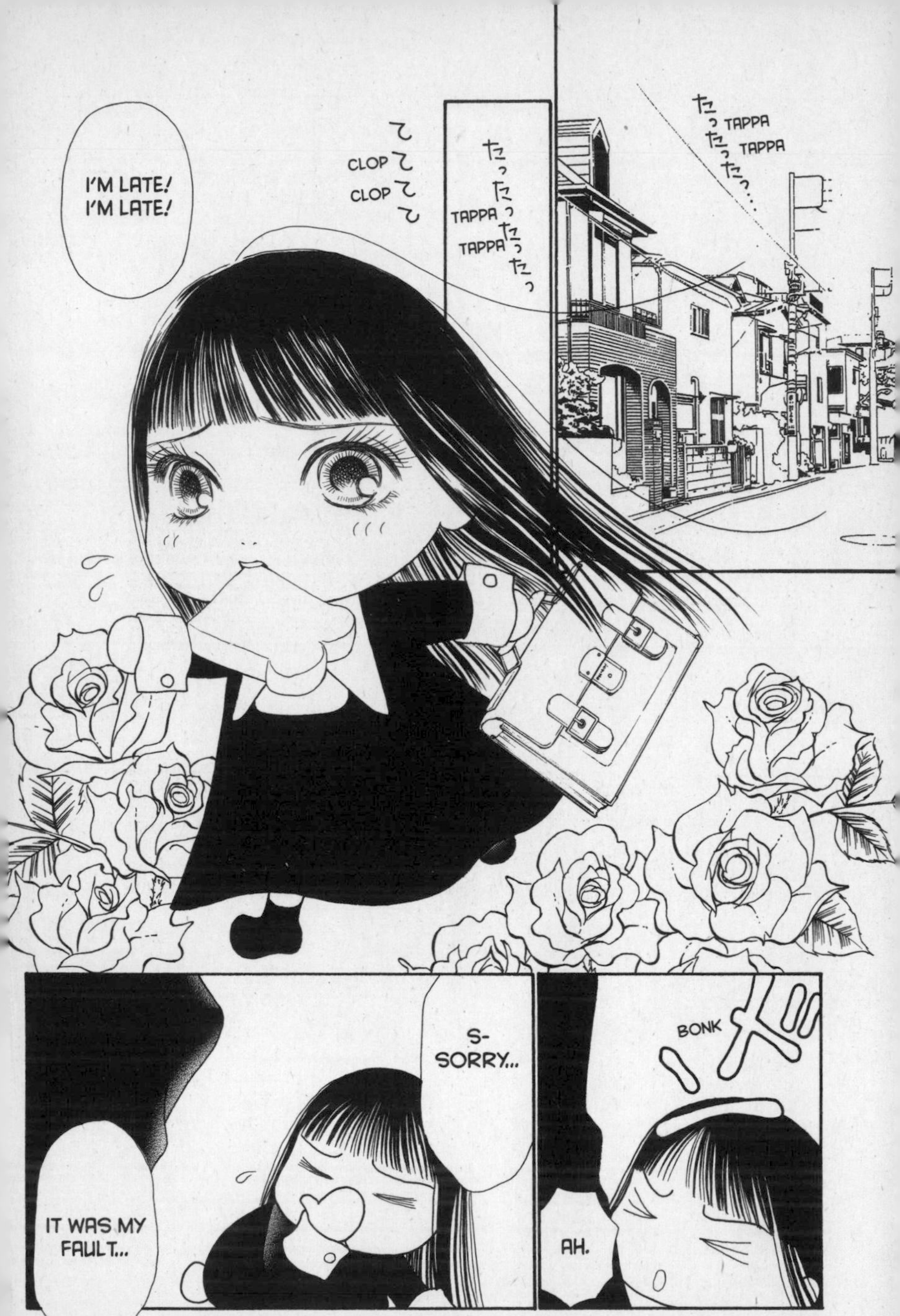

たったたっ…
TAPPA
TAPPA
たったたったっ
TAPPA
TAPPA
てててて
CLOP
CLOP
I'M LATE!
I'M LATE!
BONK
AH.
S-SORRY...
IT WAS MY FAULT...

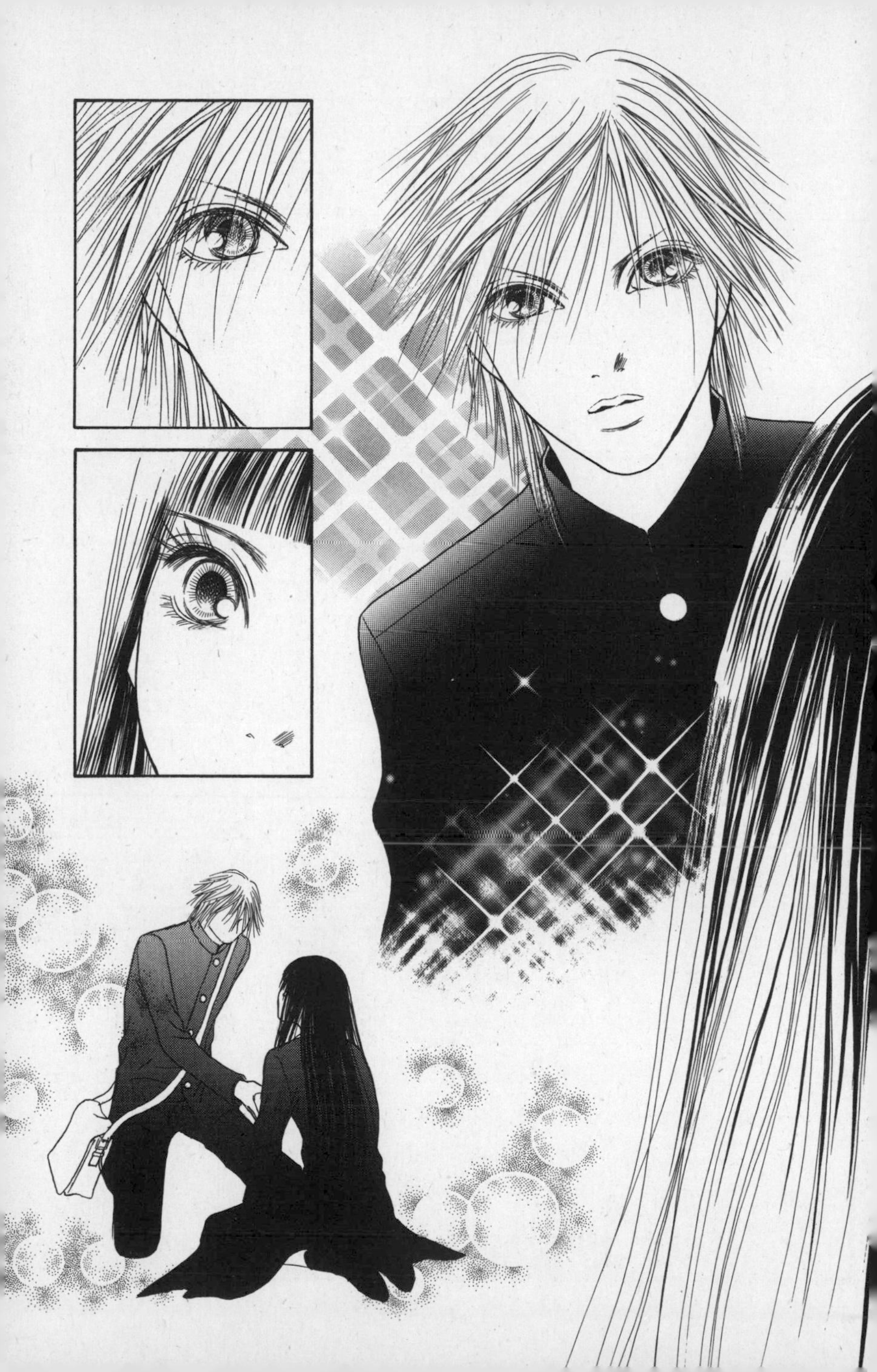

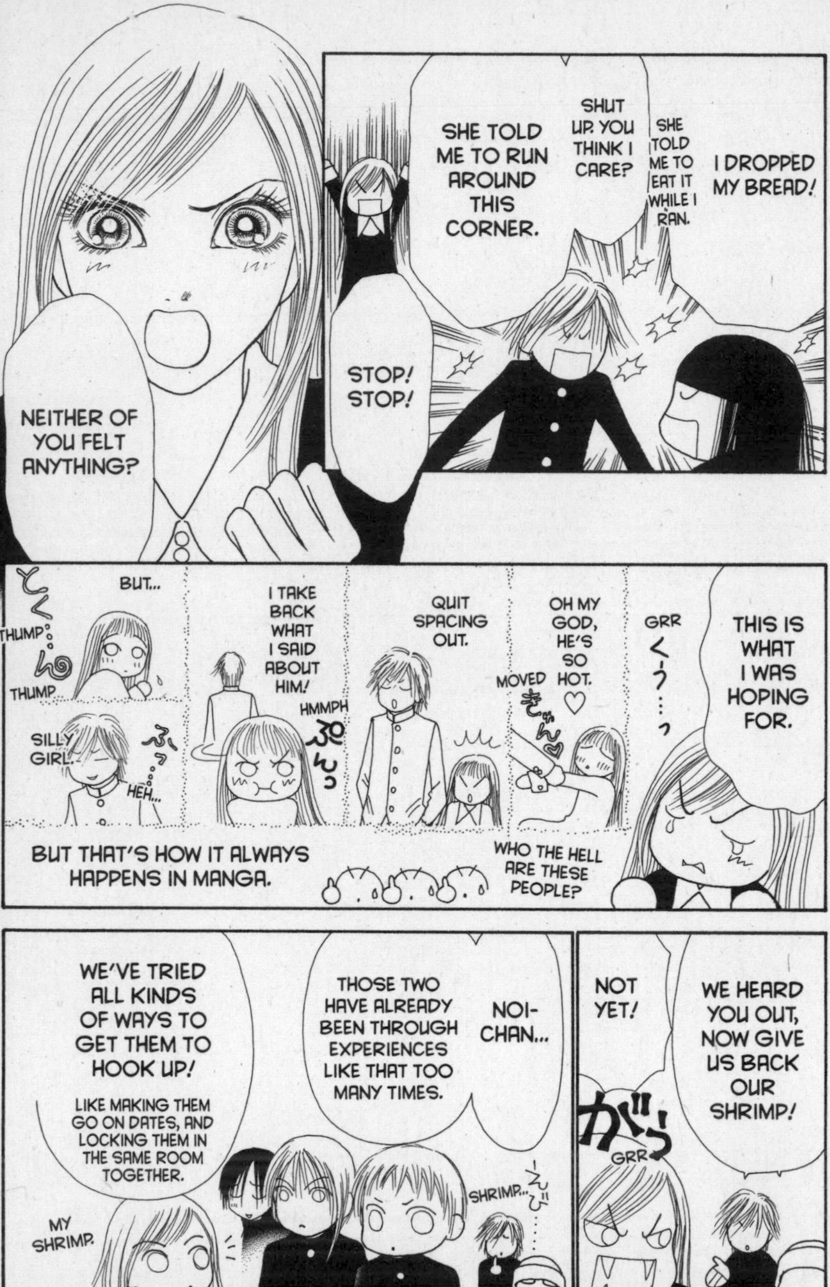
I DROPPED MY BREAD!
SHE TOLD ME TO EAT IT WHILE I RAN.
SHUT UP. YOU THINK I CARE?
SHE TOLD ME TO RUN AROUND THIS CORNER.
STOP! STOP!
NEITHER OF YOU FELT ANYTHING?
THIS IS WHAT I WAS HOPING FOR.
GRR
OH MY GOD, HE'S SO HOT.
MOVED
QUIT SPACING OUT.
WHO THE HELL ARE THESE PEOPLE?
I TAKE BACK WHAT I SAID ABOUT HIM!
HMMPH
BUT...
THUMP
THUMP
SILLY GIRL.
HEH...
BUT THAT'S HOW IT ALWAYS HAPPENS IN MANGA.
WE HEARD YOU OUT, NOW GIVE US BACK OUR SHRIMP!
NOT YET!
GRR
NOI-CHAN...
THOSE TWO HAVE ALREADY BEEN THROUGH EXPERIENCES LIKE THAT TOO MANY TIMES.
WE'VE TRIED ALL KINDS OF WAYS TO GET THEM TO HOOK UP!
LIKE MAKING THEM GO ON DATES, AND LOCKING THEM IN THE SAME ROOM TOGETHER.
SHRIMP...
MY SHRIMP.

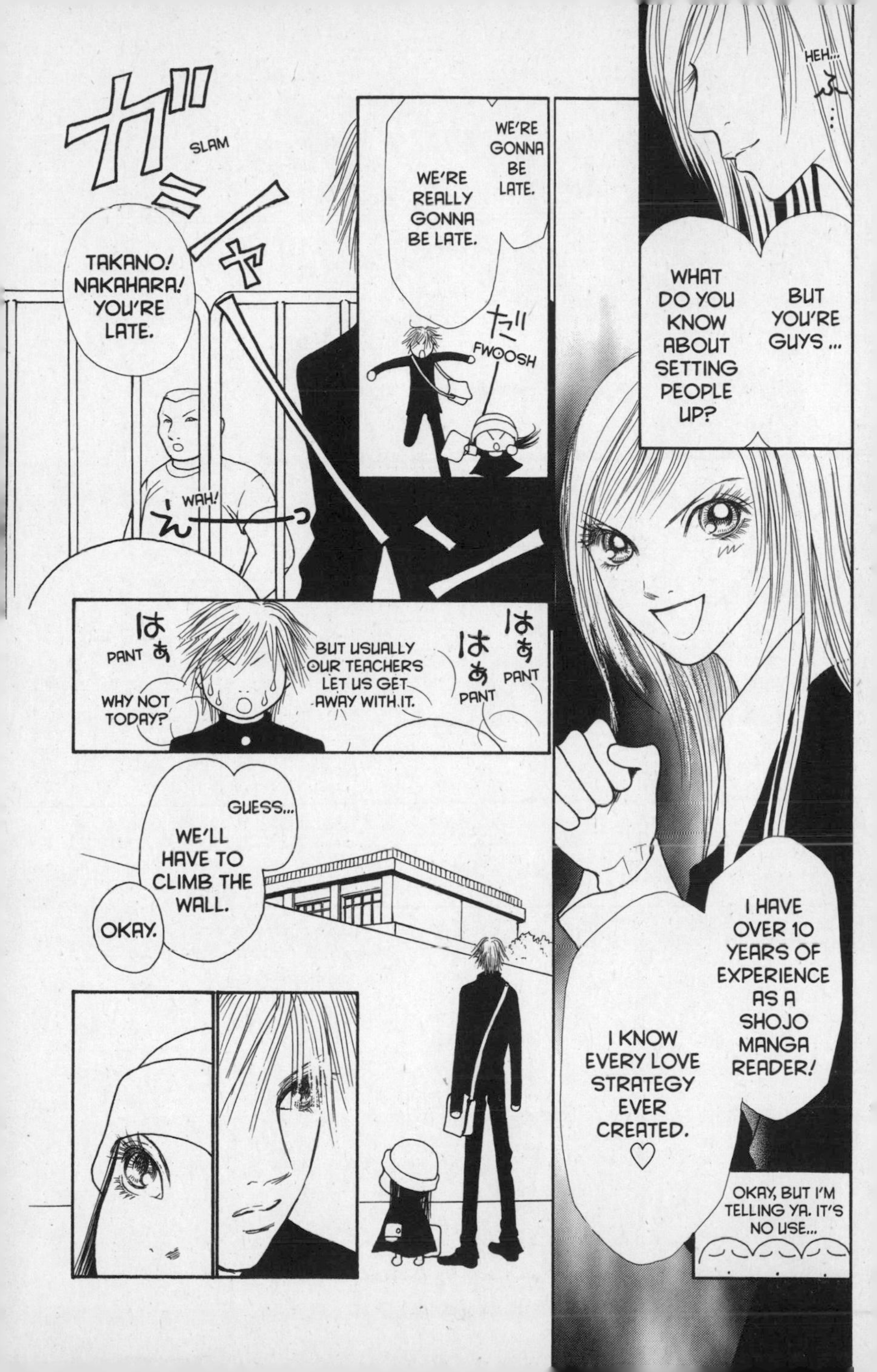
HEH...
BUT YOU'RE GUYS ...
WHAT DO YOU KNOW ABOUT SETTING PEOPLE UP?
I HAVE OVER 10 YEARS OF EXPERIENCE AS A SHOJO MANGA READER!
I KNOW EVERY LOVE STRATEGY EVER CREATED. ♡
OKAY, BUT I'M TELLING YA. IT'S NO USE...
WE'RE GONNA BE LATE.
WE'RE REALLY GONNA BE LATE.
FWOOSH
SLAM
TAKANO! NAKAHARA! YOU'RE LATE.
WAH!
PANT
PANT
BUT USUALLY OUR TEACHERS LET US GET AWAY WITH IT.
PANT
WHY NOT TODAY?
GUESS...
WE'LL HAVE TO CLIMB THE WALL.
OKAY.

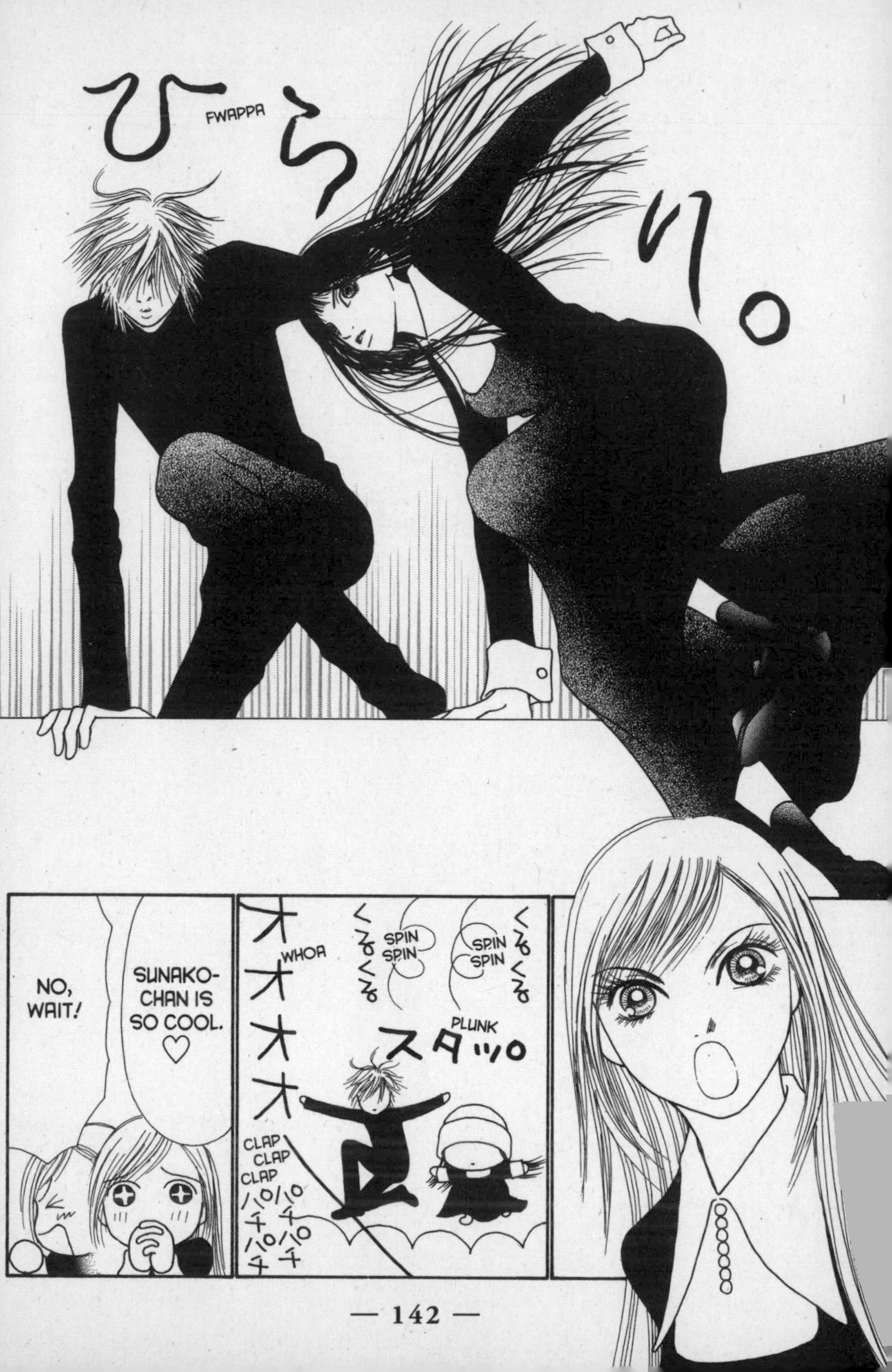
ひらり。
FWAPPA
くるくる
SPIN SPIN
くるくる
SPIN SPIN
オオオオ
WHOA
スタッ。
PLUNK
CLAP CLAP CLAP
パチパチパチパチ
SUNAKO-CHAN IS SO COOL. ♡
NO, WAIT!

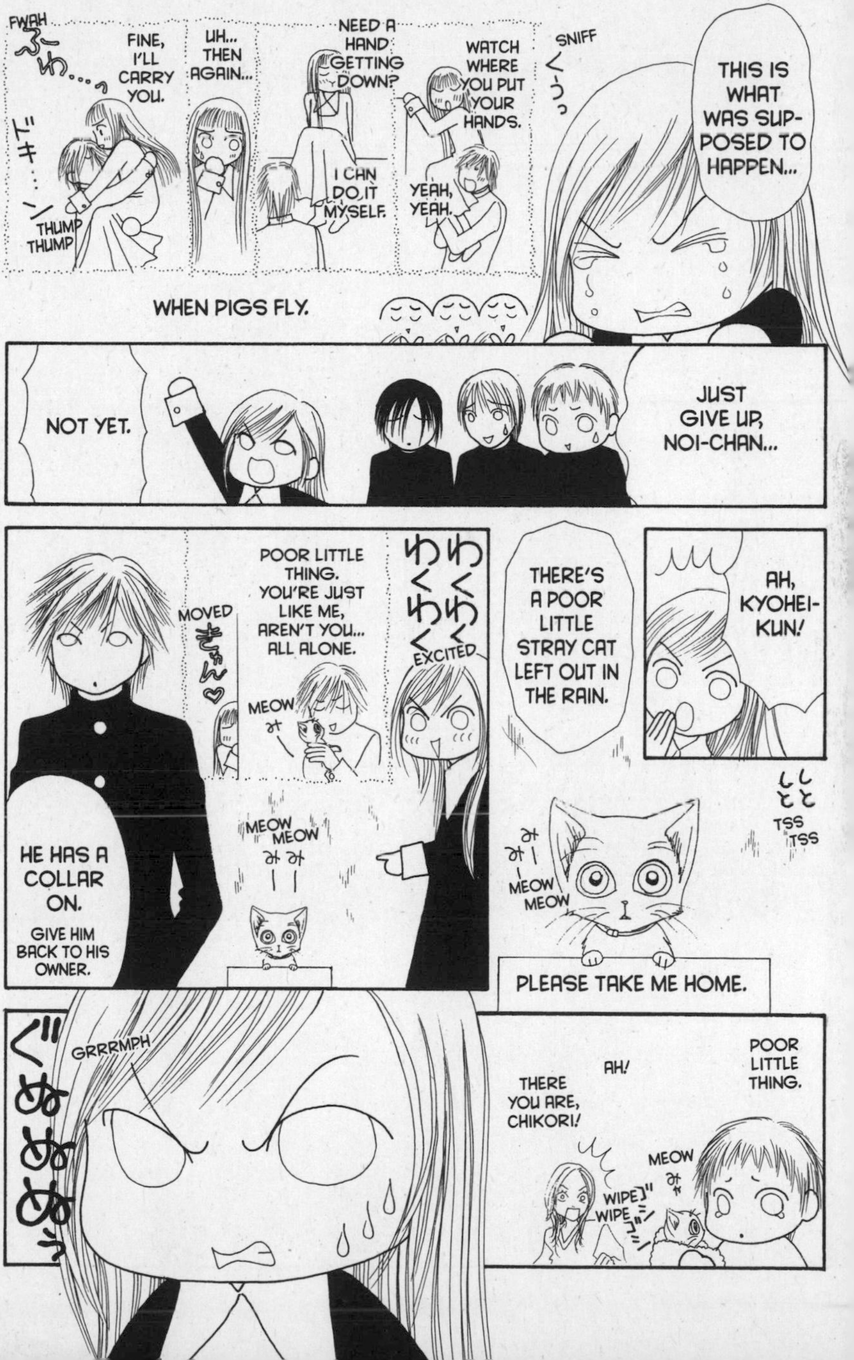
THIS IS WHAT WAS SUP-POSED TO HAPPEN...
SNIFF
く～うっ
WATCH WHERE YOU PUT YOUR HANDS.
YEAH, YEAH.
NEED A HAND GETTING DOWN?
I CAN DO IT MYSELF.
UH... THEN AGAIN...
FINE, I'LL CARRY YOU.
FWAH
ふわ…
ドキ…ン
THUMP THUMP
WHEN PIGS FLY.
JUST GIVE UP, NOI-CHAN...
NOT YET.
AH, KYOHEI-KUN!
THERE'S A POOR LITTLE STRAY CAT LEFT OUT IN THE RAIN.
しとしと
TSS TSS
みーみー
MEOW MEOW
PLEASE TAKE ME HOME.
わくわく
EXCITED
POOR LITTLE THING. YOU'RE JUST LIKE ME, AREN'T YOU... ALL ALONE.
MEOW
み
MOVED
きゅん
MEOW MEOW
みーみー
HE HAS A COLLAR ON.
GIVE HIM BACK TO HIS OWNER.
POOR LITTLE THING.
MEOW
みゃ
AH!
THERE YOU ARE, CHIKORI!
WIPE WIPE
ゴシゴシ
GRRRMPH
ぐぬぬぬぬぅ

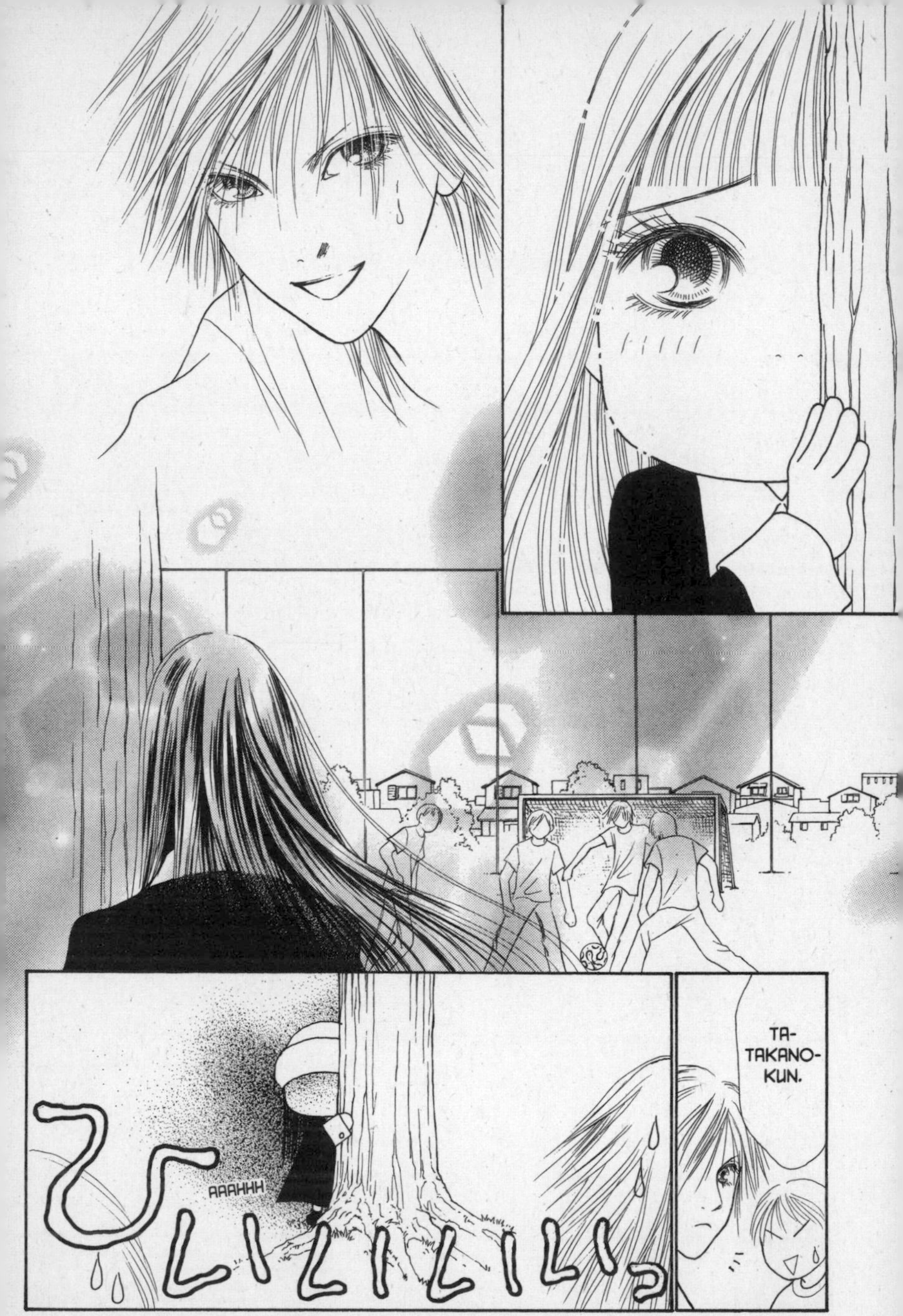

TA-
TAKANO-
KUN.
AAAHHH

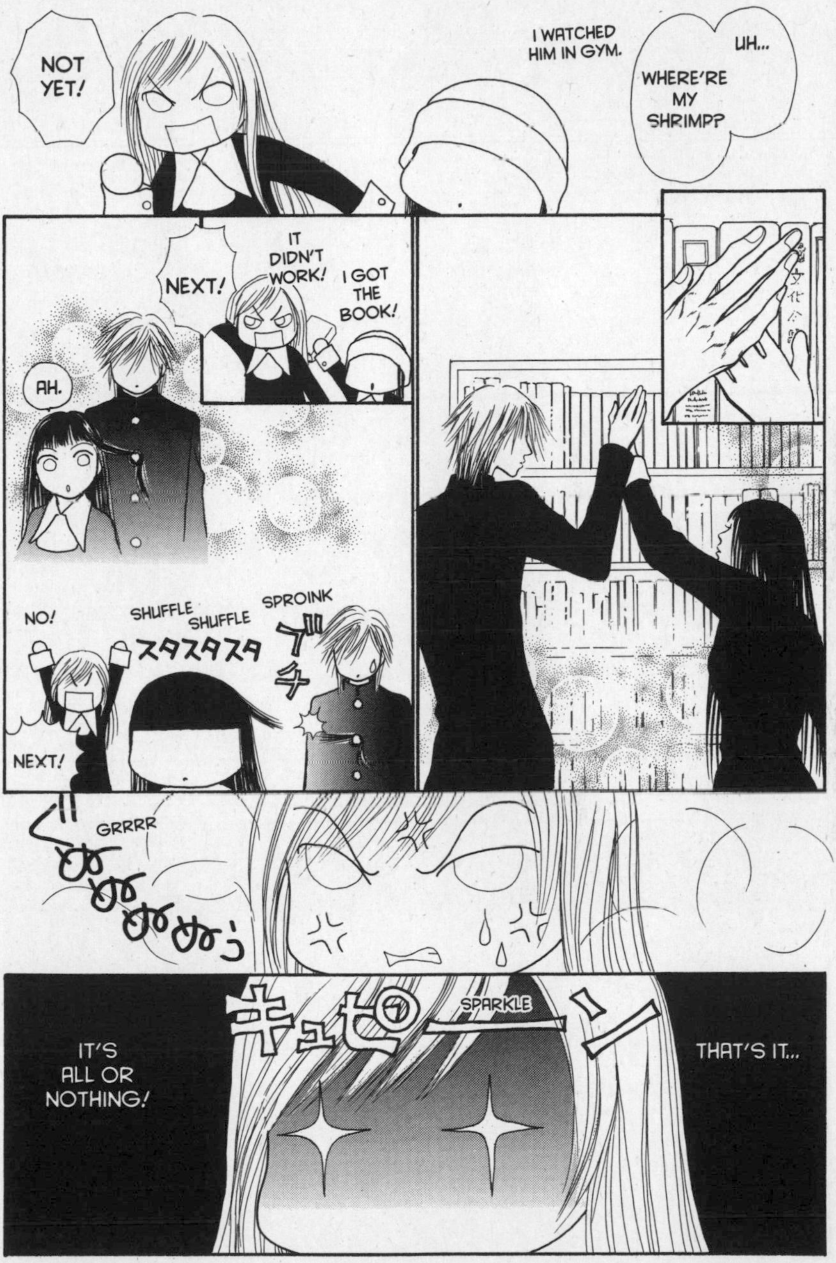
UH...
WHERE'RE MY SHRIMP?
I WATCHED HIM IN GYM.
NOT YET!
I GOT THE BOOK!
IT DIDN'T WORK!
NEXT!
AH.
SPROINK
ブチ
SHUFFLE SHUFFLE
スタスタスタ
NO!
NEXT!
GRRRR
THAT'S IT...
キュピーン
SPARKLE
IT'S ALL OR NOTHING!

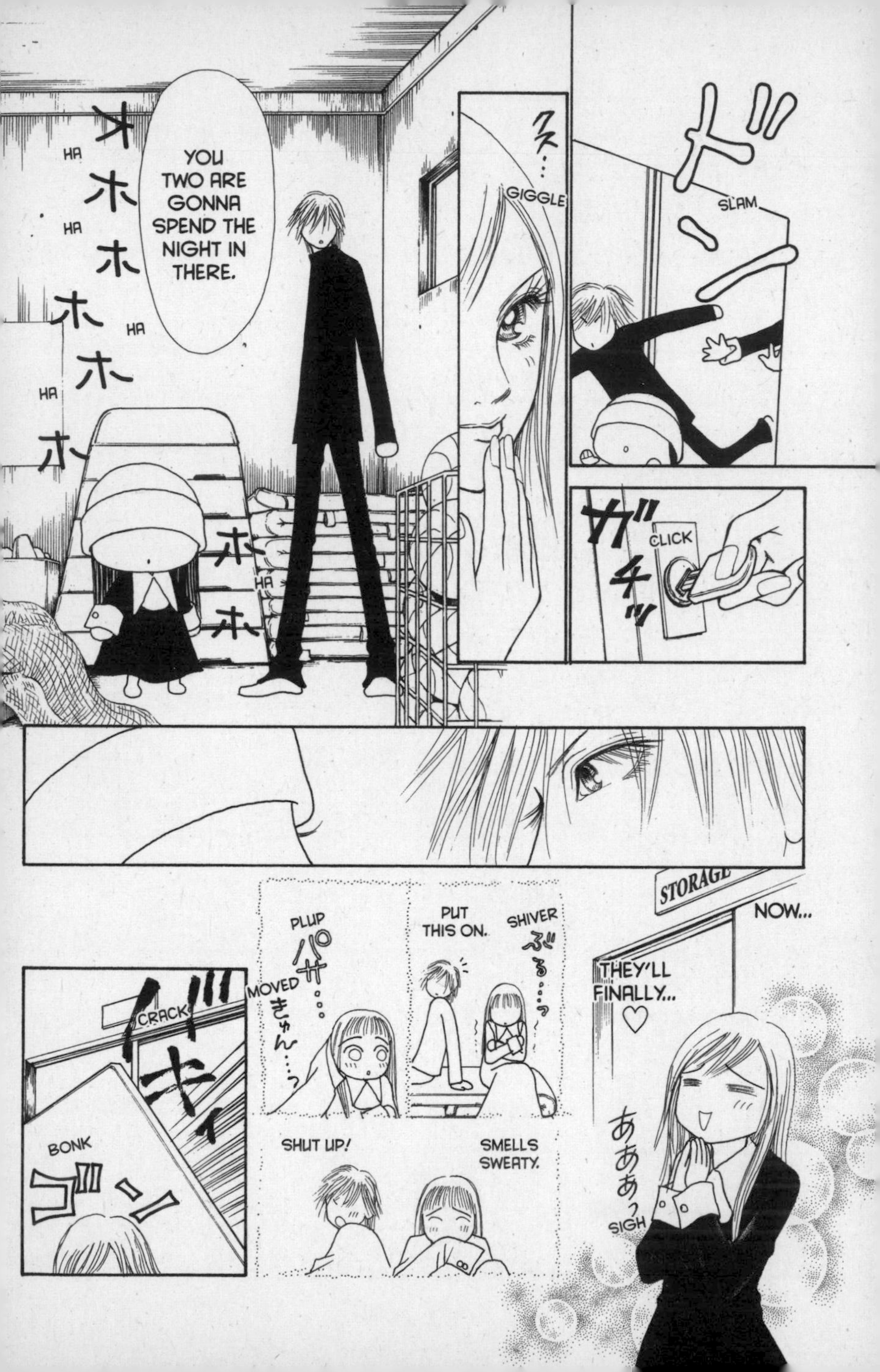

ドン
SLAM
ガチッ
CLICK
クス…
GIGGLE
YOU TWO ARE GONNA SPEND THE NIGHT IN THERE.
オホホホホ
HA
HA
HA
HA
ホホ
HA
STORAGE
NOW...
THEY'LL FINALLY... ♡
ああっ
SIGH
PUT THIS ON.
SHIVER
ぶる…っ
PLUP
パサ…
MOVED
きゅん…っ
SMELLS SWEATY.
SHUT UP!
ギィ
CRACK
ゴーン
BONK

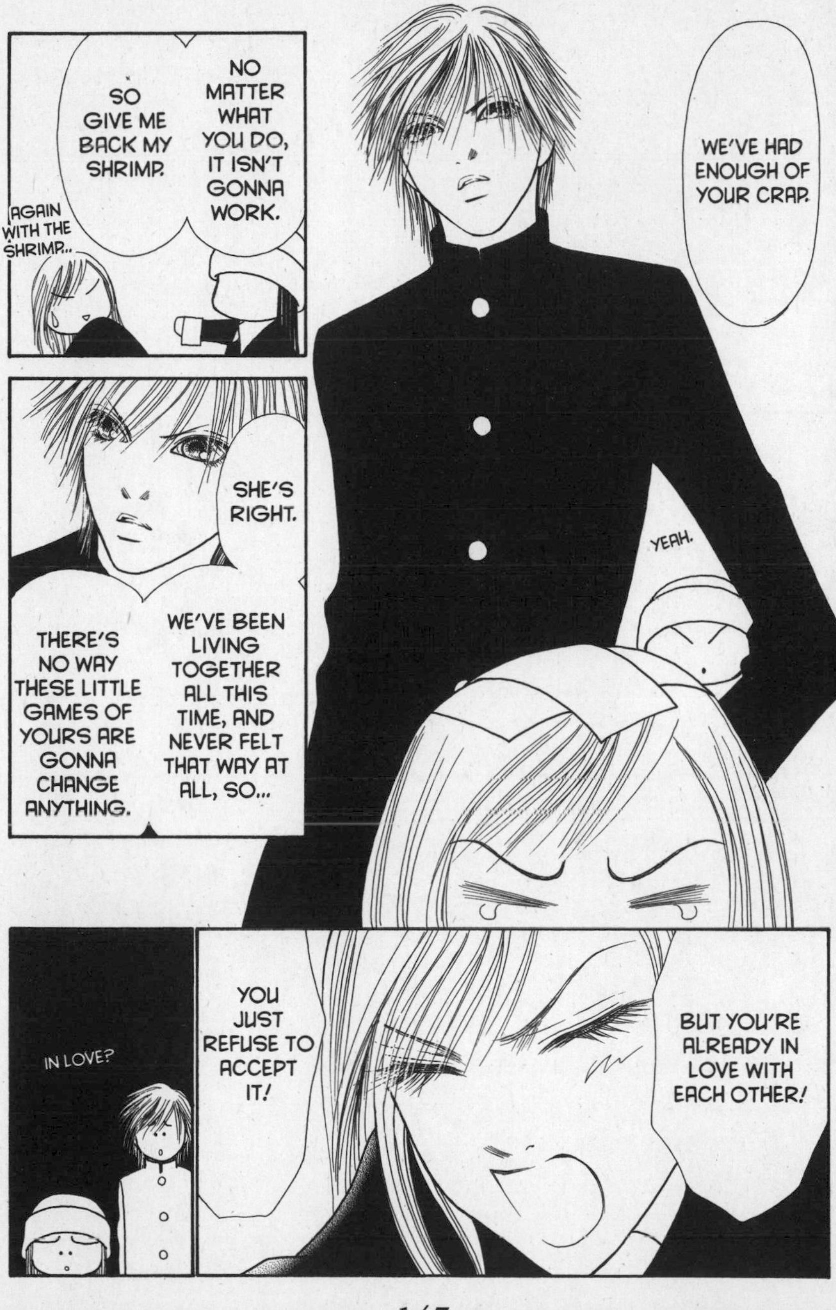
WE'VE HAD ENOUGH OF YOUR CRAP.
YEAH.
NO MATTER WHAT YOU DO, IT ISN'T GONNA WORK.
SO GIVE ME BACK MY SHRIMP.
AGAIN WITH THE SHRIMP...
SHE'S RIGHT.
WE'VE BEEN LIVING TOGETHER ALL THIS TIME, AND NEVER FELT THAT WAY AT ALL, SO...
THERE'S NO WAY THESE LITTLE GAMES OF YOURS ARE GONNA CHANGE ANYTHING.
BUT YOU'RE ALREADY IN LOVE WITH EACH OTHER!
YOU JUST REFUSE TO ACCEPT IT!
IN LOVE?

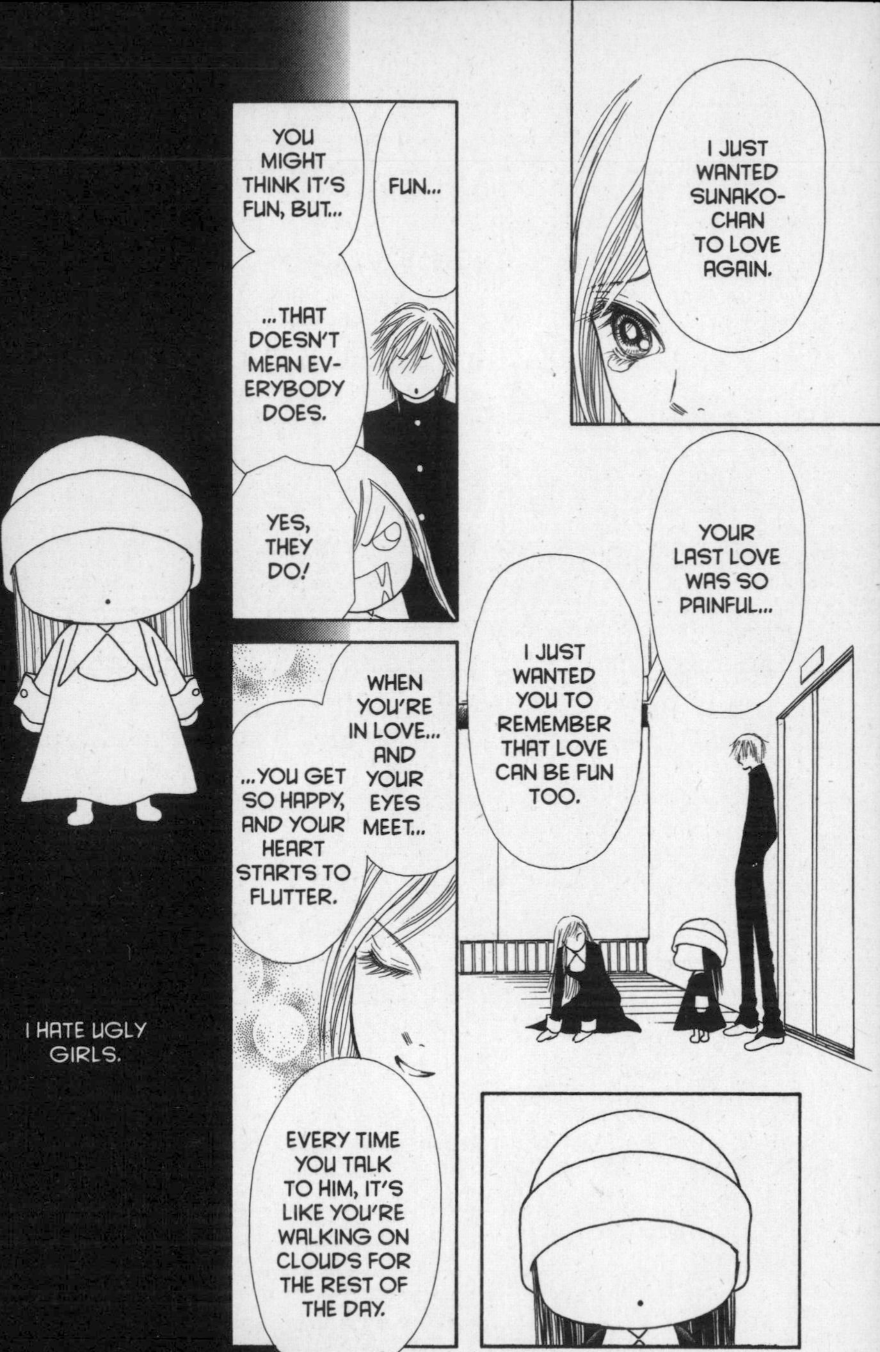
I JUST WANTED SUNAKO-CHAN TO LOVE AGAIN.
FUN...
YOU MIGHT THINK IT'S FUN, BUT...
...THAT DOESN'T MEAN EV-ERYBODY DOES.
YES, THEY DO!
YOUR LAST LOVE WAS SO PAINFUL...
I JUST WANTED YOU TO REMEMBER THAT LOVE CAN BE FUN TOO.
WHEN YOU'RE IN LOVE... AND YOUR EYES MEET...
...YOU GET SO HAPPY, AND YOUR HEART STARTS TO FLUTTER.
EVERY TIME YOU TALK TO HIM, IT'S LIKE YOU'RE WALKING ON CLOUDS FOR THE REST OF THE DAY.
I HATE UGLY GIRLS.

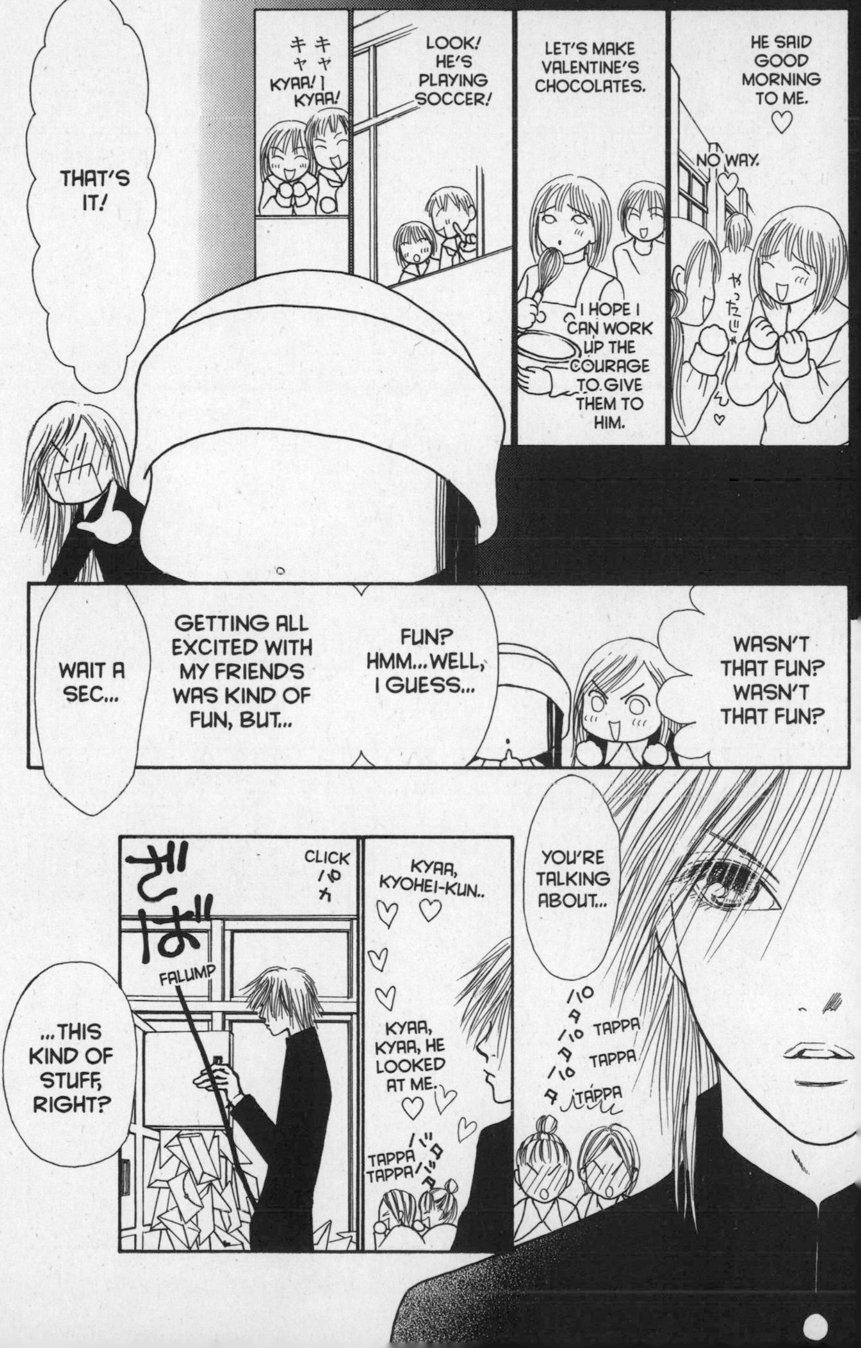
HE SAID GOOD MORNING TO ME. ♡
NO WAY. ♡
LET'S MAKE VALENTINE'S CHOCOLATES.
I HOPE I CAN WORK UP THE COURAGE TO GIVE THEM TO HIM.
LOOK! HE'S PLAYING SOCCER!
キャ キャ
KYAA! KYAA!
THAT'S IT!
WASN'T THAT FUN? WASN'T THAT FUN?
FUN? HMM...WELL, I GUESS...
GETTING ALL EXCITED WITH MY FRIENDS WAS KIND OF FUN, BUT...
WAIT A SEC...
YOU'RE TALKING ABOUT...
パタパタパタ
TAPPA TAPPA TAPPA
KYAA, KYOHEI-KUN..
KYAA, KYAA, HE LOOKED AT ME.
パタパタ
TAPPA TAPPA
CLICK
パカ
どば
FALUMP
...THIS KIND OF STUFF, RIGHT?

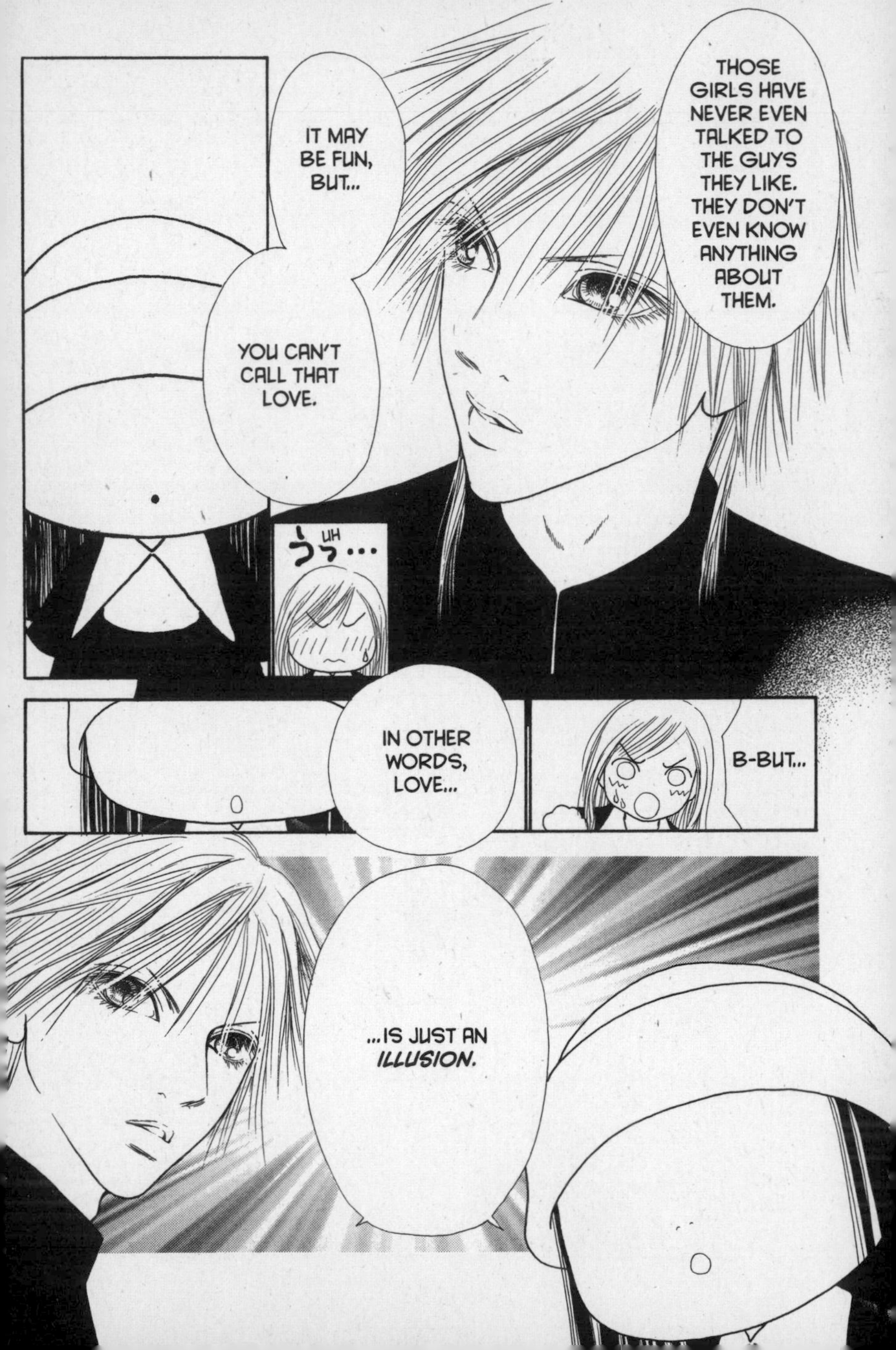
THOSE GIRLS HAVE NEVER EVEN TALKED TO THE GUYS THEY LIKE. THEY DON'T EVEN KNOW ANYTHING ABOUT THEM.
IT MAY BE FUN, BUT...
YOU CAN'T CALL THAT LOVE.
うっ… UH
B-BUT...
IN OTHER WORDS, LOVE...
...IS JUST AN *ILLUSION.*

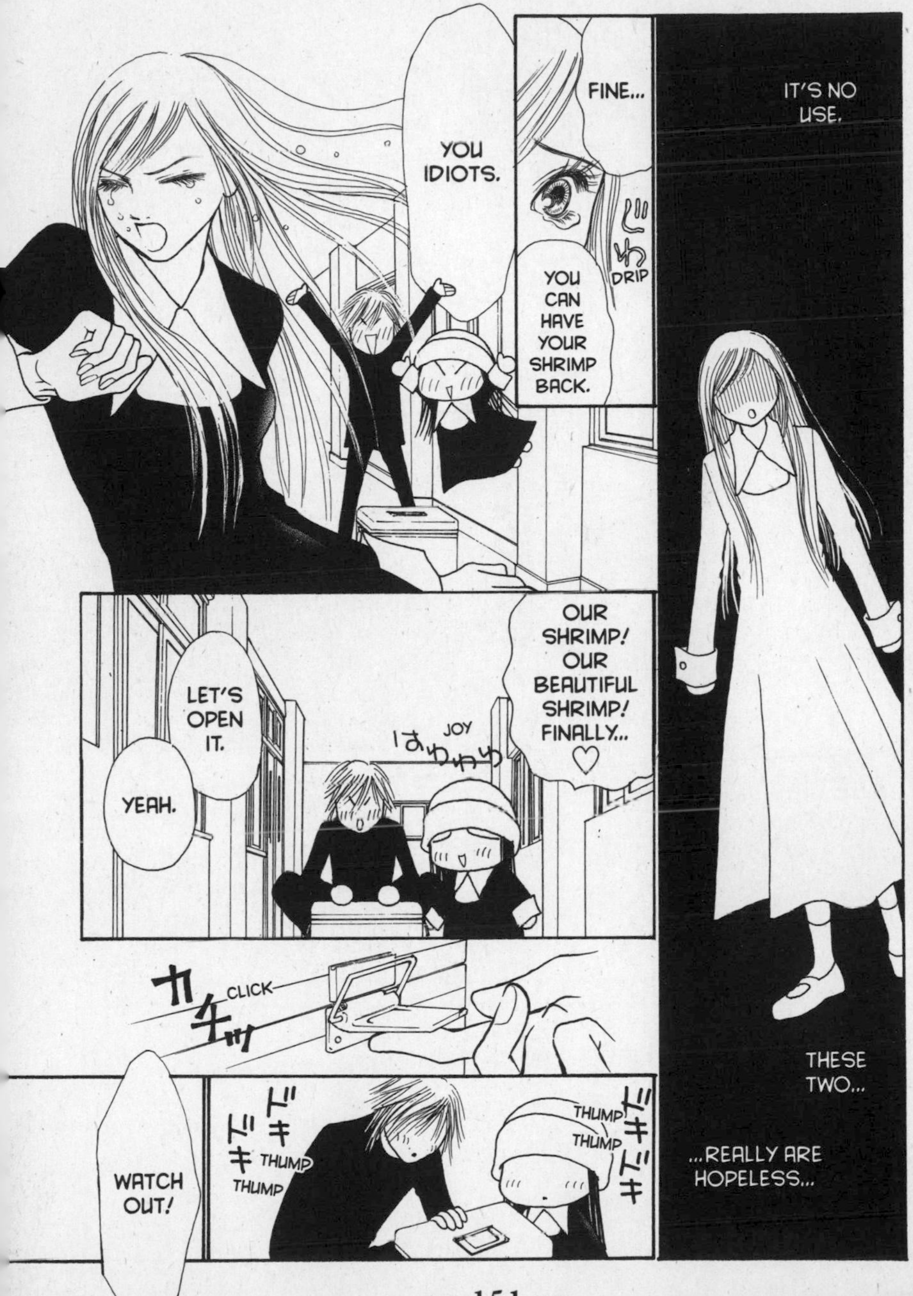
IT'S NO USE.
THESE TWO...
...REALLY ARE HOPELESS...
FINE...
じわ DRIP
YOU CAN HAVE YOUR SHRIMP BACK.
YOU IDIOTS.
OUR SHRIMP! OUR BEAUTIFUL SHRIMP! FINALLY... ♡
はわわわ JOY
LET'S OPEN IT.
YEAH.
カチッ CLICK
ドキドキ THUMP THUMP
ドキドキ THUMP THUMP
WATCH OUT!

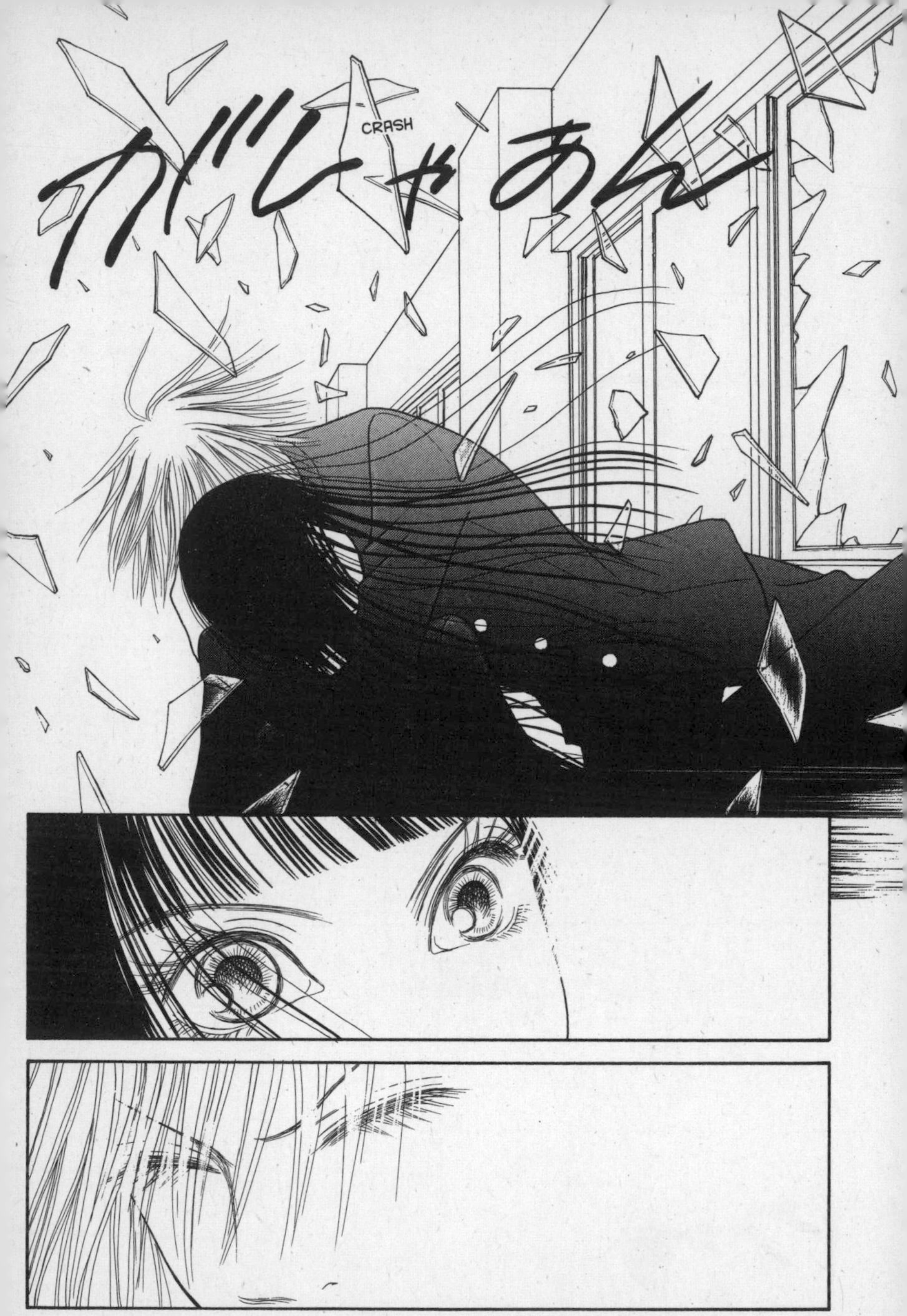
がしゃあん
CRASH

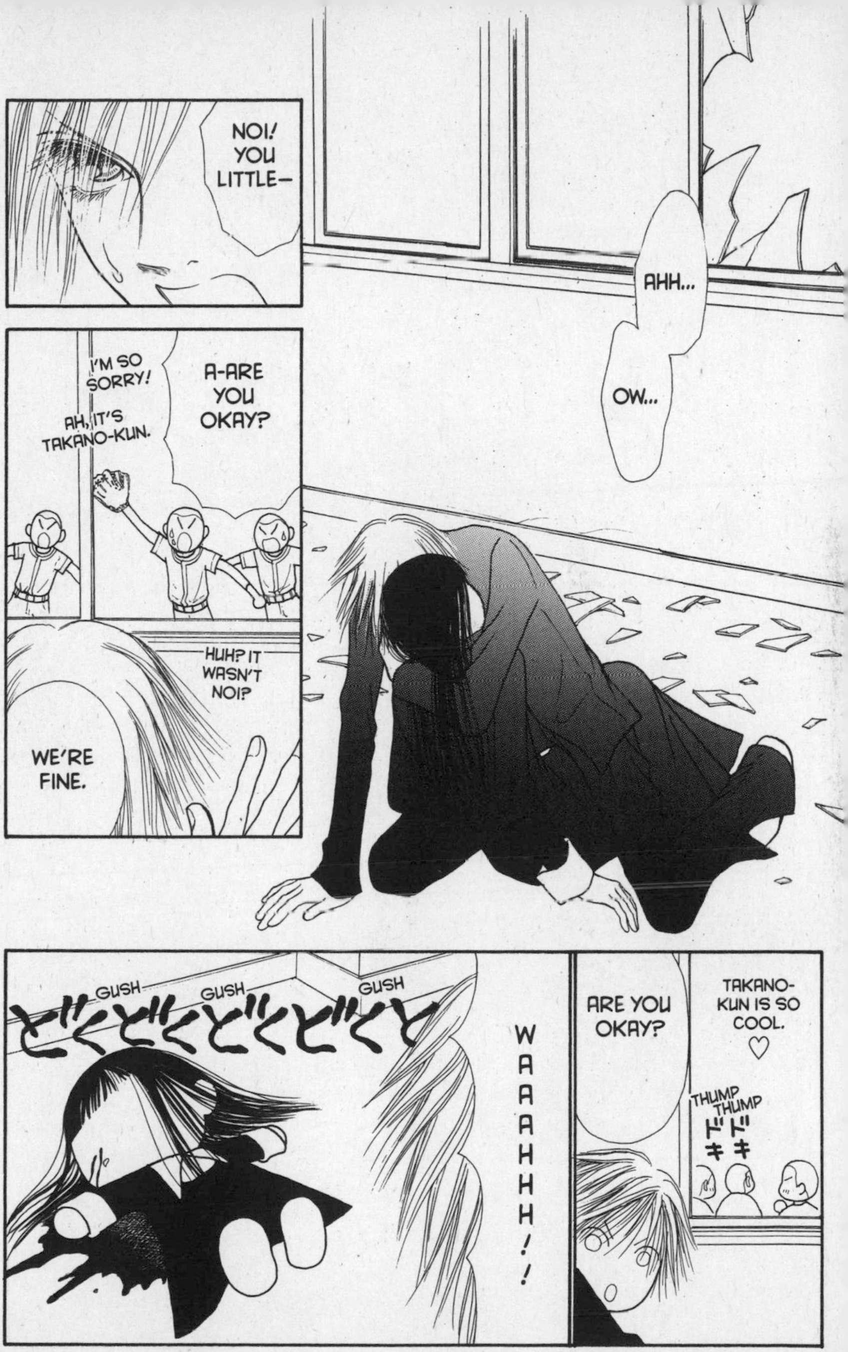
AHH...
OW...
NOI! YOU LITTLE–
A-ARE YOU OKAY?
I'M SO SORRY!
AH, IT'S TAKANO-KUN.
HUH? IT WASN'T NOI?
WE'RE FINE.
TAKANO-KUN IS SO COOL. ♡
ARE YOU OKAY?
THUMP THUMP
ドキドキ
WAAAAHHHH!!
GUSH GUSH GUSH
どくどくどくどくと

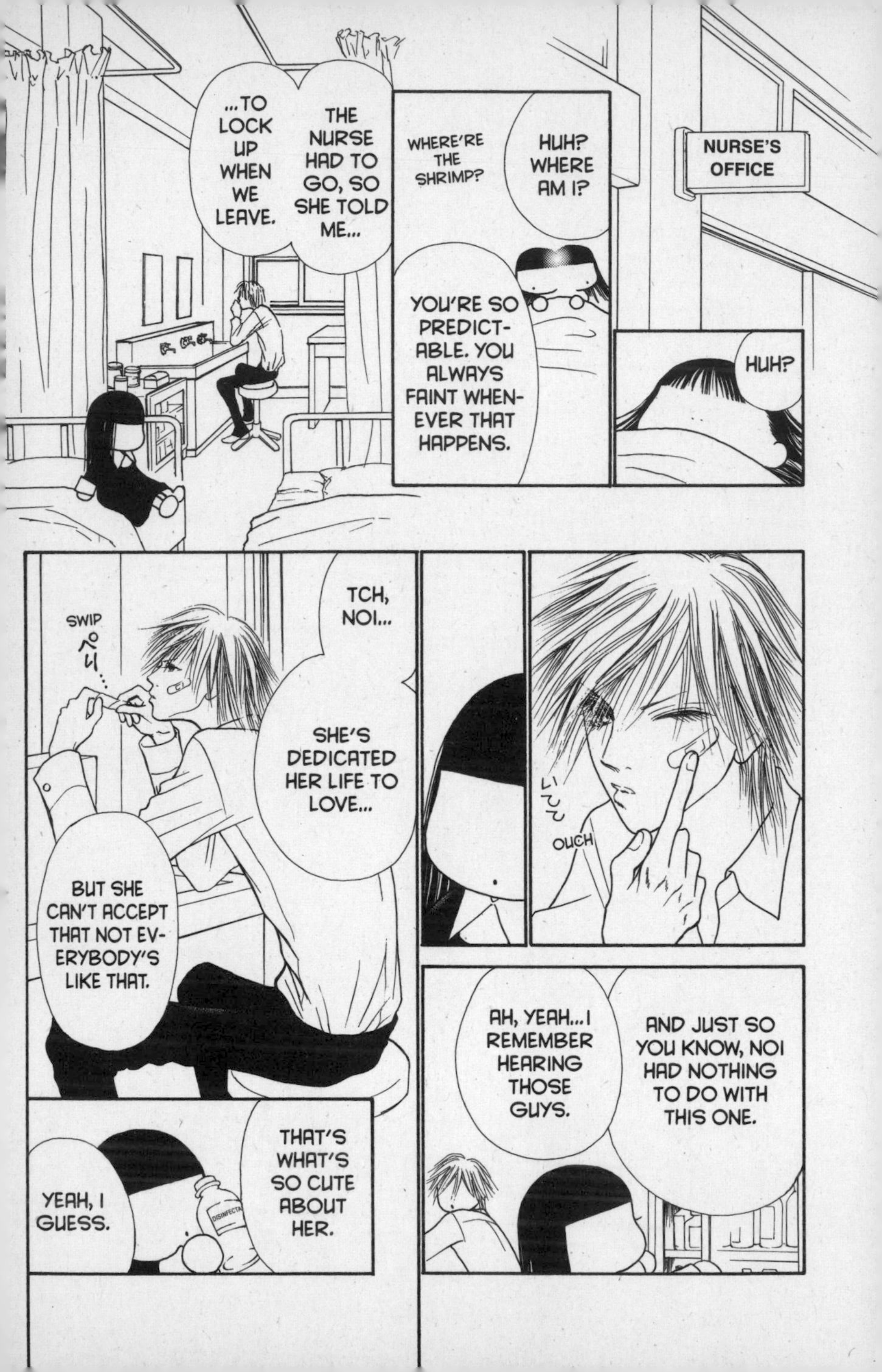
NURSE'S OFFICE
HUH?
HUH? WHERE AM I?
WHERE'RE THE SHRIMP?
YOU'RE SO PREDICTABLE. YOU ALWAYS FAINT WHENEVER THAT HAPPENS.
THE NURSE HAD TO GO, SO SHE TOLD ME...
...TO LOCK UP WHEN WE LEAVE.
OUCH
TCH, NOI...
SHE'S DEDICATED HER LIFE TO LOVE...
BUT SHE CAN'T ACCEPT THAT NOT EVERYBODY'S LIKE THAT.
SWIP
ぺり...
AND JUST SO YOU KNOW, NOI HAD NOTHING TO DO WITH THIS ONE.
AH, YEAH...I REMEMBER HEARING THOSE GUYS.
THAT'S WHAT'S SO CUTE ABOUT HER.
YEAH, I GUESS.
DISINFECTA

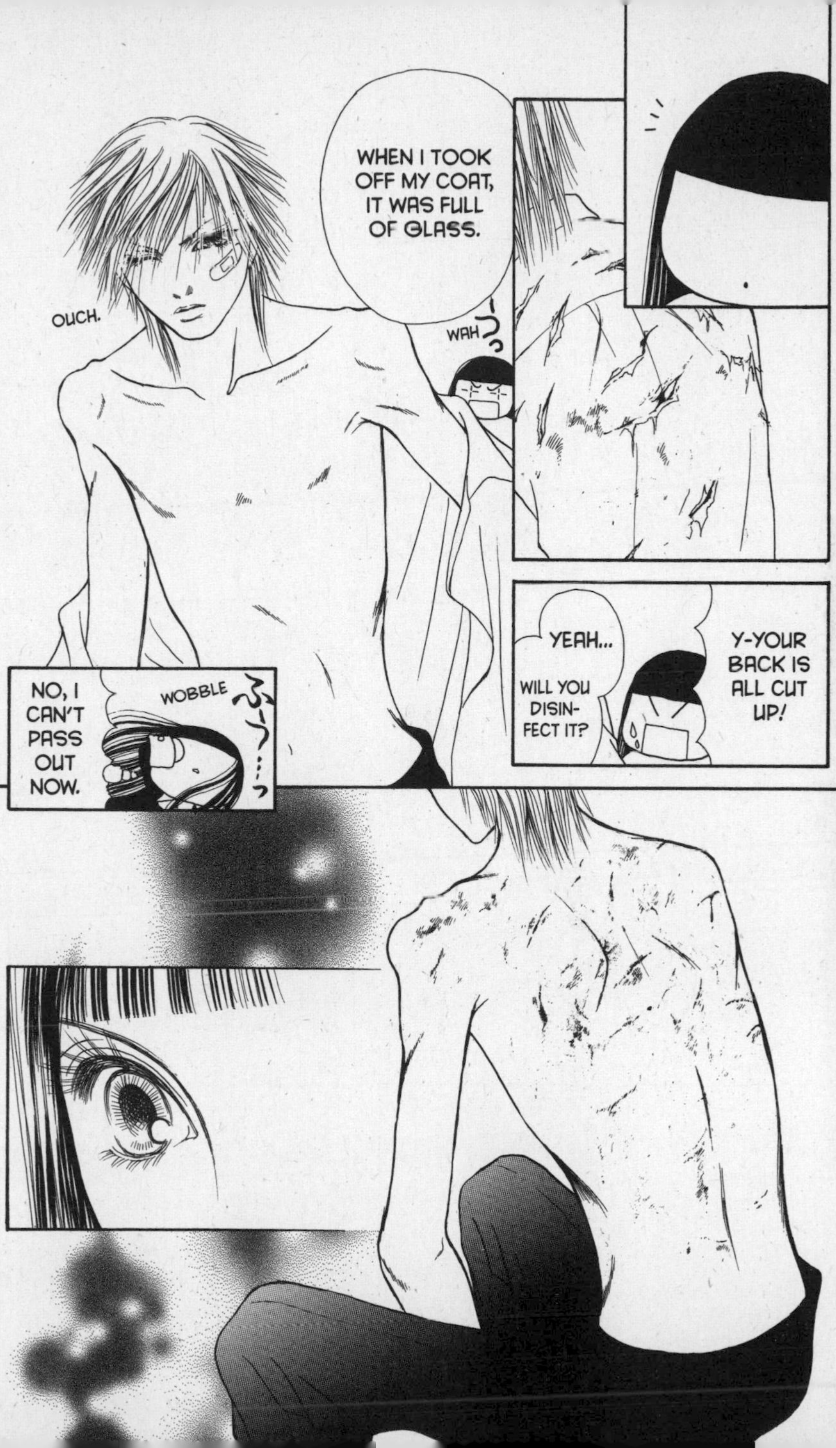
Y-YOUR BACK IS ALL CUT UP!
YEAH...
WILL YOU DISINFECT IT?
WHEN I TOOK OFF MY COAT, IT WAS FULL OF GLASS.
WAH
OUCH.
WOBBLE
NO, I CAN'T PASS OUT NOW.

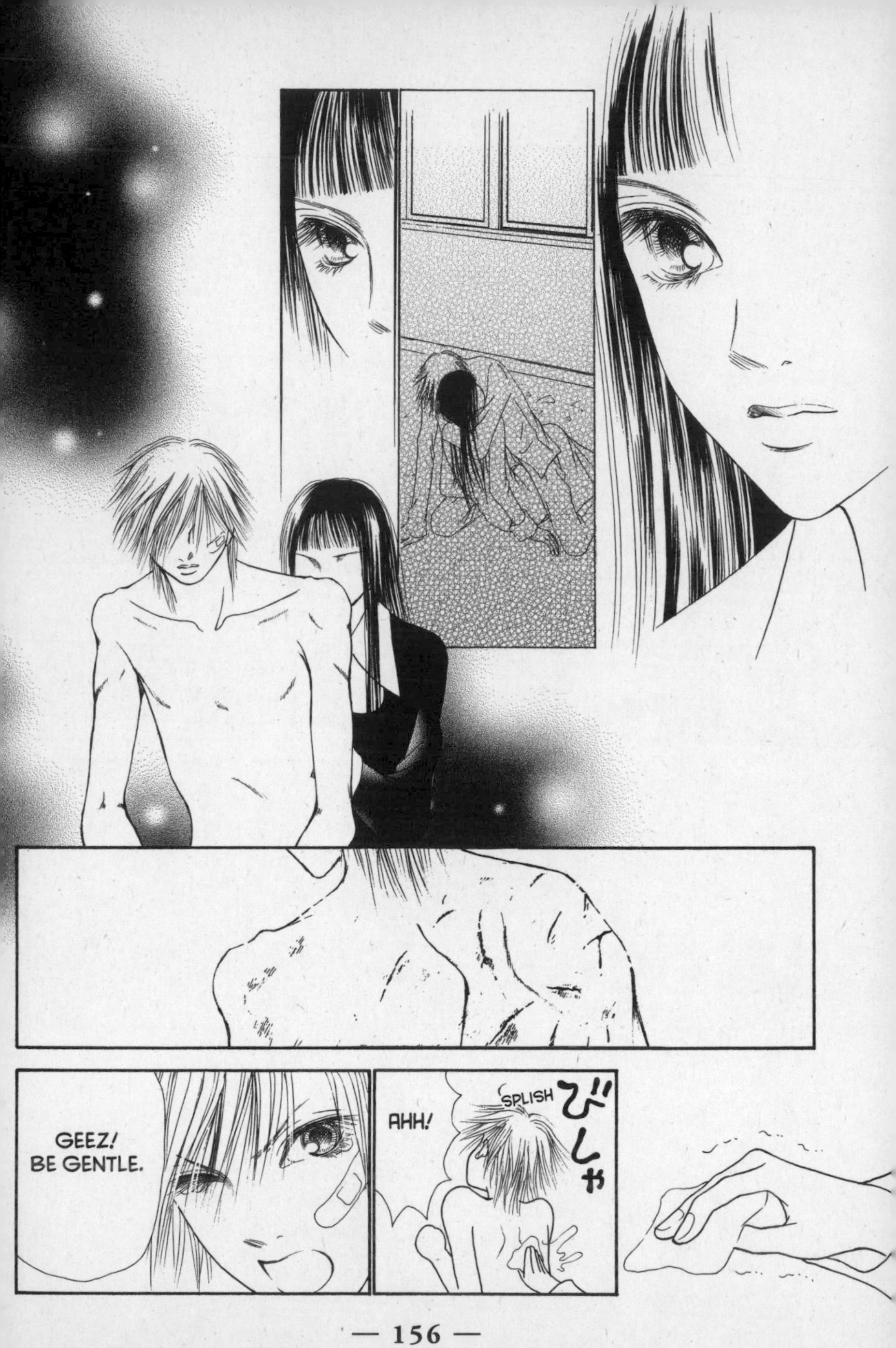
びしゃ
SPLISH
AHH!
GEEZ!
BE GENTLE.

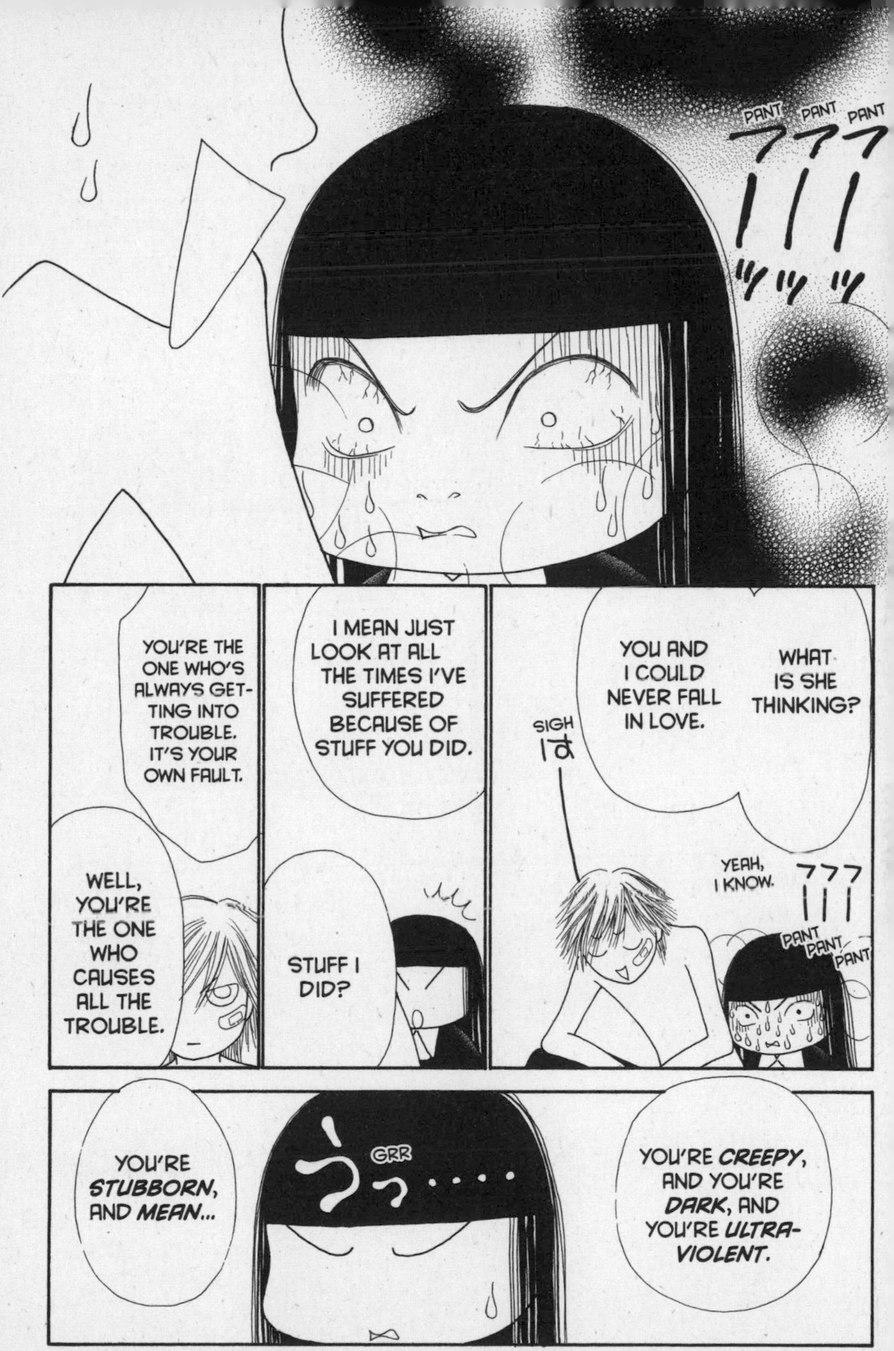
PANT PANT PANT
WHAT IS SHE THINKING?
YOU AND I COULD NEVER FALL IN LOVE.
SIGH は
YEAH, I KNOW.
PANT PANT PANT
I MEAN JUST LOOK AT ALL THE TIMES I'VE SUFFERED BECAUSE OF STUFF YOU DID.
STUFF I DID?
YOU'RE THE ONE WHO'S ALWAYS GET-TING INTO TROUBLE. IT'S YOUR OWN FAULT.
WELL, YOU'RE THE ONE WHO CAUSES ALL THE TROUBLE.
YOU'RE *CREEPY*, AND YOU'RE *DARK*, AND YOU'RE *ULTRA-VIOLENT*.
GRR
うっ....
YOU'RE *STUBBORN*, AND *MEAN*...

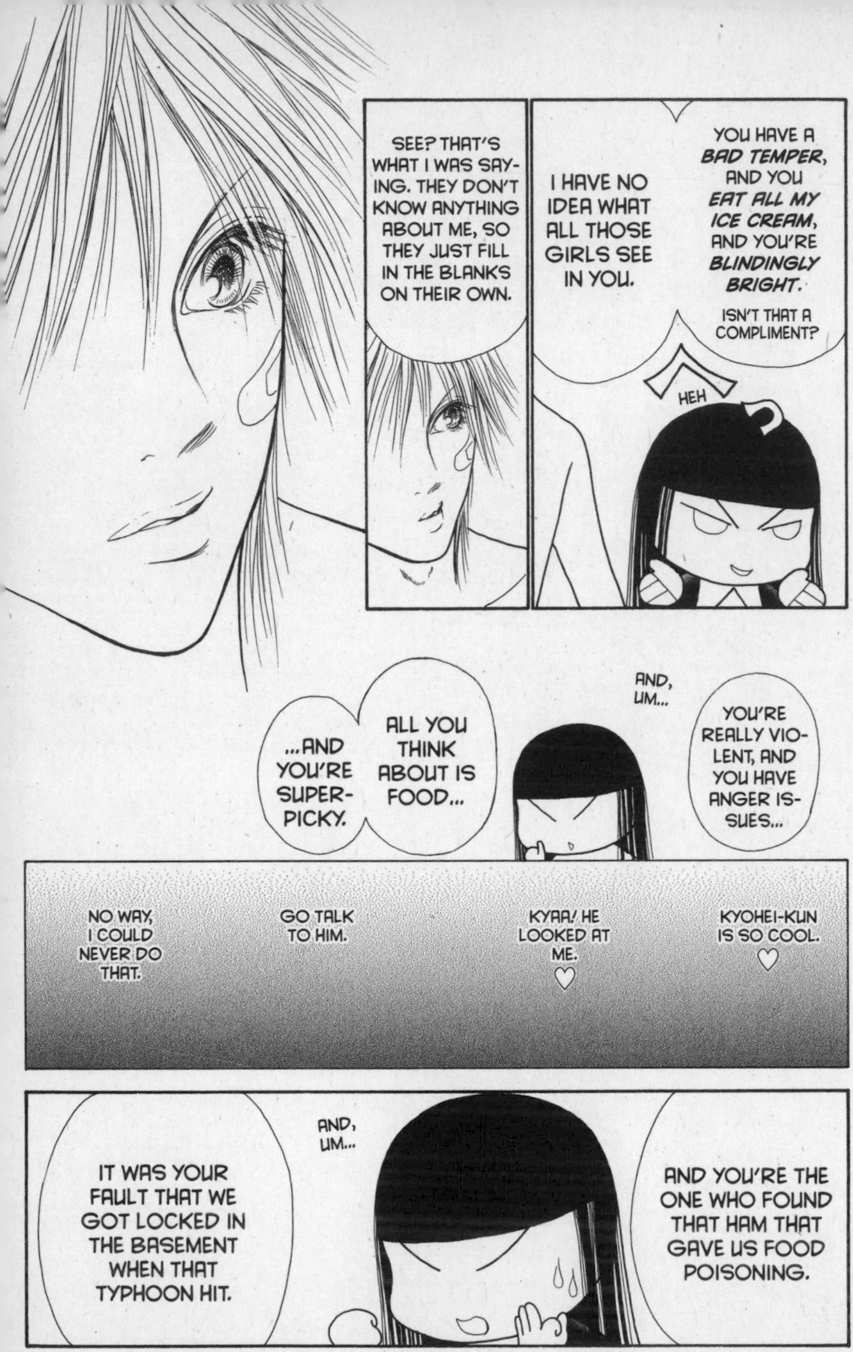
YOU HAVE A BAD TEMPER, AND YOU EAT ALL MY ICE CREAM, AND YOU'RE BLINDINGLY BRIGHT.
I HAVE NO IDEA WHAT ALL THOSE GIRLS SEE IN YOU.
ISN'T THAT A COMPLIMENT?
HEH
SEE? THAT'S WHAT I WAS SAY-ING. THEY DON'T KNOW ANYTHING ABOUT ME, SO THEY JUST FILL IN THE BLANKS ON THEIR OWN.
YOU'RE REALLY VIO-LENT, AND YOU HAVE ANGER IS-SUES...
AND, UM...
ALL YOU THINK ABOUT IS FOOD...
...AND YOU'RE SUPER-PICKY.
KYOHEI-KUN IS SO COOL. ♡
KYAA! HE LOOKED AT ME. ♡
GO TALK TO HIM.
NO WAY, I COULD NEVER DO THAT.
AND YOU'RE THE ONE WHO FOUND THAT HAM THAT GAVE US FOOD POISONING.
AND, UM...
IT WAS YOUR FAULT THAT WE GOT LOCKED IN THE BASEMENT WHEN THAT TYPHOON HIT.

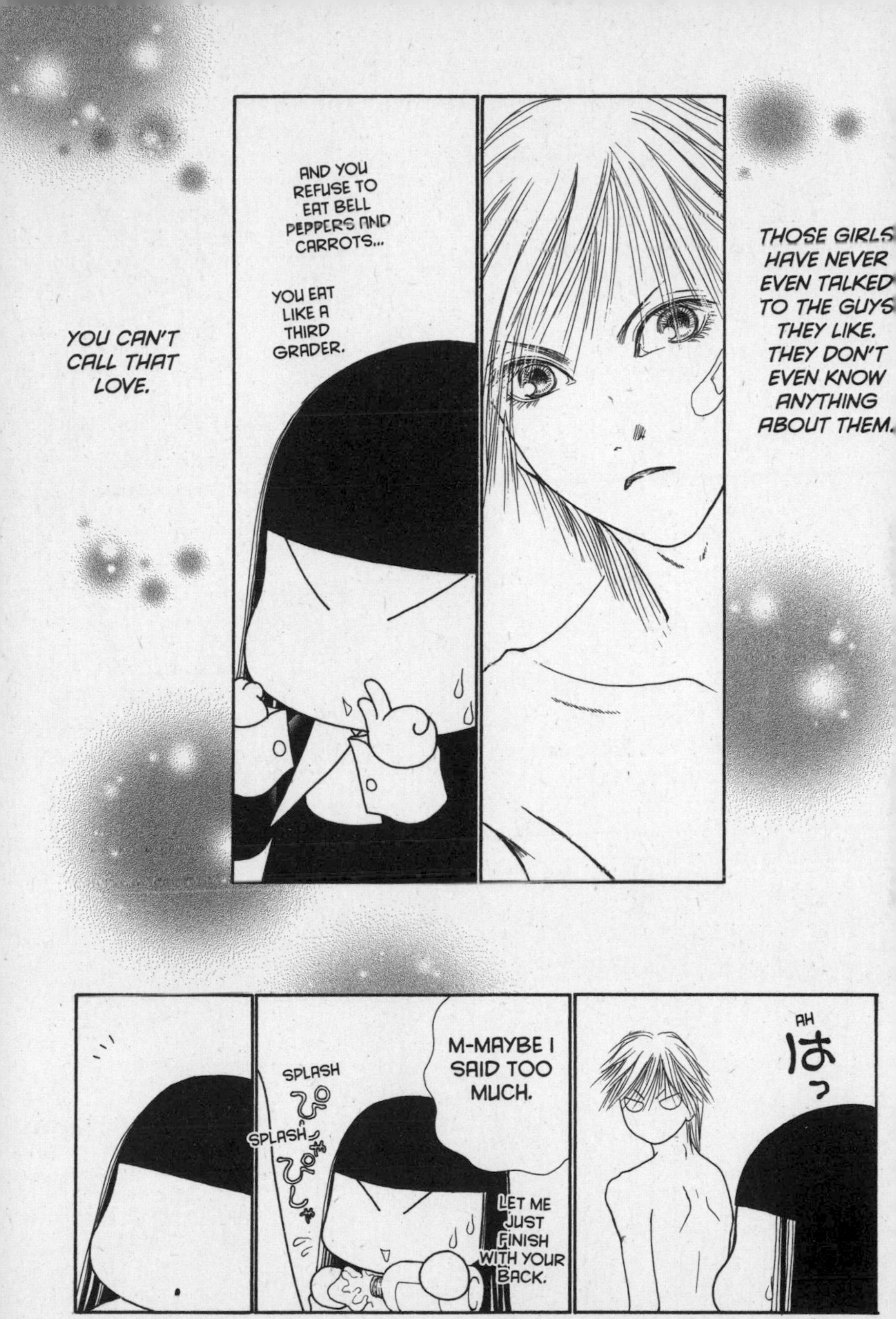
THOSE GIRLS HAVE NEVER EVEN TALKED TO THE GUYS THEY LIKE. THEY DON'T EVEN KNOW ANYTHING ABOUT THEM.
AND YOU REFUSE TO EAT BELL PEPPERS AND CARROTS...
YOU EAT LIKE A THIRD GRADER.
YOU CAN'T CALL THAT LOVE.
AH
はっ
M-MAYBE I SAID TOO MUCH.
SPLASH
ぴ
SPLASH
ぴしゃ
LET ME JUST FINISH WITH YOUR BACK.

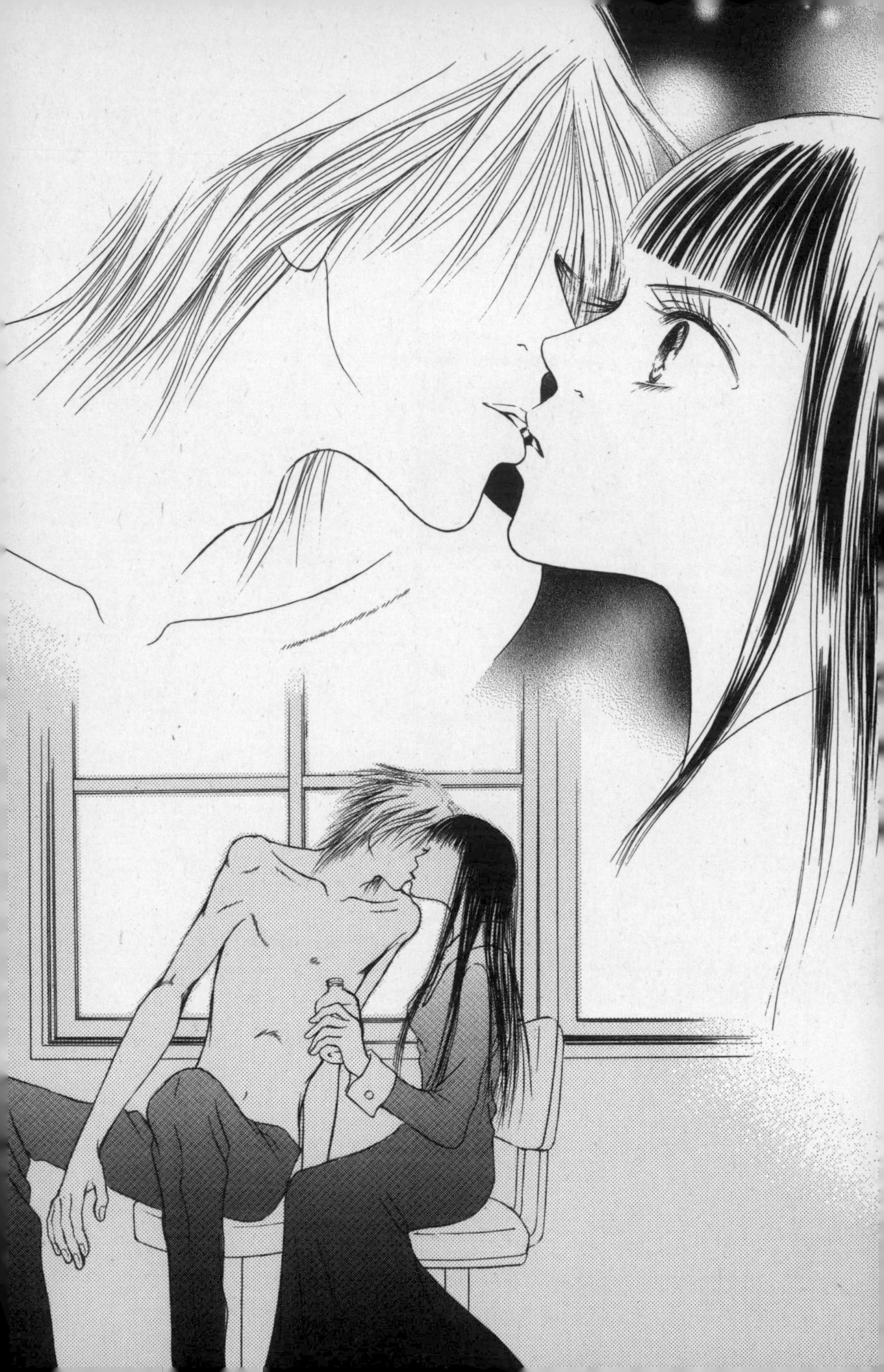

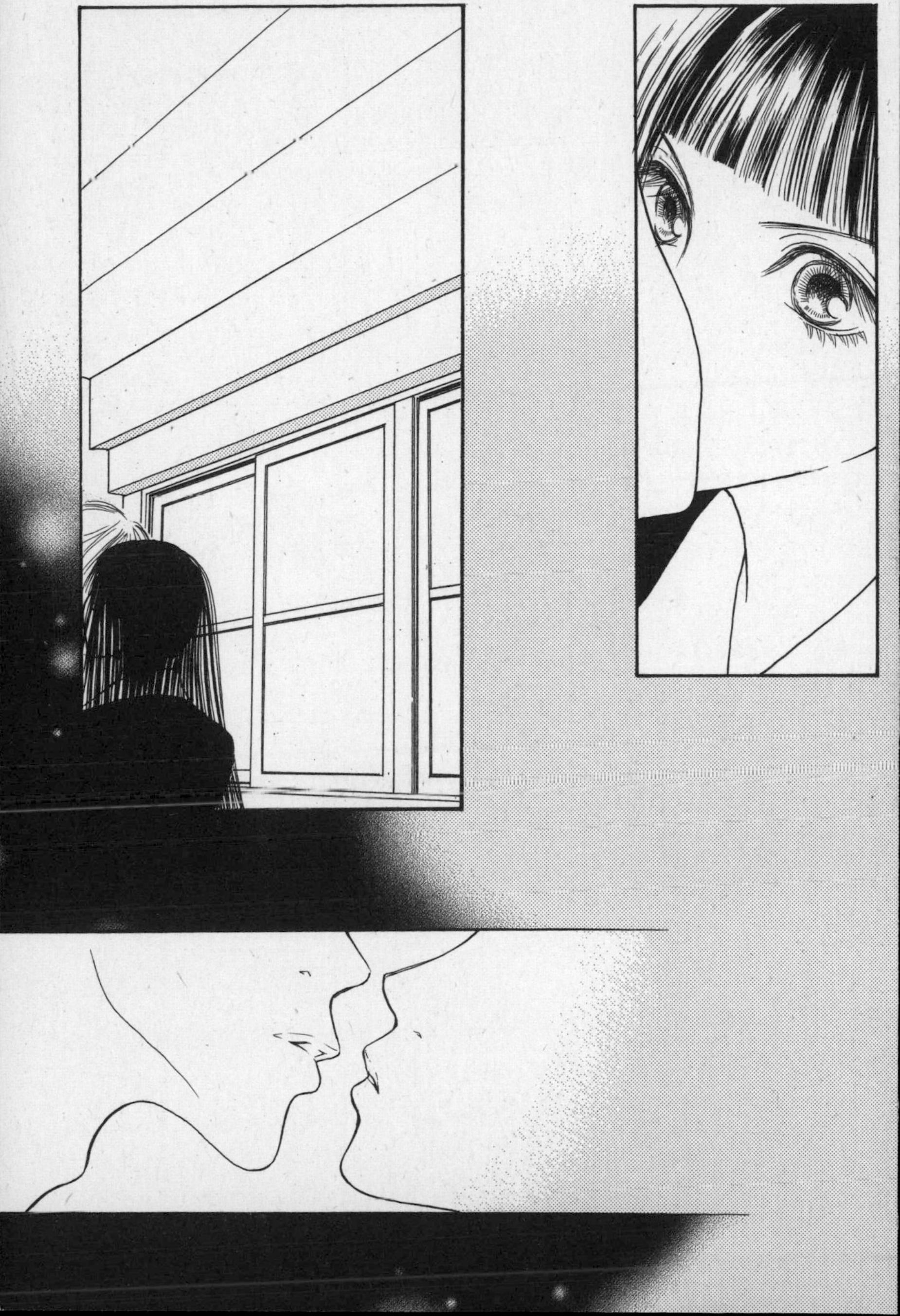

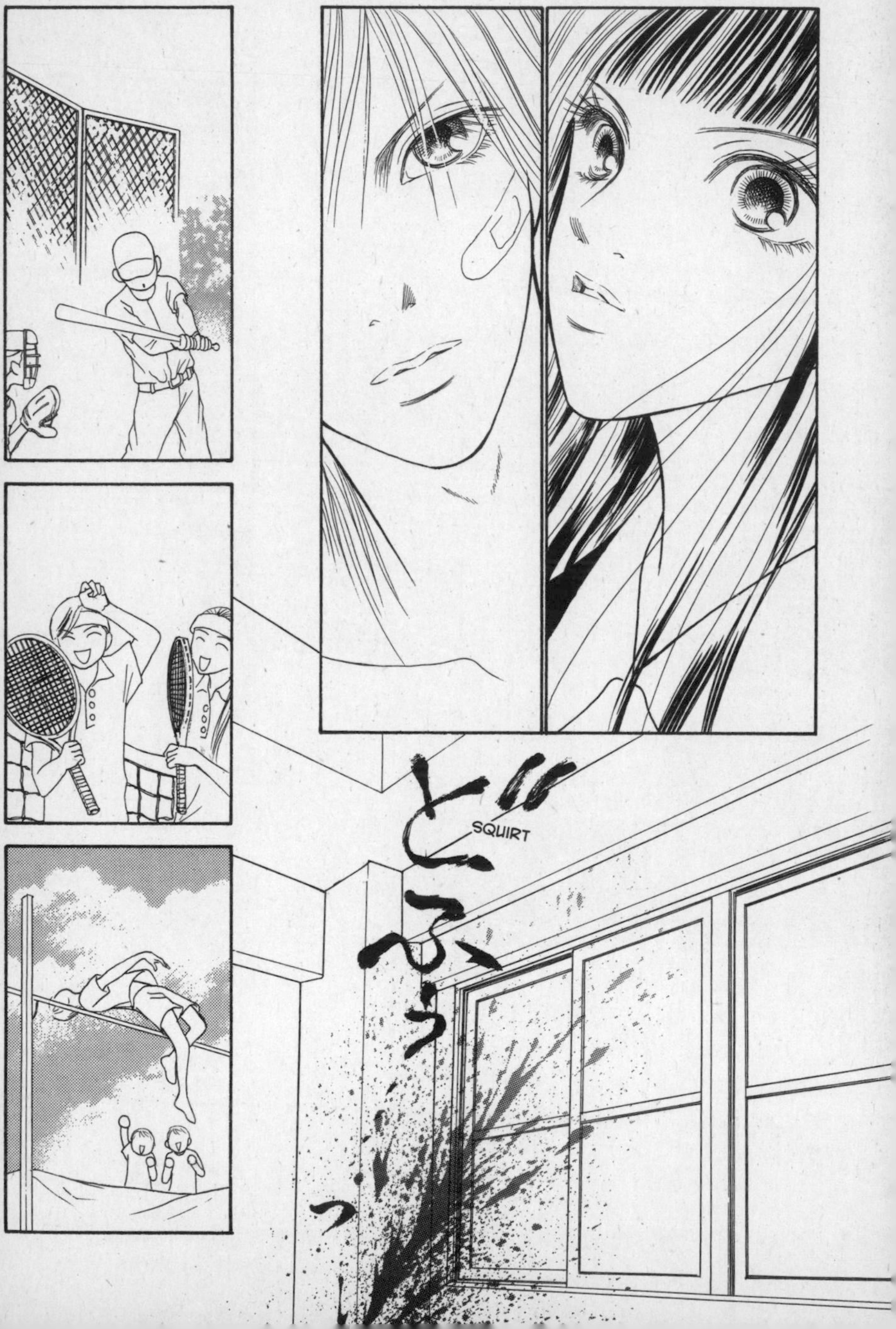
SQUIRT

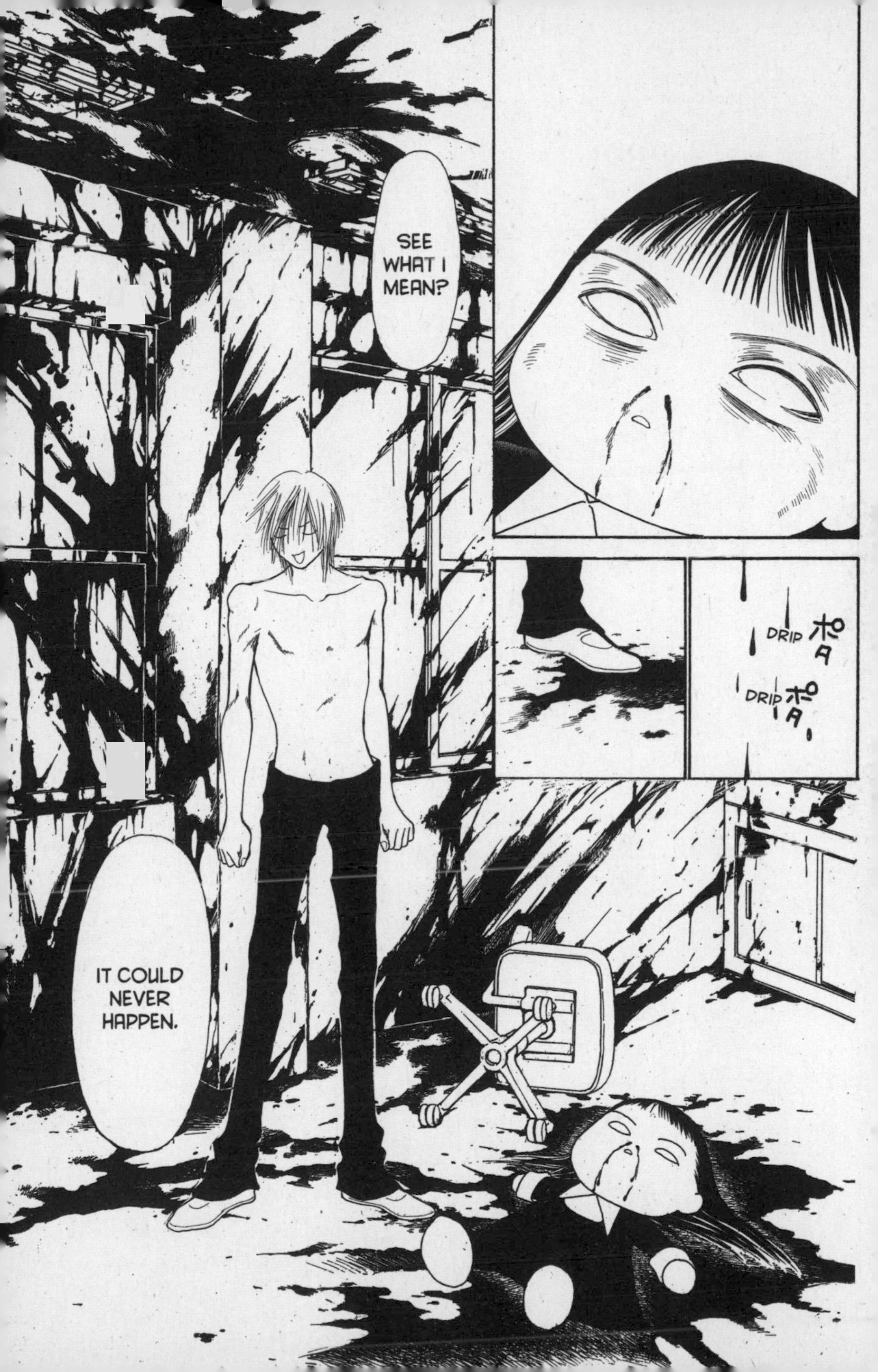
DRIP ポタ
DRIP ポタ
SEE WHAT I MEAN?
IT COULD NEVER HAPPEN.

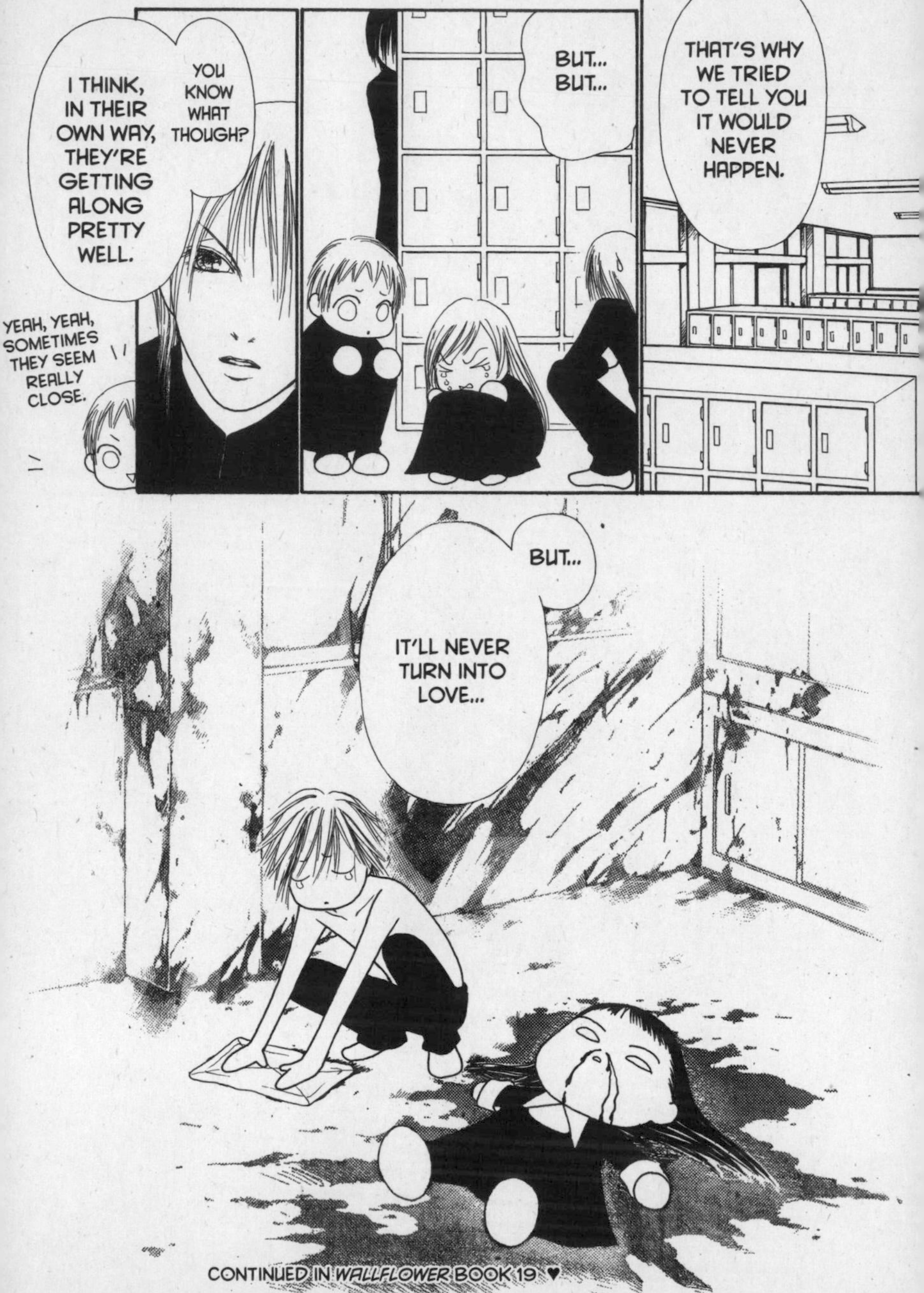
THAT'S WHY WE TRIED TO TELL YOU IT WOULD NEVER HAPPEN.
BUT... BUT...
YOU KNOW WHAT THOUGH?
I THINK, IN THEIR OWN WAY, THEY'RE GETTING ALONG PRETTY WELL.
YEAH, YEAH, SOMETIMES THEY SEEM REALLY CLOSE.
BUT...
IT'LL NEVER TURN INTO LOVE...

CONTINUED IN *WALLFLOWER* BOOK 19 ♥

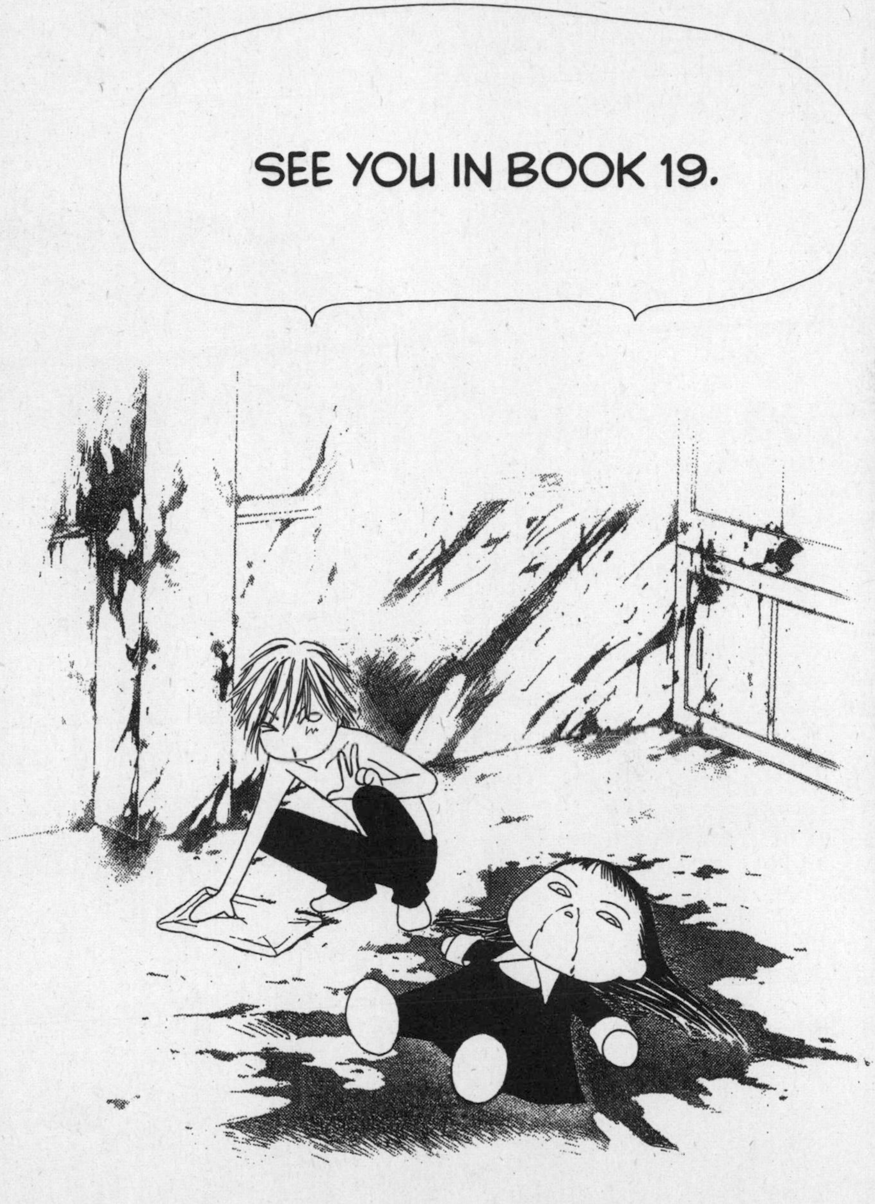
SEE YOU IN BOOK 19.

2/9/07 KIYOHARU-SAMA DID A SPECIAL CONCERT FOR HIS FAN CLUB MEMBERS, AND I GOT TO GO. ♡♡♡

I'D BEEN TOO BUSY WITH WORK TO GO TO ANY SHOWS, SO IT WAS MY FIRST CONCERT IN A WHILE. (EVEN THAT NIGHT, I WAS LATE TO THE CONCERT BECAUSE OF WORK.) SO I ENDED UP MISSING HIS PERFORMANCE OF THE SONG "ICE MY LIFE" WHICH HE ALMOST NEVER DOES LIVE. WAHH . . . I REALLY WANTED TO HEAR IT.

SAID IT BEFORE, AND I'LL SAY T AGAIN. HE'LL ALWAYS BE THE HOTTEST MAN ON EARTH. ♡ HE'S A GOD. ♡

USUALLY YOUR FAVORITE SINGER WILL CHANGE EVERY FEW YEARS, BUT NOT FOR ME. (IS IT JUST ME?) I'VE LIKED KIYOHARU FOR 10 YEARS, AND I'M STILL GOING STRONG.

HE'S THE HOTTEST MAN ON THE PLANET. ♡ ♡ ♡

HE LOOKS GREAT IN MAGAZINES AND ON TV, BUT HE'S AT HIS BEST WHEN HE'S ***LIVE IN CONCERT***. ♡ ♡ ♡

CAN'T BELIEVE HE RECORDED THE THEME MUSIC FOR MY ANIME. I MUST BE THE HAPPIEST PERSON ON EARTH. I'M SO GLAD I BECAME A MANGA ARTIST. ♡

JUST DRAWING PICTURES LIKE THIS ONE IS ENOUGH TO MAKE ME HAPPY.

NISHIOKA-SAN FROM FULL FACE REALLY HELPED ME OUT, AND NOW NISHIOKA-SAN IS QUITTING. I'LL BE SO LONESOME.

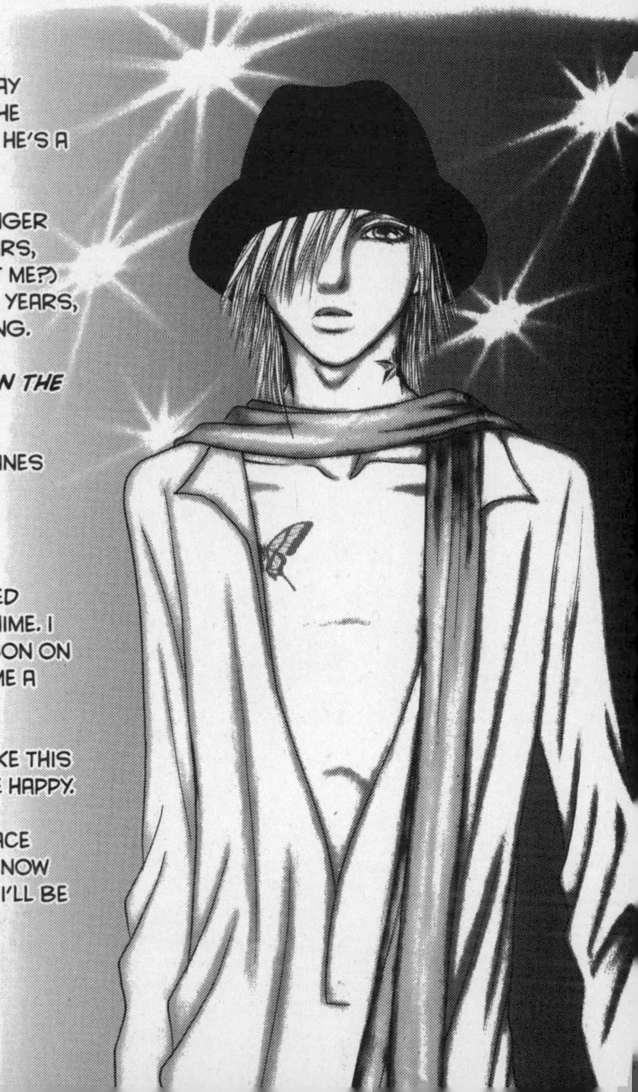

THANK YOU FOR BUYING KODANSHA COMICS ♡♡♡

AS ALWAYS, I'M FIGHTING AN EPIC BATTLE AGAINST MY BODY FAT.

AS ALWAYS, I'M KITTY CRAZY.

THANK YOU SO MUCH FOR ALL YOUR LETTERS. ♡
THEY ARE THE SOURCE OF MY POWER. ♡
I TRULY TREASURE THEM. ♡

WHEN I HAVE ENOUGH PAGES, I HOPE TO ANSWER ALL YOUR QUESTIONS. I HOPE YOU'LL STICK AROUND TILL THAT DAY.

SPECIAL THANKS

CHUBI-SAN-SAMA
TOMMY-SAMA
NABEKO-SAMA

IYU KOZAKURA-SAMA

MINE-SAMA
INO-SAMA
INNAN-SAMA
EVERYBODY IN THE EDITING DEPARTMENT

EVERYONE WHO'S READING THIS RIGHT NOW

About the Creator

Tomoko Hayakawa was born on March 4.

Since her debut as a manga creator, Tomoko Hayakawa has worked
on many shojo titles with the theme of romantic love—only to realize
that she could write about other subjects as well. She decided to pack
her newest story with the things she likes most, which led to her current,
enormously popular series, *The Wallflower*.

Her favorite things are: Tim Burton's *The Nightmare Before Christmas*,
Jean-Paul Gaultier, and samurai dramas on TV. Her hobbies are collecting
items with skull designs and watching bishonen (beautiful boys). Her
dream is to build a mansion like the one the Addams family lives in. Her
favorite pastime is to lie around at home with her cat, Ten (whose full
name is Tennosuke).

Her zodiac sign is Pisces, and her blood group is AB.

Translation Notes

Japanese is a tricky language for most Westerners, and translation is often more art than science. For your edification and reading pleasure, here are notes on some of the places where we could have gone in a different direction in our translation of the work, or where a Japanese cultural reference is used.

Floor lady, page 11

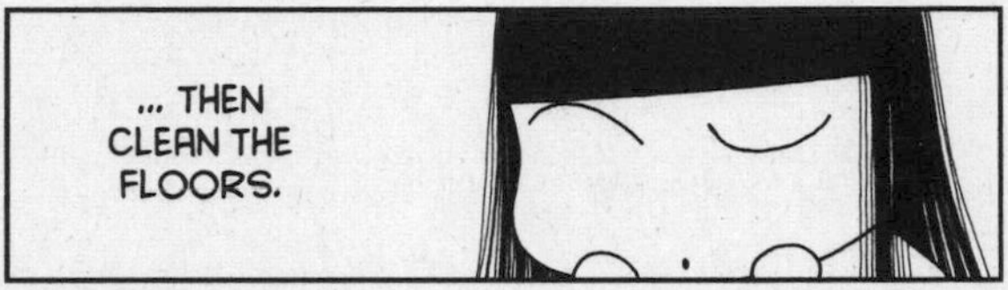
... THEN CLEAN THE FLOORS.

The Japanese term that Sunako is reading in the classifieds is actually "floor girl." This is a term for a club hostess that Sunako mistakenly believes refers to the girl who cleans the floor.

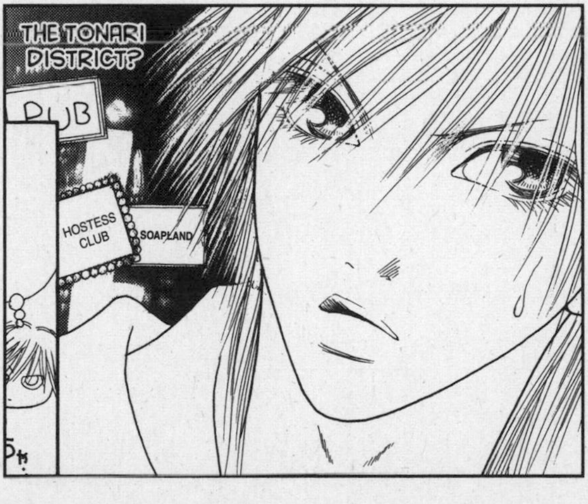
THE TONARI DISTRICT?
CLUB
HOSTESS CLUB
SOAPLAND

Red Light Districts, page 19

The Tonari district is supposed to be a red light district. The signs Kyohei is imagining illustrate what you might see in one of Japan's red light areas.

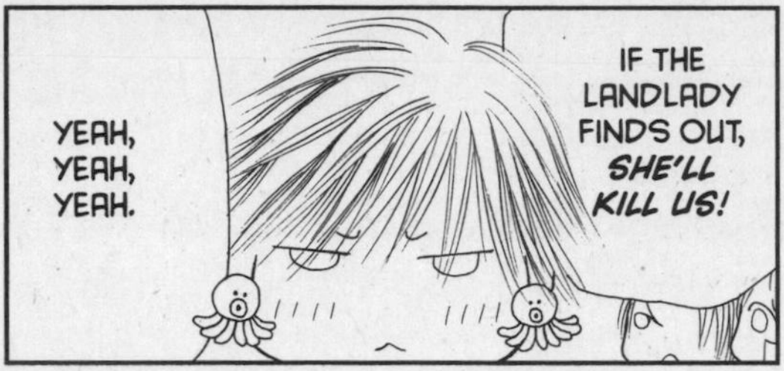
IF THE LANDLADY FINDS OUT, SHE'LL KILL US!
YEAH, YEAH, YEAH.

Octopus Ears, page 28

In Japanese the phrase "*mimi ni tako ga dekiru*" (literally to grow calluses on one's ears) is used to express the feeling of having been told something over and over again. "*Tako*" means callus, but when written with different kanji, it can also mean octopus. In this scene, Kyohei is tired of hearing the guy's complaining over and over, and so he has grown octopi on his ears. It's a common visual pun used in manga.

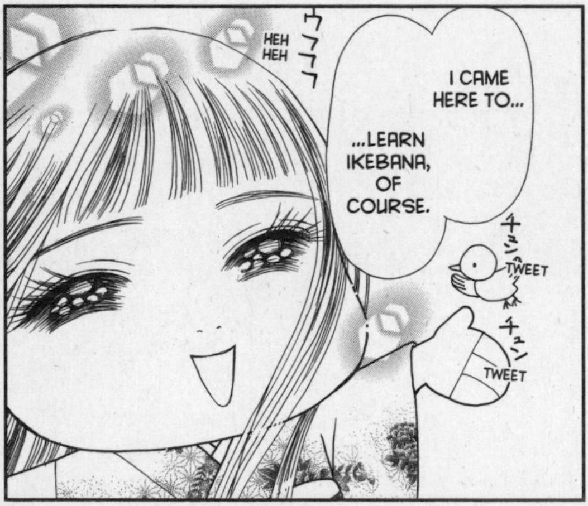
ウフフフ
HEH HEH
I CAME HERE TO...
...LEARN IKEBANA, OF COURSE.
チュン
TWEET
チュン
TWEET

Ikebana, page 47

Ikebana is the art of flower arrangement, a deeply respected art in Japan.

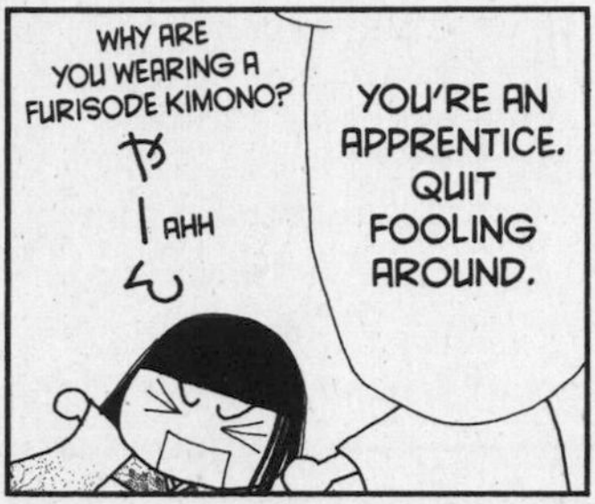
YOU'RE AN APPRENTICE. QUIT FOOLING AROUND.
WHY ARE YOU WEARING A FURISODE KIMONO?
AHH

Furisode kimono, page 51

A furisode kimono is a brightly colored, formal women's kimono usually worn for celebrations such as weddings or coming-of-age ceremonies.

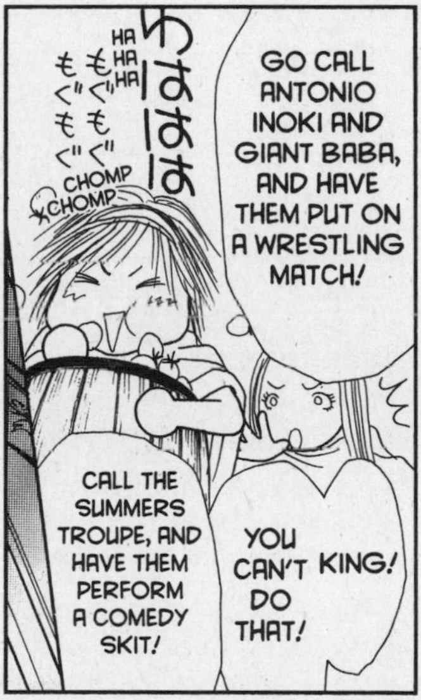
GO CALL ANTONIO INOKI AND GIANT BABA, AND HAVE THEM PUT ON A WRESTLING MATCH!
わははは
HA HA HA
もぐもぐ もぐもぐ
CHOMP CHOMP
KING!
YOU CAN'T DO THAT!
CALL THE SUMMERS TROUPE, AND HAVE THEM PERFORM A COMEDY SKIT!

Pro Wrestling, page 116

Giant Baba and Antonio Inoki were famous Japanese professional wrestlers. Inoki later became a politician.

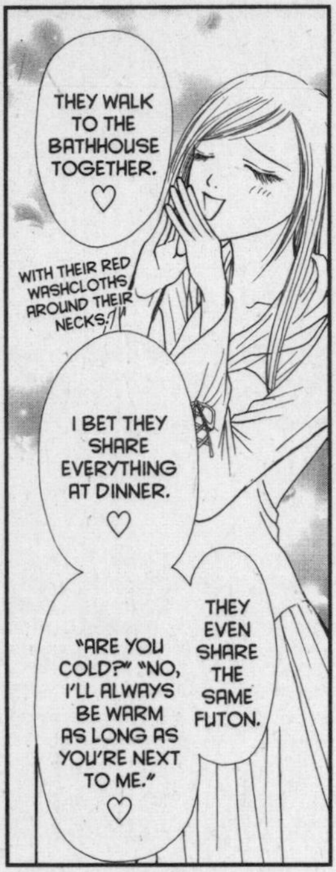
THEY WALK TO THE BATHHOUSE TOGETHER. ♡
WITH THEIR RED WASHCLOTHS AROUND THEIR NECKS.
I BET THEY SHARE EVERYTHING AT DINNER. ♡
THEY EVEN SHARE THE SAME FUTON.
"ARE YOU COLD?" "NO, I'LL ALWAYS BE WARM AS LONG AS YOU'RE NEXT TO ME." ♡

Kandagawa, page 126

Noi-chan is making a reference to a famous song by Kousetsu Minami. It's a romantic song about a poor, young couple. One verse in particular mentions them walking to the public bath with red washcloths around their necks.

Sukiyaki and Shabu Shabu, page 128

These are both beef hot pot dishes that are cooked at the table, family style. Sukiyaki is beef, veggies, and tofu boiled together in broth. Shabu Shabu consists of the same ingredients, but they are placed in a pot of boiling water briefly, and then dipped in sauce, as opposed to being cooked like a stew.

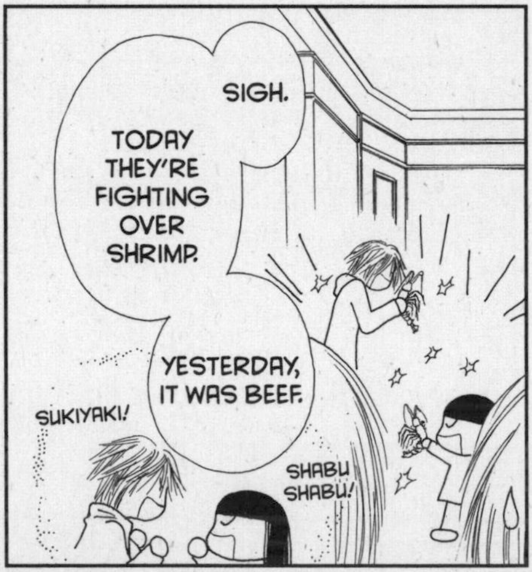
SIGH.
TODAY THEY'RE FIGHTING OVER SHRIMP.
YESTERDAY, IT WAS BEEF.
SHABU SHABU!
SUKIYAKI!

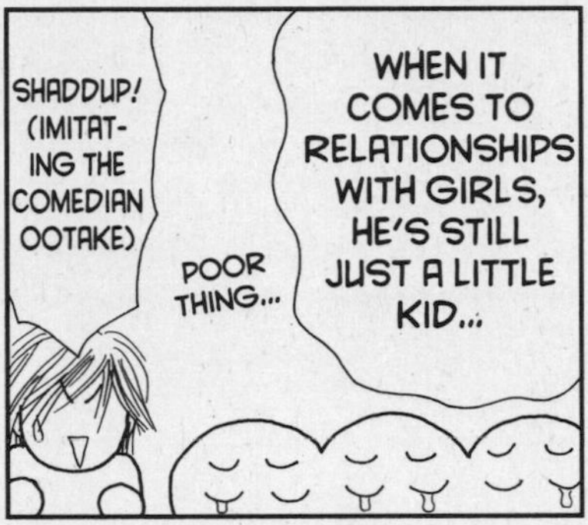
WHEN IT COMES TO RELATIONSHIPS WITH GIRLS, HE'S STILL JUST A LITTLE KID...
POOR THING...
SHADDUP! (IMITATING THE COMEDIAN OOTAKE)

Summers, page 135

Ootake is a member of the sketch comedy troupe Summers. Hayakawa makes references to Summers in nearly every volume of *Wallflower*. She must be a big fan.

Preview of Volume 19

We're pleased to present you a preview from volume 19. Please check our website (www.delreymanga.com) to see when this volume will be available in English. For now you'll have to make do with Japanese!

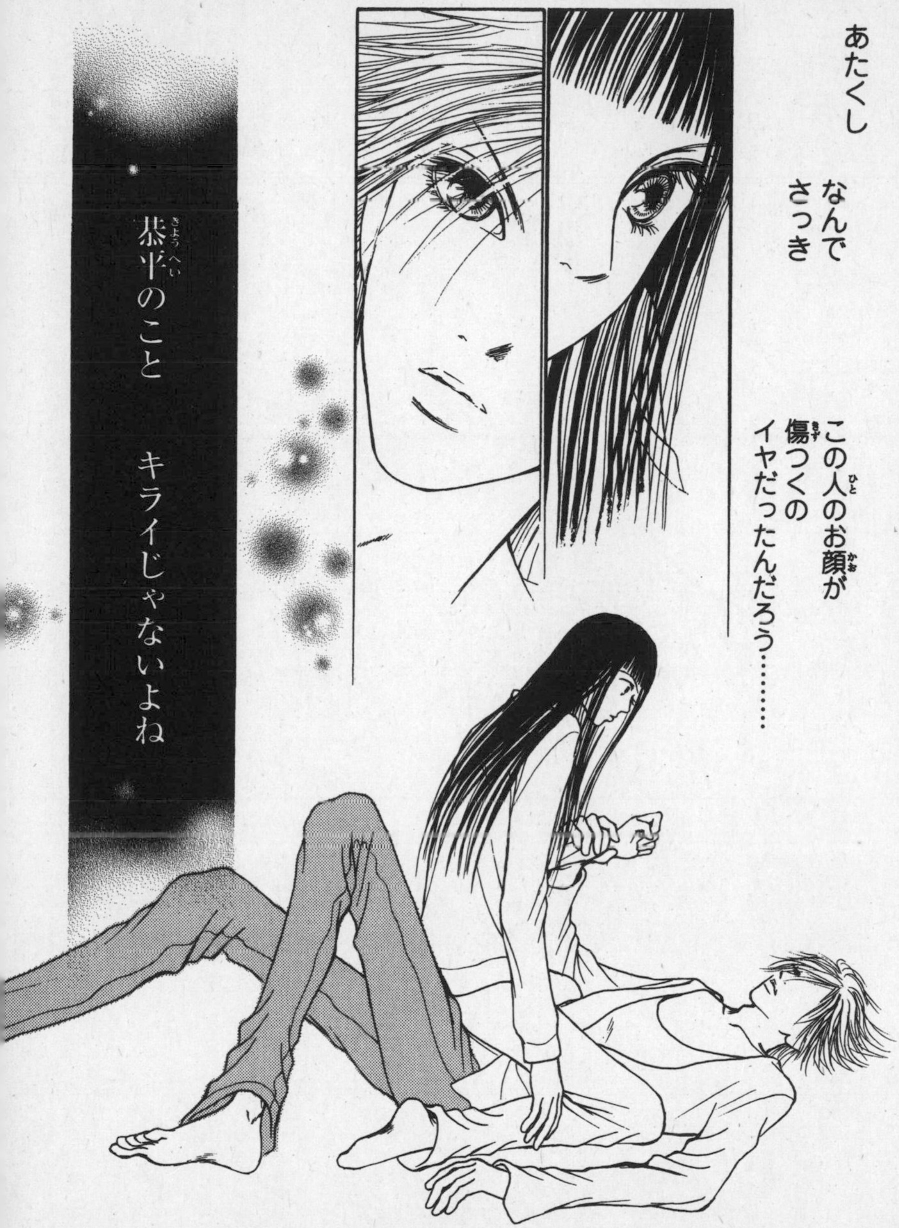
あたくし
なんで
さっき
この人のお顔が
傷つくの
イヤだったんだろう……
恭平のこと
キライじゃないよね

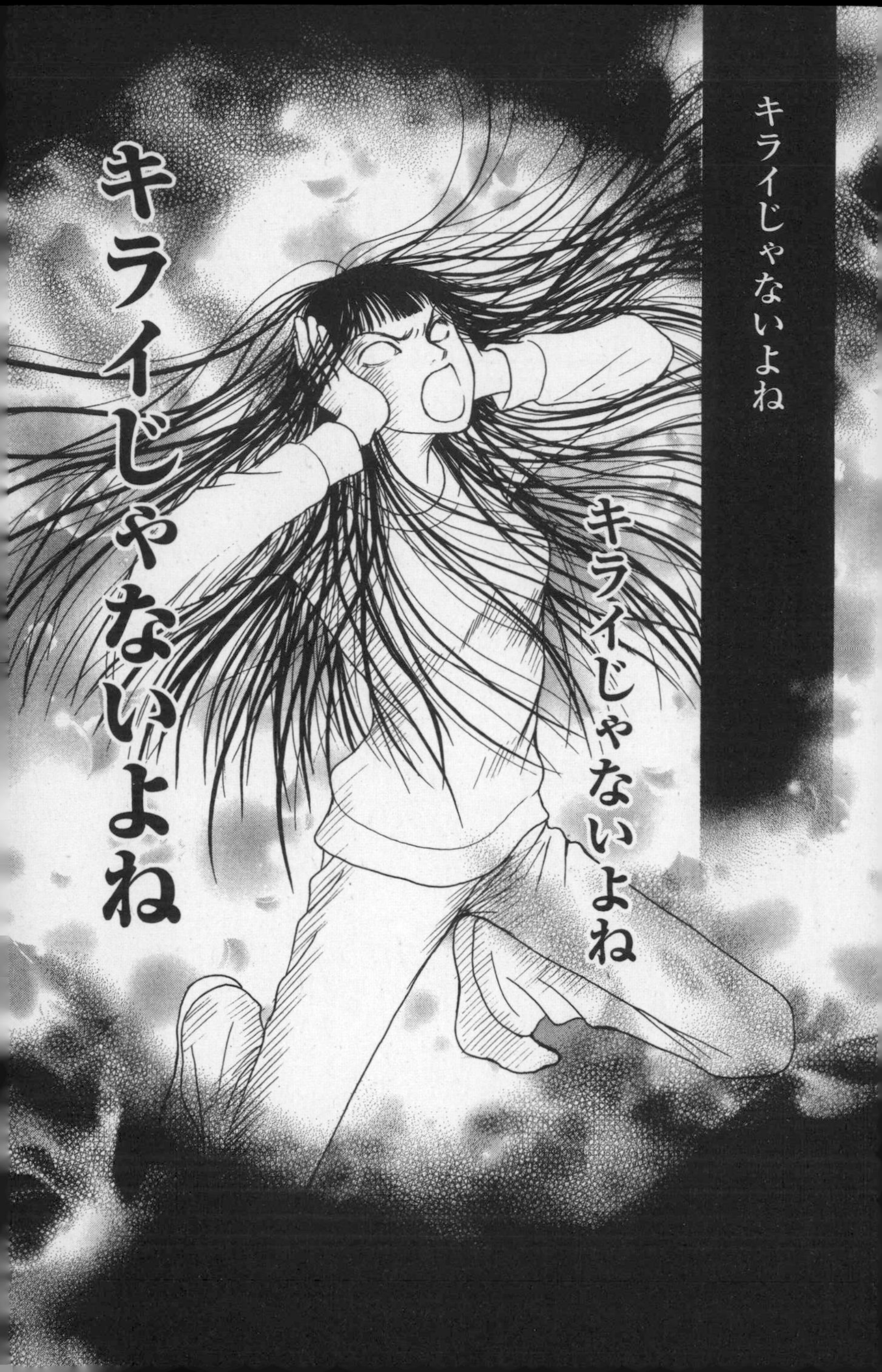
キライじゃないよね
キライじゃないよね
キライじゃないよね

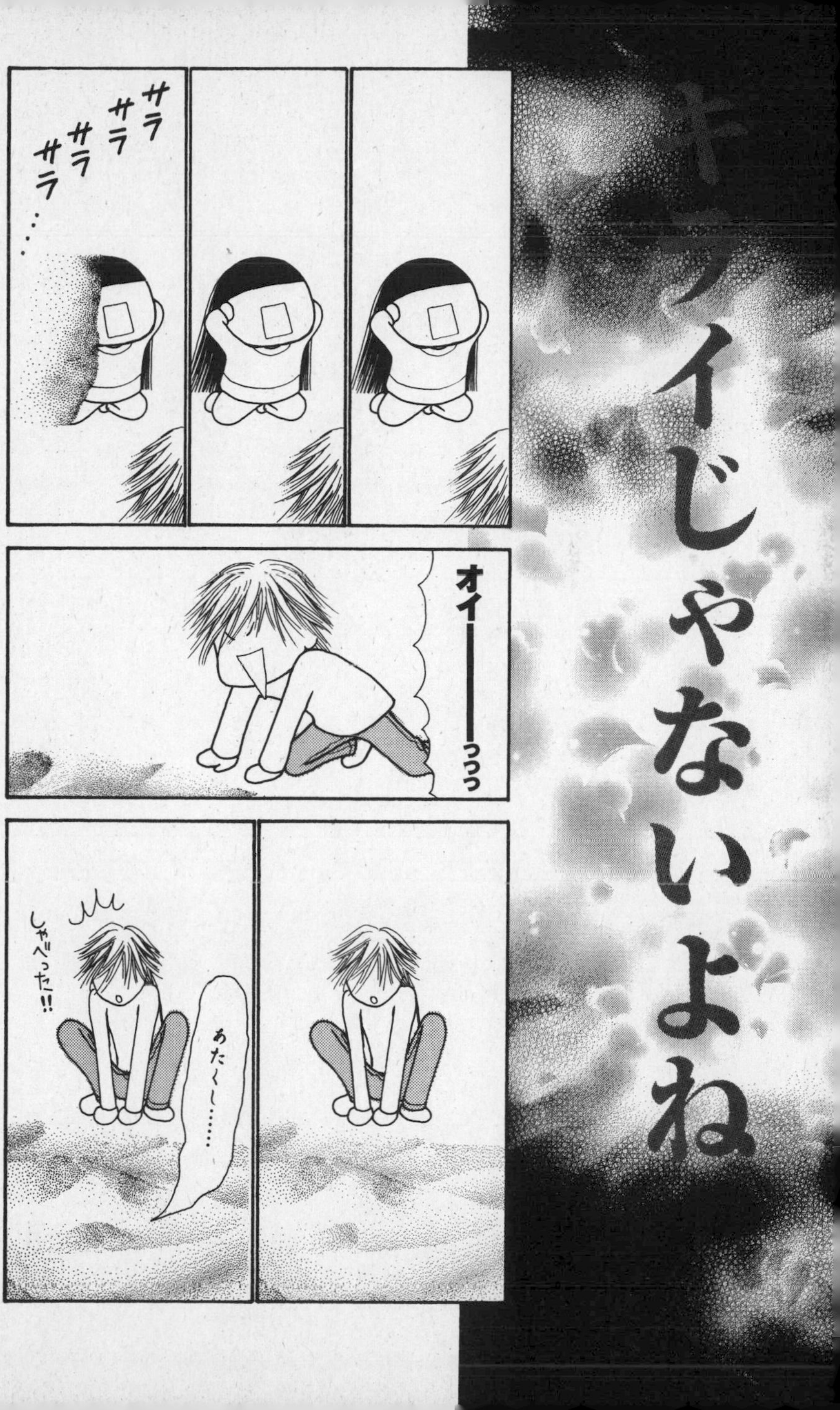
キライじゃないよね
サラ
サラ
サラ
サラ……
オイーーっっっ
あたくし……
しゃべった!!

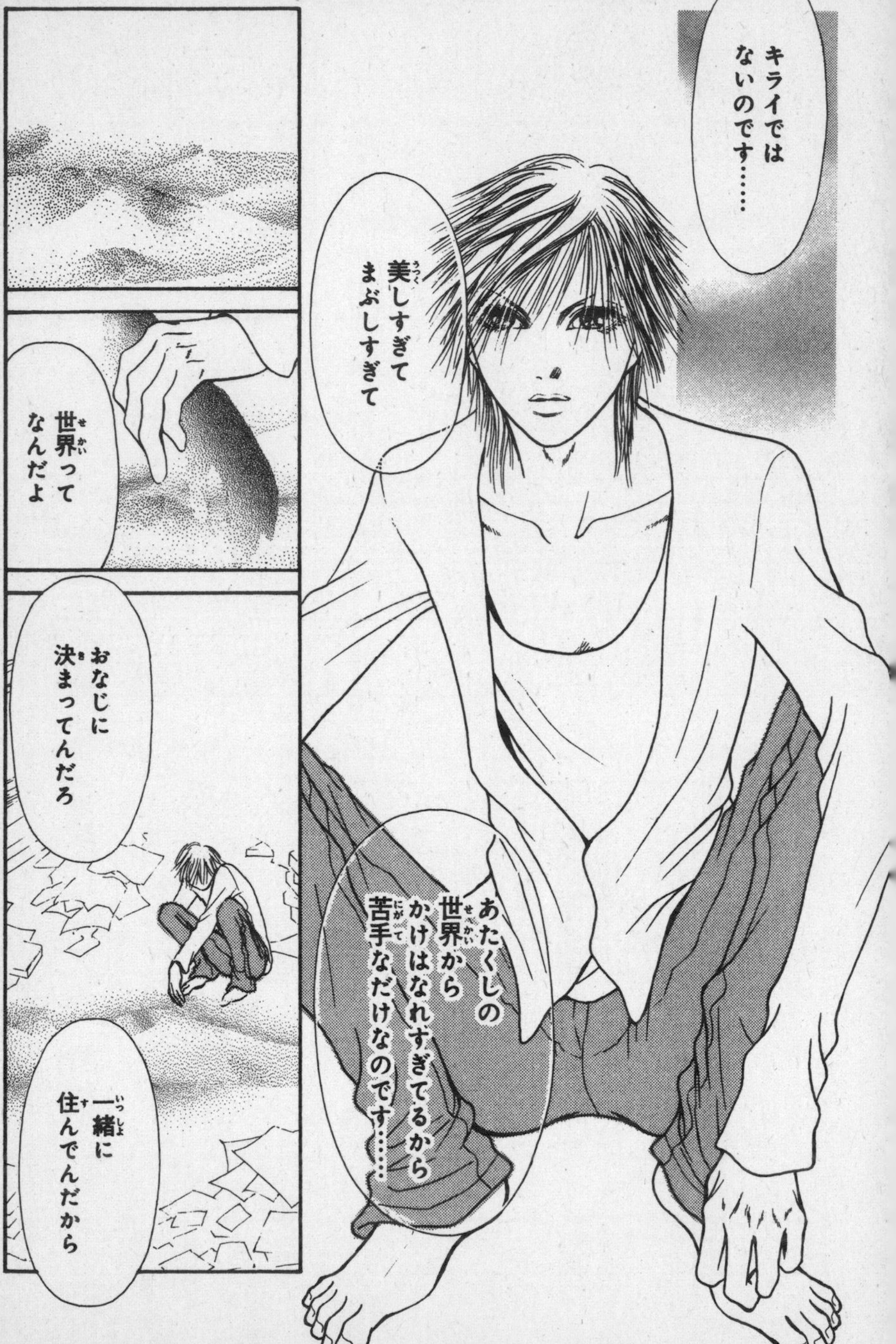
キライではないのです……
美しすぎてまぶしすぎて
あたくしの世界からかけはなれすぎてるから苦手なだけなのです……
世界ってなんだよ
おなじに決まってんだろ
一緒に住んでんだから

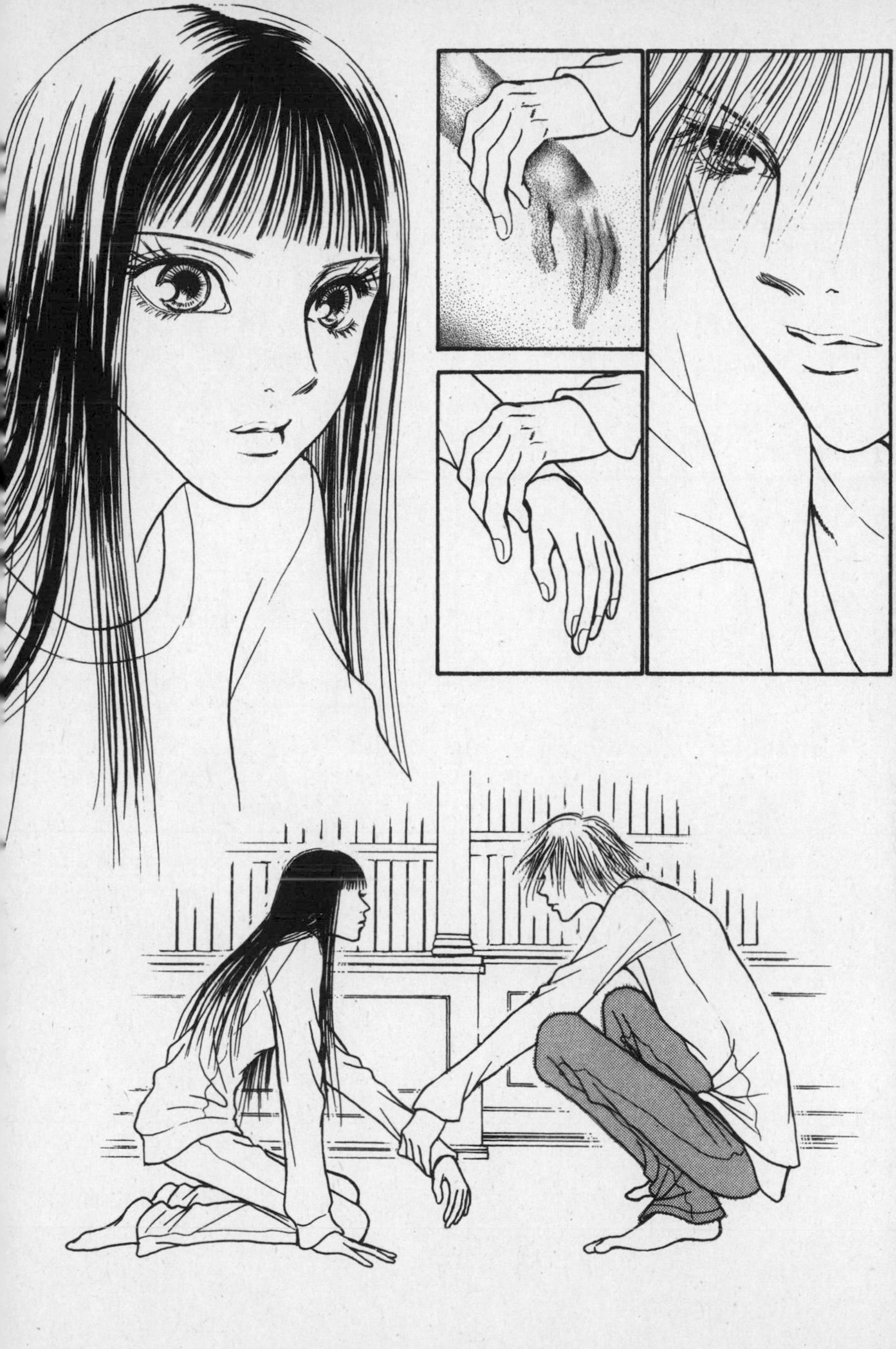

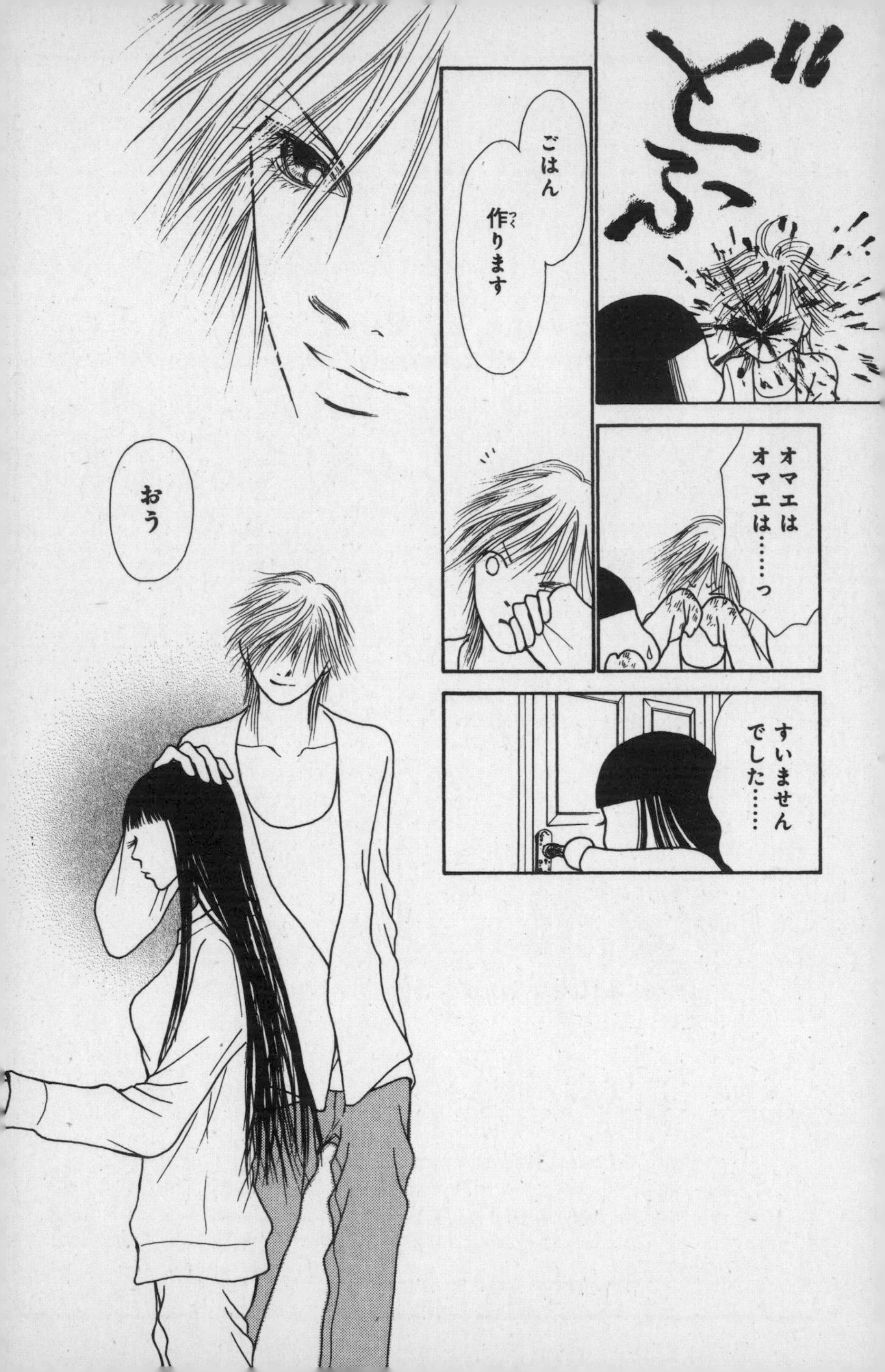

どふ
オマエは オマエは……っ
ごはん 作ります
すいません でした……
おう

STORY BY SURT LIM
ART BY HIROFUMI SUGIMOTO

A DEL REY MANGA ORIGINAL

Exploring the woods, young Kasumi encounters an ancient tree god, who bestows upon her the power of invisibility. Together with classmates who have had similar experiences, Kasumi forms the Magic Play Club, dedicated to using their powers for good while avoiding sinister forces that would exploit them.

Special extras in each volume! Read them all!

VISIT WWW.DELREYMANGA.COM TO:
• Read sample pages
• View release date calendars for upcoming volumes
• Sign up for Del Rey's free manga e-newsletter
• Find out the latest about new Del Rey Manga series

RATING   T AGES 13+

The Otaku's Choice.™

KITCHEN PRINCESS

STORY BY MIYUKI KOBAYASHI
MANGA BY NATSUMI ANDO
CREATOR OF ZODIAC P.I.

HUNGRY HEART

Najika is a great cook and likes to make meals for the people she loves. But something is missing from her life. When she was a child, she met a boy who touched her heart— and now Najika is determined to find him. The only clue she has is a silver spoon that leads her to the prestigious Seika Academy.

Attending Seika will be a challenge. Every kid at the school has a special talent, and the girls in Najika's class think she doesn't deserve to be there. But Sora and Daichi, two popular brothers who barely speak to each other, recognize Najika's cooking for what it is—magical. Could one of the boys be Najika's mysterious prince?

Special extras in each volume! Read them all!

BY MACHIKO SAKURAI

A LITTLE LIVING DOLL!

What would you do if your favorite toy came to life and became your best friend? Well, that's just what happens to Ame Oikawa, a shy schoolgirl. Nicori is a super-cute doll with a mind of its own—and a plan to make Ame's dreams come true!

Special extras in each volume! Read them all!

VISIT WWW.DELREYMANGA.COM TO:
- Read sample pages
- View release date calendars for upcoming volumes
- Sign up for Del Rey's free manga e-newsletter
- Find out the latest about new Del Rey Manga series

RATING T AGES 13+

The Otaku's Choice™

Yozakura Quartet

BY SUZUHITO YASUDA

A DIFFERENT SET OF SUPERTEENS!

Hime is a superheroine. Ao can read minds. Kotoha can conjure up anything with the right word. And Akina . . . well, he's just a regular guy, surrounded by three girls with superpowers! Together, they are the Hizumi Everyday Life Consultation Office, dedicated to protect the town of Sakurashin. And with demon dogs and supernatural threats around every corner, there's plenty to keep them busy!

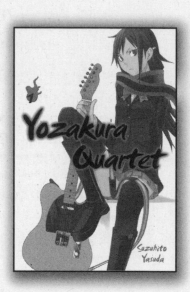

Special extras in each volume! Read them all!

VISIT WWW.DELREYMANGA.COM TO:
- Read sample pages
- View release date calendars for upcoming volumes
- Sign up for Del Rey's free manga e-newsletter
- Find out the latest about new Del Rey Manga series

RATING   T AGES 13+

 DEL REY MANGA デルレイ

The Otaku's Choice.™

TOMARE!

[STOP!]

You're going the wrong way!

Manga is a completely different type of reading experience.

To start at the *beginning*,
go to the *end*!

That's right! Authentic manga is read the traditional Japanese way—from right to left. Exactly the *opposite* of how American books are read. It's easy to follow: Just go to the other end of the book, and read each page—and each panel—from right side to left side, starting at the top right. Now you're experiencing manga as it was meant to be!